DATE DUE

HUMOR IN AMERICA

◆ HUMOR IN AMERICA ◆

A RESEARCH GUIDE TO GENRES AND TOPICS

EDITED BY
LAWRENCE E. MINTZ

Greenwood Press
New York • Westport, Connecticut • London

Library of Congress Cataloging-in-Publication Data

Humor in America.

   Bibliography: p.
   Includes index.
   1. American wit and humor—History and criticism.
2. United States—Popular culture.   3. Literary form.
I. Mintz, Lawrence E.
PS430.H86   1988   817'.009   87–17600
ISBN 0–313–24551–7 (lib. bdg. : alk paper)

British Library Cataloguing in Publication Data is available.

Library of Congress Catalog Card Number: 87–17600
ISBN: 0–313–24551–7

First published in 1988

Greenwood Press, Inc.
88 Post Road West, Westport, Connecticut 06881

Printed in the United States of America

∞

The paper used in this book complies with the
Permanent Paper Standard issued by the National
Information Standards Organization (Z39.48–1984).

10   9   8   7   6   5   4   3   2   1

Contents

INTRODUCTION   vii

1. Literary Humor
  Nancy Pogel and Paul P. Somers, Jr.   1

2. The Comics
  M. Thomas Inge   35

3. Humor in Periodicals
  David E. E. Sloane   49

4. Film Comedy
  Wes D. Gehring   67

5. Broadcast Humor
  Lawrence E. Mintz   91

6. Standup Comedy
  Stephanie Koziski Olson   109

7. Women's Humor
  Zita Dresner   137

8. Racial and Ethnic Humor
  Joseph Dorinson and Joseph Boskin   163

Contents

9. Political Humor
    Stephen J. Whitfield   195

10. Folklore Methodology and American Humor Research
    Elliott Oring   213

    INDEX   231

    ABOUT THE CONTRIBUTORS   239

Introduction

It has become conventional to begin scholarly studies of humor with two standard disclaimers: an apology is offered for the fact that the study of humor is not, of itself, funny, and attention is directed to the apparent irony that though humor is itself trivial and superficial, the study of it is necessarily significant and complex. It is not quite clear why it is expected that the study of humor be more amusing than, say, the study of sex is titillating, but somehow it seems ineluctable that the reader be warned and comforted. So be it. This is not a funny collection of essays. As to the second point, humor is deceptively light, ephemeral, inconsequential, if it is so at all. Its perpetual disguise is, of course, that it is mere entertainment, amusement, "just kidding," but most of the time the joking mode scarcely masks the fact that the issue at hand is most serious. Freud noted that some humor—simple wordplay and physical horseplay—is only tangentially tendentious, but that overwhelmingly the humorous posture was a means by which we make our confrontation of our most threatening thoughts palatable, apparently safe, or comfortable.[1] Mark Twain claimed that while humor "must not professedly preach nor professedly teach, it must do both if it is to last forever." (He went on to note that "by forever I mean twenty years.")[2] American humor has been, from its very beginning, used to preach and to teach, on just about every issue that has concerned us as a people. We employed it as a device to examine the very nature of the democracy that would characterize our social experiment, portraying the democratic hero both as a disaster and as an ironic triumph. It has served to allow us to explore our regional, class, ethnic, national, and religious differences and to deal with our sex roles and sex-role conflicts. As our society became modern, complex, urban, and industrial, our humor defined new values, attitudes, dispositions, hopes, fears, expectations, and new behavior models to laugh at and to laugh with. Our contemporary humor confronts virtually everything that is important to us in ways that make us understand ourselves and our society more thoroughly, more deeply, more meaningfully, and at the same time in ways that make it easier to cope with our often-disturbing reality.

There are many ways to approach the study of humor. Beginning with Aristotle, philosophers and critics have attempted to define and to describe it. Sociologists and anthropologists have compared and contrasted its manifestations in various social contexts. Psychologists have attempted to account for its origins in the human personality and in the structure and operation of the cognitive process. Historians have traced its development diachronically, noting differences and similarities during various historically defined periods. Educators, communications specialists, and scholars of all of the artistic and entertainment genres have noted humor's significance to their fields and have added to the literature. The international conferences devoted to humor studies (there have been seven thus far, beginning with one in Cardiff, Wales, in 1976) testify eloquently to the widespread and deep interest in the subject. Scholars from virtually every discipline including some that may surprise the uninitiated— mathematics, for instance, with its interest in the connections between logical thought, creativity, and humor; biology with its concerns over animal perception and expression and genetic origins of personality and temperament—communicate with professionals representing such fields as law and prison management (humor and interpersonal negotiation), business, the entertainment industry in its many manifestations, and the health professions, where there has been a growing awareness of the importance of humor to the well-being of the individual. These activities have provoked a parallel growth of scholarly and professional literature devoted to the study of humor, again in just about every field imaginable.[3] In short, not only is there no need to apologize for the serious study of humor, there is reason to argue that it should be at the very center of the study of human belief and behavior whatever its particular perspective.

The chapters that follow this introduction provide a good overview of the serious study of American humor in most of its major manifestations, generic and topical. While the writing is rarely ''heavy'' and never boring, the approaches are universally serious. The authors employ many of the familiar, approved methods of intellectual analysis—literary criticism, intellectual history, aesthetic description, sociology of art, communications analysis, ethnography, psychoanalytic explanation, political interpretation, linguistic and semiological decoding, and so forth. Each chapter is organized to provide an overview of either a genre of expression such as literature, the comic strip, film, broadcast humor, magazines, or standup comedy, or a topic of significance such as racial and ethnic humor, womens' humor, and political humor. After the genre or topic is introduced, the authors trace its manifestation historically, discuss the issues that are demanding further attention, and provide a bibliographical survey and checklist to facilitate further study.

Nancy Pogel and Paul P. Somers, Jr., survey the diverse expression of humor in American literature from its early pseudo-folklore roots through such major writers as Twain and Thurber, to the modern novel where humor is often found to be at the core of nearly all serious fiction. M. Thomas Inge examines the comic strip, a combination of caricature and narrative that is considered one of the truly original American art forms, and, more importantly perhaps, an often overlooked and underrated form of popular culture. David E. E. Sloane shows that humorous journalism has played a very significant role in our cultural communication since the earliest years of our national history, and Wes D. Gehring and Lawrence E. Mintz examine the more modern mass media manifestations in film and broadcasting, respectively. Stephanie Koziski Olson's exploration of the world of standup comedy performance similarly illustrates an interdisciplinary inquiry into the relationship between the performer, the text, and the audience. The most important topics recurring in American humor are singled out for separate discussion: Zita Dresner explains that the study of women and American humor—both as subjects and as creators—offers some prominent and provocative contrasts with more traditional male-centered studies; Joseph Dorinson and Joseph Boskin examine how racial and ethnic humor function similarly with regard to the extremely important and sensitive area of cultural pluralism and the pressures of assimilation; Stephen J. Whitfield notes how political humor has provided us with a licensed arena in which we might safely express dissent and political conflict; and Elliott Oring's examination of the study of American humor as folklore suggests an important link between the genres of expression, the issues behind topical communication both overt and covert, and the ways in which the scholar seeks to understand expression in its social contexts. Collectively the ten chapters and the bibliographies provide a fairly thorough introduction to the study of humor in America; they both invite and help guide further inquiry.

Are there any grand conclusions to be drawn? If there were, this introduction would not be an appropriate place for them anyway. The convenors of the humor conferences lament the absence of continuity and consensus: We can't even agree upon a central definition of humor, much less on a universal outline for understanding its significance. Some observers have cited humor as the central element in our national character; how then do we account for our frequent humorlessness and self-conscious seriousness? How can a description of national character based on humor accommodate the popularity of Joan Rivers, David Letterman, Lily Tomlin, Richard Pryor, Bill Cosby, Nancy and Sluggo, Frank Zappa, *Mad*, *The National Lampoon*, Howard Stern, and all of the other strains currently prominent? What are we to make of all of the paradoxes in humor theory such as the problem of humor as an aggressive characteristic and humor as a deflection of aggressive needs when we seek to apply all that we are learning to a study of

American culture and society? The answer is, I believe, that we are just beginning to accept how important, how complex and difficult, and how varied the study of humor can be and the answers are still out there. These chapters offer a vital insight into the nature of the questions, the best answers currently offered, and the materials with which students might build their own inquiries. A handbook need do not more.

NOTES

1. Sigmund Freud, *Jokes and their Relation to the Unconscious*, ed. James Strachey (New York: W. W. Norton, 1960), pp. 90ff.

2. Mark Twain, *The Autobiography of Mark Twain*, ed. Charles Nieder (New York: Washington Square Press, 1961), pp. 297–98.

3. There have been several volumes of essays that have come from the international conferences, including Tony Chapman and Hugh Foot's seminal books *Humour and Laughter* (New York: John Wiley, 1976) and *It's A Funny Thing, Humour* (New York: Pergamon Press, 1977). Collections of abstracts have been issued for conferences two through five, but they are less readily available. The best place to begin the study of humor theory and the academic study of humor is the two-volume *Handbook of Humor Studies*, edited by Paul McGhee and Jeffrey Goldstein (New York: Springer Verlag, 1985), which includes a good bibliography and a good discussion of the journal literature as well.

HUMOR IN AMERICA

Literary Humor

Nancy Pogel and Paul P. Somers, Jr.

OVERVIEW

American literary humor has always embodied the fundamental contradictions of our national life. Louis D. Rubin, Jr., sees the humor of "the great American joke" as arising "out of the gap between the cultural ideal and the everyday fact, with the ideal shown to be somewhat hollow and hypocritical, and the fact crude and disgusting."[1]

Stripping capitalistic democracy to its bare essentials, we have Simon Suggs' motto, "It is good to be shifty in a new country," and P. T. Barnum's, "There's a sucker born every minute." Debunking the dignity of the nation's highest office, we have President Nixon portrayed as a vampire bat in Hunter S. Thompson's *Fear and Loathing: On the Campaign Trail'72*. Contesting the ideal of "Life, Liberty and the Pursuit of Happiness," we have P. J. O'Rourke's cantankerous *Modern Manners* which tacitly assumes that for proper people the most important things in life are sex, drugs, alcohol, money, and status.

Countering patriot Patrick Henry's ringing phrase, we have Josh Billings': "Give me liberty, or give me deth—but ov the 2 I prefer the liberty." Demythifying the immigrants' dream of "streets paved with gold," we have Groucho Marx's antiproverbial, "When I came to this country I didn't have a nickel in my pocket. Now I have a nickel in my pocket."

From Benjamin Franklin's exaggeration over the promise of America in her earliest years ("The very tails of the American sheep are so laden with wool, that each has a Car or Waggon on four little wheels to support and keep it from trailing on the ground"), to Woody Allen's observation, "How wrong Emily

Dickinson was! Hope is not the thing with feathers. The thing with feathers has turned out to be my nephew. I must take him to a specialist in Zurich,'' American literary humor has been a source of laughter and an unsettling response to well-made schemes of all kinds.

As Walter Blair points out, American humor ''gave us the first American fiction that writers fashioned out of the life about them.'' That early humor was written with ''a gift not only for dramatic story-telling but for style.''[2] The spirit in American literary humor, made out of the antitheses of American life and filled with good stories and lively style, has proved to be remarkably durable through lighter and darker times in our history. American humor remains, in poetry, drama, and fiction, a vital part of our literary tradition today.

HISTORICAL DEVELOPMENT

The origins of American humor go back to the early years of colonization, to what many consider the first American art form: the tall tale. It seems the European colonists had no more landed in the New World than they were writing home lies, or at least shameless exaggerations, of its bountifulness. John Smith solemnly maintained, ''He is very bad fisher [who] cannot kill in one day with his hook and line one, two, or three hundred cods. . . . '' Amusing as we may find these tales today, it is sometimes difficult to realize that many of them were not intended to be humorous.

This is not to say that none of the colonists deliberately essayed to write humorously. Examples of colonial humor include: Thomas Morton's *The New English Caanan* (1637), George Alsop's *A Character of the Province of Maryland* (1666), Sarah Kemble Knight's *Private Journal of a Journey From Boston to New York (1704–1705)* (1825), and Ebeneezer Cook's *The Sotweed Factor* (1708).

Educated in England, William Byrd II, of Westover, Virginia, wrote *History of the Dividing Line Betwixt Virginia and North Carolina Run in The Year of Our Lord 1728*, first published here in 1841, and the racier *The Secret History of the Line*, the first part of which did not see the light until 1929. Another gentleman diarist was Dr. Samuel Sewall of Boston, whose *Diary* provides a sometimes amusing case study of one Puritan's transformation into Yankee.

It has been widely noted that the colonists' slavish attempts to imitate English neoclassical models produced little in the way of truly native humor. The glaring exception, Benjamin Franklin, learned much from the laborious exercises in composition he practiced on Addison and Steele's *Spectator*.

During the Revolution, Philip Freneau wrote eight satirical poems, such as ''George the Third's Soliloquy.'' For his stinging anti-Federalist satires, he earned from George Washington the sobriquet, ''that rascal Freneau.'' Freneau's Princeton classmate and friend Hugh Henry Brackenridge is sometimes remembered for his episodic novel *Modern Chivalry*, various installments and revisions of which appeared between 1792 and 1815.

Playing an important role in the development of American humor were the jest books and almanacs. According to Walter Blair, the English jest books provided the models for American editors to copy: "And even jest books which made an occasional attempt to develop American humor consistently retold mossy ancedotes which had nothing to do with the native scene or native life."[3] With the advent of the almanac, however—*An Almanack for New England for the Year 1639* was the first native one—a foundation was laid for native American humor and, especially, recognizably American comic stereotypes to replace the English ones borrowed from the *Spectator*. The first humorous American almanac was put out in 1687, by John Tully of Saybrook, Connecticut.

Perhaps the most influential, appearing in 1733, was Benjamin Franklin's *Poor Richard's Almanack*. Poor Richard was Richard Saunders, who, along with his wife, Bridget, was one of Franklin's most enduring personae. Franklin published the almanac until he sold it in 1758, the year he introduced Father Abraham. He also wrote the *Dogood Papers*, which introduced the no-nonsense character Silence Dogood to the readers of the *New England Courant* in 1722. Twenty-five years later, "The Speech of Polly Baker" in the London *Gentleman's Magazine* would add to America's gallery of character types.

To the stylistic influences of Addison and Steele the omnivorous reader added those of Swift and Defoe, whose works inspired "The Sale of the Hessians" (1777) and "Rules by Which a Great Empire May be Reduced to a Small One" (1773).

Franklin wrote lighter, less tendentious pieces over the years, ranging from his letter "To the Royal Academy of Brussels" in 1745 to the whimsical Bagatelles written in 1778–1780 for the amusement of his French friends. The self-deprecating "Dialogue Between Franklin and the Gout" is one of the best known of these.

Benjamin Franklin contributed to the development of American humor in several ways: to the tall tale tradition he brought whales that chased cod up Niagara Falls; to the political satire he brought wit and satire. Yet, it is for his pioneering comic personae that he most deserves to be remembered: Polly Baker, Silence Dogood, and, especially, Poor Richard and Father Abraham—not to mention Ben Franklin, himself.

Perhaps surprisingly, the next important steps were taken by Washington Irving, another young man who was steeped in the literature of eighteenth-century England. Returning to New York, he joined with his brother William and James Kirke Paulding to publish *Salmagundi* (1807–1808), an anonymous satirical periodical.

In 1809 he produced the *History of New York*, purportedly by Diederich Knickerbocker, satirizing such figures as Wouter Van Twiller, Peter Stuyvesant, and William the Testy, the young Federalist wit's representation of Thomas Jefferson.

Encouraged by Sir Walter Scott, he wrote *The Sketch Book* of Geoffrey Crayon (1819–1820). Two of the tales, "Rip Van Winkle" and "The Legend of Sleepy

Hollow,'' instantly became classics on both sides of the Atlantic and influenced American literature for generations.

Subsequent schools of American humor would find much of use in these seminal tales: the use of the narrative frame, and the mining of American materials, by which he showed a generation of American writers, among them Hawthorne and Poe, that the thin soil of America's short past could profitably be cultivated; and for his particularization, his romanticization, and transformation of older, neoclassical character types into American comic types.

As Jennette Tandy asserts, Irving's Ichabod Crane is the first literary Yankee to gain popularity, though she adjudges him but ''a dumb shadow.''[4] The character type was well evolved by the time of Ichabod's 1820 appearance.

The character of Brother Jonathan the Yankee has another aspect: that of the shrewd peddler. Wandering the wilderness armed only with his wit and the goods he carries in his pack, he will establish another element of the paradoxical American character: disapproval of the trickster mixed with nearly equal parts of admiration of his cleverness and scorn for his victims.

As far as the novel is concerned, John Neal has some historical significance as the author of *Brother Jonathan, or the New Englanders* (1825) and *The Down-Easters* (1833). The popular stage, however, did much the work of developing the Yankee type. In Royall Tyler's *The Contrast*, produced in 1787 and published in 1790, we have in Tandy's words, ''the first full portrait of the New-Englandman,'' and ''the progenitor of a long line of stage Yankees,'' the bumpkin servant, Jonathan. Blair considers Jonathan Ploughboy, who appeared in Samuel Woodworth's *The Forest Rose* (1825), as ''the first stage Yankee of national, even international, and fairly lasting appeal.''[5] By 1825, according to Tandy, the Yankee's ''stage popularity was such that he became a star part, and was, in fact, for a long time the leading comic figure of American drama. The time was ripe for Jack Downing and Sam Slick.''[6]

Something else had transpired to make the time ripe for Jack Downing et al., something more consequential than a mere proliferation of comic stage characters: the accession of Democrat Andrew Jackson to the presidency.

With admirable restraint, the New Englanders who were to become known as the ''Down East'' humorists satirized not so much General Jackson as the sort of backwoods Yankee who supported him. Seba Smith, editor of the *Portland* (Maine) *Courier*, created Major Jack Downing, of Downingville. Travelling to Washington to seek a political position in the Jackson administration, Jack became a member of Old Hickory's Kitchen Cabinet and as such reported back home with wide-eyed innocence what he observed in the corridors of power.

So popular were the Downing letters that they were widely read and acclaimed in numerous newspapers and book-length editions. Charles Augustus Davis copies Smith and published his own volumes of Downing letters. Smith's first authorized collection was *The Life and Writings of Major Jack Downing, of Downingville* (1833).

Another Yankee made his first appearance in 1836, the itinerant peddler, Sam

Slick. Created by Nova Scotian Thomas Chandler Haliburton, he was probably the best known of the Down East characters from his inception until 1860. *The Clockmaker or, The Sayings and Doings of Samuel Slick, of Slickville* was published in three series: 1837, 1838, and 1840. Readers praised his italicized aphorisms, his "knowledge of *soft sawder* and *human natur.*"

A pair of widows provided readers with considerable amusement during the forties, fifties, and sixties: Frances M. Whitcher's Widow Bedott, *The Widow Bedott Papers* (1856), and Benjamin P. Shillaber's Mrs. Partington, America's Mistress of Malapropism, *Life and Sayings of Mrs. Partington* (1854).

Least sentimental of all the Down East humorists is James Russell Lowell, whose first series of the Biglow Papers, letters purportedly written by farmer Hosea Biglow, appeared in *The Boston Courier* in 1846 and was collected in 1848. Lashing out against the Mexican War and the proslavery expansionism behind it, Lowell used Biglow himself, the pompous pastor Homer Wilbur, and Birdofredom Sawin. Sawin is a very common man who succumbed to the lure of the recruiting officer and went to fight in Mexico. For his patriotism, he was severely maimed, but remains cheerful and opportunistic.

Overall, Lowell's skill in characterization, as well as his mastery of dialect, not to mention his scarcely controlled sense of outrage, leads modern critics to rank him just behind Smith among the Down East humorists.

As Walter Blair has written, Yankee humor in the years between 1830 and 1867 developed an increasing emphasis on "accurate rendition of dialect and the authentic depiction of localized background and individualized characters."[7] In its gentle realism it foreshadowed the New England local colorists.

Another major strain of American humor had been flourishing almost coincidentally with Down East humor, but with distinct differences. Down in the backwoods and bayous of the Old Southwest, other writers were experimenting with the use of the vernacular and alternative narrative methods but with less overt commentary and, especially, through the development of oral narrative.

Traditionally, the birthdate of southwestern humor is given as 1835, the publication of Judge Augustus Baldwin Longstreet's *Georgia Scenes, Characters, and Incidents*. Antedating the publication of *Georgia Scenes* are the tales of Davy Crockett and Mike Fink. The twin lenses of folklore and political hyperbole magnified Whig Congressman David Crockett of Tennessee to a demigod. With reputed help from party publicists, he produced books such as *Sketches and Eccentricities of Col. David Crockett* (1833). Along with the less-appealing and more brutal Mike Fink, also a real person, the backwoodsman who could grin a squirrel out of a tree and shoot six cord of bear in one day helped stimulate the great national craving for all tall tales from the frontier.

Probably the major medium for the dissemination of these tales in print was William T. Porter's the *Spirit of the Times*, founded in 1831. Porter printed an increasing number of sporting yarns, many of which were set in the Southwest.

Several things distinguish these southwestern humorists from their contemporaries among writers: they were self-consciously, defensively, southerners;

they were professionals, often lawyers; and they were gentlemen, conservative Whig gentlemen, who felt superior to their backwoods neighbors.

A. B. Longstreet, whose *Georgia Scenes* signalled the rush of southwestern humorous tales into book form in 1835, was the oldest of the group and one of the most influenced by the *Spectator*. Walter Blair characterizes Longstreet's narrator, Ned Brace, as a contemporary of Pindar Cockloft, and Addisonian humorist, a link between the humor of the eighteenth and nineteenth centuries. (Poe had himself noted this in a contemporary review.) Longstreet's dirt-eating, troublemaking Ransy Sniffle occupies a prominent place among the rascals of the frontier.

Jurist Joseph G. Baldwin, author of *The Flush Times of Alabama and Mississippi* (1853), wrote essays, with little dialogue, about the liar, Ovid Bolus, Esq.

Alabama editor and lawyer Johnson J. Hooper introduced one of the most memorable of the backwoods tricksters in *Some Adventures of Simon Suggs, Late of the Tallapoosa Volunteers* (1845), a mock campaign biography. Simon is always able to exploit the "soft spots" in his fellow man, and his motto, "It is good to be shifty in a new country," will serve at once to inspire and warn.

An Ohioan transplanted to Georgia, William Tappan Thompson was known for *Major Jones's Courtship* (1843) and *Chronicles of Pineville* (1845), sedate small-town sketches considered closer to the Down East stories than to some of the more raucous and violent tales of the southwestern school. He also did much to advance the art of transferring the oral tale to paper.

Another emigrant from the north (Massachusetts), Thomas Bangs Thorpe lived for many years in Louisiana. He is the author of perhaps the most famous story in southwestern humor, "The Big Bear of Arkansas," the title story of a collection of outstanding stories published by William T. Porter in 1845. William Faulkner would base his novelette *The Bear* on the story a century later.

Other southwestern humorists include John S. Robb, *Streaks of Squatter Life* (1847) and *Far-West Scenes* (1847), Joseph M. Field, *The Drama in Pokerville* (1847), and Sol Smith, *Theatrical Apprenticeship* (1845). Henry Clay Lewis, "Madison Tensas, M.D.," wrote stories with gruesome medical details, many of which were collected in *Odd Leaves From the Life of a Louisiana Swamp Doctor* (1850).

Finally, there is George Washington Harris, Tennessee jack-of-many professions, generally regarded as the best of the southwestern humorists. He created Sut Lovingood, whose exploits are chronicled in *Sut Lovingood* (1867). Compared to Sut, Simon Suggs, who as a youth once filled his mother's pipe with gunpowder, is a choirboy. Harris' stories are noteworthy for their gratuitous cruelty: Sut inflicts pain randomly and without provocation, explaining to "George" that he, Sut, is just "a natral born durn fool."

After the Civil War, most of the gentlemen humorists faded into obscurity, displaced by a new breed of national comedians, many of whom were also comic actors. Their vogue would be long and overlap other fashions in humor.

Coexisting with the southwestern and Down East humorists even as they supplanted them, the misspellers, the phunny phellows, the literary comedians, utilized many of their devices: the tall tale, the comic essay, and a whole bag of verbal tricks relying on incongruity, anticlimax, cacography, etc. Perhaps more importantly, they continued to develop the wise fool of the regional humorists, but they declined to identify him with any particular region and thus limit his appeal. Although he was universally unlettered, giving a newly literate national reading public a chance to feel superior, he was nonetheless "sharp" and trying to get ahead. "You scratch my back & Ile scratch your back," promised Charles Farrar Browne's travelling showman, Artemus Ward. More than mere "sharpness," Jesse Bier sees in the new generation of comic personae "a pervasive amoralism abroad in the land, which furnishes capital for either humorous expose or propaganda."[8]

While the literary comedians are generally considered national, unifying forces, during the Civil War several of them enlisted in the cause and trained their typewriters on the enemy. Of these, Petroleum V. Nasby, the creation of Ohioan David Ross Locke, is the most vitriolic. A Copperhead who flees to Canada to avoid the draft, Nasby is drafted but deserts to the Confederate army. He is an unregenerate coward, hypocrite, and racist. The Nasby letters were an effective propaganda weapon for the Union.

If the North had Petroleum V. Nasby during the war, the South had its own Bill Arp, the creation of Georgian Charles Henry Smith. The first Bill Arp letter appeared in the Rome (Georgia) *The Southern Confederacy* in early 1861. Bill wrote satirical letters to "Mr. Linkhorn." In his sly and genial way, he cheered his Confederacy on through the early victories and the later defeats.

Another humorist popular during the Civil War was Robert Henry Newell, whose character, Orpheus C. Kerr, began as an "office seeker" desiring an appointment in the Lincoln administration. Throughout the course of the war Newell presented comic northern figures and vicious southern ones that reflect the author's growing hatred.

While Lincoln praised Nasby, it was the letters of Artemus Ward that he read to his cabinet, on one occasion, to warm them up for a preview of his Gettysburg Address. Ward's creator, Charles Farrar Browne, is often ranked at the top of the class of literary comedians, excepting, of course, Samuel Clemens. His first collection of letters, *Artemus Ward, His Book,* was published in 1862 and was a tremendous success, as were subsequent lecture tours. He died in March 1867, of tuberculosis. A careful editor and wordsmith, Browne had a scant six years to develop his jaundiced view of human nature.

Partly because of their topicality and, in most cases, their labored misspelling, the literary comedians are largely forgotten. In their day, however, they did much to create a national humor and to establish writing as a lucrative and, therefore, at least partly respectable profession. (Praise from England helped.) And, as critics point out, they also provided a valuable service by presenting a cynicism to counter the overwhelming sentimentality of much of the popular literature of the time.

Some of this sentimentality emanated from members of another, more "literary'' school that flourished alongside the phunny phellows, the local colorists. Studied more for their contributions to American literary realism than to American humor, these writers were genteel heirs of the southwestern humorists, striving to describe the daily life of their region to other Americans. They did so by emphasizing universal themes shared by Americans everywhere yet using "local color" to provide immediacy and interest.

Of the numerous practitioners of local color, Harriet Beecher Stowe with her *Uncle Tom's Cabin* and the more comic Joel Chandler Harris with his Uncle Remus stories are singled out by Blair as the most accomplished "in the field of humorous depiction." Bret Harte helped launch formally the local color movement with his 1868 assumption of the editorship of the *Overland Monthly*, and with the 1870 publication of *The Luck of Roaring Camp*.

In addition to these three, who probably emphasized humor more than the rest, there are numerous others, among them Edward Eggleston, Mary Wilkins Freeman, Zona Gale, Hamlin Garland, and Sarah Orne Jewett, to name a few. Blair and Hill list "fifty of the most prominent ones" in a footnote.[9] As a group, they provide a transition between the racy southwestern humor and the genteel realism of the late nineteenth century.

Studies of American humor generally touch, however briefly, upon several major nineteenth-century authors from "American Literature Proper": Cooper, Thoreau, Melville, Poe, and Whitman. Of these, Walt Whitman never tried to be funny, but sometimes achieved it unintentionally. James Fenimore Cooper is occasionally amusing, but rarely when he tries to be. His main contribution to American humor was to inspire Clemens' "Fenimore Cooper's Literary Offenses."

The humor of Henry David Thoreau has received attention in recent years. Jesse Bier argues convincingly for the comic art of *Walden* (1854), contending that "much, if not all of it, is conceived as a comic contrast to Benjamin Franklin's *Autobiography*."[10] Better known for his contributions to the Gothic and detective genres, Edgar Allan Poe produced burlesques, parodies, and examples of black comedy. The editor who reviewed Longstreet's *Georgia Scenes* in glowing terms obviously had a natural taste for the cruelty of the frontier. Herman Melville used humor extensively. Bier argues that the first quarter of *Moby Dick* (1851) was intended as "the start of a comic rather than heroic epic."[11] Ishmael says: "Better sleep with a sober cannibal than a drunken Christian." As Hennig Cohen puts it: "Not only did Poe . . . , and Melville use comic effects to temper their predominantly tragic view. They also appreciated the ridiculous for its own sake."[12]

To the West, a writer was growing up with a highly developed appreciation of the ridiculous. Born in 1835, Samuel Clemens was contemporary to and shared characteristics with writers in several "schools": the local colorists, the southwestern humorists, and the literary comedians. *Life on the Mississippi* won praise as a masterpiece of local color. Growing up in frontier conditions similar to those that produced the southwestern humorists, whose works he enjoyed,

Clemens carried to its fruition the oral tale, using a narrative frame, a distinctly characterized narrator, and faithfully rendered dialect. "The Celebrated Jumping Frog of Calaveras County" (1865), the story that brought him national attention, is a classic of this genre, as is "The Blue Jay Yarn," which appeared in *A Tramp Abroad*. As for the literary comedians, he worked with Bret Harte and Charles Farrar Browne ("Artemus Ward") and was enormously successful as a humorous lecturer in his own right.

As a journalist, Clemens toured the Mediterranean and the Holy Land and described his travels in *Innocents Abroad* (1869), the popular account of irreverent Americans faced with the grandeurs of antiquity. In *Roughing It* (1872), he satirized his western experiences, but with an ambivalence regarding the relative virtues of eastern gentility versus western democracy. With Charles Dudley Warner he wrote *The Gilded Age* (1873), a satirical novel considered a weak work, but one that introduced the indomitable Colonel Sellers. 1876 saw the publication of *The Adventures of Tom Sawyer*, Clemens' return to the Hannibal of his childhood. A subsequent European tour led to *A Tramp Abroad* (1880) and *The Prince and the Pauper* (1882). Further musing on his past produced *Life on the Mississippi* (1883), and ultimately, his masterpiece, *The Adventures of Huckleberry Finn* (1884), which has earned Clemens a place in the very top rank of American writers, humorous or otherwise. In his later years he was beset by bankruptcy and personal tragedy. *A Connecticut Yankee in King Arthur's Court* (1889) shows some of his deepening pessimism. His humor grew more and more sardonic in such works as *The Tragedy of Pudd'nhead Wilson* (1894), *The Man That Corrupted Hadleyburg* (1900), and the posthumously published *The Mysterious Stranger* (1916).

Earlier critics tended to dismiss Clemens' later works as mere products of depression induced by personal tragedy. Recent studies, however, as Pascal Covici, Jr., points out, give Clemens credit for more conscious artistry and design.[13] Richard Boyd Hauck finds deliberately nihilistic and absurd implications, not only in *Connecticut Yankee* and *The Mysterious Stranger*, but in earlier works as well.[14]

Clemens' achievement lies not so much in innovation but in the way he developed so many genres beyond what contemporary practitioners were able to accomplish. By earning such widespread popular and critical acclaim, both here and abroad, he helped legitimize local color with its realistic attention to detail, the oral tale with its narrative frame and vernacular language (leading to Ring Lardner, Sherwood Anderson, and Ernest Hemingway), and, ultimately, humor itself.

Ambrose Bierce was a man who stood almost as alone in literature as he did in life. His corrosive *Devil's Dictionary* (1911) is certainly no *Josh Billings' Farmer's Allminax*. And Samuel Clemens' moments—even hours—of despair were brief compared to the unrelenting night of Bierce's life and writings. Antithesis suited him well, as he opposed all traditional values and pieties, including capitalism, even democracy itself and the American faith in the common man: "My country, 'tis of thee,/Sweet land of felony,/'Of thee I sing—." Apparently childless in life, he did, however, leave some literary heirs: an occasional sour note in a column of Eugene Field, some of the misogyny evident in Thurber and others, and a sense of nihilism that would be shared by a number of "black humorists" in the middle-to-late part of the twentieth century.

Blair and Hill write of the turbulent decade from 1895 to 1905 as one of conflict between the older, primarily agricultural America and the new, industrial one.[15] Before taking up the more numerous adherents of the rural mode in humor let us look at a couple of urban—or rather *urbane*—practitioners, John Kendricks Bangs and Gelett Burgess.

The Columbia-educated Bangs is the best remembered, perhaps the *only* remembered of the University Wits. His literary fantasy, *A Houseboat on the Styx* (1896), enjoyed a long popularity. Gelett Burgess led a group of San Francisco wits who called themselves "Les Jeunes" in founding the *Lark*, an experimental and highly ecclectic humor magazine. His poem "The Purple Cow" gained Burgess his place in humorous American literature.

While Ambrose Bierce was stewing in his own juices out in California and Bangs and Burgess were entertaining the elite, a rather more genial bunch of fellows was dispensing humor by the column inch back in the Midwest. Bernard Duffey dates Chicago humor from

the advent of Eugene Field's column, "Sharps and Flats," in the *Daily News* in 1883 and sees it as continuing through Peter Finley Dunne's [*sic*] contributions to the rival *Chicago Evening Post* beginning in 1892. George Ade's "Fables in Slang" were added to the morning edition of the *Daily News* in 1896.[16]

While Chicago was hurrying to take its place as the nation's "Second City," many of its inhabitants—and many of its writers—were recently arrived from farms or small towns. Therefore, it is not surprising that the older, more rural, cracker-box humor was still popular.

Eugene Field came to Chicago from Denver, where he had edited the *Tribune*. Some of his humorous items, published in *The Tribune Primer* (1892), were bitter enough to be worthy of Bierce, but he gradually changed his tune. Until his death in 1895, he continued his gentle satire of Chicago's cultural affectations and not-so-gentle satires of its newly rich.

In 1893 Indiana-born George Ade and cartoonist John T. McCutcheon began to collaborate on a daily column, "Stories of the Streets and of the Town," for the *Chicago Record*. In 1897 Ade published *Fables in Slang*, the first in a series of ten such collections. Two of his most popular characters, later to have their own books, were Artie Blanchard, streetwise office boy; and Pink Marsh, savvy black shoeshine man. Although he would leave Chicago to find fame and fortune on Broadway with such plays as *The Sultan of Sulu* (1902), it is these sympathetic characters, with their mixture of wisdom and folly, and, especially, the perfectly reproduced vernacular of their urban slang, that earned him his greatest fame.

Finley Peter Dunne's Mr. Dooley stepped from the *Post* columns in 1898, with the publication of *Mr. Dooley in Peace and War*. Though urban, the Irish saloon keeper is nonetheless a descendant of the rural cracker-box philosophers, and Archey Road is a friendly neighborhood similar to a small town. No mere ethnic stereotype, Mr. Dooley is complex and depicted without condescension. Limited in knowledge and scope, he can nevertheless see through pretension, whether it be that of a genteel literary society or of President McKinley himself. Critics still praise Dunne for the accuracy and the honesty of his characterization, the frequent brilliance of his verbal devices, and the way in which he adapted elements of traditional American humor to an increasingly industrialized, urbanized, ethnicized America.

Other newspaper humorists flourished during this time, including such Chicagoans as Keith Preston, of the *Tribune* and the *Daily News* in the twenties, whose works are collected in *Pot Shots from Pegasus* (1929), and Opie Read. In Detroit, Charles B. Lewis, "The Detroit Free Press Man," was entertaining his readers as M. Quad, some of whose pieces were published in *Quad's Odds* (1875).

Kin Hubbard of the *Indianapolis News* also enjoyed widespread popularity with his wise fool, Abe Martin, of Brown County, Indiana. In his columns and self-illustrated annuals, Hubbard dispensed cracker-box humor to a vast readership, possibly rivaling that of Will Rogers. Like the Chicago humorists, he is faulted for the mildness of his satire.

Known primarily for his poetry and his association with the Harlem Renaissance, Langston Hughes is also the creator of Jesse B. Semple, "the cracker-box oracle of Harlem." "Simple," as he was nicknamed, appeared in newspapers as well as in five books, from *Simple Speaks His Mind* (1950) to *Simply Heavenly* (1963).

Contemporary of the midwestern cracker-boxers and a syndicated newspaper columnist reportedly reaching one hundred million readers a year, Will Rogers lumped himself with them when referring to "us country columnists;"[17] Rogers' multiple careers in vaudeville, radio, and films gave him a platform for his stage persona beyond anything the literary comedians could have imagined. Noriss Yates describes him as "a crackerbox sage who had discarded the crackerbox for mass media."[18] Epigrammatic and aphoristic as his wisecracks are, his books, such as *The Illiterate Digest* (1924), are lightly regarded. Many critics agree with Jesse Bier, who writes: "More and more, he became the occasionally irreverent critic but increasingly genial and harmless western type."[19] As Rogers told Max Eastman, "I don't like to make jokes that hurt anybody."[20]

Sometimes mentioned with Rogers is his friend, Kentuckian-turned New Yorker Irvin S. Cobb. In addition to him, other figures of the period persisted, survivors of some "school" of the past, perhaps local color or literary comedy, of whom historians say little more than "continued in the tradition of so-and-so."

One of these, William Sydney Porter, "O. Henry," had been a humorous newspaper columnist in the nineties. He became enormously popular for stories that dealt with the forgotten common people, "the four million" about which no one else bothered to write. He put one-dimensional characters (Jesse Bier refers to him as "the Bret Harte of Gotham")[21] into stories with ironic plot twists and surprise endings.

Following in Porter's footsteps down Broadway was Damon Runyon, popular New York columnist and short story writer. Like O. Henry, he wrote about Broadway types (*Guys and Dolls*, 1932, on which the 1950 Broadway musical was based, was one collection of these tales), and like O. Henry, he is accused of sacrificing his talent to sentimentality.

A man who created a tradition of literary and social criticism that often reached the level of invective, but exuberant, entertaining invective, was Baltimore journalist and editor, H. L. Mencken. Conservative and elitist, during the twenties he was the scourge of mediocrity, of orthodoxy, of the "booboisie." His Biercean *A Book of Burlesques* was published in 1916.

Blair and Hill entitle their chapter introducing the post–World War I humorists "The Lunatic Fringe," separating them into two groups: the Colyumnists, those "retaining vestiges of 'native' humor in daily columns," and the members of the Algonquin Round Table (also known as "the vicious circle").[22] The Colyumnists included Christopher Morley, Heywood Broun, Franklin P. Adams, and Don Marquis.

Regarded as the best of the lot, Don Marquis published in 1912 a novel, *Danny's Own Story*, reminiscent of *Huckleberry Finn*. In the same year he was hired by the *New York Evening Sun* to write a column "The Sun Dial," in which appeared archy the cockroach, the reincarnation of a free verse bard. Later, he was joined by mehitabel the cat, the reincarnation of Cleopatra. In 1927 their adventures were collected in *archy and mehitable*. Marquis created another crackerbox philosopher, this one human: Clem Hawley, the likable Old Soak. Collected columns were published as *The Old Soak* in 1921, and a dramatization was successful on Broadway in 1922. Critics have credited Marquis with depth, mastery of vernacular style, and sheer comic inventiveness.

Chicago columnist, Ring Lardner, was also a transitional figure who wrote a humorous sports column "In the Wake of the News" for the *Chicago Tribune* from 1913 to 1919. His vernacular stories, published in national magazines and collected in such volumes as *You Know Me Al* (1916), followed in the tradition of his colleagues Ade and Dunne, except that his fools were less often wise than the others; and Lardner seemed to find fewer redeeming values in his characters. (The Gullible family of *Gullible's Travels* [1917] is an exception.)

In 1919 Lardner moved with his family to New York, where in collaboration with George Kaufman, he wrote *June Moon* (1929). Critics such as Edmund Wilson and H. L. Mencken praised *How to Write Short Stories* (1924). Lardner excelled as the chronicler of the lower middle class, white folk of little education and breeding, who expose themselves with each spoken—or misspoken—word. Yet, also, in growing alienation, some of his Little Men, like the narrator of "Large Coffee" (1934), are driven to despair. It is in these later stories, characterized by Blair and Hill as "in the dead center of the lunatic fringe," [23] that Ring Lardner anticipated the dementia praecox school.

In contrast with the rural humor that remained alive in the Midwest were the "more caustic, urbane, and neurotic" wits of the Algonquin Hotel's Round Table. Participants in the verbal mayhem included Robert Benchley, George S. Kaufman, Dorothy Parker, Alexander Woolcott, and Edna Ferber, along with Ring Lardner and others who visited occasionally.

In 1925 Harold Ross published the first edition of *The New Yorker*. Characterized by witty stories and features, as well as distinctly sophisticated and sometimes off-the-wall cartoons, the magazine advertised itself as "not for the old lady in Dubuque." Early contributors included Corey Ford, Phyllis McGinley, Ogden Nash, and Clarence Day, who would become well known for *Life With Father* (1935). Algonquin Wits such as Woolcott, Parker, Lardner, and Benchley soon joined the magazine, followed by James Thurber in 1927 and S. J. Perelman in 1932. Thus was established the nucleus that would shape the character of *The New Yorker* and of American humor for years to come, as these writers refined the character of the "Little Man." As Bernard DeVoto puts it: "the literary comedians . . . presented themselves as Perfect Fools, whereas our comedians present themselves as Perfect Neurotics." [24]

One of the deadliest wits of the vicious circle belonged to Dorothy Parker, whose *bon mots* are frequently quoted. Norris Yates compares her use of language to expose idle middle-class women with that of Ade, Lardner, and Marquis. [25] Her books include *Enough Rope* (1926), *Sunset Gun* (1928), and *The Collected Dorothy Parker* (1973). She also wrote plays, screenplays, and poems: *Collected Poems: Not So Deep as a Well* (1936).

Highly popular as a lecturer and film actor, Robert Benchley developed his persona, the "normal bumbler," after the manner of the literary comedians. As a lecturer, he held forth in pedantic manner on such topics as "Through the Alimentary Canal with Gun and Camera" and "The Social Life of the Newt." The stories find him incapable of coping with one crisis after another: tying a necktie, opening a bank account, riding an elevator, etc. No matter what challenges modern life presents, Benchley's bumbler is not up to it: "It is a little terrifying, with all that I have to do this week, to discover that I have a dementia praecox into the bargain." Screenwriting and acting took up an increasing amount of Benchley's time in the forties, and eventually he gave up his other writing. Representative titles include: *20,000 Leagues Under the Sea; or, David Copperfield* (1928), *My Ten Years in a Quandry* (1936), and an excellent sampler, *Inside Benchley* (1942). Accompanied by his primitive line drawings, much of James Thurber's writing is whimsical, but frequently with an underlying note of desperation. If Benchley's neurotics are "perfect," Thurber's are a mess.

Their defeat is often total and humiliating. Critics frequently cite Thurber's misogyny, for women, especially wives, are frequently the means of the Little Man's undoing.

Early reminiscences of Columbus and Ohio State are filled with nostalgic wackiness. Other, later pieces, written during his struggles with ill health, alcohol, nervous breakdowns, and blindness, are bleak, even nihilistic. He published numerous collections, including: *The Seal in the Bedroom and Other Predicaments* (1932), *Fables For Our Time, and Famous Poems Illustrated* (1940), and *The Male Animal* (1940), a successful comedy written with Elliott Nugent.

E. B. White was Thurber's friend, collaborator, and writing instructor. He provided a wide variety of material for *The New Yorker* and worked with Thurber on *Is Sex Necessary (Or Why You Feel the Way You Do)* (1929). Blair and Hill see him as appearing "to belong with both the citified New Yorkers and countrified humorists."[26]

The youngest of the main cadre, S. J. Perelman, began contributing to *The New Yorker* in 1931, with two Marx Brothers screenplays, *Monkey Business* (1931) and *Horsefeathers* (1932) already to his credit. Unlike the Little Man of Benchley and Thurber, Perelman's has, at least at the beginning of a misadventure, delusions of grandeur. He sometimes attempts to be aggressive—he frequently throws things in his frenzy, without stopping to ask how they got there. A devotee of Henry James, Perelman writes in a much more elaborate style than Thurber or White. And, an admirer of James Joyce as a comic writer, he engages much more often in verbal pyrotechnics, frequently unleasing torrents of nonsense and *non sequitur*, puns and literalisms, burlesques and parodies, a practice that also puts him in the tradition of Benchley and earlier literary comedians such as Artemus Ward. He wrote several plays, some with his wife, Laura. *One Touch of Venus* (1943), co-written by Ogden Nash was successful as a play and as a film (1948), screenplay by Perelman. His stories and other pieces were collected in numerous books, including travel books such as *The Swiss Family Perelman* (1950) and *Westward Ha! or Around the World in Eighty Cliches* (1948). The 120 pieces in *The Most of S. J. Perelman* (1958) provide a good cross-section of his work up to that time.

Stephen H. Gale sees Perelman's work in the sixties, collected in *Chicken Inspector No. 23* (1966) and *Baby, It's Cold Inside* (1970) as reflecting "a kind of loss of innocence, a continuation of . . . ''[27] Blair and Hill see Perelman, along with Benchley, as "stopping short of satire," with the "tidal waves of banter, frivolity, and whimsy" preventing "most readers from coming away from the *New Yorker*-style material clutching any message." [28] Though inevitably defeated, their characters escape the annihilation that lurks ahead for the next generation of antiheroes.

Humor during this period was by no means confined to the newspaper columns or the pages of *The New Yorker*. So-called serious novelists were adapting humor to their ends. For example, a humorous novel, *Tortilla Flat* (1935), first drew popular attention to John Steinbeck. And of William Faulkner, M. Thomas Inge has written: "In his private life, as well as his public fiction, Faulkner practices the hyperbole and comic exaggeration that have characterized American humor from William Byrd to John Barth."[29] Although there is humor in most of his works, the following are frequently considered to be more purely comic: *The Sound and the Fury* (1929), *As I Lay Dying* (1930), *The Hamlet* (1940), and *The Reivers* (1963). Faulkner's fellow heir to the southwestern humorous tradition, Erskine Caldwell, depicts poor whites in *Tobacco Road* (1932) and *God's Little Acre* (1933).

Perelman's brother-in-law, Nathaniel West, was praised by critics but ignored by the book-buying public during his lifetime. His bleak, mocking novels are *The Dream Life of Balso Snell* (1931), *Miss Lonelyhearts* (1939). He is frequently discussed as a predecessor of the black humorists.

The postwar era saw a proliferation of novels concerned with the development of suburbia, as various writers, some of them known for other themes, took potshots at the remote land where the Man in the Gray Flannel Suit hung his hat and briefcase. Representatives include: Max Shulman, *The Zebra Derby* (1946), *The Many Loves of Dobie Gillis* (1951), and *Rally Round the Flag, Boys* (1957); Peter DeVries, *Comfort Me with Apples* (1956); and Jean Kerr, *Please Don't Eat the Daisies* (1957).

The term "black humor" has been used widely—and loosely—since the mid-sixties to refer to a growing body of fiction reflecting what Brom Weber characterizes as: "its rejection of morality and other human codes ensuring earthly pattern and order, from its readiness to joke about the horror, violence, injustice, and death that rouses its indignation, from its avoidance of sentimentality by means of emotional coolness, and from its predilection for surprise and shock"[30] the concept was not new; there were European precedents, and, as we have seen, examples of black humor may be found in the work of American writers including Poe, George Washington Harris, Melville, Twain, Bierce, West, and others.

Reputed practitioners of black humor, along with a sampling of their works, include: John Barth, *The Floating Opera* (1956), *The End of the Road* (1958), and *The Sot-Weed Factor* (1960); Bruce Jay Friedman, *Stern* (1962) and *A Mother's Kisses* (1964); Joseph Heller, *Catch-22* (1961); Donald Barthelme, *Snow White* (1967), *Unspeakable Practices, Unnatural Acts* (1968); Thomas Pynchon, *V* (1963), *The Crying of Lot 49 (1966),* and *Gravity's Rainbow* (1973); Ken Kesey, *One Flew Over the Cuckoo's Nest* (1962); Terry Southern, *The Magic Christian* (1959) and *Candy* (1964); J. P. Donleavy, *The Ginger Man* (1958); and Kurt Vonnegut, *Mother Night* (1961), *Cat's Cradle* (1963), *God Bless You, Mr. Rosewater* (1965), and *Slaughter-House Five* (1969); Vladimir Nabokov, *Lolita* (1955); Walker Percy, *The Moviegoer* (1961) and *Love in the Ruins* (1971); Robert Coover, *The Universal Baseball Association, Inc., J. Henry Waugh, Prop.* (1968); and James Purdy, *Cabot Wright Begins* (1964).

Although, as Max Schulz writes, black humor was a "phenomenon of the sixties,"[31] its concerns are still very much in evidence, both in subsequent works of the writers listed above and in works by other contemporary novelists in whose books comedy is a major concern. Philip Roth, *Goodbye, Columbus* (1959), *Portnoy's Complaint* (1969), *Our Gang* (1971), *The Breast* (1972), and *The Great American Novel* (1973); J. D. Salinger, *The Catcher in the Rye* (1951); Henry Miller, *Tropic of Cancer* (1934) and *Tropic of Capricorn* (1939); Saul Bellow, *The Adventures of Augie March* (1953) and *Henderson The Rain King* (1959); Richard Brautigan, *A Confederate General from Big Sur* (1964), *Trout Fishing in America* (1967), and *Revenge of the Lawn* (1971); Richard Fariña, *Been Down So Long It Looks Like Up to Me* (1966); John Irving, *The World According to Garp* (1978) and *The Hotel New Hampshire* (1981); Erica Jong, *Fear of Flying* (1973); John Hawkes, *The Lime Twig* (1961) and *Second Skin* (1964); Ishmael Reed, *The Freelance Pallbearers* (1967) and *Flight to Canada* (1976); Tom Robbins, *Even Cowgirls Get the Blues* (1976) and *Still Life With Woodpecker* (1980); Tom McGuane, *The Sporting Club* (1969) and *The Bushwhacked Piano* (1971); Wallace Markfield, *To an Early Grave* (1964); Stanley Elkin, *Boswell: A Modern Comedy* (1964); John Nichols, *A Ghost in the Music* (1979); John Kennedy Toole, *A Confederacy of Dunces* (1980); Rita Mae Brown, *Rubyfruit Jungle* (1973) and *Southern Discomfort* (1981); Charles Portis, *True Grit* (1968) and *Masters of Atlantis* (1985); and Lisa Alther, *Kinflicks* (1975).

The theater, like the novel, was influenced by the rise of black humor, with the additional impetus of Samuel Beckett's Theater of the Absurd, as evidenced by the works of Edward Albee, *Zoo Story* (1960), *The Sandbox* (1960), *The American Dream* (1961), and *Who's Afraid of Virginia Woolf? (1962); Arthur Kopit, Oh Dad, Poor Dad, Mama's Hung You in the Closet and I'm Feelin' So Sad* (1962), *The Day the Whores Came Out to Play Tennis* (1965), and *Indians* (1969); and Murray Schisgal, *The Tiger* (1963), *Luv* (1964), and *All Over Town* (1974). Still farther off-Broadway, Terrence McNally, *Next* (1968), *Witness* (1968), *Where Has Tommy Flowers Gone? (1971)*, and the less black but more farcical *The Ritz* (1975); John Guare, *Rich and Famous* (1976) and *Bosoms and Neglect* (1979); and Jules Feiffer, *Feiffer's People* (1968), *Little Murders* (1967), and *Knock Knock* (1976).

Broadway's popular Neil Simon has seldom impressed the critics with what most consider to be weakly plotted, gag-dominated plays, such as *Barefoot in the Park* (1963), *The Odd Couple* (1965), and *The Sunshine Boys* (1972), but financially he is considered to be the most successful playwright ever.

Newspaper columnists continue to supply their readers with humor, as the success of several widely different representative ones will attest. Erma Bombeck has attained great popularity with her gentle, self-satires of domestic life, including *At Wit's End* (1967) *I Lost Everything in the Post-Natal Depression* (1973) and *The Grass Is Always Greener Over the Septic Tank* (1976) and *Motherhood, the Second Oldest Profession* (1983). The columnist most consistently concerned with political matters is Art Buchwald whose collections include: *Son of the Great Society* (1966), *I Never Danced at the White House*

(1978), *While Reagan Slept* (1983), and *You Can Fool All of the People All of the Time* (1985).

Others deal with politics occasionally: Russell Baker, author of *Washington: City on the Potomac* (1958), *All Things Considered* (1965), *Poor Russell's Almanac* (1972), *So this Is Depravity*, and *The Rescue of Miss Yaskell* (1983); *The Nation* columnist Calvin Trillin, author most recently of *With All Disrespect: More Uncivil Liberties* (1985); and Georgian Roy Blount, Jr., who writes for *The Atlantic Monthly* and is the author of *Crackers* (1980), *About Three Bricks Shy of a Load* (1981), *One Fell Soup* (1982), *What Men Don't Tell Women* (1984), and *Not Exactly What I Had in Mind* (1985).

While Erma Bombeck inhabits some vague, universal suburb and Baker and especially Buchwald are associated with Washington, D.C., Mike Royko is an urban cracker-box throwback from Chicago; he'll share with his national readership the foibles of whatever mayor is trying to run the city, and he'll take on the quiche-eaters of San Diego at the drop of a National League Pennant. Two collections of his columns are *I May Be Wrong, But I Doubt It* (1968) and *Slats Grobnik and Some Other Friends* (1973), *Sez Who? Sez Me* (1982), and *Like I Was Sayin'* (1984).

Another cracker-box survivor, although not a columnist, is Garrison Keillor. His meandering tales of Lake Wobegon, Minnesota, "where all the women are strong, all the men are good-looking, and all the children are above averaage," appeared in *The New Yorker* and were broadcast on public radio. This material is dealt with in *Happy to Be Here* (1982), *Lake Wobegone Days* (1985), and *Happy to Be Here: Even More Stories and Comic Pieces* (1986). In a more cynical, epigrammatic and urban mode are Fran Lebowitz's *Metropolitan Life* (1978) and *Social Studies* (1981) and P. J. O'Rourke's *Modern Manners* (1983). O'Rourke has also written *The Bachelor Home Companion* (1987) and *Republican Party Reptile* (1987), the latter a self-proclaimed example of that rarity, humor from the conservative Republican point of view.

ISSUES

Writing about literary humor has never been easy. Nobody wants to see a favorite joke "dissected"; even important humorists like Mark Twain and Woody Allen worry that comedy isn't very "grown-up"; and in scholarly circles, achieving respectability for anything popular or funny is usually an uphill battle. To make matters worse, today we find ourselves in a world that looks to many observers like Emmeline Grangerford's funereal drawings: "blacker mostly than is common."

Given this state of affairs, the decade-old debate between Jesse Bier's analysis of post–World War II American literary humor in *The Rise and Fall of American Humor* and Walter Blair and Hamlin Hill's perspective in *America's Humor* is still very much alive. In 1968 Bier argued that with 1960's "black humor,"

American humor had reached its nadir in "hopelessness . . . noncommunication and pessimism." Thus, although he did not deny possibilities for recovery, modern writing represented for him the "decline" of the American literary humor tradition.[32] Conversely, Blair and Hill concluded their history of *America's Humor* on a more positive note. According to them, many contemporary humorists are still producing "dark gray" rather than "black humor," and since even black humor "is a distinct strain from traditional popular humor and underground humor . . . it allows for an even wider range of potential comic mixtures that the contemporary humorist can exploit."[33] Blair and Hill saw a pluralism and cross-generic fertilization occurring in contemporary American humor as it is constantly infused and enlivened by "oral stories and exchanges." In this light, they asked, "How can American humor ever fade away?"[34]

Although S. J. Perelman's phrase, "Baby It's Cold Inside," holds true for many writers today, and Bier's viewpoint appears to be on the ascendant, historically, American humor as well as its theory and criticism have tended to be surprisingly and incongruously oppositional. Happily, even in the face of an overdeterminate cultural ideology, writers and critics of humor alike have continued to find loopholes in apparently closed systems.

To our advantage, postmodern literary theory and practice continue to stress the pluralism that characterized Blair and Hill's point of view. However, as Matei Calinescu observes, "the very notion of plurality is frequently resorted to . . . for purposes of subversion and disruption of the One" and seldom for the "affirmation of the many." He calls instead for a more genuine "pluralistic renaissance."[35] Borrowing the terminology as well as the mood of Mikail Bakhtin's study of the Rabelaisian novel as polyphonous or "dialogic,"[36] Calinescu, with a contemporary understanding of his own (and his opponents') paradoxical positions, nevertheless argues that while "total reducibility, absolute uniqueness of truth, total predictability or perfect linguistic consistency [are] untenable," there are many "happy dwelling places of the mind."[37] Calinescu, pleading a familiar case with a new conditional sensitivity for its difficulties, reminds us that "when a choice is made in full awareness of the meaning and possibilities offered by other alternatives, the chances are that this choice will be more fruitful, more satisfying, and more insight producing."[38]

Much as Blair and Hill perceived the future of humor production as an unending series of "exchanges" and "infusions," contemporary pluralism such as Calenescu espouses tends to see all cultural and literary criticism and theory in process. Applied to the study of American literary humor, a pluralistic approach would encourage a variety of critical and scholarly perspectives in a "dialogic" climate. Such an outlook fosters a rich interweaving of traditional and revisionist entrances to texts—a convergence of different voices and languages within text.

From this point of view, greater diversity is needed in several areas. Perhaps the most immediate absence that deserves remedy involves retrieving the "comedic" in contemporary writing. We recall that even the late works of Mark Twain contain moments of recovery, that few writers are able to sustain a constant mood of despair; in fact, it may be in the midst of hopelessness that ludicrous moments are best defined. While admitting to its often "painful" nature, Jerome Klinkowitz celebrates the "hilarious self-conscious artistry" of contemporary fiction.[39] And Ronald Wallace emphasizes "humor" from an affirmative tradition along with "blackness" in contempoary comic novels.[40] Most critics today, however, are less inclined to concentrate on this tension. Not only in fiction, but in drama and poetry, there is need to recover the humorous and to study how it works within a variety of recent texts. Moreover, in view of contemporary linguistic theory and the tendency to see texts as hermetic, literary humor's efficacy as a corrective to social and political problems remains an important part of the general debate.

The principles involved in a pluralistic approach hold as well for critical readings of individual writers' texts. In the wake of structuralist, poststructuralist, Marxist, feminist, and psychoanalytical theory, American literary humor should receive more attention as a field of concentration. All is frontier again in light of newer stategies such as Norman Holland's brand of reader-response theory. Ideally, the newer perspectives would inform the old and vice-versa, as they do, for instance, in interpretations, such as Cathy N. Davidson's *The Experimental Fictions of Ambrose Bierce*. By using Bierce's own language together with the terminology of reader-response theory, and by grounding the newer approach upon a thorough understanding of traditional scholarship, Davidson combines a sense of history with a contemporary critical outlook to illuminate her subject.

Critical terminology related to the study of literary humor also invites further discussion within historical, cross-cultural, and intergeneric contexts and with an eye to their use within a pluralistic set of critical assumptions. Just so, self-parody, parody, irony, reflexivity, metafiction, and intertextuality—terms that particularly fascinate contemporary writers and critics—refer to devices that have always been characteristic of literary humor to some extent; both terms and techniques warrant reexamination and redefinition within a historical continuum. Traditional literary humor texts deserve reconsideration in light of contemporary terminology, while newer works should be examined in view of tradition. Linda Hutcheon's *A Theory of Parody* makes a valiant effort in tracing the history of the term "parody" and clarifying its contemporary use. Despite the questionable results, the process in which Hutcheon engages her subject provides an example of the way that studies of terminology might move.

Similarly, as Ronald Wallace's (*The Last Laugh*) and only a few other American studies have begun to point out, "black" humor is not merely a recent phenomenon and deserves to be considered historically and from an international perspective. Indeed, with the very nature of genre under siege by semiologists, phenomenologists, structuralists, and poststructuralists, not merely black humor, but a number of literary genres and humorous subgenres should be reexamined with a greater awareness of historical and social contexts. The issues for literary humor studies are those that concern all of literary study, and the problems, like all critical problems, are broadly social, political, and epistemological. The knottiest "issues" for students and researchers of literary humor today are intimately tied to the concerns of postmodern literary, communications, linguistic, and cultural theories. The study of American literary humor now means studying a much larger communication process than many traditional studies encompassed.[41]

Thus, researchers also need to deal more consistently with how literary humor texts are produced, and to pay attention not only to the commercial and sociocultural climates in which these texts are made, but to examine who the people are that read the humor, and who also help to shape it within their particular times and cultures. In this spirit, Louis J. Budd's discussion of Mark Twain as "our" creation is a particularly noteworthy analysis.

A pluralistic attitude toward the study of literary humor also appears to require more broadly representative histories of American literary humor that go beyond the "canon." Modernized as well as traditional humor anthologies should include minor as well as major texts, and the representation of those writers whose exclusion has largely been the result of cultural elitism.[42] In concert with such aims, too, we have need for more comprehensive bibliographies geared to fill a particular role in a world of high technology. In his evaluation of the recent proliferation and homogenization of reference guides, Willis J. Buckingham points out that in an age of on-line computerized bibliographies, individualizing the formats of resource guides in print to the particular topic under consideration, annotating with care, and discovering sources not generally included by on-line bibliographies becomes a special task.[43] The production of such individualized, well-researched, and well-annotated up-to-date bibliographies of American literary humor remains a priority issue.

To create a rich pluralistic, "dialogic" interchange we also need many more intercultural and intracultural studies, more cross-disciplinary studies such as those that converse with sociological, psychological, and anthropological research, more studies of neglected genres and neglected works. A handful of articles and just one full-length contemporary study of humor in poetry only begin to suggest the nature of such gaps in literary humor studies. The appearance of James C. Austin's *American Humor in France* is heartening in this regard, but too few such cross-cultural American studies are presently available. Sarah Blacher Cohen's newly announced series for Wayne State University Press, *Humor in Life and Letters* promises to offer "serious not somber, titillating not tedious" original book-length studies of humor in a number of disciplines, from literature and anthropology to women's studies. The series which will include collections of original essays, anthologies of primary materials, and reprints of classic texts in humor, should satisfy a number of diverse needs in the field.

A critic's style is also a consideration. Blair and Hill's work is a model of informal "humorous" prose style that does not kill the spirit of the comic texts it analyzes. While more solemn approaches to humor today tend to abandon that example, some deconstructionist criticism, filled with paradox, pun, and wordplay, offers a later, though extreme example for the interplayfulness of critic and text. More accessible are experiments with critical style in books such as Neil Schmitz's *Huck and Alice: Humorous Writing in American Literature*. Schmitz's study allows us to see a reading in process, and because of its self-consciousness, it provides a recent idea of the sorts of stylistic games critics of literary humor can play.

All of this falls into what Walter Blair might call "fighting for a faith." The hope is that in these anxious times when moments that combine insight and delight are rare, literary humor is still one of our most valuable fictions. If inconclusiveness still permits choice, we can choose to believe that American literary humor, its criticism, and theory are moribund, or we can hope that our favorite works of literary humor, as well as the theory and criticism that help us read them, will stubbornly refuse to come to the funeral our culture seems determined to arrange. Some years ago at a Modern Language Association American Literature Section meeting, John S. Tuckey, in a quietly oppositional spirit, put a challenge to scholars who liked solemnly to discuss only the relentless defeat in Mark Twain's late works. That challenge, which Tuckey put in Twain's own words—to "dream other dreams and better,"—remains a good suggestion for students of American literary humor even today.

NOTES

1. Louis D. Rubin, Jr., "The Great American Joke," in Louis D. Rubin, Jr., ed., *The Comic Imagination in American Literature* (New Brunswick, N.J.: Rutgers University Press, 1973), p. 12.

2. Walter Blair and Raven McDavid, Jr., eds., *The Mirth of a Nation* (Minneapolis: University of Minnesota Press, 1983), p. xi.

3. Walter Blair, *Native American Humor* (San Francisco: Chandler, 1937), p. 11.

4. Jennette Tandy, *Crackerbox Philosophers in American Humor and Satire* (New York: Columbia University Press, 1925), p. 11.

5. Blair, *Native American Humor*, p. 38.

6. Tandy, *Crackerbox Philosophers*, p. 11.

7. Blair, *Native American Humor*, p. 62.

8. Jesse Bier, *The Rise and Fall of American Humor* (New York: Holt, Rinehart and Winston, 1968), p. 82.

9. Walter Blair and Hamlin Hill, *America's Humor: From Poor Richard to Doonesbury* (New York: Oxford University Press, 1978), pp. 264–65.

10. Bier, *Rise and Fall*, p. 363.

11. Ibid., p. 316.

12. Hennig Cohen, "A Comic Mode of the Romantic Imagination," in Rubin, ed., *The Comic Imagination in American Literature*, p. 93.

13. Pascal Covici, Jr., "Mark Twain," *Dictionary of Literary Biography, American Humorists: 1800–1950*, Vol. 2 (Detroit: Gale Research, 1982), p. 553.

14. Richard Boyd Hauck, *A Cheerful Nihilism: Confidence and "The Absurd" in American Humorous Fiction* (Bloomington: Indiana University Press, 1971), p. 151.

15. Blair and Hill, *America's Humor*, pp. 367–68.

22 Nancy Pogel and Paul Somers, Jr.

16. Bernard Duffey, "Humor, Chicago Style," in Rubin, ed., *The Comic Imagination in American Literature*, p. 208.

17. Quoted in Norris W. Yates, *The American Humorist: Conscience of the Twentieth Century* (Ames: Iowa State University Press, 1964), pp. 116–17.

18. Ibid., p. 125.

19. Bier, *Rise and Fall*, p. 199.

20. Max Eastman, *The Enjoyment of Laughter* (New York: Simon and Schuster, 1936), p. 338.

21. Bier, *Rise and Fall*, p. 198.

22. Blair and Hill, *America's Humor*, pp. 405–6.

23. Ibid., p. 413.

24. Bernard DeVoto, "The Lineage of Eustace Tilly," *Saturday Review of Literature* 16 (September 25, 1937), p. 20.

25. Yates, *American Humorists*, pp. 265–73.

26. Blair and Hill, *America's Humor*, p. 440.

27. Stephen H. Gale, "S. J. Perelman," *Dictionary of Literary Biography, American Humorists: 1800–1950*, p. 339.

28. Blair and Hill, *America's Humor*, p. 436.

29. M. Thomsa Inge, "William Faulkner," *Dictionary of Literary Biography, American Humorists: 1800–1950*, p. 135.

30. Brom Weber, "The Mode of Black Humor," in Rubin, ed., *The Comic Imagination in American Literature*, p. 365.

31. Max F. Schulz, *Black Humor Fiction of the Sixties* (Athens: Ohio University Press, 1973), p. 15.

32. Bier, *Rise and Fall*, pp. 467–75.

33. Blair and Hill, *America's Humor*, p. 506.

34. Ibid., p. 529.

35. Matei Calinescu, "From the One to the Many: Pluralism in Today's Thought," in Ihab Hassan, ed., *Innovation/Renovation* (Madison: University of Wisconsin Press, 1983), pp. 272–73, 284.

36. Ibid., pp. 269–70. Also see M. M. Bakhatin, *The Dialogue Imagination*, Michael Holquist, ed., Caryle Emerson and Michael Holquist, trans. (Austin: University of Texas Press, 1981), especially "From the Prehistory of Novelistic Discourse," pp. 41–83 and Mikhail Bahktin, *Rabelais and His World*, Helene Iswolsky, trans. (Bloomington: Indiana University Press, 1984).

37. Calinescu, "From the One," p. 285.

38. Ibid., p. 279.

39. Jerome Klinkowitz, *Literary Disruptions* (Urbana: University of Illinois Press, 1975), p. x.

40. Ronald Wallace, *The Last Laugh* (Columbia: University of Missouri Press, 1979), pp. 2–3.

41. John G. Cawelti, "The Question of Popular Genres," *Journal of Popular Film & Television* 13, 2 (1985): 57–60.

42. For a general discussion regarding new literary histories, see Annette Kolodny, "The Integrity of Memory: Creating a New Literary History of the United States," *American Literature* 57, 2 (1985): 290–307.

43. Willis J. Buckingham, "The G. K. Hall Reference Guides in Literature Series: A Second Appraisal," *Resources for American Literary Study* 12, 1 (1982): 67–77.

BIBLIOGRAPHICAL SURVEY

In spite of Dorothy Parker's complaint that every time she tried to describe the comic, she "had to lie down with a cold wet cloth on [her] head,"* brave students of literary humor should probably strike up a frustrating acquaintanceship with humor theory. Paul Lauter's *Theories of Comedy* excerpts several major theoretical texts and makes for a good introduction. Not quite contemporary, Lauter's collection ends with selections from Suzanne K. Langer's *Feeling and Form* and Martin Grotjahn's *Beyond Laughter*. Curiously, D. J. Palmer's *Comedy Developments in Criticism* lacks excerpts from Freud, but a section on "Twentieth Century Views" represents some theorists omitted from Lauter's book. Robert W. Corrigan's collection, *Comedy: Meaning and Form* also contains additional theoretical writings.

Other relevant studies include Max Eastman, *The Enjoyment of Laughter*, Charles R. Gruner, *Understanding Laughter*, Walter Kerr, *Tragedy and Comedy*, Morton L. Gurewitch, *Comedy: The Irrational Vision*, Robert Bechtold Heilman, *The Ways of the World: Comedy and Society*, Richard Keller Simon, *The Labyrinth of the Comic*, and Mahadev L. Apte, *Humor and Laughter: An Anthropological Approach*. Most of these discussions like Neil Schaeffer's *The Art of Laughter*, John Morreall's *Taking Laughter Seriously*, Edward L. Galligan's *The Comic Vision in Literature*, and George McFadden's *Discovering the Comic* begin with summaries and critiques of past theory. Galligan's views are derived from Arthur Koestler's and William Lynch's theories and are discussed at length. Also see Norman Holland's provocative contemporary perspective in *Laughing, A Psychology of Humor*.

The two volumes of *American Humorists, 1800–1950* in the *Dictionary of Literary Biography* (*DLB*) Series, edited by Stanley Trachtenberg, are among the best places to begin gathering bibliography about American literary humor. Together the volumes include relatively up-to-date (1982) lists of primary works and well-selected lists of secondary works for most major and some minor literary humorists. A number of entries also cite research collections. To find additional collections, see Lee Ash, *Subject Collections*, 6th ed. (1985). Bibliographies also appear in Walter Blair and Hamlin Hill's *America's Humor* (up through 1976) and in Jesse Bier's *The Rise and Fall of American Humor* (up through 1967). Bier's is alphabetical and unannotated. Blair and Hill annotate sparingly but tellingly and the bibliography also serves as notes for the chapters in their history; thus, the arrangement is chronological and topical.

References will also be found in standard literary bibliographies such as Lewis Leary's, *Articles on American Literature, 1900–1950 and 1950–1967*; Jacob

---

*The Dorothy Parker quote comes from William Cole's introduction to *The Fireside Book of Humorous Poetry* (New York: Simon and Schuster, 1959), p. xiii, via Ronald Wallace's introduction to *God Be With the Clown* (Columbia: University of Missouri Press, 1984), p. 10.

Blanck's *Bibliography of American Literature*, and Lawrence McNamee's *Dissertations in English and American Literature, 1865–1964*. Popular humor items appear in Larry N. Landrum's well-indexed and cross-referenced *American Popular Culture: A Guide*. In addition, see Louis D. Rubin, Jr., ed., *A Bibliographical Guide to the Study of Southern Literature* and the checklist by Charles E. Davis and Martha B. Hudson in *The Frontier Humorists*. *Abstracts of American Literary Scholarship* summarizes and annotates some of the more significant studies each year as does the more frequently published *Abstracts of English Studies*. Strong selected lists of contemporary humor studies can be found in Sarah Blacher Cohen's *Comic Relief: Humor in Contemporary American Literature* and in Ronald Wallace's *The Last Laugh*. Notes to his *God Be With the Clown* provide references to critical studies of humor in poetry. Also see Janice Radway's "Verse and Popular Poetry" in *Handbook of American Popular Culture*, Vol. 2, M. Thomas Inge, ed.

Researchers seeking additional sources should consult the annual *MLA International Bibliography* and the *Arts and Humanities Citation Index*. Those with access to computers and modems will find the *MLA Bibliography* since 1970 on-line via DIALOG information system and the *Arts and Humanities Citation Index* since 1980 on-line via Bibliographical Retrieval Services (BRS). For literary humor items in popular magazines, *The Magazine Index* is on-line via both DIALOG and BRS. *Abstrax 400*, also on-line via BRS, indexes 400 popular journals from December 1982 to date and will provide brief abstracts of articles.

Such specialized journals as *Studies in American Humor* and *Thalia* (a Canadian scholarly journal of humor) contain reviews in each issue. Prior to merging with *Studies in American Humor* in 1983, *American Humor: An Interdisciplinary Newsletter*, included annotated bibliographies and book reviews of studies in American literary humor in each edition and an annual bibliography as well. *Studies in American Humor* is supposed to be carrying on that tradition; however, that helpful journal has been published only irregularly since 1983. AMS Press has recently collected and reprinted several volumes of *American Humor, An Interdisciplinary Newsletter*. In addition, many scholarly literary journals contain relevant reviews and/or a bibliography in each issue.

Full-length bibliographical studies and reference guides are available for a number of major figures in American literary humor. Space limitations prevent a complete listing here; the most important are cited in the *DLB American Humorists* volumes. Of particular interest is the G. K. Hall "Reference Guides to Literature Series," which includes many volumes devoted to American literary humorists. The *Encyclopedia of American Humorists*, edited by Steven H. Gale, is a reference text of brief critical-bibliographical essays about approximately 150 major and minor literary humorists. The articles contain reference material on the life and most important works of the writers along with an overview which summarizes his or her place in American literature. Each article includes an analysis of the humorist's themes and techniques, as well as bibliographies of primary and secondary sources.

Collections of critical essays also provide an entrance into the field. Several of these, like Louis Rubin's *The Comic Imagination in American Literature* and Harry Levin's *Veins of Humor* are arranged in an historical pattern. Levin's collection deals with both European and American literature. Also see O. M. Brack, Jr.'s edition of *American Humor: Essays Presented to John C. Gerber*. Sarah Blacher Cohen's well-edited *Comic Relief: Humor in Contemporary American Literature* features essays about individual authors such as Nabokov, Roth, and Bellow as well as about types of humor (science fiction, black humor, and absurdist humor) and about humorous devices (tall tale, cruelty, regional, ethnic humor). Maurice Charney's edition of the New York Literary Forum's *Comedy: New Perspectives* includes essays on theory as well as on comedy in drama and literature. Also see Don L. F. Nilsen and Alleen Pace Nilsen's *The Language of Humor The Humor of Language*, which abstracts papers presented at the 1982 Western Humor and Irony Membership (WHIM) Conference. The collection includes a healthy section on humor in American fiction, as well as relevant sections on poetry, bilingual humor, children's literature, feminist studies, linguistics, and "prose styles." A recent collection of essays is William Bedford Clark and W. Craig Turner's *Critical Essays on American Humor* in the Critical Essays on American Literature series edited by James Nagel. It contains a brief introductory historical overview and a section on "Documents in an Evolving Criticism," which reprints essays and excerpts from Jennette Tandy, J. DeLancey Ferguson, Constance Rourke, Bernard DeVoto, Louis J. Budd, Arlin Turner, Hamlin Hill, Jesse Bier, and James M. Cox. In a section devoted to "New Essays," Clark and Turner present the perspectives of Walter Blair on German antecedents to American humor, Robert Miklus on colonial humor, Milton Rickels on southwestern humor and the grotesque, David B. Kesterson on literary comedians, and Sanford Pinsker on modernist humor. Heralding the growing interest in women humorists, Emily Toth writes an important essay, "A Laughter of Their Own: Women's Humor in the Unitied States" to conclude the book's second part. In a "Postscript," Hamlin Hill discusses "The Future of American Humor: Through a Glass Eye, Darkly." The book is well indexed, and the notes to each essay invite further reading.

Another recent collection, Arthur Power Dudden's, *American Humor*, deals with more than literature, but it does include several essays on literary humor. Noteworthy are Peter M. Briggs' "English Satire and Connecticut Wit," Alan Gribben's "The Importance of Mark Twain," and Nancy Walker's, "Humor and Gender Roles: The Funny Feminism of the Post-World War Two Suburbs." Joseph Boskin and Joseph Dorinson's "Ethnic Humor: Subversion and Survival," deals in part with literary humor, for it provides a helpful description of the literary and journalistic backgrounds to ethnic humor in stand-up comedy, radio, film, and television. Researchers should also consult "special issues" of scholarly journals such as *American Quarterly*'s "American Humor" issue (vol. 37, 1), *Thalia's* "Southern Humor" issue (vol. 6, 2), and *Perspectives on Contemporary Literature*'s "20th Century Humor" issue (vol. 7). Also see

"Humor in America," a special issue of *Open Places* published by Stephens College in Spring 1985.

The most comprehensive historical/critical overviews of literary humor are Walter Blair and Hamlin Hill's *America's Humor* and Jesse Bier's *The Rise and Fall of American Humor*. The Appendix to the second volume of the *DLB American Humorists* contains historical/critical essays on "Eastern" humor by Stanley Trachtenberg, "Midwestern" humor by Nancy Pogel, "Western" humor by David B. Kesterson, and "Southern and Southwestern" humor by Sandy Cohen. Willard Thorp's Minnesota Pamphlet *American Humorists* is a short historical overview.

Such broad studies should entice readers to consult more specific historical/ critical works such as Carl Holliday's *The Wit and Humor of Colonial Days* and W. Holland Kenney's introduction to *Laughter in the Wilderness: Early American Humor to 1783*. Martin Roth's *Comedy in America: The Lost World of Washington Irving* makes a bridge between eighteenth- and nineteenth-century American humor. For discussions of nineteenth-century humor, see Jennette Reid Tandy's *Crackerbox Philosophers*, Walter Blair's *Horse Sense in American Humor* and *Native American Humor*, Constance Rourke's *American Humor*, M. Thomas Inge's *The Frontier Humorists: Critical Views*, Kenneth Lynn's *Mark Twain and Southwestern Humor*, Noris W. Yates' *William T. Porter and the Spirit of the Times: A Study of the Big Bear School of Humor*, and David E. E. Sloane's *The Literary Humor of the Urban Northeast, 1830–1890*. Also see Ben C. Clough's edition of *The American Imagination at Work: Tall Tales and Folk Tales*, Hennig Cohen and William B. Dillingham's *Humor of the Old Southwest*, Franklin J. Meine's *Tall Tales of the Southwest*, Wade Hall's *The Smiling Phoenix: Southern Humor from 1865 to 1914*, and Claude Simpson's *The Local Colorists*. Several of these books are collections of primary materials that are noteworthy for their valuable introductions and/or headnotes.

Among the most significant studies of the early twentieth-century and the post–World War I period is Norris Yates' *The American Humorist: Conscience of the Twentieth Century*, which deals with humorists of the nineties and with the rise of "little man" humor in the East. James DeMuth's *Small Town Chicago: The Comic Perspective of Finley Peter Dunne, George Ade, and Ring Lardner* looks at Chicago humor as a mediator between rural and urban traditions during the early twentieth century. Also see Kenny J. Williams and Bernard Duffey's *Chicago's Public Wits: A Chapter in the American Comic Spirit*, and Lawrence Mintz's "American Humour in the 1920s."

Max Schulz's *Black Humor Fiction of the Sixties* provides a transition into the contemporary period. Harry Levin's *Veins of Humor* includes essays by Mathew Winston, "Humour Noir and Black Humor," and by W. M. Frohock, "The Edge of Laughter: Some Modern Fiction and the Grotesque." Other discussions of recent trends in literary humor are Ihab Hassan's "Laughter in the Dark," Brom Weber's "The Mode of 'Black Humor' " in Rubin's *The Comic*

Imagination, Hamlin Hill's, "Black Humor and the Mass Audience," in *American Humor: Essays Presented to John C. Gerber*, and "Modern Amerian Humor: The Janus Laugh." Also see Sanford Pinsker's "The Greying of Black Humor," Stanley Trachtenberg's "Counterhumor: Comedy in Contemporary American Fiction," Richard Poirier, "The Politics of Self-Parody," and William Harmon's " 'Anti-Fiction' in American Humor" in Rubin's *Comic Imagination*. Bruce J. Friedman's *Black Humor* and Douglas M. Davis' *The World of Black Humor* are important black humor anthologies with introductions.

Although it covers earlier periods as well, Richard Boyd Hauck's *A Cheerful Nihilism* is among the best of several studies that emphasize a modernist approach; it includes chapters on Faulkner and Barth as absurdist writers. Like Hauck's study, Ronald Wallace's *The Last Laugh: Form and Affirmation in the Contemporary American Comic Novel* is a lively and coherent discussion that places recent comic fiction within an affirmative historical tradition, but also delineates its contemporary characteristics. Wallace has chapters on Barth, Hawkes, Nabokov, Kesey, and Coover. Also see Charles B. Harris' *Contemporary American Novelists of the Absurd* and David D. Galloway's *The Absurd Hero in American Fiction*. Fred Miller Robinson's *The Comedy of Language: Studies in Modern Comic Literature* examines how characters create a sense of the world through language and convey a sense of reality as metaphysical flux. Robinson's book includes studies of comedy in Faulkner, Wallace Stevens, and Beckett.

Students of modern drama will also want to consult Martin Esslin's important study, *The Theater of the Absurd*. J. L. Styan's chapter on "The Theatre of the Absurd: Beckett and Pinter," in *Modern Drama in Theory and Practice*, and Styan's *Dark Comedy: Development of Modern Comic Tragedy*. Ronald Wallace's *God Be With the Clown* is a full-length study of humor in American poetry that includes discussions of Whitman, Dickinson, Frost, Stevens, and Berryman, as well as a chapter on humor in contemporary poetry. Also read John Vernon's "Fresh Air: Humor in Contemporary Poetry," in Cohen's *Comic Relief*. James C. Austin's *American Humor in France* documents French reception of American literature's "comic spirit" over the last two centuries.

For anthologies of primary materials see Enid Veron's *Humor in America*, which has headnotes, a brief history of humor in American Literature, a glossary of critical terms, and a section on comic theory. Other anthologies are William Cole's *The Fireside Book of Humorous Poetry*, William Harmon's edition of *The Oxford Book of American Light Verse*, Bennett Cerf's *An Encyclopedia of Modern American Humor*. Walter Blair and Raven McDavid's *The Mirth of a Nation* collects dialect humor. See also Brom Weber, *An Anthology of American Humor*, Henry C. Carlisle, *American Satire in Prose and Verse*, E. B. and Katherine White, *A Subtreasury of American Humor*, Kenneth S. Lynn, *The Comic Tradition in America*, George William Koon, *A Collection of Classic Southern Humor, Fiction and Occasional Fact*, and Mordecai Richler, *The Best of Modern Humor*. A number of older primary works as well as some important critical studies have been reprinted by AMS Press, which has also begun publishing reprints of twentieth-century humorists' work in a series edited by M. Thomas Inge.

A listing of the numerous studies of individual writers is beyond the scope of this brief bibliographical survey, but the biographical/critical essays about individual humorists in Trachtenberg's *DLB* volumes are a good place to start. Of special interest, too, are books dealing with humor in the works of traditional American writers such as Melville, James, and Thoreau. Jane Mushabac's *Melville's Humor: A Critical Study* is a strong representative of its type. Also consult special issues of literary journals dedicated to individual figures; the two special "Thomas Berger" issues of *Studies of American Humor* (n.s. vols. 1,1 and 2,1) are exemplary. Important book-length interpretations of contemporary writers and humor such as Sarah Blacher Cohen's *Saul Bellow's Enigmatic Laughter* and Daniel Fuchs' *The Comic Spirit of Wallace Stevens* warrant attention as well. Among recent studies of individual writers are Susan K. Harris, *Mark Twain's Escape from Time* (1982); Louis J. Budd, *Our Mark Twain* (1983); Robert Keith Miller, *Mark Twain* (1983); John J. Pullen, *Comic Relief: The Life and Laughter of Artemus Ward, 1834–1867* (1983); Cathy N. Davidson, *The Experimental Fictions of Ambrose Bierce* (1984); Everett Emerson, *The Authentic Mark Twain* (1984); Catherine McGhee Kenney, *Thurber's Anatomy of Confusion* (1984); Kimball King, *Augustus Baldwin Longstreet* (1984); Anita Lawson, *Irvin S. Cobb* (1984); Nancy Pogel, *Woody Allen* (1987); Thomas Shirer, *Mark Twain and the Theatre* (1984); Paul P. Somers, Jr., *Johnson J. Hooper* (1984); and Kate H. Winter, *Marietta Holley, Life with "Josiah Allen's Wife"* (1984).

CHECKLIST AND ADDITIONAL SOURCES

Ash, Lee. *Subject Collections: A Guide to Special Book Collections and Subject Emphases as Reported by University, College, Public and Special Libraries and Museums in the United States and Canada.* 6th ed. New York: R. R. Bowker, 1985.

Austin, James C. *American Humor in France.* Ames: Iowa State University Press, 1978.

Bier, Jesse. *The Rise and Fall of American Humor.* New York: Holt, Rinehart and Winston, 1968.

Blair, Walter. *Horse Sense in American Humor from Benjamin Franklin to Ogden Nash.* Chicago: University of Chicago Press, 1942.

———. *Mark Twain and Huck Finn.* Berkeley: University of California Press, 1960.

———. *Native American Humor.* New York: American Book Co., 1937; rpt. New York: Chandler, 1960.

——— and Hamlin Hill. *America's Humor: From Poor Richard to Doonesbury.* New York: Oxford University Press, 1978.

——— and Raven McDavid, Jr., eds. *The Mirth of a Nation: America's Great Dialect Humor.* Minneapolis: University of Minnesota Press, 1983.

——— and Franklin J. Meine, eds. *Half Horse Half Alligator: The Growth of the Mike Fink Legend.* Chicago: University of Chicago Press, 1956.

Blanck, Jacob. *Bibliography of American Literature*. New Haven, Conn.: Yale University Press, 1955.

Boatright, Mody C. *Folk Laughter on the American Frontier*. New York: Macmillan, 1949; rpt. 1961, Collier Books.

Brack, O. M., Jr. *American Humor: Essays Presented to John C. Gerber*. Scottsdale, Ariz.: Arete Publications, 1977.

Brooks, Van Wyck. *The Ordeal of Mark Twain*. New York: Dutton, 1920; rev., 1933.

Budd, Louis J. *Critical Essays on Mark Twain 1867–1910*. Boston: G. K. Hall, 1982.

————. *Our Mark Twain: The Making of His Public Personality*. Philadelphia: University of Pennsylvania Press, 1983.

Carlisle, Henry C. *American Satire in Prose and Verse*. New York: Random House, 1940.

Cerf, Bennett, ed. *An Encyclopedia of Modern American Humor*. New York: Modern Library, 1954.

Charney, Maurice. *Comedy High and Low*. New York: Oxford University Press, 1978.

————, ed. *Comedy: New Perspectives*. New York: New York Literary Forum, 1978.

Chittick, V.L.O. *Thomas Chandler Haliburton: A Study in Provincial Toryism*. New York: Columbia University Press, 1924.

Clark, William Bedford and W. Craig Turner, eds. *Critical Essays on American Humor*. Boston: G. K. Hall, 1984.

Clemens, William M. *Famous Funny Fellows*. New York: John W. Lovell Co., 1882.

Clough, Ben C., ed. *The American Imagination at Work: Tall Tales and Folk Tales*. New York: Alfred A. Knopf, 1947.

Cohen, Hennig and William B. Dillingham, eds. *Humor of the Old Southwest*. Boston: Houghton Mifflin, 1964; 2nd ed. Athens: University of Georgia Press, 1975.

Cohen, Sarah Blacher, ed. *Comic Relief: Humor in Contemporary American Literature*. Urbana: University of Illinois Press, 1978.

————. *Saul Bellow's Enigmatic Laughter*. Urbana: University of Illinois Press, 1974.

Cole, William, ed. *The Fireside Book of Humorous Poetry*. New York: Simon and Schuster, 1959.

Cook, Albert. *The Dark Voyage and the Golden Mean: A Philosophy of Comedy*. Cambridge, Mass.: Harvard University Press, 1949.

Corrigan, Robert W., ed. *Comedy: Meaning and Form*. San Francisco: Chandler, 1965.

Covici, Pascal, Jr. *Mark Twain's Humor: The Image of a World*. Dallas: Southern Methodist University Press, 1962.

Cox, James M. *Mark Twain: The Fate of Humor*. Princeton, N.J.: Princeton University Press, 1966.

Davidson, Cathy N. *The Experimental Fictions of Ambrose Bierce: Structuring the Ineffable*. Lincoln: University of Nebraska Press, 1984.

Davis, Douglas M., ed. *The World of Black Humor*. New York: E. P. Dutton, 1967.

Day, Donald. *Will Rogers*. New York: David McKay, 1962.

DeMuth, James. *Small Town Chicago: The Comic Perspective of Finley Peter Dunne, George Ade, and Ring Lardner*. Port Washington, N.Y.: Kennikat Press, 1980.

DeVoto, Bernard. *Mark Twain's America*. Boston: Little, Brown, 1932.

D'Itri, Patricia Ward. *Damon Runyon*. Boston: Twayne, 1982.

Dorson, Richard M. *Jonathan Draws the Longbow*. Cambridge, Mass.: Harvard University Press, 1946.

Dudden, Arthur Power, ed. *Amercan Humor*. New York: Oxford University Press, 1987.

Eastman, Max. *The Enjoyment of Laughter*. New York: Simon & Schuster, 1936.

Elgin, Don D. *The Comedy of the Fantastic, Ecological Perspectives on the Fantasy Novel*. Westport, Conn.: Greenwood Press, 1985.

Emerson, Everett. *The Authentic Mark Twain: A Literary Biography of Samuel L. Clemens*. Philadelphia: University of Pennsylvania Press, 1984.

Esslin, Martin. *The Theater of the Absurd*. Garden City, N.Y.: Doubleday, 1961; rev. ed. Anchor-Doubleday, 1969.

Ferguson, J. Delancey. "The Roots of American Humor." *American Scholar* 4 (Winter 1935): 41–49.

Fiedler, Leslie. "Come Back to the Raft Ag'in, Huck Honey!" *Partisan Review* 15 (June 1948): 664–71.

Ford, Corey. *The Time of Laughter*. Boston: Little, Brown, 1967.

Ford, James L. "A Century of American Humor." *Munsey's Magazine* 25 (July 1901): 482–90.

Fowler, Douglas. *S. J. Perlman*. Boston: Twayne, 1983.

Freud, Sigmund. *Jokes and their Relation to the Unconscious*. (1905) tr. James Strachey. New York: W. W. Norton, 1960.

Friedman, Bruce J., ed. *Black Humor*. New York: Bantam Books, 1965.

Frye, Northrop. *Anatomy of Criticism*. Princeton, N.J.: Princeton University Press, 1957.

Fuchs, Daniel. *The Comic Spirit of Wallace Stevens*. Durham, N.C.: Duke University Press, 1963.

Gaines, James R. *Wit's End: Days and Nights of the Algonquin Round Table*. New York: Harcourt, Brace, Jovanovich, 1977.

Gale, Steven H., ed. *Encyclopedia of American Humorists*. New York: Garland, 1987.

Galligan, Edward L. *The Comic Vision in Literature*. Athens: University of Georgia Press, 1984.

Galloway, David D. *The Absurd Hero in American Fiction*. Rev. ed. Austin: University of Texas Press, 1970.

Gill, Brendan. *Here At the New Yorker*. New York: Random House, 1975.

Grotjahn, Martin. *Beyond Laughter*. New York: McGraw-Hill, 1957.

Gruner, Charles R. *Understanding Laughter: The Workings of Wit and Humor*. Chicago: Nelson-Hall, 1978.

Gurewitch, Norton L. *Comedy: The Irrational Vision*. Ithaca, N.Y.: Cornell University Press, 1975.

Habegger, Alfred. "Nineteenth-Century American Humor: Easygoing Males, Anxious Ladies, and Penelope Lapham." *PMLA* 51 (1976): 884–99.

Hall, Wade H. *The Smiling Phoenix: Southern Humor from 1865 to 1914*. Gainesville: University of Florida Press, 1965.

Hancock, Ernest L. "The Pressing of the American Comic." *Bookman* 22 (September 1905): 78–84.

Harmon, William, ed. *The Oxford Book of American Light Verse*. New York: Oxford University Press, 1979.

Harris, Charles B. *Contemporary American Novelists of the Absurd*. New Haven, Conn.: College and University Press, 1971.

Harris, Susan K. *Mark Twain's Escape from Time*. Columbia: University of Missouri Press, 1982.

Harrison, John M. *The Man Who Made Nasby*. Chapel Hill: University of North Carolina Press, 1969.

Hassan, Ihab. "Laughter in the Dark." *American Scholar* 33 (Autumn 1964): 636–40.

Hassler, David M. *Comic Tones in Science Fiction*. Westport, Conn.: Greenwood Press, 1982.

Hauck, Richard Boyd. *A Cheerful Nihilism: Confidence and "The Absurd" in American Humorous Fiction*. Bloomington: Indiana University Press, 1971.

Heilman, Robert Bechtold. *The Ways of the World: Comedy and Society*. Seattle: University of Washington Press, 1978.

Hill, Hamlin. *Mark Twain and Elisha Bliss*. Columbia: University of Missouri Press, 1964.

————. *Mark Twain: God's Fool*. New York: Harper & Row, 1973.

————. "Modern American Humor: The Janus Laugh." *College English* 25 (December 1963): 170–76.

Hodge, Francis. *Yankee Theatre*. Austin: University of Texas Press, 1964.

Holland, Norman. *Laughing, A Psychology of Humor*. Ithaca, N.Y.: Cornell University Press, 1982.

Holliday, Carl. *The Wit and Humor of Colonial Days*. New York: Frederick Ungar, 1960.

Hoole, W. Stanley. *Alias Simon Suggs: The Life and Times of Johnson Jones Hooper*. University: University of Alabama Press, 1952.

Howe, Will D. "Early Humorists." In *The Cambridge History of American Literature*, Vol. 2. New York: Macmillan, 1948, pp. 703–27.

Howells, William Dean. "Our National Humorists." *Harpers* 134 (February 1917): 442–45.

Hughes, Langston, ed. *The Book of Negro Humor*. New York: Dodd, Mead, 1966.

Hutcheon, Linda. *A Theory of Parody: The Teachings of Twentieth-Century Art Forms*. New York: Methuen, 1985.

Inge, M. Thomas, *The Frontier Humorists: Critical Views*. Hamden, Conn.: Archon, 1975.

Kaplan, Justin. *Mr. Clemens and Mark Twain*. New York: Simon & Schuster, 1966.

Kenney, Catherine McGhee. *Thurber's Anatomy of Confusion*. Hamden, Conn.: Archon Books/Shoestring Press, 1984.

Kenney, W. Holland, ed. *Laughter in the Wilderness: Early American Humor to 1783*. Kent, Ohio: Kent State University Press, 1976.

Kern, Edith. *The Absolute Comic*. New York: Columbia University Press, 1980.

Kerr, Walter. *Tragedy and Comedy*. New York: Simon & Schuster, 1967.

Kesterson, David B. *Bill Nye*. Boston: Twayne, 1981.

————. *Josh Billings*. Boston: Twayne, 1983.

King, Kimball. *Augustus Baldwin Longstreet*. Boston: Twayne, 1984.

Kittredge, George Lyman. *The Old Farmer and His Almanac*. Williamstown, Mass.: Cornerhouse, 1904.

Koestler, Arthur. *The Act of Creation*. New York: Dell, 1967.

Koon, George William. *A Collection of Classic Southern Humor, Fiction and Occasional Fact*. Atlanta: Peachtree Publishers, 1984.

Landrum, Larry N. *American Popular Culture: A Guide*. Detroit: Gale Research, 1982.

Lauter, Paul, ed., *Theories of Comedy*. Garden City, N.Y.: Doubleday Anchor Books, 1964.

Lawson, Anita. *Irvin S. Cobb*. Bowling Green, Ohio: Bowling Green University Press, 1984.

Leacock, Stephen B. *Humor and Humanity: An Introduction to the Study of Humor*. New York: Henry Holt, 1938.

Leary, Lewis. *Articles on American Literature, 1900–1950 and 1950–1967*. Durham, N.C.: Duke University Press, 1954, 1970.

———, ed. *A Casebook on Mark Twain's World*. New York: Crowell, 1962.

Levin, Harry. *Veins of Humor*. Cambridge, Mass.: Harvard University Press, 1972.

Lukens, Henry C. "American Literary Comedians." *Harper's*, 80 (April, 1890): 783–97.

Lynn, Kenneth S. *The Comic Tradition in America: An Anthology of American Humor*. Garden City, N.Y.: Doubleday Anchor Books, 1958.

———. *Mark Twain nd Southwestern Humor*. Boston: Little, Brown, 1959.

McFadden, George. *Discovering the Comic*. Princeton, N.J.: Princeton University Press, 1982.

McNamee, Lawrence. *Dissertations in English and American Literature, 1865–1964*. New York: R. R. Bowker, 1968.

Masson, Thomas L. *Our American Humorists*. New York: Dodd, Mead, 1922.

Meine, Franklin J. *Tall Tales of the Southwest*. New York: Alfred A. Knopf, 1930.

Meredith, George. *An Essay On Comedy and the Uses of the Comic Spirit*. New York: Charles Scribner's Sons, 1897.

Miller, Robert Keith. *Mark Twain*. New York: Frederick Ungar, 1983.

Mintz, Lawrence. "American Humour in the 1920's." *Thalia* 4,1 (Spring/Summer 1981): 26–32.

Morreall, John. *Taking Laughter Seriously*. Albany: State University of New York, 1983.

Mushabac, Jane. *Melville's Humor: A Critical Study*. Hamden, Conn.: The Shoestring Press, 1981.

Nash, Walter. *The Language of Humour: Style and Technique in Comic Discourse*. New York: Longman, 1985.

Nilsen Don L. F. and Alleen Pace Nilsen, eds. *The Language of Humor The Humor of Language*. Tempe: Arizona State University, 1983.

Olson, Elder. *A Theory of Comedy*. Bloomington: Indiana University Press, 1968.

Paine, Alfred Bigelow. *Mark Twain: A Biography*. 3 vols. New York: Harper, 1912.

Palmer, D. J. *Comedy Developments in Criticism*. London: Macmillan, 1984.

Parrington, Vernon Louis, ed. *The Connecticut Wits*. New York: Harcourt Brace, 1926.

Pinsker, Sanford. "The Greying of Black Humor." *Studies in the Twentieth Century* 9 (Spring 1972): 15–33.

Pogel, Nancy. *Woody Allen*. Boston: Twayne, 1987.

Poirier, Richard. "The Politics of Self-parody." *Partisan Review* 35 (Summer 1968): 339–53.

Poirier, William R. *The Comic Sense of Henry James; A Study of the Early Novels*. London: Chatto & Windus, 1960.

Pullen, John J. *Comic Relief: The Life and Laughter of Artemus Ward, 1834–1867*. Hamden, Conn.: Archon Books/Shoestring Press, 1983.

Radway, Janice. "Verse and Popular Poetry." In *Handbook of American Popular Culture*, ed. M. Thomas Inge. Vol. 2. Westport, Conn.: Greenwood Press, 1980.

Richler, Mordecai, ed. *The Best of Modern Humor*. New York: Alfred A. Knopf, 1983.

Rickels, Milton. *George Washington Harris*. New York: Twayne, 1964.

———. *Thomas Bangs Thorpe, Humorist of the Old Southwest*. Baton Rouge: Louisiana State University Press, 1962.

Robinson, Fred Miller. *The Comedy of Language: Studies in Modern Comic Literature*. Amherst: University of Massachusetts Press, 1980.

Rosenberry, Edward H. *Melville and the Comic Spirit*. Cambridge, Mass.: Harvard University Press, 1955.

Roth, Martin. *Comedy in America: The Lost World of Washington Irving*. Port Washington, N.Y.: Kennikat Press, 1976.

Rourke, Constance. *American Humor: A Study of the National Character*. New York: Harcourt, Brace, 1931. rpt. Doubleday Anchor, 1955.

Rubin, Louis D., Jr., ed. *A Bibliographical Guide to the Study of Southern Literature*. Baton Rouge: Louisiana State University Press, 1969.

——, ed. *The Comic Imagination in American Literature*. New Brunswick, N.J.: Rutgers University Press, 1973.

Schaaf, Barbara. *Mr. Dooley's Chicago*. Garden City, N.Y.: Doubleday, 1977.

Schirer, Thomas. *Mark Twain and the Theatre*. Nurnberg: Verlag Hans Carl, 1984.

Schmitz, Neil. *Of Huck and Alice: Humorous Writing in American Literature*. Minneapolis: University of Minnesota Press, 1983.

Schulz, Max, *Black Humor Fiction of the Sixties*. Athens: Ohio University Press, 1973.

Seelye, John D. *The True Adventures of Huckleberry Finn*. Evanston, Ill.: Northwestern University Press, 1970.

Shackford, James Atkins. *David Crockett, the Man and the Legend*. Chapel Hill: University of North Carolina Press, 1956.

Simard, Rodney. *Postmodern Drama*. New York: University Press of America, 1984.

Simon, Richard Keller. *The Labyrinth of the Comic: Theory and Practice from Fielding to Freud*. Tallahassee: Florida State University Press, 1985.

Simpson, Claude M., ed. *The Local Colorists*. New York: Harper & Row 1960.

Sloane, David E. E., ed. *The Literary Humor of the Urban Northeast, 1830–1890*. Baton Rouge: Louisiana State University Press, 1983.

Smith, Henry Nash, ed. *Mark Twain: A Collection of Critical Essays*, Englewood Cliffs, N.J.: Prentice-Hall, 1963.

——. *Mark Twain: The Development of a Writer*. Cambridge, Mass.: Harvard University Press, 1962.

Somers, Paul P. Jr. *Johnson J. Hooper*. Boston: Twayne, 1984.

Styan, J. L. *Dark Comedy: Development of Modern Comic Tragedy*. New York: Cambridge University Press, 1962.

——. *Modern Drama in Theory and Practice*. 3 vols. New York: Cambridge University Press, 1981.

Sypher, Wylie, ed. *Comedy*. Garden City, N.Y.: Doubleday Anchor Books, 1956.

Tandy, Jennette Reid. *Crackerbox Philosophers in American Humor and Satire*. New York: Columbia University Press, 1925.

Thompson, Harold W. and Henry Seidel Canby. "Humor." In *Literary History of the United States*, Vol. II. New York: Macmillan, 1948, pp. 728–57.

Thorp, Willard. *American Humorists*. Minneapolis: University of Minnesota Press, 1964.

Trachtenberg, Stanley, ed. *American Humorists, 1800–1950*. Detroit: Bruccoli-Clark/Gale Research Co., 1982. 2 vols. [*Dictionary of Literary Biography*]

——, "Counterhumor: Comedy in Contemporary American Fiction." *Georgia Review* 27 (Spring 1973): 33–48.

Tuckey, John S. *Mark Twain and Little Satan: The Writing of "The Mysterious Stranger"*. West Lafayette, Ind.: Purdue University Press, 1963.

Turner, Arlin. "Realism and Fantasy in Southern Humor." *Georgia Review*, 12 (Winter 1958): 451–57.

Van O'Connor, William. "Why *Huckleberry Finn* Is Not the Great American Novel." *College English* 17 (October 1955): 6–10.

Veron, Enid. *Humor in America*. New York: Harcourt Brace, Jovanovich, 1976.

Wade, John Donald, *Augustus Baldwin Longstreet*. New York: Macmillan, 1924; new edition, edited by M. Thomas Inge. Athens: University of Georgia Press, 1969.

Wagenknecht, Edward. *Washington Irving: Moderation Displayed*. New York: Oxford University Press, 1962.

Wagner, Linda W. *Phyllis McGinley*. New York: Twayne, 1971.

Walker, Nancy. *The Tradition of Women's Humor in America*. Huntington Beach, Calif.: American Studies Publishing, 1984.

Wallace, Ronald. *God Be With the Clown*. Columbia: University of Missouri Press, 1984.

———. *The Last Laugh: Form and Affirmation in the Contemporary American Comic Novel*. Columbia: University of Missouri Press, 1979.

Weber, Brom. *An Anthology of American Humor*. New York: Thomas Y. Crowell, 1962. rpt. as *The Art of American Humor*, 1970.

Whicher, George F. "Minor Humorists." In *Cambridge History of American Literature*, Vol. III. New York: Putnam's, 1921.

White, E. B. and Katherine S. White, eds. *A Subtreasury of American Humor*. New York: Random House, 1941.

Williams, Kenny J. and Bernard Duffey, eds. *Chicago's Public Wits: A Chapter in the American Comic Spirit*. Baton Rouge: Louisiana State University Press, 1983.

Winter, Kate H. *Marietta Holley, Life with "Josiah Allen's Wife"*. Syracuse, N.Y.: Syracuse University Press, 1984.

Yates, Norris W. *The American Humorist: Conscience of the Twentieth Century*, Ames: Iowa State University Press, 1964.

———. *William T. Porter and The Spirit of the Times: A Study of the Big Bear School of Humor*. Baton Rouge: Louisiana State University Press, 1957.

♦ *2* ♦

The Comics

M. Thomas Inge

OVERVIEW

Historians of the comic strip have traced its origins back to a number of sources in Western art and culture—the pictorial narrative of the medieval Bayeux tapestry, the eighteenth-century print series of such artists as William Hogarth and Thomas Rowlandson, the illustrated European broadsheet, illustrated novels and children's books, and European and American humorous periodicals. Usually the interest in making such connections is to dignify and make respectable what is considered a low-brow form of entertainment, and while it may reflect the influence of all these antecedents, the comics as we know them are a distinct form of artistic expression primarily American in its origin and development.[1]

The comic strip is an open-ended dramatic narrative, usually without beginning or end, about a recurring set of characters on whom the reader is always dropping in. Relationships have been established before we arrive, and they continue with or without our attention, even beyond the life of the comic strip in a world seldom bound by or conscious of time, except in such stories in which characters age as in *Gasoline Alley* or in such intentionally anachronistic strips as *B.C.* The story is told or the daily joke made through a balance of narrative text and visual action with a proper aesthetic balance between the two (that is, both the picture and the words are essential to a full understanding of the meaning). Very few strips rely entirely on the visuals, like *Henry*, or the words, as in the heavily textual Sunday *Prince Valiant*. Dialogue is contained in seeming puffs of smoke called balloons, a feature that goes back to medieval art and early political cartoons, and the strips are published serially in daily newspapers, to be followed by readers in much the same way as the public followed the novels serialized in nineteenth-century periodicals.

The comic strip draws on many conventions associated with the theater, such as dialogue, dramatic gesture, background or scene, compressed time, a view of the action framed by a rectangular structure, and a reliance on props and various stage devices. It also anticipated most of the techniques associated with film, such as montage (before Eisenstein), angle shots, panning, cutting, framing, and the close-up. Beginning photographers and film makers are often referred to such well-designed and highly visual strips as *Buzz Sawyer* and *Steve Canyon* for rudimentary lessons in effective framing and angle shots. Yet the comic strip remains quite unlike the play or the film in that it is usually the product of one artist (or a writer and artist team) who must fulfill simultaneously the roles of scriptwriter, scene designer, director, and producer. The actors must be brought to life in the flat space of a printed page, engage our interest such that we want to return to them on a daily basis, and take less than a minute of our reading time. Working in the contexts of these characteristics establishes the challenge to the comic artist and contributes to the particular features of an art form very unlike any of its related forms in literature and the fine arts.

HISTORY OF COMICS

Any effort to identify the first comic strip is open to challenge, but the artist who helped establish many of its basic features was Richard Outcault in his depiction of the adventures of a street urchin in the low-class immigrant section of New York City called *The Yellow Kid*. First produced for the *New York World* in 1895 as a single-panel cartoon, Outcault's focus on a central character (clad in a yellow shift with dialogue printed across it) and his move to a progressive series of panels with balloon dialogue essentially defined the art form. Despite the enormus popularity of *The Yellow Kid*, its use of the coarse reality of urban life would not prove to be usual fare for American comic strips, although such writers as Stephen Crane, Frank Norris, and Theodore Dreiser were bringing naturalistic views of city life into the mainstream of American literature. It would be two decades before the tensions of urban existence fully entered the comics, and even then it was in the safe midwestern worlds of Sidney Smith's *The Gumps* in 1917 and Frank King's *Gasoline Alley* in 1918, both of which emphasized the pathos of lower middle-class life and the impact of industrialism and technology on the ordinary family. By and large, however, critical realism was never to be a common attitude among comic artists.

What would prove to be an abiding presence in the comic strip was the American sense of humor. Most of the popular titles that came in the wake of *The Yellow Kid* for three decades were primarily characterized by humor and fantasy. These included Rudolph Dirks' *The Katzenjammer Kids*, whose hijinks on an island that was an absurd world unto itself would continue for over eighty years under other hands and titles; Frederick Burr Opper's wonderfully wacky creations *Happy Hooligan*, *Maude the Mule*, and the eternally polite *Alphonse and Gaston*; Richard Outcault's *Buster Brown*, a naughty Lord Fauntleroy whose continual "Resolutions" provided a kind of penance for Outcault's illiterate, dirty Yellow Kid; Winsor McCay's dream fantasy *Little Nemo in Slumberland*, the most beautifully drawn and aesthetically pleasing Sunday page ever to grace the weekly color supplements; Bud Fisher's *Mutt and Jeff*, the first daily comic strip that featured the first successful comic team outside vaudeville with a breezy style all their own; George Herriman's *Krazy Kat*, a classic in abstract absurdist fantasy and a uniquely lyrical love poem; Cliff Sterret's *Polly and Her Pals*, a family situation comedy drawn in an oddly out-of-kilter style reflecting elements of cubism and surrealism; George McManus' *Bringing Up Father*, whose featured players Maggie and Jiggs became a part of marital comic folklore; Billy DeBeck's inspired portrayals of the sporting life and the Appalachian mountaineer in *Barney Google and Snuffy Smith*; Elzie Segar's *Thimble Theatre*, which, after a ten-year run, introduced Popeye, our first and still most popular superhero; and Frank Willard's *Moon Mullins*, a farce about boarding house life that has far outlasted the existence of the boarding house.

These were the years in which the terms *comics* and *funnies* naturally, suitably, and inseparably became identified with this new form of entertainment so outrageously popular that the world sometimes seemed to wait on developments in certain titles (according to one story, the stock market once suspended operations to see if Uncle Bim got married in *The Gumps*), and many a newspaper would owe its very survival to the popularity of these attractive features. Then after three decades of fun and frolic several new elements entered the funnies with the introduction of adventure and dramatic suspense. These had appeared to a certain degree as early as 1906 in *Hairbreadth Harry*, an inventive burlesque of melodrama by C. W. Kahles. The adventure comic strip was established, however, in 1924 by Roy Crane in his vividly rendered *Wash Tubbs* and by Harold Gray whose *Little Orphan Annie* was a successful combination of gothic characterization, exotic suspense, and homespun reactionary philosophy, which gave us our favorite picaro outside Huckleberry Finn.

The adventure strip would not become a dominant genre, however, until 1929 when Richard W. Calkins and Phil Nolan introduced *Buck Rogers*, the first science fiction strip, and Edgar Rice Burroughs' classic primitive hero *Tarzan* was given his first translation into comic strip form (most admirably drawn in the early days by Harold Foster and later by Burne Hogarth). Directly on their heels the 1930s and 1940s would witness a great expansion in this category: Chester Gould's gothic morality play in the police detective mode *Dick Tracy*, Vincent Hamblin's combination of advanced technology and prehistory in *Alley Oop*, Milton Caniff's realistically drawn and effectively plotted tales in *Terry and the Pirates* and his postwar *Steve Canyon*, Alex Raymond's futuristic visions and space fiction in *Flash Gordon*, Lee Falk's men of magic and mystery *Mandrake the Magician* (drawn by Phil Davis) and *The Phantom* (drawn by Ray Moore), Fred Harman's nicely stylized western *Red Ryder*, Frank Harman's masked cowboy *The Lone Ranger* (drawn by Charles Flanders), Harold Foster's grand contribution to the Arthurian romance *Prince Valiant*, Alfred Andriola's well crafted detective stories in *Charlie Chan* and *Kerry Drake*, Roy Crane's second contribution to the tradition with a World War II setting *Buzz Sawyer*, and Will Eisner's gently satiric and impressively rendered masterpiece of crime fiction *The Spirit*. Because of their use of mystery and suspense, the soap opera strips also belong in the adventure category. The best known of these are Allen Saunders and Dale Connor's *Mary Worth*, the matronly Miss Lonelyhearts of the Geritol set; writer Nicholas Dallis's several professionally oriented melo-dramas *Rex Morgan, M.D., Judge Parker*, and *Apartment 3-G*; and Stanley Drake's fashionplate love story *The Heart of Juliet Jones*.

During the 1950s and 1960s satire flourished and dominated comic strips, although it was consistently present at least from 1930 when Chic Young's *Blondie* satirized at first flappers and playboys of the jazz age and subsequently the institution of marriage in what would prove to be for decades the most popular comic strip in the world. Al Capp's hillbilly comedy of 1934, *Li'l Abner* (with little of the authentic Southern humor Billy DeBeck had used in *Snuffy Smith*), evolved into an influential forum for ridiculing the hypocrisies and ab-surdities of the larger social and political trends of the nation. Just as Capp used the denizens of Dogpatch as vehicles for his satire, other artists of postwar America would follow his example and use even more imaginative vehicles, such as the fantasy world of children in *Peanuts* by Charles Schulz, the ancient form of the animal fable by the master of comic mimicry Walt Kelly in *Pogo*, an anachronistic military life in the durable *Beetle Bailey* by Mort Walker, an imagined world of prehistoric man by Johnny Hart in *B.C.*, and the absurd world of a medieval kingdom in *The Wizard of Id* by Johnny Hart and Brant Parker. During the 1970s, this trend would continue in such strips as Dik Browne's *Hagar the Horrible*, which relies on a farcical recreation of life among Viking plunderers, but it would also move in interesting new directions. Russel Myers' *Broom Hilda* a wacky ancient witch, lives in a totally abstract world in the imaginative tradition of Herriman's *Krazy Kat*, while Garry Trudeau's *Doones-bury* moved into the realistic world of the radical student generation of the last decade (but recently updated to follow his characters into their postgraduate lives). Jeff MacNelly's *Shoe* and Jim Davis' *Garfield* have both returned to animals as effective ways of reflecting on the eccentricities of human behavior, as has Berk Breathed's *Bloom County*, which mixes talking animals and humans in a delightful satire of contemporary politics, public trends, and modern neu-roses.

RESEARCH ISSUES AND PROBLEMS

Because of the widespread development of strips of a serious caste devoted to adventure and melodrama, and the efforts of artists to render these stories in a more life-like style, critics and historians of comic art have never been satisfied with the use of the word *comics* and have found even more objectionable the word *funnies*. It is true, they say, that in the beginning comic strips were devoted to humorous stories and situations, but the development of adventure strips calls for another broader term. In response to this concern, some commentators have suggested alternative terms, such as pictorial fiction and visual narratives, none of which have gained widespread acceptance.

It can be argued, however, that the use of the word *comic*, as in the plural noun *comics* or as an adjective in *comic art*, is appropriate and suitable for this form of creative expression, in spite of the great range of topical categories that have been developed, such as domestic drama, science fiction, western and detective stories, medieval romance, war and crime stories, adventure in exotic places, fantasy, satire, situation comedy, and slapstick humor. Not all things "comic" necessarily cause laughter or are overtly funny. Comedy implies an attitude toward life, an attitude that trusts in man's potential for redemption and salvation. Since comic strips always conclude with resolutions in favor of morality and a trust in the larger scheme of truth and justice, as do Dante's *Divine Comedy* or Shakespeare's *Hamlet*, they too affirm a comic view of the social and universal order. While such strips as *Krazy Kat* and *Smokey Stover* may appear absurd, they do not reflect on the world around them as being irrational or devoid of meaning, as in the drama of the absurd. Comic art is supportive, affirmative, and rejects notions of situational ethics or existential despair. For this reason, modern social concerns such as drugs, homosexuality, premarital sex, and abortion seldom enter the funnies, and when they do, as in *Doonesbury* and *Mary Worth*, they rest uncomfortably. It is difficult to treat these ambiguous issues with the full complexity they require.

Most of the popular adventure and suspense titles also reflect a satiric stance on the part of the author/artist—this includes the grotesque villains of Chester Gould's *Dick Tracy*; the romantic and often adolescent adventures of the characters in Milton Caniff's *Terry and the Pirates* and *Steve Canyon*; the exotic and exaggerated antics of such supporting characters as Wash Tubbs, Roscoe Sweeney, and Pepper Sawyer in the works of Roy Crane; the smug cynicism of Dr. Keith Cavell and the exaggerated villains in *Rex Morgan, M.D.*; the arrested adolescent love play of Sam Driver and Abbey Spencer in *Judge Parker*; or the inherent sense of visual and literary parody that invests the world of Will Eisner's *The Spirit*. Such strips as *Li'l Abner, Pogo, Peanuts, Doonesbury*, and *Bloom County* have never been alone in their overt satire and witty criticisms of the status quo.

To satirize life and institutions is to believe in a better mode of conduct that people fail to live up to, and humor may serve as a gentle but sometimes bitter and angry corrective. From the self-conscious parody of the superhero in C. C. Beck's Captain Marvel to Stan Lee's neurotic and insecure Peter Parker, Spider-Man's alter ego, comic books also partake of the pervasive spirit of satire. The underground comic books such as *Zap, Fritz the Cat*, the *Fabulous Furry Freak Brothers*, and *Wonder Wart-Hog* were almost exclusively devoted to debunking not only society but the very form of comic art itself. When a contemporary comic artist decides to treat the Holocaust and the survival of his own parents, as Art Spiegelman has done in his work-in-progress *Maus*, he resorts to the satiric tradition of animal fable and the imagery of funny animal comic books and animated cartoons, the effect of which is to make the subject all the more terrifying because of the incongruity between theme and visual imagery.

In its depictions of characters, physical objects, and landscape, all comic art seems to draw upon and belong to the tradition of caricature and comic exaggeration. There is no such thing arguably as realism to be found in the comics, certainly in the photographic sense or as employed in painting. Even comic strips that have been praised for their authentic detail and meticulous draftsmanship, such as *Terry and the Pirates*, *Buzz Sawyer*, *Prince Valiant*, or *Scorchy Smith* (as drawn by Noel Sickles), do not for all their obvious qualities succeed in bringing to the flat printed page any sense of visual depth or dimensional reality. Realism may be incompatible with comic art, the virtues of which reside in the distinctive and inimitable drawing styles and points of view of the individual comic artists. Steve Canyon and Buzz Sawyer are not better than *Smilin' Jack* because they are more realistic but because Caniff and Crane are more effective stylists and artists than Zack Mosely. *Dick Tracy* does not continue to hold the interests of readers because of its use of authentic police methods, a point in which Chester Gould took pride, but because of its grotesque villains (with ugly exteriors to match their warped souls), stylized violence (long before Arthur Penn's film *Bonnie and Clyde*), and an uncompromising belief in evil and incorrigibility (the number of reformed criminals in the strip can be counted on the fingers of one hand). It is interesting to note that some of the most popular and enduring strips—*Krazy Kat, Peanuts, Pogo, Li'l Abner*, or *Nancy*—have intentionally opted for the abstract, the nonrepresentational, and the art of caricature through either exaggeration or oversimplification.

The comics also belong in the major divisions or patterns of American mainstream humor. The three major comic strips set in the South—*Li'l Abner, Snuffy Smith* (without Barney Google but as created by Billy DeBeck), and *Pogo*— all owe allegiance to the lively school of Southern frontier humor in the nineteenth century whose authors used regional dialects, folk humor, and outrageous actions to puncture the pretensions and hypocrisies of polite society. Some of Snuffy Smith's antics, in fact, were directly inspired by DeBeck's readings in the Sut Lovingood yarns of George Washington Harris; and surely in his study of Georgia dialects before creating Pogo Possum, Walt Kelly must have encountered the Uncle Remus stories of Joel Chandler Harris.

The wise fool who speaks more truth than he knows, from Benjamin Franklin's Poor Richard to Will Rogers and Archie Bunker, has his counterparts in Li'l Abner, Pogo, and Popeye. The timid soul or the little man trapped in the complexities of modern life, as represented by James Thurber's Walter Mitty, Charlie Chaplin's tramp, or Woody Allen's on-screen persona, has his comic strip existence in a multitude of characters, including Andy Gump, Krazy Kat, Casper

Milquetoast, Skeezix Wallet, Dagwood Bumstead, Mickey Mouse, Charlie Brown, Jiggs, Beetle Bailey, Ziggy, and the Perfesser in *Shoe*. The school of zany anarchy and irreverent ridicule to which S. J. Perelman, the Marx Brothers, and Robert Benchley belonged finds its practitioners in the comic strip work of George Herriman, Rube Goldberg, Bill Holman (*Smokey Stover*), and Milt Gross, the last bridging the two worlds of literature and comics with his columns and books using Yiddish-dialect humor and his screwball comic strips such as *Nize Baby, Count Screwloose*, and *That's My Pop!*

The comics have been produced within a narrow set of limitations throughout their existence—the space allowed them on a printed page, which has been gradually reduced over the past decade to an extremely small size today, the necessity to carry forth the action or deliver the punch line daily within three or four panels at most, the limited number of words allowable in a speech balloon, and the difficulties of maintaining a distinctive style of art in the available space. These restrictions have worked against the form and discouraged some artists, yet numerous others have seen these as challenges and have brought the comics to unusual levels of distinction.

It can be argued that despite such bright spots as *Krazy Kat, Pogo, Peanuts*, and *Doonesbury*, the comic strip has not reached its aesthetic potential or become a valid art form, as has film. These very accomplishments, however, are sufficient to suggest its genuine potential as an art form for the future. Given the fact that we have entered an age in which nearly all information is conveyed by visual means (film, television, and computer screens), and assuming that the Gutenberg age has approached its end, it is possible that the comics of the future may remain one of our last links with the printed word.

In any case, the comics clearly belong to the great body of humor that Americans cherish in their oral traditions, literature, stage entertainments, film, radio, and television. They soften the impact of reality by providing comic distance on life's dangers, disasters, and tragedies, and enable us to laugh at ourselves as the pretentious creatures we often become. Yet the comics are a form of cultural expression we have come neither to understand nor appreciate. When we do, the comics will be found to be one of those humanistic forces that add quality to life and enable us to believe in man's promise through the saving grace of comedy.

NOTE

1. This chapter contains revised material drawn from my essays "Comic Art," *Handbook of American Popular Culture*, Vol. 1 (Westport, Conn.: Greenwood Press, 1978), and "What's So Funny About the Comics?" to appear in a special issue of the German journal *Amerikastudien* on American humor edited by Hamlin Hill.

BIBLIOGRAPHICAL SURVEY

The sound bibliographical and reference work that must precede historical and critical research has not been adequately accomplished yet for the comics, but a few tentative efforts have been made and much good work is in progress. What should be a useful checklist of secondary material—the *International Bibliography of Comics Literature* by Wolfgang Kempkes—is marred by inaccuracies, incomplete data, and inconvenient arrangement. The entries are divided into eight general categories, such as histories, structure, readership, etc., and then subdivided by country of origin, with twenty nations represented. A subject cross-index in the first edition was unfortunately deleted in the revised edition, thus making it impossible to locate entries on specific artists and titles, the major use for such a checklist. The book, however, is the only convenient source of information on criticism published outside the United States up to 1974 and illustrates the extent to which a comprehensive study of American comics has been taking place abroad, especially in France, Germany, and Italy, rather than in the United States. Once again, the Europeans prove capable of perceiving the important creators of American culture before we do, from Edgar Allan Poe and William Faulkner to Winsor McCay and George Herriman.

While *The Comic Book Price Guide* by Robert M. Overstreet began in 1970 as a selling price reference for dealers and collectors, it has grown through annual revisions and expansions into the single most important source of information on the history of the comic book. A comprehensive listing of comic book titles from 1933 to the present, dates of first and last issues, publishing companies, and important artists has been supplemented with updated information on comic book collecting and preservation, fan publications, comic book conventions, a history of the development of comic books, and other special features. The text is copiously illustrated with comic book covers. A standard source of biographical data on artists and writers is *The Who's Who of American Comic Books* in four volumes, edited by Jerry Bails and Hames Ware. Conscientiously compiled and edited, with information obtained directly from the artists and writers, each entry provides birth dates, pen names, art schools attended, major influences, and career data, including major publishers and comic book credits. The first volume of *The Encyclopedia of Comic Book Heroes* by Michael L. Fleisher contains over one thousand entries on every major and minor character to appear in the Batman stories, with one hundred pages alone devoted to the life and adventures of Batman himself. The second and third volumes provide similar coverage for Wonder Woman and Superman, respectively. Although eight volumes were announced, only three were published. The underground comic book publishing phenomenon is thoroughly documented by Jay Kennedy in *The Official Underground and Newave Comix Price Guide*.

The main body of *The World Encyclopedia of Comics*, edited by Maurice Horn, consists of more than twelve hundred cross-reference entries arranged alphabetically and devoted either to an artist, a writer, a comic strip title, or a comic book character, prepared by an international group of contributors. Additional materials include a short history of the development of comics, a chronology from the eighteenth century to 1975, an original analytic inquiry into the aesthetics of comics by Horn, a history of newspaper syndication, a glossary, a selected bibliography, and several appendixes and indexes. Unfortunately there are many typographical errors in the text and the critical comments are often idiosyncratic or biased. A promised revised and corrected edition has never appeared. *The World Encyclopedia of Cartoons*, also edited by Maurice Horn, contains another twelve hundred entries by twenty-two contributors on cartoonists, animators, editors, producers, and the works they have created in the fields of animation, gag cartoons, syndicated comic panels, editorial cartoons, caricature, and sports cartoons. The entries are supplemented by an overview of caricature and cartoons, a brief history of humor magazines, a world summary of animated films, a chronology of important events in the history of cartooning, a glossary of terms, and a history of the humor periodicals *Puck*, *Life*, and *Judge* by Richard Marshall. Both of the encyclopedias are thoroughly illustrated in black and white and in color.

Because so little sound bibliographic and historic research has been completed, almost every single book published on the comics contains errors and mistaken assumptions. Although the Overstreet *Price Guide* contains extensive data on the beginning and concluding dates of comic book titles, no such reliable list exists for the major or minor comic strips. Many authors assume that the starting date for a comic strip was its first appearance in a local newspaper, or the first date on which it was syndicated, whereas it may have begun months earlier. The syndicates themselves have kept very few records and even incomplete files of proof sheets for the strips they distribute. The most knowledgeable and meticulous scholar of the comics, Bill Blackbeard, is writing a history for Oxford University Press that will establish for the first time much of this factual information, but until his book appears all of the existing histories must be used with caution.

A History of American Graphic Humor by William Murrell was the first history of the development of pictorial satire and cartooning in America to include attention to the comics. While he devotes only a few appreciative pages to comic strips, the work is still valuable as a panorama of the forms of visual art that have influenced the comics. The first full-length work entirely devoted to American comic art was Martin Sheridan's *Comics and Their Creators* in 1942. Not actually an organized history or study, it consisted primarily of biographical sketches and interviews with the artists and writers of over seventy-five of the most popular newspaper comics, copiously illustrated with portraits and reproductions of the strips. It remains a useful resource for primary data on the views and working habits of many important cartoonists. The earliest history and analytic study was *The Comics* by Coulton Waugh, a practicing comic artist and devoted scholar of the subject. While many of his facts are faulty, Waugh attempted a comprehensive survey of the important movements and types of comic strips from *The Yellow Kid* through the first decade of the comic book. His insights into the reasons for the popularity of certain strips, his comments on the aesthetic principles behind them, and his early effort to define the medium make Waugh's pioneering effort a work of lasting interest, although he had little appreciation for the comic book and he appeared to accept without question some of the highbrow standards often applied to popular art by the self-appointed guardians of high culture.

The next effort on the part of a single author to chart the history of the medium was Stephen Becker's *Comic Art in America*. Becker's interests were broader than Waugh's in that he ambitiously envisioned his book, according to its subtitle, as "A social history of the funnies, the political cartoons, magazine humor, sporting cartoons, and animated cartoons." Casting his net so broadly led to much superficiality, and his commentary is often derivative, but the volume is a useful storehouse of over 390 illustrations and sample drawings. The text is kept to a minimum and the illustrations are at a maximum in *The Penguin Book of Comics* by George Perry and Alan Aldridge, aptly described in its subtitle as "A slight history." Originally published in French in conjunction with an exhibition of comic art at the Louvre, and the joint product of six contributors headed by Pierre Couperie, *A History of the Comic Strip* contains some of the best discussion and provocative comments yet ventured on the aesthetics, structure, symbolism, and themes in comic art. Another general survey undertaken by one author, comic artist Jerry Robinson, is *The Comics: An Illustrated History of the Comic Strip*. Robinson provides a readable and interesting text complemented by thirteen original essays by eminent artists about the theories behind their work.

Although assembled as a catalog for an exhibition at the University of Maryland, Judith O'Sullivan's *The Art of the Comic Strip* contains a brief history with emphases on Winsor McCay, George McManus, George Herriman, and Burne Hogarth, a compilation of short biographies and bibliographic references on 120 comic artists, a chronology of important dates, and a bibliography. What appears to be the most ambitious effort yet undertaken to describe the "history of the comic strip" has yielded so far only the first massive volume, *The Early Comic Strip* by David Kunzle, which reaches the year 1825 before the comic strip as we know it actually begins. Kunzle traces the full development of narrative art in the European broadsheet, which he sees as an antecedent to the comic strip as he has defined it in the introduction. The complete corpus of reproductions of broadsheets in the oversized volume make it of greater interest to art historians than comics scholars. No further volumes have been published. In *Backstage at the Strips*, Mort Walker provides an engaging insider's tour of the world of comic strip artists, how the strips are created, and who the people are who draw and read them. Ron Goulart's *The Adventurous Decade* is an informal and subjective history of the adventure comic strips during the 1930s when the funnies came of age. The interviews Goulart conducted with living veterans of the period enrich the volume, which tends to adopt an intentionally controversial stance in its critical judgments of the work of classic artists.

Several thematic studies have been published, mostly by Maurice Horn. His *Comics of the American West* is a heavily illustrated historic survey of the major Western comic strips and books and their basic symbolic themes, and his *Women in the Comics* surveys in a similar fashion the images and roles of women as reflected in the comics. Horn's third book in this series is *Sex in the Comics*, an informal discussion of the presence of sexual behavior in comic strips and comic books of the mainstream and underground varieties primarily in the United States but in select foreign countries as well. Horn finds that despite associations of nostalgia and innocence, from the start comics have flirted with or strongly suggested sexuality and eroticism, and in the last decade through adult fantasy and science fiction comic books, writers and artists have been explicitly concerned with normal and abnormal sexual activity. Horn seldom documents his sources or mentions dates of publication, so his work is not as useful as it might be to the scholar, but his frequent use of illustrations is a major strength. *Women and the Comics* by Trina Robbins and Catherine Yronwode is a thoroughly researched first effort to chart the careers of hundreds of generally unknown women who have worked in the comic art field. The result of four years of research, this study documents the contributions of over five hundred women writers and cartoonists and admirably elucidates a largely ignored area of comics history. A chapter is also devoted to female cartoonists in Europe, Japan, and Australia.

Comics: Anatomy of a Mass Medium is a broad effort by two German scholars, Reinhold Reitberger and Wolfgang Fuchs, to relate the comics to their social context and developments in other mass media. It is an admirable example of foreign scholarship, but faulty secondary sources and inaccessible primary material led to a number of factual and other errors that no one corrected in the process of translation. A British perspective is found in Denis Gifford's *The International Book of Comics*, a fully illustrated, broad survey of the cultural and historic development of comic strips and comic books in America and Great Britain, from nineteenth-century caricature and humorous periodicals through the underground comix movement. This comparative approach demonstrates the degree to which influences have worked internationally in the shaping of comic art. *A Nation of Nations*, edited by Peter Marzio, contains an essay by M. Thomas Inge and Bill Blackbeard that first discusses the influence of European comic art on American culture and then the later influence of the fully developed American comic strip and book on the culture of the world at large.

The first full-length volume on the comic book was neither a history nor an appreciation. The purpose of *Seduction of the Innocent* by psychologist Fredric Wertham, published in 1954, was to prove that comic books, especially of the crime and horror variety, were a major contributor to juvenile delinquency. Although his data was scientifically invalid, Wertham's book upset many parent and teacher groups and added to the general hysteria of the McCarthy era, resulting in a congressional investigation chaired by Estes Kefauver. Anticipating the investigation, in October 1954, the Comics Magazine Association of America moved to adopt a self-regulating Comics Code Authority with the most stringent code ever applied to any of the mass media. Wertham's book, therefore, remains of significant cultural and historic interest.

The first writer to inaugurate what he claimed would be a full-scale history of the comic book was James Steranko, himself a talented comic book artist. Volume 1 of *The Steranko History of Comics* finds that pulp fiction of the 1930s was the single most important source of inspiration to the development of the comic book and then traces the histories of Superman, Batman, Captain America, Captain Marvel, and the D. C. comic books. Volume 2 continues the coverage of Captain Marvel and related Fawcett superheros, the Blackhawks and other airborne characters, Plastic Man and the Quality titles, and Will Eisner's Spirit. Encyclopedic in detail, there is more information in these two volumes than most readers can easily assimilate, but Steranko's contributors have a high regard for the distinctive qualities of comic book art and view it as a part and reflection of the total context of popular culture. Unfortunately, none of the promised following four volumes have appeared. Though primarily an anthology of selected stories, Jules Feiffer's *The Great Comic Book Heroes* has a lengthy introduction in which artist/author Feiffer reminisces about his days in the comic book industry and provides his personal commentary on the meaning of the superhero. Published as a catalog for an exhibition held at Ohio State University, M. Thomas Inge's *The American Comic Book* contains a brief history of the subject, an analysis of selected stories from the EC science fiction comic books, interviews with publishers Stan Lee and Jenette Kahn, and additional essays by Stan Lee, Will Eisner, and Ray Bradbury.

A single-volume history is *Comix: A History of Comic Books in America* by Les Daniels. Daniels provides a sensible outline of the major developments and reprints over twenty stories, four of them in color. His final chapter deals with the development of underground comic books, generally called "comix" to distinguish them from the traditional publications. Partly a radical rejection of the Comics Code Authority and partly a natural development of the counterculture underground press, comix provided artists with unrestricted freedom to write and draw to the limits of their imagination, something that has seldom been possible in comic art. While shameless obscenity and bad taste abound, several striking talents emerged from the movement—Robert Crumb remains the best known—and much highly original work was accomplished. Mark James Estren attempted to produce *A History of the Underground Comics*, which is difficult to accomplish because the publishing centers have ranged from California to the Midwest to New York, and the artists have never been eager to cooperate with researchers and critics. While much of his commentary is debatable, Estren has assembled an excellent cross-section of representative art by the major figures, many of them are allowed to speak for themselves through interviews and letters, and a useful checklist of underground titles by comix scholar Clay Geerdes concludes the volume. It is an engaging grab bag of reading matter about an important cultural development.

Throughout the years popular magazines, newspapers, and journals have published hundreds of articles and essays on the comics, many of them worthwhile. A selection of some of the best can be found in *The Funnies: An American*

Idiom, edited by David Manning White and Robert H. Abel. Two excellent collections of essays, mainly on comic book figures, are *All in Color for a Dime,* edited by Dick Lupoff and Don Thompson, and *The Comic-Book Book,* edited by Thompson and Lupoff. *The Comic-Stripped American* by social scientist Arthur Asa Berger is a collection of his pieces on the ways comics reflect our culture, many of them stimulating but also highly debatable. At a minimum, Berger is always provocative.

Things appear very promising for the study of comic art at present. Numerous projects are under way to reprint the works of classic artists, either in selected anthologies or in projected sets of complete works. Biographies and appreciative studies of major figures, as well as several historic works, have been announced. Specialized journals and publications are thriving, and major museums are mounting exhibitions devoted to the comic arts. By the end of the century, it is possible that the comics, the most scorned of the mass media and humorous arts, will achieve the appreciation they deserve as an influential part of the cultural life of the nation.

CHECKLIST AND ADDITIONAL SOURCES

Bails, Jerry and Hames Ware, eds. *The Who's Who of American Comic Books.* 4 vols. Detroit: Jerry Bails, 1973–1976.

Becker, Stephen. *Comic Art in America.* New York: Simon & Schuster, 1959.

Berger, Arthur Asa. *The Comic-Stripped American.* New York: Walker, 1973.

Couperie, Pierre et al. *A History of the Comic Strip.* Tr. Eileen B. Hennessy. New York: Crown, 1968.

Daniels, Les. *Comix: A History of Comic Books in America.* New York: Outerbridge & Dienstfrey, 1971.

Estren, Mark James. *A History of Underground Comics.* San Francisco: Straight Arrow Books, 1974.

Feiffer, Jules. *The Great Comic Book Heroes.* New York: Dial Press, 1965.

Fleisher, Michael L. *The Encyclopedia of Comic Book Heroes.* Vol. 1: *Batman.* Vol. 2: *Wonder Woman.* Vol. 3: *Superman.* New York: Macmillan, 1976–1978.

Gifford, Denis. *The International Book of Comics.* New York: Crescent Books, 1984.

Goulart, Ron. *The Adventurous Decade.* New Rochelle, N.Y.: Arlington House, 1975.

Horn, Maurice. *Comics of the American West.* New York: Winchester Press, 1977.

————. *Sex in the Comics.* New York: Chelsea House, 1985.

————. *Women in the Comics.* New York: Chelsea House, 1977.

————, ed. *The World Encyclopedia of Cartoons.* New York: Chelsea House, 1980.

————, ed. *The World Encyclopedia of Comics.* New York: Chelsea House, 1976.

Inge, M. Thomas. *The American Comic Book.* Columbis: Ohio State University Libraries, 1985.

———— and Bill Blackbeard. "American Comic Art." In *A Nation of Nations,* edited by Peter Marzio. New York: Harper & Row, 1976.

Kempkes, Wolfgang. *International Bibliography of Comics Literature.* Detroit: Gale Research Co., 1971. Rev. ed.: New York: R. R. Bowker/Verlag Dokumentation, 1974.

Kennedy, Jay. *The Official Underground and Newave Comix Price Guide*. Cambridge, Mass.: Boatner Norton Press, 1982.

Kunzle, David. *The Early Comic Strip*. Vol. 1: *History of the Comic Strip*. Berkeley: University of California Press, 1973.

Lupoff, Dick and Don Thompson, eds. *All in Color for a Dime*. New Rochelle, N.Y.: Arlington House, 1970.

Murrell, William. *A History of American Graphic Humor*. 2 vols. New York: Whitney Museum/Macmillan, 1933–1938.

O'Sullivan, Judith. *The Art of the Comic Strip*. College Park: University of Maryland Department of Art, 1971.

Overstreet, Robert M. *The Comic Book Price Guide*. Cleveland, Tenn.: Robert M. Overstreet, 1970 (and subsequent annual editions, now distributed by Harmony Books).

Perry, George and Alan Aldridge. *The Penguin Book of Comics*. New York: Penguin Books, 1969, rev. 1971.

Reitberger, Reinhold and Wolfgang Fuchs. *Comics: Anatomy of a Mass Medium*. Tr. Nadia Fowler. Boston: Little, Brown, 1972.

Robbins, Trina and Catherine Yronwode. *Women and the Comics*. Guerneville, Calif.: Eclipse Books, 1985.

Robinson, Jerry. *The Comics: An Illustrated History of Comic Strip Art*. New York: G. P. Putnam's Sons, 1974.

Sheridan, Martin. *Comics and Their Creators*. Boston: Hale, Cushman & Flint, 1942.

Steranko, James. *The Steranko History of Comics*. 2 vols. Wyomissing, Penn.: Supergraphics, 1970–1972.

Thompson, Don and Dick Lupoff, eds. *The Comic-Book Book*. New Rochelle, N.Y.: Arlington House, 1973.

Walker, Mort. *Backstage at the Strips*. New York: Mason/Charter, 1975.

Waugh, Coulton. *The Comics*. New York: Macmillan, 1947.

Wertham, Fredric. *Seduction of the Innocent*. New York: Holt, Rinehart and Winston, 1954.

White, David Manning and Robert H. Abel, eds. *The Funnies: An American Idiom*. New York: The Free Press, 1963.

♦ 3 ♦

Humor in Periodicals

David E. E. Sloane

OVERVIEW

In August 1875, Brander Matthews wrote in the columns of *The American Bibliopolist* that "the history of comic journalism in America is merely a list of tombstones." He was expanding on a soliloquy by Orpheus C. Kerr's gravedigger in the "Cloven Foot," which ran in the pages of the New York *Punchinello* in 1870. The mortuarist, in identifying the graves, pointed to a row of projectors of "American *Punches*": "Next, Original Projector of American *Punch*; next, Projector of Rural Newspaper; next, another projector of American *Punch*—indeed, all the rest of that row is American *Punches*." It may be that a list of humor periodicals in America amounts to a mortuary volume, dotted with the tombstones of the chronically short-lived. However, an equally strong case can be made that in fact Mathews was responding negatively to what is actually a wild profusion of unbridled frontiersmanship and unruliness typifying the comic Yankee Democracy—particularly in the North where mercantile enterprise and the literary salon combined the talent and money necessary for such ventures, but also in the regions. It is true that comic magazines of the first one hundred years of the republic seemed unprofitable ventures, although a number lasted for several years. In comparison to the increasingly distinguished London *Punch*, then a lusty adult after somewhat sickly beginnings in the early 1840s, Mathews' and Kerr's observation had some merit. With another one hundred years of perspective, however, the history of American comic periodicals emerges more clearly as an incredibly dynamic, vibrant, and diverse profusion of modes, materials, and intentions. The history of American humor magazines thus becomes a record of vitality—a chronicle of rambunctious invasions of sacrosanct territory in politics, social pretension, and sexual mores almost unrivalled in any comparable literary genre.

The history begins in 1765, before the founding of the republic itself, and continues through the present. Within its boundaries can be found quips, cartoons, jokes, comic narratives, ironic and sarcastic criticism, bitter propaganda and invective, narration, occasional essays, poetry and doggerel, captioned photos, and every other available format in print. In one medium or another, something exists to exacerbate and offend virtually any shade of social belief or personal opinion. There are a number of humor magazines that claim no social responsibility whatever except to amuse themselves and their readers and sell issues.

Following Frank Luther Mott's *A History of American Magazines*, the major work in the history of American periodicals, magazines are defined as having the intent to publish serially on a regular basis with a motive of public distribution, either generally or to a defined group of subscribers. Identifying and cataloging American humor magazines would seem fairly easy on that basis. Among modern magazines, *The National Lampoon* would be an obvious choice. *Life, Judge*, and *Puck*, the triad of great later nineteenth- and early twentieth-century humor magazines, would immediately occur as obvious representatives of the genre, particularly to readers knowledgeable in cartoon art. Political cartoons, including Thomas Nast's attacks on the Tweed Ring in New York City, or the archly seductive beauties of Charles Dana Gibson posed in their mildly ironic social settings fall comfortably in the humor category and are widely known to modern readers: *Nast's Weekly* would be an obvious choice, although *Harper's*, which published Nast's drawings, was not predominantly humorous in mode or content. From the Civil War era, *Vanity Fair*, famous both for its caricatures by H. L. Stephens and its Artemus Ward columns, is an obvious representative, along with the earlier Boston *Carpet-Bag* edited by B. P. Shillaber and the first national publisher in 1852 of Artemus Ward, John Phoenix, and Mark Twain. Each of these magazines has in common regular weekly or monthly publication, a fixed newsstand or subscription price, and an editor selecting various materials primarily humorous or satiric in intention. The ratio of cartoons to comic copy varies, politics and social viewpoint vary, and life span and publication histories are dissimilar. But the earmarks of caricature, burlesque, exaggerated wordplay, and ironic inversion so permeate the material generally that the humor genre is the only fitting one for these publications.

Unaccommodated under this definition are the almanacs, of course, among whose outstanding editors is the writer-publisher Benjamin Franklin, who used humor often as a mode but never edited anything that flatly belongs in the category of humor magazines or comic papers. A vast range of similar comic material, including the *Crockett Almanacs* and a number of offsprings through Josh Billings' burlesque almanacs in the 1870s, are tangentially related to humor magazines.

Comic columns in otherwise serious journals also stretch categories: *Harper's Weekly* featured humor columns in the 1850s, as did *Graham's*, and in the early 1870s, *The Galaxy* even captured Mark Twain for a "Memoranda" column lasting about a year. Many later newspapers and magazines offered regular humor departments. Street and Smith's *New York Weekly* in the middle 1870s published columns by Josh Billings, Mark Twain, and Doesticks—the last so popular that they continued for two years after his death. The New York *Sunday Mercury* of the 1860s has provided texts of several fugitive Mark Twain items. All of these humor columns and pages are well before the advent of the Sunday "funnies" or comic sections, a different phenomenon, made immortal as an institution of American culture by Major Fiorello LaGuardia's readings over the radio in 1945.

In the 1870–1910 period particularly, almost every hometown newspaper in America had its own humorist on staff. The same desire for comic relief brought humor columns and pages to the great middle-class popular magazines of the twentieth century, including the *Saturday Evening Post, Colliers, Look*, and others of the 1900–1950 era, as well as men's magazines such as the slick *Playboy*; each scattered cartoons throughout its pages of fiction, offered joke pages, and otherwise catered to the need for mild amusement of a general readership.

In the 1920–1960 period, numbers of general magazines including comic copy and cartoons spun off annual collections of humor. Cartoons by Peter Arno, Coburn, and a large number of others were complemented by annual *Best Cartoons of the Year*, edited for many years from 1942 into the fifties by Lawrence Lariar. *Reader's Digest* offered cartoons and comic items faithfully issue after issue, and continues to be known for its "Humor in Uniform" and similar sections, but never saw itself as a humor magazine; nevertheless, it issued humor books collecting its own material: *Fun Fare* (1949) and *Reader's Digest Treasury of Wit and Humor* (1958), to name two. *The New Yorker* of the 1980s is similarly problematical because of the extent it has departed from its 1920s whimsey and sophisticated disrespect for the little old lady in Dubuque. Particularly noticeable during the Vietnam War era was its change in primary orientation toward serious content treated directly rather than through irony, sarcasm, or burlesque. *The New Yorker 25th Anniversary Album, 1925–1950*, however, is a stunning sampling of American social cartooning—and nothing else, no prose, and no serious illustrations is offered. *Look, Esquire*, and others did likewise.

Problematical though an exact narrowing of "humor" may be, the description of humor magazines and comic periodicals produces about three hundred obvious choices of titles for study, having runs from one or two issues up to forty or fifty years. In addition, a range of important humor magazines can be established to round out the history of the genre as a significant contributor to the definition of American popular culture since the founding of the republic. The range of dates is from 1765 to 1985, with the most important eras seeming to lie in the 1800–1820, Civil War, Mauve Decade, and post–World War I eras. Sizes run from subpocket-size digests to mammoth newspapers, with various sizes and shapes between. Names like *Scrouge, Wasp, Firefly*, and *Bee* are typical of the early intent to sting that preoccupied many of the Federalist-era editor-authors, although the longest lived appear more benignly as *Salmagundi, The Portfolio, The Tickler*, and *The Farmer's Museum*. Later, following the lead of English humor in the 1860s, *Vanity Fair* and *Mrs. Grundy* appeared, matching and appearing more creative in their social criticism than *Yankee Notions, The Plantation*, or other similarly American titles, but all showing the influence of the English *Punch* to some extent. It is only in the later nineteenth century that mass circulation brought about the expansion in distribution and advertising that sustained the greatest of the American humor magazines, including the original *Life, Puck*, and *Judge*, and a host of shorter-lived followers. After the turn of the present century, the iconoclasm of *The American Mercury* was matched by lesser known examples such as *Hot Dog*, (Cleveland, Ohio) and *Jim Jam Jems* (both harassed for four years in the courts on charges of obscenity), *Ziffs*, and *Sagebrush Philosophy* from the far West, all of the 1900–1930 period. Another of these little magazines from 1900 to 1930 began as an iconoclastic magazine in Canada—*The Calgary Eye-Opener*—but moved to Minneapolis under the editorship of Captain Billy Fawcett's ex-wife and ended up as a competitor to his *Whizbang*. These were fitting counterparts in their era to the journals of a century before: the Baltimore *Monument* and the Salem (Mass.) *Scourge*. In the twentieth century, the new sexual vitality enters, bringing titles like *Captain Billy's Whizbang, Pepper, Paris Nights, Broadway Humor*—for a sampling of earlier twentieth-century titillation—and later *TNT, Zowie, Gaze, TV Girls and Gags, From Sex to Sexty*, and *Screw*.

HISTORICAL DEVELOPMENT

The earliest date for a publication unquestionably belonging in the category of humor magazines is 1765. The publication is titled *The Bee*. It was published in Philadelphia by "William Honeycomb," and was printed at the shop of John Armbruster. *The Bee* lasted for three weekly eight-page numbers. It was directly immersed in Pennsylvania politics, at that time hotly contested, brutal, and dangerous. Honeycomb had lived in the country, so he announced in the first issue, and had trained his *Bee* to gather information at the Philadelphia coffeehouses and return with the grotesque parodies and stories of the dullness and moral laxity of the king's governor, whom it found as distasteful as it found Penn and the tax-gatherers of the Penn party. Its first number offers a roundhouse burlesque of the governor keeping court in a brothel presided over by an allegory of the Spirit of Dullness. The later two numbers pretended to be answers to this viewpoint by different pens. There is no indication of why *The Bee* perished, but politics in this region in 1765 was in turmoil over frontier atrocities and corresponding lynchings of peaceful Indians, and bitter invective was considered a powerful and dangerous tool. Thus the beginnings of American humor magazines lie at the center of controversy even before the American Revolution.

The next known humor magazine, *The Omnium Gatherum*, in 1795, was much milder, with a more Addisonian cast to its essays. It lasted only ten numbers, and was more generally literary than humorous, but it carried a genuine New England tall tale or two that have survived in various versions as part of the New England folk tradition up to the present time.

The early Federal period and the development of an educated urban class can be seen as fostering periodicals and the impulse to periodical publication in a comic vein. Joseph Dennie and Royall Tyler thus entered into the *Farmer's Weekly Museum* in the seemingly unlikely town of Walpole, New Hampshire, with Dennie becoming editor in 1796. Dennie's satiric "Farrago" essays on American society were a popular feature of the *Farmer's Museum* before Dennie took up the editorship, and he intended to sustain another magazine, *The Tablet*, briefly alive in the summer of 1795, with them as well. Tyler and Dennie joined together again in Philadelphia after the turn of the century in *The Port Folio*, where some of Dennie's best satire appeared during the next several years, including reprints of most of the Farrago pieces. By the 1800s, humorous magazines seemed to develop along two lines: one was political, the other literary. Philadelphia and Boston were the notable centers of this sort of publishing, with New York emerging as the dominant center of publication only in the 1850s. George Helmbold of Philadelphia stands out among several enterprising editors as the greatest of the comic editors of the early Federal period. His *Philadelphia Tickler* appeared in 1809 and lasted until Helmbold left to fight in the War of 1812; he later succeeded himself with the *Independent Balance* in 1817, which outlived him. Both papers are outstanding examples of the growth of urban social and political irony and popular speech as a humorous medium. He commented on civic corruption, borrowed extensively from foreign sources, and juxtaposed plain language and Augustan items of news and literature. Even corrupt bridge contractors for the city of Philadelphia came in for their share of ridicule under the corrective scourge of the *Tickler*.

Other journals worthy of note in this period include *Salmagundi* in New York under the hands of Washington Irving (1807–1808) and James Kirke Paulding (1809–1811), which was most literary in its orientation, with a characteristic Irvingesque view of the Knickerbocker world. There is some evidence that Irving was influenced by Dennie before him, and Dennie's conservatism as "Oliver Oldschool" might well have influenced the chronicler of Gotham's Dutch history as Diedrich Knickerbocker. Dennie was the most acerbic of the social critical humorists of the period, barely stopping short of the virulent animadversions of Peter Porcupine in *The Rush-Light*, animadversions so strong that William Cobbett, the author, was forced to flee the country as a consequence. Dennie himself was indicted for sedition in 1804—for a piece that was relatively mild in comparison to other writings.

Most humor magazines of the early Federal period openly expressed a desire to correct society through the scourge of satire, and the name *The Scourge* was popular. *The Wasp* appeared in 1804. New York's *The Corrector* in 1804 corrected the Burr/Hamilton disputes. Among journals that had to retract to escape lawsuits were Helmbold's *Tickler*, the Boston *Firefly*, and a number of others. In fact, the historic Zenger case in 1733–1734, in which colonial license of the press was significantly advanced, was based on satiric remarks published in Zenger's paper. Since the courts held that the greater the truth the greater the libel, it can be imagined how advocacy positions could easily lead to judicial penalty, and comic journalists were not fully released from this predicament until a century or more later. Tentatively, William Cobbett's *Porcupine's Political Censor* and *Rush-Light* might be included in a study of humor as invective, although Cobbett seems to have little in common with humorists generally.

The humor of the 1800–1830 period reflects the spirit of the Addisonian and Swiftian models, but also bears traces of increasing American characterizations. Elaborate jokes were developed around supposed sightings of sea serpents in Boston Harbor. Yankee bumpkin types appeared sometimes as butts, sometimes as pen names. Acerbic attacks on rival editors and political parties were typical. In Hudson, New York, in 1802, the Federalist *Wasp* stung it out with the Democratic-Republican *Bee*. Other journals merely attempted to be compendiums of humorous matter. *The Fool* and *Moonshine*, both of 1807, were typical of brief-lived comic magazines lampooning European styles affecting Americans or the majestic public itself. The *Thistle* (1807) and Portland, Maine's *Abracadabra* (1808) were general humorous offerings. Baltimore in 1810 and Boston in 1811 each had their *Scourge*. Washington, D.C., as the national capital acquired *The———*, by Nonius Nondescript in 1826, and *The Champagne Club* for a few issues in 1834–1835. Frank Luther Mott's *History of American Magazines* and David E. E. Sloane's *American Humor Magazines and Comic Periodicals* extend and deepen this necessarily sketchy listing.

In the 1830s, magazine and newspaper publishing expanded rapidly, probably as a result of the growth of American cities and a somewhat expanded readership capable of cash subscriptions, as well as the development of cheaper sources of paper and ink than had prevailed in earlier times. In this period, editors like Joseph C. Neal, himself to become known as the American Dickens for his "Charcoal Sketches" of previously unrecorded city down-and-outers, began actively fostering native talent; in Neal's case, Frances M. Whitcher, (The Widow Bedott) and John S. Robb are particularly notable discoveries. Generally, the era of "American" humor and comic literary burlesque replaced the Federalists.

Two journals, neither intended to be humor magazines, require special attention in this period because of their central position in the encouragement of periodical humor in America: William Trotter Porter's *The Spirit of the Times* (1831–1861) and Lewis Gaylord Clark's *Knickerbocker Magazine* (1833–1865). Porter's *Spirit* was founded as a sporting magazine addressed to the horse world and the plantation, but broadened to include a wide splay of American frontier humor. Among others appearing in its pages were Thomas Bangs Thorpe, C.F.M.

Nolan, Johnson Jones Hooper, and George Washington Harris—all associated with the "southwestern" school of regional humor. Porter also published humor from other regions, but the interest in "uniquely American types" has tended to focus scholarly attention away from these and toward the roughhouse school of the Southwest. The fortunes of the magazine were mixed throughout its career, but as a publisher and republisher of regional humorists, it is a major source of American comic writing in its period and is closely identified with the prototypical frontier American humor story, "The Big Bear of Arkansas," by Thorpe, which appeared in its pages in 1841. Clarke's *Knickerbocker* was a general magazine that also provided a wide variety of comic fare, including regional material, short stories, and editorial items in the humorous mode. It was never as rambunctious as *Spirit*, but offered humor from the northeastern and southwestern regions with an equal hand. John Phoenix, Doesticks, and a host of others were reprinted in the "Editor's Table," and a varied run of humorists made up the regular contents. In Volume 49, for example, Charles G. Leland, Frederic S. Cozzens, and forgotten writers like "Swanquill" and Henry Brent appear along with reviews of Stoddard, Curtis, and Burton's *Cyclopedia of Humor*, and Phoenix in the "Editor's Table."

Benjamin Penhallow Shillaber's Boston *Carpet-Bag* (1851–1853)—which published George Horatio Derby, Charles F. Browne, and Samuel L. Clemens in one issue—is an important example of the increasingly burlesque literary tone of comic papers no longer restricted to the elite or the political. City life and literary topics became the currency of discussion; urban language and tone began to replace neoclassical restraint. Shillaber's own Mrs. Partington became a popular success, and reprints of her comic urban experiences appeared well into the 1890s. The plaguey boy Ike and the malapropisms of an old woman baffled by the new-fangled ways of Boston in the 1840s opened up middle-class experience as the subject matter of the next generation of northern humorists. Other significant journals of the 1850s include Corbyn's comic New York paper *Figaro!*, *Diogenes Hys Lanterne*, and running throughout the decade and opening up even more of the lower crust of New York life the *New York Picayune*, which lasted from 1847 through 1860 and featured W. H. Levison, T. B. Gunn, Frank Bellew, and Doesticks at one time or another. The San Francisco *Hombre* was a West Coast addition; *Yankee Notions*, from 1852 to 1875, was T. W. Strong's magazine reprinting humor of the period. Several other long-lasting journals began in this period, including *Frank Leslie's Budget of Fun*, from 1858 through 1896; J. C. Haney's *Comic Monthly*, from 1859 through 1881; and the *Phunny Phellow*, from 1859 through 1876. The literary burlesque became a fully entrenched mode of American periodical humor. Slang and plain language, neologisms, and vernacular as used brilliantly by Doesticks, Artemus Ward, Mark Twain, and a host of lesser literary comedians and phunny phellows appeared as staples in this era, leaving behind elevated humor of the essay form in favor of illustrated pieces pointedly responding to sentiment and romance in contemporary fiction.

Social issues came increasingly to the attention of the better of these journal editors, and acid barbs were directed at mill owners, city policy, and other types of urban bullies. *Vanity Fair* in 1859, founded by loyal Democrats, was dragged into politics by the importance of the issues of the day, although the Stephens brothers as founders and editors wished to be nonpolitical. Harsh toward Lincoln, their most effective cartoons pilloried "Buck" Buchanan for his refusal to strongly advance the interests of the Union as it dissolved into two camps before Lincoln's inauguration. *Vanity Fair* was edited by both Charles G. Lelend and Artemus Ward, and its bohemian cleverness and its brilliant cartoons by Stephens cause it to be rated as one of the best of the American comic papers. Ultimately taking the "War Democrat" position, it was itself a casualty of the Civil War in 1863, when paper costs tripled and lowered purchases in railways and through an increasingly polarized readership doomed it to extinction. Shortly after the war, *Mrs. Grundy*, another promising journal, failed and became the occasion of the first laments over the deaths of American humor magazines, including Brander Matthews' comments cited at the beginning of this chapter.

After the Civil War, American life became increasingly dominated by mercantile and industrial problems. The expansion in salaried families, urban workers with middle- and upper-class ideals—and disposable cash pocket money—created a new environment for American humor magazines. This new environment was less bohemian and literary than before the war. It included problems of social mobility and local and suburban life, and it expanded significantly in generalizing humorous views of life from the local to the national, and in some cases merely "general." The greatest beneficiaries of this new mass potential for the distribution of humor magazines were *Life, Puck*, and *Judge*. Each took advantage of major developments in printing techniques to offer better engravings than the older woodcuts, and to provide increasingly gorgeous color illustrations as advances in paper and inking techniques allowed. Furthermore, each of the three journals seemed to have found a wide segment of the American reading population to which to appeal. In part, newsstand marketing dictated a large size and flamboyant covers. The great age of American illustration, however, provided a pool of talent from which to draw that seems unrivalled in the annals of American illustration.

Puck's Keppler and *Life*'s Charles Dana Gibson—as unpromising as both seemed in their earliest work—came naturally to dominate their age in illustration. *Puck* lasted from 1877 through 1917. H. C. Bunner edited the weekly from 1878 through 1896 with the boldly colored cartoons of Joseph Keppler its dominant feature; anti-Tweed and anti-Blaine in the early years, *Puck* was a strong opponent of political corruption and became a major force in politics through its cartoonists' illustrations. *Judge* lived from 1881 until the early thirties, although it limped along after its initial bankruptcy in 1932. Prior to that time, it had reached a circulation amounting to a quarter of a million copies in the twenties. Originally backed by Republicans to counter the Democratic *Puck, Judge* was against Bryan and the antitrust legislators. Its illustations proved so popular that, as with *Puck*, a variety of hardcover reprints, quarterlies, and related publications were spun off from it. By 1912, at a circulation of 100,000, Frank Luther Mott places *Judge* as the largest circulating American humor periodical. *Life* lasted from 1883 until it was dismembered in 1936. It began as a brainchild of three Harvard men who wished to establish a satirical weekly. Charles Dana Gibson made his Gibson girl famous in its pages and ended up with a controlling interest in the magazine in 1920. Committed to neither political party, *Life* boldly attacked whatever issues it wished, but maintained considerable interest in the social mores of the city socialite and the developing middle and upper crusts of America.

The tenure of *Life, Puck,* and *Judge* tend to diminish other American humor magazines, but there was considerable expansion taking place in the field. The great age of sex in humor, as analyzed later by Alexander King, began when Charles Dana Gibson discovered that he could lift the eyebrows of a woman an inch on her forehead and make her sexily haughty. He gave her an upperclass *desengagé* manner and established the identity of a generation and gave it its image. By the turn of the century, local color figures were also becoming popular, however. *Sis Hopkin's Own Book* and *Magazine of Fun* (single and in united form spanning the years from 1899 to 1911) are typical, along with *Uncle Remus's Home Magazine* (1908–1913); a profusion of such lower middle-class popular humor magazines appeared around the turn of the century. Sweet and Knox's *Texas Siftings* (1881–1897), Opie Read's *Arkansas Traveler* (1882–1916), and other regional offerings with shorter lives, such as the *Kansas Knocker* (1900–1901) followed regional lines.

The "little magazines" after the turn of the century also provided their share of humor magazines. *The Lark* and *Epi-Lark* (1895–1897) set the standard, published on bamboo paper that made them all but unsavable and featuring the whimsy of the San Francisco literati led by Gelett Burgess. Elbert Hubbard's *Philistine* (1895–1915) was the longest lived of these chapbooks with a circulation of over 100,000 for much of its run.

By 1900, the American cartoon was a major component of every humor magazine, completely dominating many. Furthermore, popular newspapers and the rise of literacy in Europe and America encouraged a vast growth in the medium of comic art—and many books on cartooning essentially begin, after cursory reference to Ben Franklin and Thomas Nast, at 1900. So, roughly did H. H. Windsor's *Cartoons Magazine* (1912–1922), one of the finest and most thoughtful reprinters of journalistic cartoons ever to appear—a sister publication to *Mechanics Illustrated*. Comic art had come of age, and *Cartoons*, including a special 1914 issue, *War in Cartoons*, often listed as a separate entry, chronicled an age with a clarity and sensitivity to politics and social experience that is rare enough in any medium.

A range of local spokesmen for the skeptical in revolt from the village emerged around 1900—*The Calgary Eye Opener* in Canada and *Sagebrush Philosophy* in Wyoming are examples. "Consider the Sphinx he ain't had no fun in five thousand years" wrote the editor of the latter, attacking prune-faced do-gooders.

At a national level, *The American Mercury*, begun in 1924 by H. L. Mencken and George Jean Nathan after their years with *The Smart Set*, was to attack the American booboisie. At the same time, *The New Yorker* would decline to write for the little old lady in Dubuque.

The entrance of overt sensuality in American humor was forecast by *New Varieties* as early as 1873 and carried forward by the Gibson girl. Captain Billy Fawcett opened the spigot with *Captain Billy's Whizbang* (1919–1932)—referred to in the musical *The Music Man*—"Do you want your children reading *Captain Billy's Whizbang* behind the outhouse?"—as a degenerate threat to small-town American morality. Capt. Billy followed his own success with *Smokehouse Monthly*, featuring hobo humor, and his henna-haired ex-wife revamped *The Calgary Eye-Opener* into *Red Pepper*, a journal with cuties and comic cuts. *Paris Nights, Snicker Snacks, Broadway Nights*, and a host of others represent the breaking loose of American humor in conjunction with pin-ups and sexual jokes in the late twenties and early thirties. Some were unlucky, the editor of *Jim Jam Jems* was under indictment for four years for obscenity in the mails before gaining vindication. A whole genre of silk-stocking quips, gals 'n gags, and cheesecake/joke magazines with names like *Zowie* and *Comic Cuties* would eventually emerge in the 1940s, 1950s, and 1960s.

More significant is *Ballyhoo* as a classic innovator. Several magazines of the teens and twenties are important in terms of their literary and social vision: *Art Young Quarterly, Americana, Ziffs*, Mencken's *The Smart Set*, Ross's *The New Yorker*, and Mencken's *The American Mercury*—all but *Americana* and *Ziffs* having received some degree of serious attention. Harold Ross' *New Yorker* from 1925 intended to expose the human side of city life and culture through wit and gayety. Eustace Tilley, its cover dandy appearing each February as the nation's first sign of spring, is a lineal descendent of Diedrich Knickerbocker. With E. B. White, James Thurber, and Peter Arno leading the twentieth century's best metropolitan wits, it performed brilliantly and continues to perform at present. Mencken's career has also been carefully examined by popular and scholarly writers. But most ignored is *Ballyhoo*, which burst on the American scene in 1931 in the face of the Great Depression. Its advent is an important phenomenon of modern magazine publishing history, for its freedom of format, sarcasm, and acerbic anti-establishment burlesques of advertising and the capitalist enterprise marked out the lines of the major innovators of the 1950s and 1960s—*Mad* and *The National Lampoon*. Edited by Norman Anthony and a product of Floyd Dell's Dell Publishing Co., *Ballyhoo*'s first issue appeared in cellophane wrap— "Kept Fresh by Cellophane" its cover boasted insincerely—and it continued to burlesque every form of advertising puff from then on. It was a sort of gin-mill late-twenties production—a maturing of the flapper era blended with the social urgency of *Art Young Quarterly* and *Americana*, two notable comic magazines of the twenties espousing social reform and existential belief, respectively. *Ballyhoo*'s Elmer Zilch—a suitable Zero figure to represent the little guy in American life—was the hero of the magazine and its leading comic figure, with a presence as profound as Alfred E. Neuman's for *Mad* two generations later. Full-page burlesque ads stayed close to the originals in noncomic magazines, outraging some, embarrassing others, but delighting most—some of the targets even asked *Ballyhoo* for more chaff directed at their own products. Circulation on this speculative magazine soared into the millions. Knock-offs with names like *Aw*, *Nerts!*, *Boloney*, and *Bunk* make *Ballyhoo*'s inspiring cultural position under Anthony even clearer. By the middle of the decade, Anthony and the magazine started to become stale, but a racier more open format had been established.

Predictably, World War II humor supplanted Jazz Age and Depression humor with titles like *Army Fun*, *Army Laughs*, *War Laffs*, *TNT*, and *Squad Riot!* In the late thirties, the size of many of these magazines either condensed to digest-size at 5 1/2 by 7 1/2 inches or expanded to 10 1/2 by 13 with only twenty to forty pages. Pictorial humor—particularly cheesecake and comic-caption girlie pics—became prominent components of magazines like *Laff*, *Hit*, *Gags*, and *Wit*. Humor turned to Hitler and the G.I. One of the best covers—on the 1941 *Hooey Annual*, a late survivor of the *Ballyhoo* period—shows Hitler landing on the seat of his pants, when the cover flap is lifted, a stork is seen goosing his behind.

In the 1950–1980 period, domestic comedy replaced war comedy. Dell resurrected *Ballyhoo* in a format akin to an editorialized teen-age comic book. Magazines like *Good Humor* and *Cartoon Cavalcade* emphasized plays on suburban life, office sexuality, and middle-class habits. Consequently, political humor retreated to the columnists in regular newspapers, leaving the field open for counterculture politics in Paul Krasner's *The Realist* of the 1960s and early 1970s, and local kitchen-table publications. Counterculture "comix" appeared in the late 1960s and early 1970s, featuring distsorted drawings and "drop out" political positions. They continue to be a notable feature of counterculture publishing, particularly as represented in California-based comix publications.

Mad Magazine did much to further the comix form of comic illustration under editor Harvey Kurtzman, with the commitment not to single jokes but to gag serial strips burlesquing a novel, poem, or TV series over several pages, all in slightly grotesque comic drawings with inappropriately exaggerated episodes and talk. *Mad*, too, was experimental when it first began and its phenomenal growth suggested another new wave of American humorous thought, antagonistic to the commonplace analysis of life in conventional literature, TV, and schools. *Mad*'s artwork was also a drop-out alteration in conventional line-drawing of cartoons. Several of the comix are clearly its counterculture descendents, including *Zap* comix, featuring the Fabulous Furry Freak Brothers, and other efflorescences of the California hippie culture. All show the knobby roughness and cluttered eccentricity of the Harvey Kurtsman/Robert Crumb school of illustration with exaggerated sex, drug, and "raunchy" physical themes. Others, like *The Stark Fist of Removal* from Dallas, Texas, reflect the drop-out ethics of regional cultists of comic dissent.

The National Lampoon emerged with a somewhat more distinguished lineage, but a grosser sense of the ability of tits and ass to sell an adult humor magazine. Shooting dogs and bombing Vietnamese children were all part of the comic mix that *Lampoon* saw, and such an inclusive sense of black humor offended many people who prefer to deal with social atrocities by ignoring them—another cultural commonplace developed to a high art during the Vietnam era.

Still publishing is Carlton Press with *Cartoon Carnival* and *Good Humor*, alternate bimonthly publications selling about 17,000 copies an issue, having peaked at 50,000 in the late 1970s. They feature adult, sexually oriented jokes. Both are edited by one woman at a desk in Derby, Connecticut. Neither attempts to crusade or intends any change in format. This characteristic seems typical of the sexy humor publications of the 1950–1980 period: publication of alternate titles bimonthly by one publisher to allow longer shelf life, unchanging format mixing picture and cartoons or solely sexual humor, an increasingly physical view of sex, fidelity, and social acts.

The present standing of humor periodicals is mixed. *The New Yorker* in 1985 announced a determination to return to a more humorous format, having become increasingly serious over the preceding twenty years. *The National Lampoon, Mad*, and a few imitators continue as viable publications. College humor magazines seem largely vanished. A few speciality humor magazines, like *CARtoons*, seem able to maintain runs of some duration, sustained by teenage audiences. Academic humor magazines, most noticeably *Scholia Satyrica*, and regionals, like *Lone Star*, from Texas, seem to appear and disappear as did earlier humor magazines of the preceding century. Thus, the American comic periodical scene appears much as it has from the beginning. At one time or another, one or another segment of a widely read public seems ready to purchase humor magazines. Social and political content, and sexual content in this era, continue to provide irritants to established authorities. There seems to be room in the pantheon for humor both with and without purpose. New humor publications, some of significant merit, continue to appear.

KEY ISSUES FOR RESEARCH

Because humor is considered ephemera, it is sometimes difficult to obtain source material. Humor magazines are even more ephemeral still, as are comic newspapers. Consequently, the mere cataloging of American humor periodicals and major periodical contributors, both writers and illustrators, represents a significant task. The central issue for research in the field at present is merely a definition of the field. A complete list of comic periodical publications in America is probably an impossibility, although Mott has provided excellent surveys of periods and Sloane extends the major listings up to the 1980s. Even copyright listings provide scant help in identifying names and dates. Although many humor magazines of the 1900–1980 period bear copyright notices, there is no evidence that required issues of the magazines were ever cataloged into the record maintained by the federal government. Therefore, the natural source of information is unhelpful. Similarly, few libraries consider humor magazines of significance, and the *Union List of Serials* has a number of inaccuracies. No listings are available for humor magazines for the post–1930 period, and the sexual content of many of them make collection by college or public libraries unlikely. Ephemera they are, and ephemera they are likely to remain unless students of popular culture collect and analyze them.

An assessment of the relation of jest books, joke books, songsters, almanacs, and even serially published books to magazine humor and newspaper column humor would be worthwhile. Even as substantial and important a book as *Burton's Cyclopedia of American Humor*, produced by Appleton in 1857, was issued in twenty-four semimonthly numbers rather than as a single volume. Without pretending to make additional problems, it is fair to say that American humor was often presented as fugitive humor in periodical forms for a popular readership. A full evaluation of its impact on its audience and what it represents about that audience is both intriguing and debatable. In any case, the lines between periodical and book application are very hazy. Since periodicals are so widely scattered among different libraries, little attempt has been made to evaluate them by content. Yet such an attempt would add information to our understanding of literary and popular developments throughout several eras.

Many of the major magazines up to 1930 are capably discussed in Frank Luther Mott's *A History of American Magazines*, and more magazines are given careful attention in David Sloane's *American Humor Magazines and Comic Periodicals*. However, scholarly treatment has still not been carried out to the extent that is merited for many individual magazines. George Helmbold of Philadelphia and his *Philadelphia Tickler* and *Independent Balance* of the 1800–1820 period should be a scholar's first choice for study. Norman Anthony's *Ballyhoo* in the 1930s springs immediately to mind. *Mad* and *The National Lampoon* are covered by essays in *American Humor Magazines* but can certainly absorb extended analysis as representatives of contemporary culture. Even such a magazine as *Film Fun*, which ran from 1916 to at least 1942, deserves thoughtful analysis because of its duration; it has yet to be fully studied, or even collected. *Americana*, around 1932, *Ziffs* in the middle twenties, and many of the smaller regional magazines deserve attention both in their regions and nationally. It is safe to say that relatively few humor periodicals have been studied at all, for their own sake, for their place in their times, or for other reasons.

College humor represents another gigantic open field in the periodical publication of humor. The Jazz Age saw humor magazines on every campus in America. Some had been distinguished for many years—Harvard *Lampoon*, Williams *Purple Cow*, and a host of others. However, the profusion of them in the twenties and thirties is astounding. In fact, commercial magazines, most notably *College Humor*, derived all their material from the collegiate sources and sustained significant national sales. The disappearance of college humor in the 1960s and the emergence of counterculture comix and counterculture humor periodicals obscures the importance of collegiate humor magazines in their era.

Most articles and anthologies dealing with college humor may be charitably described as superficial.

Comic books and counterculture comix are allies to humor periodicals. Whether or not they should be considered primarily humor periodicals is an open question. The author of this chapter classes them separately because, particularly in the case of comic books, their purpose is dramatic rather than comic. Comics are illustrated stories aimed often at a juvenile audience. Obviously, a *Mad Magazine* or similar magazines following *Mad* blur this distinction, for they are oriented toward adults and use humor for satiric purposes. Counterculture comix probably do belong in the study of humor periodicals because their reason for existence is social criticism; humor, illustration, and story lines are used for that purpose. The only comprehensive listings of these magazines are commercial listings designed for collectors and purchasers, not for analysts; in this case, the collectors' market is leading the academic student.

The area of sexual humor is also problematical. Mott includes *New Varieties*, publishing in the period around 1873, among humorous periodicals. *New Varieties* did use comic art for satiric purposes, but many of its illustrations were intended to be titillating rather than comic. It was particularly fond of cartoons depicting Satan leering over leggy showgirls doing the high kick-step—the showgirls are always in the front. Its melodramatic emphasis on sexual news is not humorous in intent. On the other hand, Al Goldstein's *Screw* magazine of the 1970s and 1980s is blatantly sexual in orientation, but Goldstein's medium is consistently burlesque, irony, or sarcasm: does this classify as a humor magazine? Transposing the grinning face of New York Mayor Ed Koch onto the pornographic picture of a man undergoing fellatio, as one issue did, must be a comic rather than serious form of commentary—and such contrivances are a consistent feature of *Screw*. For purposes of analysis, it is humor, just as the politically oriented humorous journals of the 1810–1840 period belong in any study of the comic medium. Many of the comic magazines of the 1910–1930 period were harassed by postal regulators and local police on charges of indecency. Authors treating girlie magazines regularly show covers of 1940s humor magazines including *Titters* and *Grin*. *TV Girls and Gags* in the 1950s supplies a title for the genre of such gals-and-gags cheesecake, which degenerated into sleazecake by the 1960s and 1970s, when it seems to have largely died out. It is safe to say that complete files of these magazines will be as difficult to obtain one hundred years from now as are their politically controversial ancestors from the previous century at present.

Because of the complexity of defining the field, it is easy to overlook the value to be found by studying individual publishers and contributors as magazine writers. Humor writers of the 1900–1950 period particularly were magazine writers, and their contributions help define their own canons. Similarly, the role of certain publishers is well worth special interest: Carleton in the 1850s and 1860s—who turned down Mark Twain's *Jumping Frog* book; Frank Leslie; T. W. Strong; Dell in the 1920–1950 period—who encouraged Norman Anthony and *Ballyhoo*, among a host of others; Charlton Press in Derby, Connecticut, still publishes two of the longer running cartoon-humor magazines now in decline—*Cartoon Cavalcade* and *Good Humor*—but is worth study to understand the waning of a tradition they represent. The social, sexual, and political and apolitical attitudes of major writers and cartoonists are all but untouched by scholarly critics. The range of various magazines over the period of a year or two would give insights into how American writers adjusted their works for the popular audience. H. L. Mencken's influence through *The American Mercury* has been so studied and *The New Yorker* and *Esquire* have received a reasonable amount of attention, but lesser magazines have not gotten attention beyond mention in occasional surveys of periods. Histories of individual editors and their influence are worthwhile enterprises. William Helmbold and the Philadelphia humorous publishers, beginning with *The Bee* in 1765, deserve a book-length study, as do the comic periodicals of New York, Boston, San Francisco, and the "regions." There are almost as many topics as there are authors and journals, either singly or in groups by locale, period, style, or coterie of contributors.

BIBLIOGRAPHICAL SURVEY

Frank Luther Mott's five-volume *A History of American Magazines* from Harvard University Press rightfully deserves primary standing in any study of American magazines, and the field of humor is no exception. Each of Mott's volumes, with the exception of the last posthumously published covering the 1905–1930 period, offers a concise description of the humorous periodical publications of the era, naming major titles and footnoting minor ones. Mott's discussions are cogent and intelligent, always interesting, and provide an excellent grounding in the field. His work did not go beyond 1930, and effectively cuts off about 1900. In addition to the summaries of humorous periodicals, Mott also offers five- to fifteen-page studies of major titles. Consequently, excellent, lengthy treatments of most of the magazines cited in this chapter can be found in the Mott volumes. He provides a full review of publishing history, major contributions and contributors and editors, and available circulation statistics. Theodore Peterson's *Magazines in the Twentieth Century* is an attempt to complete Mott's work through the 1960s but pays only scanty attention to comic periodicals.

American Humor Magazines and Comic Periodicals by David E. E. Sloane offers over seventy studies of individual comic periodicals by various scholars along with over two hundred brief studies of publications through 1985. The intent is to give a complete reference guide to the field, including listings of all available titles by name and date. Although some material necessarily covers the same ground as Mott's volumes, a number of secondary magazines and magazines from 1900 to the present are treated for the first time.

Analysis of humor magazines has not been extensive. However, a few articles are worthy of study and should be noted here. Brander Matthews' "The Comic Periodical Literature of the United States," *American Bibliopolist*, poses the issue of survivability of magazines of humor and gives a partial listing of important magazines to that date. "The Comic Paper Question" in Frederick Hudson's *Journalism in the United States from 1690 to 1872* (New York: Harper, 1873), 688–96, raises similar issues. Walter Blair's "The Popularity of Nineteenth-century American Humorists," in *American Literature*, 3 (May 1931), 175–94, gives full coverage to the newspaper humor writing and popular humorists of the post-Civil War period. Alexander King's, "The Sad Case of the Humorous Magazines," *Vanity Fair*, December 1933, is an intelligent brief statement on American humor magazines that offers provoking insights. Richard Marshall and Carol J. Wilson's "Selected Humorous Magazines (1820–1950), in Stanley Trachtenberg, ed., *American Humorists, 1800–1950*, gives an extensive listing and shows many covers offering a visual sense of comic periodical history.

Valuable bibliographies can be found in several places. Walter Blair's bibliography in *Native American Humor* (San Francisco: Chandler Publishing Co., 1960), originally compiled in 1937, is very broad and helpful. Ideally, the *Catalogue of Copyright Entries: Periodicals* (Washington, D.C.: U.S. Government Printing Office, 1906—), the copyright list of periodicals compiled by the Library of Congress since 1906 would offer information on humor magazines by title and date, but it lists only those magazines that actually submitted copyright copies. It is a testimony to the fleeting status of humor publications that many such magazines listing copyright on their editorial pages never in fact submitted issues for copyright protection. Therefore, there are no established data in the copyright records. Similarly, *The Union List of Serials*, edited by Edna Brown Titus, the other great repository of data concerning American magazines, lists only those magazines that librarians report, and where few or no libraries have collected runs of magazines, there is no information.

Some help for humor magazines of the earlier periods is available in *American Periodicals 1741–1900*, edited by Jean Hoornstra and Trudy Heath. Owing to their ambitious photoreproduction of American serials, particularly in the "American Periodicals" project, many humor magazines of the late eighteenth and nineteenth centuries are available in microfilm made from the one or two extant runs.

CHECKLIST AND ADDITIONAL SOURCES

Brigham, Clarence S. *History and Bibliography of American Newspapers, 1690–1820*. Hamden, Conn.: Archon Books, 1962, reprinted from the American Antiquarian Society.

Chielens, Edward E. *American Literary Magazines: The Eighteenth and Nineteenth Centuries*. Westport, Conn.: Greenwood Press, 1986.

———. *The Literary Journal in America to 1900*. Detroit: Gale Research, 1975.

Fulton, Lee, ed. *International Directory of Little Magazines and Small Presses*. 12th ed. Paradise, Calif.: Dustbooks, 1976, noncumulative indexing.

Garry, Leon, ed. *Standard Periodical Directory*. 4th ed. New York: Oxbridge Publishing Co., 1973, updated regularly.

Hoornstra, Jean and Trudy Heath. *American Periodicals 1741–1900*/An Index to the Microfilm Collections. Ann Arbor, Mich.: University Microfilms International, 1979.

Inge, M. Thomas. "Collecting Comic Books." *American Book Collector* 5 (March-April 1984), n.s.:3–15.

Katz, Bill, ed. *Magazines for Libraries*. New York: R. R. Bowker, 1969, updated regularly.

Kennedy, Jay. *The Official Underground and Newave Comix Price Guide*. Cambridge, Mass.: Boatner Norton Press, 1982.

Kery, Patricia F. *Great Magazine Covers of the World*. New York: Abbeville, 1981.

King, Alexander. "The Sad Case of the Humorous Magazines." *Vanity Fair* 41 (December 1933):26–27, 68–71.

Koppe, Richard et al. *A Treasury of College Humor*. New York: Wm. Penn, 1950.

Kribbs, Jane K. *An Annotated Bibliography of American Literary Periodicals, 1741–1850*. Boston: G. K. Hall, 1977.

Marshall, Richard and Carol J. Wilson. "Selected Humorous Magazines." In *American Humorists, 1800–1950*, ed. Stanley Trachtenberg. Detroit: Gale Research, 1983, 2:655–78.

Matthews, Brander. "The Comic Periodical Literature of the United States." *American Bibliopolist* 7 (August 1875):199–201.

Mott, Frank Luther. *American Journalism*. New York: Macmillan, 1941.

———. *A History of American Magazines*. 5 vols. Cambridge, Mass.: Harvard University Press, 1938–1965.

Murrell, William. *A History of American Graphic Humor*. New York: Whitney Museum, 1933.

Overstreet, Robert M. *The Comic Book Price Guide*, 14th ed. New York: Harmony Books, 1984. Annual price guide.

Peterson, Theodore. *Magazines in the Twentieth Century*, 2nd ed. Urbana: University of Illinois Press, 1964.

Serials in Microform, 1984. Ann Arbor, Mich.: University Microfilms International, 1984, updated annually.

Sloane, David E. E. *American Humor Magazines and Comic Periodicals*. Westport, Conn.: Greenwood Press, 1987.

Tebbel, John. *The American Magazine: A Compact History*. New York: Hawthorn, 1969.

Titus, Edna Brown, ed. *Union List of Serials in Libraries of the United States and Canada*, 3rd ed. New York: H. W. Wilson Co., 1965, updated regularly.

Ulrich's International Periodicals Directory, 22nd ed. New York: R. R. Bowker Co., 1983, updated regularly.

Wood, James P. *Magazines in the United States*. New York: Ronald, 1949.

Various hardcover reprints of *Life, Colliers, Reader's Digest, Saturday Evening Post, Esquire, Playboy*, and *The New Yorker* humor and cartoons, and now even counterculture and other humor as well as various period anthologies like *Clips from Jonathan's Jacknife* as early as the 1870 period, may be located individually.

♦ 4 ♦

Film Comedy

Wes D. Gehring

OVERVIEW AND HISTORICAL DEVELOPMENT

To better facilitate so challenging an enterprise as a chapter overview of American film comedy, its history has been broken into three distinctive periods: the silents, the studio era, and the post–World War II period.

The Silents

American humor has always placed a high premium upon physical comedy. Thus, even our great literary comedians frequently showcase this phenomenon; witness Mark Twain's comic description of bouncing about in a stagecoach from *Roughing It* (1872) or James Thurber's delightfully unofficial autobiography, *My Life and Hard Times* (1933), whose very episode titles create cartoon pictures: "The Night the Bed Fell," "The Day the Dam Broke," "The Dog that Bit People."

Appropriately coupled with this fascination is the widespread belief that the silent era (specifically, the 1920s) was the golden age of American film comedy. Boasting a comedy pantheon composed of Charlie Chaplin, Buster Keaton, Harold Lloyd, and Harry Langdon (the most traditionally showcased foursome), it makes for a good argument. But many significant events predate the 1920s.

The birth of American film comedy coincides with the very beginnings of film in this country. The earliest whole film on record is the comic *Fred Ott's Sneeze* (1891, from the American father of movies, Thomas Edison).[1] Ott was an Edison engineer and resident comic whose one-routine comedy "film" lasted merely seconds, but now holds this double distinction of being the first film and the first comedy.

American film comedy into the twentieth century was seldom more complex. The early leaders in film comedy were the French, particularly George Méliès and Max Linder. Not until the early 1910s would Mack Sennett, creator of the Keystone Kops, emerge as the father of American film comedy.

Sennett had been a journeyman performer in a cross-section of popular entertainment forms (circuses, burlesque, vaudeville, legitimate stage) before finally achieving success in film, originally under the tutelage of the great film pioneer D. W. Griffith. Sennett, a large, naive farm boy, came to New York early in the twentieth century to sing opera but instead found work as the rear end of a horse at the Bowery Burlesque. While not the standard route to the Met, this was an appropriate beginning for a man whose future comedy would be based largely in slapstick irreverence. His later description of why he enjoyed burlesque comics could just as aptly be applied to his film work:

the cops and tramps with their bed slats and bladders appealed to me as being funny people. Their approach to life was earthy and understandable. They whaled the daylights out of pretension. They made fun of themselves and the human face. They reduced convention, dogma, stuffed shirts, and Authority to nonsense, and then blossomed into pandemonium.[2]

For the student of American film comedy, this description is also appropriate for a great deal of what would follow Sennett.

Sennett was at his best when doing parody, especially comedy send-ups of melodramatic narratives with last-minute rescues—which also just happened to be the forte of Griffith. In fact, Sennett had come to understand the Griffith melodrama so well he had even scripted a classic early example of it: Griffith's *The Lonely Ville* (1909). Thus, later Sennett parodies of the master were devastating dissections.

Sennett's greatest gift to film comedy was making slapstick totally cinematic for the first time. His company was also an important early "laboratory" for the careers of such later comedy giants as Chaplin, Langdon, and director Frank Capra. Moreover, Sennett had intuitively tapped into the twentieth century's most fundamental contribution to humor—the world's ever-accelerating comic absurdity.

While Sennett might be likened to the more recent parody artist Mel Brooks, America's first film comedy star, John Bunny, anticipates the antiheroic persona of W. C. Fields. Both were film comedy fifth columnists, frequently working behind married lines (their own), as they attempted manly things. Examples include Bunny's poker-playing needs in *Cure for Pokeritus* (1912), or Fields' desire to see a wrestling match in *The Man on the Flying Trapeze* (1935).

Within Bunny's film career (1910–1915), his put-upon husband also anticipates many characteristics of newspaper cartoonist George McManus's antiheroic

Jiggs, from the acclaimed *Bringing Up Father* (1913) strip. For example, Bunny's losses to his frequent female nemesis Flora Finch are obvious forerunners of the comic domination Jiggs suffers from his rolling-pin-packing wife Maggie.

Great as Bunny's comedy success was, at the time of his death he was already being eclipsed by a comedian who would become cinema's most celebrated figure: Charlie Chaplin. It is hard to overestimate the significance of Chaplin to film comedy. He remains *the* standard against which all cinema clowns are measured. His balancing of equally celebrated pathos has become an ever-elusive goal for other comedians. Because so many have failed (Langdon and Jerry Lewis are the most famous examples), film biographer Bob Thomas has labeled the fixation the "Chaplin disease."[3] Directly related to this phenomenon was Chaplin's ability to wear all the production hats; he wrote, directed, scored, starred in, and produced his own films. Many comedians have since failed in the attempt to duplicate this accomplishment, but it remains as another standard. For example, 1980s comedy star Eddie Murphy has frequently mentioned this as a goal.[4]

Before further examining Chaplin and his fellow 1920s pantheon members, it is important to note that the teens produced a number of other excellent comedians. Two of the best were former Chaplin colleagues at Sennett's Keystone (Chaplin spent 1914 with Sennett) Fatty Arbuckle and Mabel Normand. Arbuckle was an agile fat man whose films oozed energetic innocence. The beautiful Normand, known at the time as the "female Chaplin," projected the same energetic innocence. In the early 1920s scandal would ruin Arbuckle's career and seriously handicap that of Normand, but during the teens films like Sennett's *Fatty and Mabel Adrift* (1916) made them two of America's early comedy favorites.

Another important comedy figure predating the 1920s was Douglas Fairbanks, Sr. Though better known today as an early swashbuckling version of Indiana Jones, during the late teens Fairbanks did a series of delightful parodies (1915–1920). Handsome, dashing, and athletically optimistic, Fairbanks playfully attacked everything from American mores to popular film genres.

These have been important pre–1920 film comedy figures, but silent comedy is largely defined through the Jazz Age work of the "pantheon four" (though all but Langdon had begun filmmaking in the teens). With Chaplin still a dominant within the pantheon, the three remaining members are most informatively showcased in comparison with the creator of Charlie the Tramp.

The greatest creative rival to Chaplin was Keaton, although his work never knew the same contemporary critical and commercial success. For example, *The General* (1926), Keaton's greatest film and the only work by a pantheon member considered an equal to Chaplin's masterpiece *The Gold Rush* (1925), was a decidedly critical and box office failure upon its release. It was not until the 1960s that Keaton began to receive the recognition he so long deserved.

As is appropriate for Chaplin's only serious rival, the screen worlds of the two are decidedly different. First, Chaplin's position constantly reflected social statement, as if addressing the inequities of his Dickensian childhood. Chaplin was about underdogs winning—a midget Rocky pulling the upset of upsets. In *The Pilgrim* (1923), Charlie pantomimes the story of David and Goliath—it is a footnote to the source of all Charlie stories. The Keaton way was a commentary on endurance. If Sisyphus were given a mask, there could be no more appropriate visage than the Keaton face—the unchanging, enduring mask that even earned the nickname "The Great Stone Face." If one scene encapsulates the Keaton milieu, it is the impossibly comic walk into the tornado in *Steamboat Bill Jr.* (1928). This comedy code of endurance was an outgrowth of a slapstick childhood in vaudeville where he was literally ihe "body" of his family's act. Billed as "The Human Mop," little "Buster" was thrown about the stage at the "creative" whim of his father.

Second, the Chaplin film is full of nineteenth-century Dickensian emotion that so frequently focused on the child. No better example of this exists than the saga of Charlie and little Jackie Coogan in *The Kid* (1921). Of course, Chaplin tempers all this with laughter for his patented gift of pathos. Still, the student of Chaplin is invariably first moved by the Tramp emotionally. In contract, Keaton's deadpan is a twentieth-century defense to the absurdities of the modern world. Keaton is much more apt to move our minds, period. Thus, he knocks heroines off pedestals, seeming to prefer appearing opposite huge machines, such as the title-playing train in *The General*. However, Keaton eventually masters these machines, something true twenti-th-century antiheroes such as Laurel and Hardy can never do.

Third, because Charlie is so gifted a mime, i.e., transforming a clock into a miniature patient in *The Pawnshop* (1916) or dinner rolls into dancing feet in the delightful "Oceana Roll" of *The Gold Rush*, Chaplin the filmmaker exercised minimal interference. Editing and special effects would make the viewer question the authenticity of his gift. Keaton, who was equally fascinated by machines in real life, was not averse to camera trickery for comedy. Still, he, too, knew the importance of the long take or long shot in guaranteeing the authenticity of his physical skills. Unlike Chaplin, however, Keaton minimized the closeness of the camera—allowing himself to be visually overpowered both by his props and the vast expanses surrounding him.

In Lloyd, Chaplin had his greatest 1920s commercial rival. Lloyd was the boy-next-door type, anxious to be a success. His greatest film, *Safety Last* (1923), with its now celebrated skyscraper-climbing scene, is the perfect metaphor for the Lloyd story—"climbing" to success. *Safety Last* is also, of course, Lloyd's best example of thrill comedy, a phenomenon synonymous with his name.

The Lloyd film did not have the artistry of Chaplin's and Keaton's. Lloyd's bespectacled character (glasses being his person's only real costume prop) had nowhere near the depth of character instilled in Charlie the Tramp. Moreover, Lloyd's films lacked the narrative tightness of Keaton's, where even gags were sacrificed for story continuity. Lloyd himself was without the physical grace and skills of Chaplin and Keaton, but he compensated for this with a nonstop manner consistent with his Puritan Work Ethic tendencies—a latter-day Horatio Alger on speed. Still, the Lloyd films are very funny because they merge ageless gags (the merely basted-together suit that begins to come undone in *The Freshman*, 1925) and a central character whose ambitious innocence is still winsome, though without the emotional complexities that make the Tramp so fascinating.

Harry Langdon knew only a brief success at the top with three features: *The Strong Man* (1926), *Tramp, Tramp, Tramp* (1926), and *Long Pants* (1927). He resembled, in the words of film critic James Agee, "an elderly baby" or "a baby dope fiend" (not unlike the face of Pee Wee Herman), who survived only through the grace of God.[5] But, like Peter Sellers' Inspector Clouseau, who also has a guardian angel, both characters are not even remotely aware such aid is being given. Examples include Langdon's mistaken belief he has scared away the cyclone in *Tramp, Tramp, Tramp* and Sellers' complete obliviousness to the bumbling assassination attempts that become the comic centerpieces of the Pink Panther films.

Langdon was the only pantheon member not fully cognizant of why his persona worked. His success is largely tied to the molding of Frank Capra, from whom he broke in 1927, seemingly afflicted by and about to be the victim of the "Chaplin disease." Capra soon achieved solo comedy greatness; Langdon went into comedy decline.

Langdon's comedy gift lacks the physical skills of the other three. It is largely a matter of the visage,[6] such as the struggle for understanding that plays across his baby face while he attempts to comprehend a cow's udder in *Soldier Man* (1926), or the ever-so-slow awakening of sexual fear in *The Strong Man* when Langdon thinks a worldy woman plans to compromise him. Coming to the screen at the near height of the silent era, his small but subtle mime was a refreshing variation for the mid–1920s audience, especially one missing a less-productive Chaplin (whose pathos Langdon's persona most resembled). Sometimes today's viewer, because he or she is not immersed in the rich silent comedy mosaic that was the 1920s, misses the subtle greatness of Langdon. As Agee has so poetically described it, "it seemed as if Chaplin could do literally anything, on any instrument in the orchestra. Langdon had one queerly toned, unique little reed. But out of it he could get incredible melodies."[7]

There are several additional names that merit attention. Laurel and Hardy, teamed and molded by Leo McCarey, deserve near-pantheon status. Though the duo was not so dependent upon McCarey as Langdon was on Capra, McCarey was as instrumental in their success as he was in the evolution of the comic antihero in American film, of which Laurel and Hardy are excellent examples.[8]

Film historian Walter Kerr makes a strong argument for the inclusion of now neglected sophisticated comedian Raymond Griffith for near pantheon status.[9] Award-winning compilation filmmaker Robert Youngson is equally eloquent on Charley Chase's part in *Four Clowns* (1970). Cross-eyed Ben Turpin, though not of pantheon status, is now a celebrated silent comedy figure whose mere casting guaranteed the success of such inspired Sennett parodies as *The Shriek of Araby* (Turpin as Valentino, 1923) and *The Pride of Pikesville* (Turpin as Erich von Stroheim, 1927).

The Studio Era

The addition of sound defused the comic centralness of the silent clowns, shifting the comedy emphasis to a more structured realm. While Mast over-emphasizes this with his blatant "Sound comedy is structural, not physical," there is no denying the change the spoken word brought to film comedy.[10] This was best demonstrated in the 1934 birth of the screwball comedy, a genre where only picture-plus-sound could adequately showcase the marriage of slapstick to witty dialogue. The genre was at its best when a Cary Grant or a Carole Lombard starred, yet any number of 1930s actors successfully piloted screwball waters. The new genre was based upon the old "boy meets girl" formula—gone topsy-turvy. It generally presented the eccentric, female-dominated courtship of the American rich, with the male target seldom being informed that open season had arrived, such as Katharine Hepburn's hunting down of timid Professor Cary Grant in Howard Hawks' *Bringing Up Baby* (1938) or the similar male massacre of professorial Henry Fonda by Barbara Stanwyck in Preston Sturges' *The Lady Eve* (1941). The genre took an antiheroic situation and dressed up the surround-ings and added beautiful people. In contrast to screwball comedy's musical-chairs casting, seemingly no comedian could have replaced a Chaplin in *The Gold Rush* or a Keaton in *The General*. Thus, while the dominant genre of silent comedy was that of the personality comedian, mainstream studio film fare pro-vided three choices: screwball comedy, populist comedy, and a largely new cast of personality comedians.

Understanding these comedy tracks necessitates noting three variables (besides the coming of sound) that had major impact upon post–1930 film comedy: changes in humor, economics, and censorship. First, American humor was undergoing a major period of transition. The dominant comedy character had been the capable cracker-barrel Yankee type of a Will Rogers; it was now becoming a frustrated antihero best exemplified by *The New Yorker* writing of Robert Benchley and James Thurber or by the film short subjects of Laurel and Hardy. The antihero is a young urban character who appears all the younger because of his utter incompetency at any and every task. His childlike nature is underlined by the fact that he knows little of employment: His every moment is consumed with the frustrations of leisure time. Moreover, he is so frustrated by domestic, daily problems (largely female) that he never approaches the political issues that dominate the cracker-barrel's life.

The cracker-barrel Yankee, in contrast, was an older rural or small-town figure full of wisdom learned through years of experience. Unlike the antihero, when a character in the crackerbarrel world found himself in a comic dilemma, it was due to his own incompetency. The assumption was that the world was rational, and that the character could right himself by making his own life well-ordered.

Appropriately, McCarey's antiheroic Laurel and Hardy were the silent comedians who made the most successful transition to sound. (The incomparable
Chaplin's successful transition to limited sound was actually no transition at all,
since the Tramp remained silent until the end of *Modern Times*, 1936.) Because
screwball comedy would soon build upon the antiheroic transition, it is also not
surprising that McCarey would eventually surface as a pivotal screwball director,[11] such as with his Oscar-winning direction of the genre classic and standard
The Awful Truth (1937).

Second, as 1930s America suffered through its worst economic depression,
its film comedy indirectly reflected this in three ways. First, while the beginning
of the antihero transition predated the economic collapse, a comedy movement
that keyed upon frustration and often displayed anarchistic violence was no doubt
fed by the disillusionment and anger of the Great Depression. Thus, the tit-for-
tat self-destructive violence of a Laurel and Hardy, or even the much cruder
slapstick of the Three Stooges, was perferctly in keeping with this comic frustration. The Marx Brothers, though not antiheroic in the sense that they were
victims (they tended to comically victimize others), reflected the antiheroically
irrational nature of 1930s America. Physically and verbally, especially in their
propensity for outrageous puns and malapropisms, the Marx Brothers declared
that nothing, including the English language, was what it seemed. At their best,
they took on everything from government on high to high art.

A second way in which 1930s film comedy indirectly reflected the period was
in the ages and attitudes of its personality comedians. Hard times seemed to
encourage the popularity of hard, older, cynical comedians: W. C. Fields, the
Marx Brothers (particularly Groucho), Mae West, and Jimmy Durante. Fields'
famous motto, ''Never give a sucker an even break'' (also the title of a great
1941 Fields film) might as well have served as the calling card for all these
comic con artists.[12] Fields' roles, however, often fluctuated between the huckster
and the antihero. When the Marx Brothers moved from Paramount to M-G-M,
Irving Thalberg toned down their irreverence.

This worldly slant was in direct contrast to the previous decade and its favored
comedians. Both the Jazz Age and its clowns were generally optimistic and
youthful.

A final way in which 1930s film comedy indirectly reflects the decade's
economic debacle was in its fascination with the world of the wealthy. Certainly
this type of escapism is always a movie open sesame, but never more so than
in a depression. Thus, high society literally became a genre convention in screwball comedy, also frequently surfacing in the genres of both personality comedian
and populist comedy. The rich took it upon the chin in all cases, but much more
gently in screwball comedy, where they were often eccentrically and/or incom-
petently endearing, such as the Bullock family of *My Man Godfrey*, with Irene
Bullock (Carole Lombard) being delightfully described by a contemporary reviewer as ''a one-track mind with grass growing over its rails.''[13] Outside screwball comedy, things were much rougher for the cinema rich. For example, a

stuffy mountain of a dowager named Margaret Dumont was the perennial high-society target of the Marx Brothers, off whom they bounced roughhouse comedy and assorted fruit whenever she was towed into range.

The third variable having a major impact upon 1930s film comedy was film censorship. Though a Motion Picture Production Code of do's and don't's was established in 1930, largely through the action of a special interest group, The Catholic Legion of Decency, it was not until 1934 that it began to be strictly enforced. Essentially, the Code meant movies should neither lower the standards of their audiences nor encourage audiences to relate to characters of crime and sin.

The Code's most immediate comedy victim was the queen of the double entendres, Mae West. From her first screen utterance (in *Night After Night*, 1932), where her response to "Goodness, what beautiful diamonds!" was "Goodness had nothing do to with it, dearie," West was controversial. She was at her best—meaning her most uncensored—in *She Done Him Wrong* (1933), a film so commercially successful it is often credited with saving its parent company, Paramount, from Depression receivership. In *I'm No Angel* (1933), West was a lady lion tamer "who lost her reputation but never missed it." Commercial success continued, but the combined pressures of the Code and American blue-noses methodically chipped away at her then unique comic parody of sexuality. By 1937 she had all but retired from films, though there would be sporadic reappearances, most notably with W. C. Fields in *My Little Chickadee* (1940). While still amusing, West by this time had been reduced to a parody of a sexual parody.

While censorship diffused the West bombshell, it was probably a contributing factor to the birth of screwball comedy. Though this genre is most dependent upon the antiheroic transition, a formula of suppressed sexuality-eccentricity should not be ignored, nor should the parallel 1934 starting dates. The title of film critic Andrew Sarris' article on the subject best addresses this comic sexual tension: "The Sex Comedy Without Sex."[14]

Censorship also encouraged the resurgence of the populist, patriotic film during the second half of the 1930s, a time when America was beginning to believe in its institutions again as pre–World War II nationalism returned. This is best articulated in film comedy by Frank Capra's *Mr. Deeds Goes to Town* (1936) and *Mr. Smith Goes to Washington* (1939), where young Yankee figures go forth to solve national political woes in the commonsense cracker-barrel Yankee tradition of Jack Downing.

The Capra films filled a Yankee void created by the untimely death in 1935 of Will Rogers, the last cracker-barrel figure of national significance. Rogers had been a major box office figure in the fist half of the 1930s, an upbeat and sometimes sentimental exception to his more cynical contemporary personality comedians. Yet he too often used con-man techniques to insure the proper course. For example, Rogers' *A Connecticut Yankee* (1931), where he masters King

Arthur's court with modern technology, even leaves him with the title "Sir Boss."

Despite the success of Rogers and Capra, the Yankee had already become something of an anachronism. For Rogers, this frequently meant hedging on current problems with settings from an earlier, simpler time. Capra's Yankees did not retreat into the past, but after *Deeds* they displayed compromised victories. Then the chaos of the war years forever dampened America's love affair with the cracker barrel; the "catch–22" nature of the world made it impossible to relate to such a capable figure. In Capra's *It's a Wonderful Life* (1946), a former archetype of this character nearly commits suicide and the storyline must introduce a deus ex machina in the form of a second-class angel sent to preserve order. It was as if Capra had taken a suggestion from the influx of fantasy into screwball comedy in the late 1930s, when ghosts and spirits proved to be a new source of genre eccentricity. Whereas fantasy spelled resiliency for screwball comedy, it portended decline for the cracker-barrel figure.

The war years naturally also spawned a host of service comedies, with the hot new comedy team of Abbott and Costello almost cornering the market, as they seemed to salute nearly every branch of the service, starting with their first and best patriotic outing, *Buck Privates* (1941). Laurel and Hardy were also still active and frequently service-bent, such as in *Great Guns* (1941) and *Air Wardens* (1943). But their 1940s work pales beside their classic silent shorts or 1930s features like *Sons of the Desert* (1934).

The new solo comedian was Bob Hope. And although he was *Caught in the Draft* (1941) more than once, his biggest impact was as part of the unofficial comedy team of Hope and Crosby—who began their series of Road pictures in 1940.

The Post–World War II Era

American film comedy since World War II will be examined along five genre tracks: personality comedian, populist cracker barrel, screwball comedy, parody, and black comedy.

While the war years had generally been an attempt to maintain the entertainment status quo, some changes that had taken place did not fade. Most obvious was the new breed of personality comedians who could fluctuate between the most incompetent of comic antiheroes and the cool, egotistical wiseguy. Bob Hope was the unquestionable master, from the Road pictures to such diverse solo outings as his attempt to be a film noir detective in *My Favorite Brunette* (1947) or the Damon Runyon title character in *The Lemon Drop Kid* (1951).

Hope's comic duality complements modern humor's fascination with the schizophrenic. In fact, Woody Allen, today's greatest film comedian and most self-consciously shrink-oriented, follows the same antihero to wise guy and back pattern. In *Play It Again, Sam* (1972), Allen bounces frenetically between being a Bogart clone and the shlemiel of the week. Indeed, Allen, an admitted Hope disciple, at times even sounds like Hope. Comedy historian Maurice Yacower notes that Allen's comment to a guard protecting all that remains of the evil leader in *Sleeper* (1973)—''We're here to see the nose. We hear it's running''— is pure Hope.[15]

In the 1940s and 1950s this antihero/wise-guy equation was sometimes given to two performers, or what was supposed to be two. For example, Danny Kaye frequently played dual roles in his films and he was at his best in *Wonder Man* (1945), where he played the most opposite of twins.

Martin and Lewis, *the* comedy team of the 1950s, often operated on the same antihero/wise-guy formula. Jerry Lewis' screen persona, which he called the Idiot, is probably the ultimate antihero. Dean Martin has just as strongly been associated with the wise guy. Interestingly enough, Lewis' greatest solo work, *The Nutty Professor* (1963), finds him playing the same antihero/wise-guy duality, a duality often compared to the make-up of the Martin and Lewis team: Lewis plays both an absent-minded professor and a wise-mouthed crooner.[16]

While the duality has traditionally emphasized the antihero, sometimes to near neglect of the wise-guy persona, such as the excellent Red Skeleton vehicles *The Fuller Brush Man* and *A Southern Yankee* (both 1948), some current film comedy personalities are reversing the emphasis. Both Bill Murray and Eddie Murphy are essentially cool comics who can weather antiheroic situations. While they do this in radically different ways (Murray is the original Mr. Laid Back; Murphy is the master of comic intensity), they comically deny the loss of control. Thus, unlike so many of their comedy predecessors, they are able to maintain their outrageousness in establishment positions. Murphy feigns angry outrage as he cheekily dresses down dangerous situations with an inimitable comic brassiness. In contrast, Murray's Mr. Cool character is based upon never seeming to be caught off-guard. While Murphy creates the comic situation by confrontation, Murray's forte is responding to it.

While Murray and Murphy have been very influential (see especially the Murray-like nature of Michael Keaton and Tom Hanks), the emphasis on the antihero in the antihero/wise-guy duality still dominates. Three of the best contemporary examples are Dudley Moore, Steve Martin, and Chevy Chase. At their best, they tend to demonstate this combination in their screwball genre films. This is most true of Dudley Moore, who, as an economy-sized Cary Grant, has starred in such recent screwball delights as *10* (1979), *Arthur* (1981), *Unfaithfully Yours* (1984, which even improves upon Preston Sturges's long-celebrated 1948 original), and *Micki & Maude* (1984).

Just as the genre of personality comedian had evolved in the 1940s, so did the other comedy genres. The postwar screwball comedy moved to the suburbs, or what was still even the country. Thus, a film like *Mr. Blandings Builds His Dream House* (1948) offered a familiar screwball cast (Cary Grant, Myrna Loy, Melvyn Douglas) in an older, more sedate setting. Grant and Loy are a married couple with children; Douglas is their lawyer/best friend who attempts to help them in their comic housing problems. To the audiences of the baby-booming, housing-shorted 1940s, the film was as topical as it was comic. The same type of domesticated screwball comedy continued through the 1950s, such as Howard Hawks' *Monkey Business* (1952), where everyone's favorite screwball professor (Cary Grant) returns to academia fourteen years after *Bringing Up Baby*. Other than Hawks' *Man's Favorite Sport* (1964), the genre fell on hard times in the 1960s. However, since Peter Bogdanovich's *What's Up, Doc?* (1972), essentially an unacknowledged remake of *Bringing Up Baby*, the genre has reentered the 1930s-style fast lane. This shedding of domesticity has continued into the 1980s. Appropriately, today's top screwball director, Blake Edwards (*10*; *Victor/Victoria*, 1982; *Micki & Maude*), traces his filmmaking beginnings to Leo McCarey.

With the decline of the cracker-barrel figure, the genre of populist comedy also underwent change. After the deus ex machina needs of *It's a Wonderful Life*, Capra went one step further when, in *State of the Union* (1948), he has his hero forgo a chance at the presidency because of the corruptness of political life. It was a far cry from the impassioned involvement of *Mr. Smith Goes to Washington*.

In *Meet John Doe* (1941) Capra had suggested that a Yankee could be misused—be fashioned into a puppet demagogue. After the witch-hunting days of Joseph McCarthy, Elia Kazan's *A Face in the Crowd* (1957) warns that the cracker-barrel type could misuse the power himself—once his populist traits brought him to high position.

A likeable 1950s cracker-barrel type was rare, unless he became the clown, like the very commercially successful Ma and Pa Kettle series (starring Marjorie Main and Percy Kilbride), not to mention the down-home wisdom of Francis the talking mule and his conversational partner Donald O'Connor. The transition from benefactor to buffoon had no doubt been softened by the nostalgic 1940s folk comedies, which gave the simpler, paternalistic past antiheroic roots, such as *Meet Me in St. Louis* (1944), *Life With Father* (1947), and *Cheaper by the Dozen* (1950). On a more contemporary note there was *Father of the Bride* (1950) and its sequel, *Father's Little Dividend* (1951). As if reading from an antiheroic script, the all-knowing male was taking a back seat to the female. George Stevens said it more directly with *I Remember Mama* (1948). In fact, the closest thing to Capra's prewar populist, cracker-barrel films showcased females; witness the Oscar-winning performances of Loretta Young in *The Farmer's Daughter* (1947) and Judy Holliday in *Born Yesterday* (1950).

Like screwball comedy, the populist, cracker-barrel film went into 1960s decline, though both buffoon and benefactor models continued on television, in *The Beverly Hillbillies* and *The Andy Griffith Show*. Again paralleling screwball comedy, a subdued populist film resurfaced in the 1970s and 1980s as America recovered from Watergate and celebrated its bicentennial. It was best displayed in such Robert Redford works as *The Electric Horseman* (1979) and *The Natural*

(1984), but a truly eclectic group began to embrace it, from Clint Eastwood's *Bronco Billy* (1980) to Goldie Hawn's *Protocol* (1984, which might better have been titled *Ms. Smith Goes to Washington*).[17]

The parody film genre has never been absent from any period, but it has become progressively more important since World War II. As in the personality comedian genre, one can trace a significant parody line between Bob Hope and Woody Allen. Their antihero/wise-guy persona was the perfect guise with which to parody genres that starred either stoical tough guys or flamboyant swashbucklers. Hope parody classics like his Western trilogy (Hope's top grossing *The Paleface*, 1948; *Son of Paleface*, 1952; *Alias Jesse James*, 1959) were released to not fully appreciative markets, and Allen's work generally made parody take a backseat to contemporary satire. But the most influential American film parodist since Sennett is Mel Brooks.

Brooks' work, particularly his first and best parody features, *Blazing Saddles* (1974) and *Young Frankenstein* (1976), had a timely impact for five reasons. First, because of a more sophisticated audience and a greater appreciation of film history in general, the parodist could now be much more ambitious in his work. Second, while American film comedy has always milked direct address to the camera (and thus to the audience), from a wink by Charlie to an aside by Groucho, radio and television made things even more intimately suitable for the most tongue-in-cheek of parody. The self-conscious dialogue of the Road pictures, such as the line in the third Road film, *The Road to Morocco* (1942)— I'll lay you eight to five that we'll meet Dorothy Lamour''—proved a harbinger of things to come. Third, the film criticism and filmmaking of the 1950s French New Wave, particularly of François Truffaut, frequently paid homage to earlier American film comedy—providing both greater credibility and blueprint-like encouragement for the affectionately self-conscious parodist. Fourth, the 1950s training ground of television's *Your Show of Shows*, which frequently focused on film parody (such as the classic *From Here to Eternity* take-off, *From Here to Obscurity*) utilized such major future film parodists as Mel Brooks, Woody Allen, Carl Reiner, and Neil Simon. Fifth, Brooks' *Blazing Saddles* and *Young Frankenstein*, besides being thoroughly funny, were thoroughly researched along spoof lines; they also parodied the Western and horror films, the two genres most familiar to American audiences.

The black comedy has never found the acceptance of the aforementioned genres, even after World War II, when the events of Hiroshima and Nagasaki and the immediate descent of the Iron Curtain would seem to have made it the most natural to succeed. Chaplin's comically macabre *Monsieur Verdoux* (1947) was one of the very few, although Britain took the hint with it's delightful Ealing Studio's ''little'' comedies. Naturally, earlier American precedents exist. In fact, one might even label Chaplin's *Gold Rush* a black comedy since it was inspired by the Donner Party tragedy. Other examples would include two Hitler satires, Chaplin's *The Great Dictator* (1940) and Ernst Lubitsch's *To Be or Not to Be*

(1942; Lubitsch is best known for satires that focus more on love and money, such as *Trouble in Paradise*, 1932).

While black comedies would sporadically appear during the next twenty years, such as Alfred Hitchcock's *The Trouble with Harry* (1955) and Billy Wilder's *Some Like It Hot* (1959), it was Stanley Kubrick's *Dr. Strangelove or: How I Learned to Stop Worrying and Love the Bomb* (1964) that established a new era for the black comedy. (Director Frank Tashlin's satires were never so dark, being more cartoon-like putdowns of 1950s fetishes.) Since then, examples of the genre have escalated rapidly, from other war stories like *M.A.S.H.* and *Catch–22* (both 1970) to offbeat romances such as *The Graduate* (1967), *Harold and Maude*, (1972), and *Prizzi's Honor* (1985). *M.A.S.H.* director Robert Altman has been the most prolific, receiving his greatest critical recognition for *Nashville* (1975), a dark mosaic of the American scene, from the country record industry to Watergate.

The *Dr. Strangelove* of the 1970s was *Network* (1976), about a losing television network that will do anything for ratings. The entertainment industry continues to be a popular target, with such films as *Being There* (1979) starring Peter Sellers, Richard Rush's superb but neglected *The Stunt Man* (1980), and Jerry Lewis as victim in *The King of Comedy* (1983). But black comedy of the 1980s is more frequently mixed with horror and parody. This is best exemplified by John Landis' *An American Werewolf in London* (1981), a devastating parody of the horror genre and the darkest of comedies. Gross horror scenes are made palatable by comic surprise. Conversely, comic surprise never packed so much wallop, as if Jonathan Swift's classic "A Modest Proposal" had included a more detailed look at eating babies. A nervous laughter is the result, not unlike the impact of thrill comedy.

These, then, have been the five key genre threads of post–World War II American film comedy. All have been greatly influenced by the evolution of the comic antihero, yet all have roots in the most fundamental of precinema worlds— an often contrary and difficult world. That is the tradition, the bittersweet beauty, the preciousness, of comedy.

THEMES AND ISSUES

The area most in need of future research is the division of film comedy into several distinctive genres. Thus far cinema scholarship has been most apt simply to call comedy the broadest of genres and lump a number of types together. To date, screwball comedy has generated the most specific comedy-as-genre attention, although it has hardly been overwhelming (see the "Bibliographical Survey"). Of course, individual clowns and teams have inspired more total studies, but it has seldom been applied toward some broader personality comedian genre. Ironically, while film comedy lies richly waiting, genre study has been busy dissecting areas not nearly so broad. For example, under the crime film umbrella one can now find a multitude of genres—the gangster film, film noir, the thriller, the detective film. Certainly, comedy's time has come.

At present this author is addressing the subject in a handbook of film genres to be published by Greenwood Press.[18] Five comedy genres are being examined: personality comedian, screwball comedy, cracker-barrel populist comedy, parody, and black comedy. (These are discussed briefly in the "Overview and Historical Development" above.)

In the future more divisions could, and no doubt should, be made, but initially it is most important to explore the most fundamental of camps. As it is, the breakdown might have stopped with the even more generalized: personality comedy, romantic comedy, social comedy, and parody.

The personality comedy has its emphasis on a specific clown or clowns, from Charlie Chaplin to the Marx Brothers. Romantic comedy is triggered by the interaction of a comic couple. Thus, a screwball comedy is dependent upon the unique chemistry of a Cary Grant and Irene Dunne teaming, or Grant and Katharine Hepburn. But with the female-dominated courtship, screwball comedy is also part parody of the traditional "boy meets girl" story.

The social comedy attempts to present society with a specific message, frequently of a political nature. It can occur in the populist milieu of a Frank Capra, where the people are celebrated, and one underdog can make a difference. Or, it can take the black comedy route of Stanley Kubrick's *Dr. Strangelove*, where human society is seen much less ideally—warning that it is only a matter of time before some contemporary cowboy like Slim Pickens (ominously a traditional populist type) literally rides The Bomb to everyone's Armageddon.

The parody film, like the social comedy, has a message, but it is invariably lighter in tone: Do not take a specific genre and/or artist quite so seriously. The parody film is often associated with the personality comedies, because of the propensity of certain comedians (like Bob Hope and Woody Allen) to excel in the area. But it is fundamentally structural—more dependent upon the comic interaction of ideas than bodies. However, while a social comedy builds a structure (such as the escalating absurdity of man's actions in *Dr. Strangelove*), parody beings with a structure (the conventions and expectations of a given genre or director's milieu) and systematically dismantles it.

Naturally, there are few pure examples of these types, with even the most seemingly classic of examples dovetailing into other categories. For example, Mel Brooks' *Blazing Saddles* is an archetype parody film. Yet, by its conclusion a strong social statement has been made about the inherent racism and violence of the Western.

Anoher blurring of lines occurs in the inspired antics of the Marx Brothers in *Duck Soup* (1933). Here are definite personality comedians, but this film is also a decidedly black comedy send-up of government and war. Now considered their greatest film, *Duck Soup* was initially so poorly received it also ended their film careers.

It is important to dwell on these variations as one addresses comedy genre distinctions. Otherwise, generalization can establish false genre norms. For example, a key misunderstanding of screwball comedy has been the tendency to include the films of Capra. But after *It Happened One Night*, this director's career took a fascinating but decidedly nonscrewball turn. The Capra heroes who follow, like the classic trio of Mr. Deeds, Mr. Smith, and John Doe, are centered upon cracker barrel populism. In contrast, screwball comedy begins and ends with the most antiheroic of madcap romance. Film critic Jim Leach, who also places Capra in the populist map, observes:

Capra's vision is not really screwball at all. . . . whereas the only positive strategy in screwball comedy is to accept the all-pervasive craziness, the populist comedy argues that what society regards as crazy (Mr. Deeds' attempt to give away his fortune) is really a manifestation of the normal human values with which society has lost touch.[19]

Besides a concerted effort to explore the many genres of American film comedy, there are two ongoing issues the interested student needs to keep forever in mind. First, it is necessary to study the whole of American comedy history, as well as your favorite comedy medium. For example, much of the revisionist film comedy history by this author has simply come from examining the big picture in terms of American humor. In fact, that is the beauty of the book in hand—it provides one with that all-important cross-section. In addition, few comedy filmmakers are without roots in other media, whether it is W. C. Fields' copyrighted stage sketches or Mel Brooks and television's *Your Show of Shows*.

Second, the student of American film comedy needs to balance the past and the present of his or her medium. There is a need for the writer who can put a given comic phenomenon into historical perspective. Historians are guides to past and present. Considering the richness of American film comedy, there is a definite need for more overview works.

There is also a frequent deficiency of sympathetic examinations of contemporary film comedy, regardless of the historical age. Granted, all disciplines are more likely to honor those hoary with age. But comedy, to apply Rodney Dangerfield's motto more broadly, still tends to receive less respect than the "serious" arts. It is time everyone got more serious about laughter.

NOTES

1. Gerald Mast, *A Short History of the Movies*, 3rd ed. (Indianapolis: Bobbs-Merrill Educational Publishing, 1981), p. 15.

2. Mack Sennett, with Cameron Ship, *King of Comedy* (1954; rpt. New York: Pinnacle Books, 1975), pp. 28–29.

3. Bob Thomas, *Bud & Lou* (Philadelphia: J. B. Lippincott, 1977), p. 130.

4. See especially Gene Lyons (with Peter McAlevey), "Crazy Eddie," cover article for *Newsweek*, January 7, 1985, pp. 53, 55; "*Ebony* Interview with Eddie Murphy," cover article for *Ebony*, July 1985, p. 46.

5. James Agee, "Comedy's Greatest Era," in *Agee on Film*, Vol. 1 (New York: Grosset and Dunlap, 1969), p. 8 (originally appeared in *Life*, September 3, 1949).

6. Gerald Mast, *The Comic Mind: Comedy and the Movies*, 2nd ed. (Chicago: The University of Chicago Press, 1979), p. 166.

7. Agee, "Comedy's Greatest Era," p. 12.

8. See the author's *Leo McCarey and the Comic Anti-Hero in Film* (New York: Arno Press, 1980).

9. Walter Kerr, "The Unexpected Raymond Griffith," in *The Silent Clowns* (New York: Alfred A. Knopf, 1975), pp. 298–308.

10. Mast, *The Comic Mind*, p. 199.

11. See the author's *Screwball Comedy: A Genre of Madcap Romance* (Westport, Conn.: Greenwood Press, 1986). See also note 8.

12. See the author's *W. C. Fields: A Bio-Bibliography* (Westport, Conn.: Greenwood Press, 1984).

13. *My Man Godfrey* review, *New York Times*, September 18, 1936, p. 18.

14. Andrew Sarris, "The Sex Comedy Without Sex," *American Film*, March 1978, pp. 8–15.

15. Maurice Yacowar, *Loser Take All: The Comic Art of Woody Allen* (New York: Frederick Ungar, 1979), p. 156.

16. For example, see Andrew Sarris, "Jerry Lewis," in *The American Cinema: Directors and Directions, 1929–1968* (New York: E. P. Dutton, 1968), pp. 242–43.

17. See the author's "The Electric Horseman: A 'Capra' Film for the 1980s," *Journal of Popular Film and Television*, Winter 1983, pp. 175–82.

18. Wes D. Gehring, ed., *Handbook of American Film Genres* (Westport, Conn.: Greenwood Press, 1988).

19. Jim Leach, "The Screwball Comedy," in *Film Genre: Theory and Criticism*, ed. Barry K. Gant (Metuchen, N.J.: The Scarecrow Press, 1977), pp. 82–83.

BIBLIOGRAPHICAL SURVEY

This section examines key references for the study of American film comedy. There is always a temptation to note every source of related interest, but this can open such a floodgate of material that pivotal works are shortchanged. Thus, this bibliographical survey attempts the most disciplined of configurations—a brief research guide, not an all-encompassing bibliography. The focus is on significant comedy overviews, excluding works devoted to a single figure. The pivotal materials discussed are also listed in the checklist at the end of the chapter.

All works are divided by length. Book-length sources are considered first, followed by shorter material, which includes articles, book chapters, and monographs.

Books

The book with which to begin is Gerald Mast's *The Comic Mind: Comedy and the Movies*. Both an ambitious history and an analytical guide to American film comedy, it is an insightful work in an area (the historical overview) where

few competitors exist. Probably the most-well-known rival volume is John Montgomery's pioneering 1954 work *Comedy Films: 1894–1954*. While not without
interest (it also includes British film comedians), it just does not compare to the
Mast book. If the Mast text has a flaw, it would be in not devoting enough time
to sound comedy's personality comedians, who are herded together into one
chapter. Surprisingly, the 1930s work of Will Rogers is not even cited.

The Stuart Byron- and Elisabeth Weis-edited *Movie Comedy* anthology is also
a valuable source. Essays on American film comedy are arranged under five
headings: "The Silent Era," "The Sound Era," "Spoofing," "Sex and Marriage," and "Social Satire." As the final three section titles suggest, *Movie
Comedy* frequently addresses its subject in a structural, quasi-genre approach.
But a balance is still maintained between this and the personality comedians.

British film historian Raymond Durgnat's *The Crazy Mirror: Hollywood Comedy and the American Image* is another important, always critically provocative,
volume. However, the material is often rather eclectic, as the author attempts
to touch base with a seemingly limitless number of comic references, resulting
in an almost stream-of-consciousness style to the book, as if Virginia Woolf
were its coauthor. Consequently, gems of astuteness often share the page with
rather peripheral material.

A more structured examination is prolific critic and author Leonard Maltin's
The Great Movie Comedians: From Charlie Chaplin to Woody Allen. Each of
twenty-two chapters is devoted to a single comedian, or team. Besides the
universally celebrated, Maltin also has sprinkled in chapters on important but
neglected figures, such as Raymond Griffith and Marie Dressler. More recent
figures of neglect, such as Danny Kaye and Red Skelton, also receive chapters.
As with almost all of Maltin's writing, it is informatively direct.

A final recommended survey is David Robinson's *The Great Funnies: A
History of Film Comedy*. Robinson, a British film historian who frequently
focuses on humor, addresses a world overview here, though his focus is generally
American. It is much more modest in length than the aforementioned works and
largely taken up with stills, but his commentary is perceptive, if brief.

Among the book-length studies that have a more specialized subject, critic
Walter Kerr's *The Silent Clowns* is easily the best. Besides serving as an in-
depth look at seemingly every silent comedian of note, including the often-
neglected silent films of W. C. Fields, the book showcases a large number of
beautiful stills. Other silent comedy volumes of note are Donald W. McCaffrey's
4 Great Comedians: Chaplin, Lloyd, Keaton, Langdon; Kalton C. Lahue's *World
of Laughter: The Motion Picture Comedy Short, 1910–1930*, and Lahue and
Samuel Gill's *Clown Princes and Court Jesters*. The last volume is comprised
of fifty short chapters, each of which is devoted to a silent comedian or team.
However, it avoids being a silent comedy version of Maltin's *The Great Movie
Comedians* (which it predates), by often focusing on the lesser known comedians,
purposely omitting Chaplin, Keaton, and Lloyd.

McCaffrey's *The Golden Age of Sound Comedy* does for the 1930s what Kerr's work does for the silents. While not quite on a par with *The Silent Clowns*, it is an excellent look at both the decade's personality comedians and its more structured comedy genres (though not noted as such). A good companion to this work is Leonard Maltin's *The Great Movie Shorts*, an affectionately detailed look at the short subjects of the 1930s and 1940s.

Film comedy is often equated with various teams, and there are two volumes of note that survey this phenomenon: Leonard Maltin's *Movie Comedy Teams* and Jeffrey Robinson's *Teamwork: The Cinema's Greatest Comedy Teams*. Robinson's book briefly examines the careers of Laurel and Hardy; the Marx Brothers; the Ritz Brothers; Hope, Crosby and Lamour; Abbott and Costello; Martin and Lewis, and Lemmon and Matthau. The Maltin book examines more teams (including Wheeler and Woolsey, Olsen and Johnson, and the Three Stooges) in more detail.

Garson Kanin's *Together Again! Stories of the Great Hollywood Teams* devotes one-half of its space to comedy teams, but the emphasis is on romatic comedy couples such as Cary Grant and Irene Dunne. It is not up to normally high Kanin standards. Team chapters are often superficial, and mistakes are not uncommon. There are three conventional teams examined: Laurel and Hardy, Hope and Crosby, and the Marx Brothers.

Because the division of film comedy into *several* genres has not received the attention it deserves (see ''Themes and Issues'') there has been little conscious exploration of the subject. When it has occurred, screwball comedy has been the most visible. There are three book-length studies of the screwball genre: Ted Sennett's *Lunatics and Lovers*, Stanley Cavell's *Pursuits of Happiness: The Hollywood Comedy of Remarriage*, and Wes Gehring's (this author) *Screwball Comedy: A Genre of Madcap Romance*.

Sennett's work is most valuable as a reference, with appendixes on players, directors, writers, and films. Otherwise, it is too broad in scope to define the genre adequately. Cavell's work looks through the other end of the telescope and focuses on a mere handful of films. It is at times weakened by a self-imposed narrowness aggravated by a meandering, pedantic writing style. Still, its theoretical stance occasionally offers brilliant insights, and it is always thought-provoking, regardless if the reader is in agreement. The Gehring volume takes a middle ground between Sennett and Cavell, attempting to more thoroughly balance history and theory. It keys upon the significance of American humor's transition to the antihero on the screwball genre.

With America's ongoing fascination for the parody film, there should eventually be a spate of books on this genre. But for the present the best survey source is Nick Smurthwaite and Paul Geder's *Mel Brooks and the Spoof Movie*. The title notwithstanding, it devotes considerable space to the parodies of Woody Allen and other Brooks contemporaries.

Two final comedy overview entries are William and Rhoda Cahn's *The Great American Comedy Scene* and Albert Bermel's *Farce*. They close this portion of the bibliographical section because neither limits itself to film humor. *But* enough is so directed that it seems more logical to posit them here rather than to cull X-number of essays for the section on shorter works that follows. They are interesting but flawed works. Most pointedly, the Cahn volume is rather a thin work (and it shows) with which to cover the whole American humor scene. Bermel's work (though much more ambitious) seems desirous of claiming everything this side of the banana peel for the label farce.

Shorter Works

Easily the most significant of all shorter works on American film comedy is gifted writer James Agee's often-anthologized essay, "Comedy's Greatest Era." It was this work that firmly established the silent comedy pantheon of Chaplin, Keaton, Lloyd, and Langdon—a grouping that continues to be reflected in more recent overviews, such as McCaffrey's *4 Great Comedians*. It has been the starting point for serious study of silent film comedy since it appeared in the September 3, 1949, issue of *Life*.

While Agee's focus is the foursome, he addresses a number of other comedy figures, both silent and sound, from Mack Sennett to Bob Hope. The work endures because it combines insight with poetry of expression (see earlier Agee comparison of Chaplin and Langdon). Its only flaw seems the harshness with which sound comedians are dealt, with only W. C. Fields emerging with his greatness intact.

An excellent companion piece to Agee's essay and a logical extension of its focus is Gerald Mast's "A Comparison of The Gold Rush and The General." The work originally appeared in the Spring 1970 issue of *Cinema Journal*; it later appeared in Mast's own *A Short History of the Movies*, where it surfaced in expanded form as part of Chapter 6, "Movie Czars and Movie Stars." Its seemingly more narrow perspective is included here because Mast applies it in a broader silent comedy context and the expanded version goes on to include other comedy figures. Mast's history text also boasts another pertinent comparison piece in Chapter 5, "The Comics: Mack Sennett and the Chaplin Shorts," which does for the early two-reelers what Chapter 6 did for the features.

Other silent surveys of special interest include Chapter 40 from Kevin Brownlow's *The Parade's Gone By*, "We're Not Laughing Like We Used To"; Chapter 15 from William K. Everson's *American Silent Film*, "Comedy"; Donald W. McCaffrey's "The Mutual Approval of Keaton and Lloyd," and Chapter 8 of Iris Barry's *Let's Go to the Movies*, "Comedians." Barry's essay is especially fascinating because it is an early (1926) antecedent for the celebrated Agee piece. An excellent era-closing essay (1931) is Caroline Alice Lejeune's "Slapstick," from *Cinema*, which examines the physical comedy losses sustained by the coming of sound.

Andrew Bergman's *We're in the Money: Depression America and Its Films* provides two provocative essays on 1930s comedy. His Chapter 3, "Some Anarcho-Nihilist Laff Riots," explores the dark side of the Marx Brothers and

W. C. Fields, particularly *Duck Soup* and *The Fatal Glass of Beer* (both 1933). Bergman's Chapter 10, "Frank Capra and Screwball Comedy, 1931–1941," defines this director as an archetype for the genre. While this author does not subscribe to Bergman's thesis (see earlier references to Capra within this chapter), it is an essay that has been influential. Revisionist historians today often place Capra in the populist camp. Examples of this position are found in Jim Leach's "The Screwball Comedy" from the Barry K. Grant anthology *Film Genre: Theory and Criticism*, and this author's monograph, "Screwball Comedy: Defining a Film Genre," and "Screwball Comedy: An Overview." (See also this author's "McCarey vs. Capra: A Guide to American Film Comedy of the '30s" and "Frank Capra: In the Tradition of Will Rogers and Other Yankees.")

Another provocative essay on the screwball genre comes from pluralist film critic Pauline Kael's "Raising Kane," from her controversial *The Citizen Kane Book*. While the central purpose of both the essay and the book was to shift the limelight from Orson Welles to Herman J. Mankiewicz, Kael's writing also celebrates the 1930s film comedy and the neglected screenwriter. Yet, just as she overstates her main thesis, antiauteurist Kael would seem to overreact to screenwriter neglect by suddenly granting writers the lion's share of the credit.

Defining screwball comedy as a result of censorship code implementation is best addressed in Andrew Sarris's "The Sex Comedy Without Sex." It should also have the subtitle "With Review," because the essay's main strength is in its examination of earlier sociological positions. Finally, the best period reflection on the genre is in film critic Otis Ferguson's 1940 "While We Were Laughing." Ferguson even reveals that it was *My Man Godfrey* that inspired the applying of the term "screwball" to the genre.

Chapter 10 of Sarris's *The American Cinema: Directors and Directions, 1929–1968*, "Make Way for the Clowns!" provides knowing capsulizations on several of the era's personality comedians: W. C. Fields, the Marx Brothers, Mae West, and Harold Lloyd (who was active but less prominent in the 1930s), as well as the 1950s and 1960s world of Jerry Lewis. The Lewis segment also examines Martin and Lewis and, briefly, other teams.

A good overview of American film comedy in the 1940s comes, appropriately enough, in Chapter 10 of Charles Higham and Joel Greenberg's *Hollywood in the Forties*, although they woefully miss the mark on the Hope and Crosby Road pictures (finding them no longer funny).

Gordon Gow provides a similar service for the following decade in his *Hollywood in the Fifties*. Gow's survey is thorough but, as his chapter title—"When Shall We Laugh?"—suggests, it seems unduly harsh.

Two more focused companion pieces to the Higham/Greenberg and Gow essays are Peter W. Kaplan's "On the Road with Bob Hope" and Ian Cameron's "Frank Tashlin and the New World." The former article is as much a brief overview of American film comedy as it is an overdue celebration of Hope. It ranges from a comparison of the Chaplin-Hope personae to Hope's influence on Woody Allen. It reminds the reader of Frank Tashlin's amusingly astute observation that the two most popular male performers to emerge from World War II were the cowardly braggarts Bob Hope and Donald Duck. As is necessary in any revisionist work, the author also addresses a prominent early Hope distractor (the Agee of "Comedy's Greatest Era").

Cameron's Tashlin piece also works in a broad context for two reasons. Besides being one of the most creative of 1950s and early 1960s comedy directors, Tashlin worked with many of the period's greatest personality clowns, including Bob Hope, Martin and Lewis, Lewis as solo, and Danny Kaye. Cameron manages to chart a path through this maze of Tashlin-directed comedians, be it Hope in *Son of Paleface* or Lewis in *Rock-A-Bye Baby* (1958, which manages to be both widely informative and still consistent to a Tashlin world view).

The best of the more recent film comedy essays is Chapter 7 of James Monaco's *American Film Now*, "The Importance of Being Funny: Comics and Comedians." This gifted historian of contemporary cinema, who has already coined the witty but wonderful "genre genre" label for the contemporary scene's fascination with parody, manages to amusingly discerning as he examines more recent comedy trends. His pantheon consists of Neil Simon, Mel Brooks, and Woody Allen, though unlike Agee, he is not averse to discussing flaws in his kingpins. Monaco also devotes considerable space to what might be called "parody fascination versus straight comedy." Though not overly enamored of parody, he judiciously discusses it (something Dave Kehr does not manage in his angry 1982 *Film Comment* overview, "Funny Peculiar"). Moreover, Monaco intelligently discusses the film comedy repercussions of the monologue versus the sketch. Finally, he is frequently prophetic, from the more obvious—Mel Brooks eventually running out of genres to parody—to the more knowing anticipation of Albert Brooks' film comedy arrival.

The best close to this section, both in astuteness and foreshadowing of comedy things to come, is Chevy Chase's article-length letter to the *New York Times*— "Chevy Chase: I'm Not Mr. Cruel." It was provoked by Richard Whelan's earlier "Cruelty vs. Compassion Among the Comics" (from the October 2, 1977, *New York Times*). Essentially, Whelan had found the comic irreverence of Groucho Marx more palatable than that of the *Saturday Night Live* crowd because Marx humanized his comedy attacks with periodic self-abasement.

Chase, drawing from a wide comedy base (past and present) convincingly counters Whelan's claim, especially with both a sociological stance (the changing times and the nature of comedy on the edge), and more correctly noting that Marx was still primarily an attack comedian.

The between-the-lines significance of the piece is that *Saturday Night Live* is fast becoming to contemporary film comedy what *Your Show of Shows* was to 1960s and 1970s film comedy—a comic laboratory for new players and new directions. *SNL* alumni who have gone on to film comedy success include Bill Murray, Eddie Murphy, the late John Belushi, Dan Akroyd, and Chevy Chase. With regard to new direction, *Saturday Night Live* is to dark, or even black, comedy what *Your Show of Shows* was to parody.

One cannot disregard the significance of Britain's Monty Python to black comedy (which is easier to trace, since the troupe largely moved en masse from television to film). But *Saturday Night Live*, both the show and its filmmaking alumni, has brought a more distinctly American stamp to it.

Consequently, while Richard Whelan's piece seems misdirected, he did correctly focus on what has become a rich source and force in contemporary American film comedy. If the history of film comedy teaches anything, filled as it is through the years with countless Richard Whelan-type pieces, it is: *Never sell contemporary film comedy short.*

CHECKLIST

Agee, James. "Comedy's Greatest Era" (from *Life*, September 3, 1949). In *Agee on Film*. Vol. 1. New York: Grosset and Dunlap, 1969.

Barry, Iris. "Comedians." Chapter 8 in *Let's Go to the Movies*, London: Chatto and Windus, 1926.

Berman, Andrew. "Some Anarcho-Nihilists Laff Riots," and "Frank Capra and Screwball Comedy, 1931–1941." Chapters 3 and 10 in *We're in the Money: Depression America and its Films*. 1971; rpt. New York: Harper and Row, 1972.

Bermel, Albert. *Farce*. New York: Simon and Schuster, 1982.

Brownlow, Kevin. "We're Not Laughing Like We Used To." Chapter 40 in *The Parade's Gone By*, 1968; rpt. New York: Ballantine Books, 1970.

Byron, Stuart and Elisabeth Weis, eds. *Movie Comedy*. New York: Penguin Books, 1977.

Cahn, William and Rhoda Cahn. *The Great American Comedy Scene*, 2nd ed. 1957. (Originally titled *The Laugh Makers*); rpt. New York: Monarch, 1978.

Cameron, Ian. "Frank Tashlin and the New World." In *Frank Tashlin*, ed. Claire Johnston and Paul Willemen. Colchester, England: Vineyard Press, 1973.

Cavell, Stanley. *Pursuits of Happiness: The Hollywood Comedy of Remarriage*. Cambridge, Mass.: Harvard University Press, 1981.

Chase, Chevy. "Chevy Chase: 'I'm Not Mr. Cruel.'" *New York Times*, October 30, 1977, p. D.35.

Durgnat, Raymond. *The Crazy Mirror: Hollywood Comedy and the American Image*. 1969; rpt. New York: Dell, 1972.

Everson, William K. "Comedy." Chapter 15 in *American Silent Film*. New York: Oxford University Press, 1978.

Ferguson, Otis. "While We Were Laughing" (1940). In *The Film Criticism of Otis Ferguson*, ed. Robert Wilson. Philadelphia: Temple University Press, 1971.

Gehring, Wes D. "Frank Capra: In the Tradition of Will Rogers and Other Yankees." *Indiana Social Studies Quarterly*, Fall 1981, 49–56.

———. "McCarey vs. Capra: A Guide to American Film Comedy of the '30s." *The Journal of Popular Film and Television* 7:1 (1978): 67–84.

———. *Screwball Comedy: A Genre of Madcap Romance*. Westport, Conn.: Greenwood Press, 1986.

———. "Screwball Comedy: An Overview." *The Journal of Popular Film and Television*, Winter 1985.

———. "Screwball Comedy: Defining a Film Genre." Muncie, Ind.: Ball State University Press Monograph Series, 1983.

Gow, Gordon. "When Shall We Laugh?" In *Hollywood in the Fifties*. New York: A. S. Barnes, 1971.

Higham, Charles and Joel Greenberg. "Comedy." Chapter 10 in *Hollywood in the Forties*. New York: A. S. Barnes, 1968.

Kael, Pauline. "Raising Kane." In *The Citizen Kane Book*. Boston: Little, Brown, 1971.

Kanin, Garson. *Together Again! Stories of the Great Hollywood Teams*. Garden City, N.Y.: Doubleday, 1981.

Kaplan, Peter W. "On the Road with Bob Hope." *Film Comment*, January-February 1978, 18–20.

Kehr, Dave. "Funny Peculiar." *Film Comment*, July-August 1982, 9–11, 13–16.

Kerr, Walter. *The Silent Clowns*. New York: Alfred A. Knopf, 1975.

Lahue, Kalton C. *World of Laughter: The Motion Picture Comedy Short, 1910–1930*, 1966; rpt. Norman: University of Oklahoma, 1972.

Lahue, Kalton C. and Samuel Gill. *Clown Princes and Court Jesters*. New York: A. S. Barnes, 1970.

Leach, Jim. "The Screwball Comedy." In *Film Genre: Theory and Criticism*, ed. Barry K. Grant. Metuchen, N.J.: The Scarecrow Press, 1977.

Lejeune, Caroline Alice. "Slapstick." In *Cinema*. London: Alexander Maclehose, 1931.

McCaffrey, Donald W. *4 Great Comedians: Chaplin, Lloyd, Keaton, Langdon*. New York: A. S. Barnes, 1968.

———. *The Golden Age of Sound Comedy*. New York: A. S. Barnes, 1973.

———. "The Mutual Approval of Keaton and Lloyd." *Cinema Journal*, 6 (1966–1967): 9–15.

Maltin, Leonard. *The Great Movie Comedians: From Charlie Chaplin to Woody Allen*. New York: Crown, 1978.

———. *The Great Movie Shorts*. New York: Bonanza Books, 1972.

———. *Movie Comedy Teams*. 1970; rpt. New York: Signet, 1974.

Mast, Gerald. *The Comic Mind: Comedy and the Movies*. 2nd ed., 1973; rpt. Chicago: University of Chicago Press, 1979.

———. "The Comics: Mack Sennett and the Chaplin Shorts." In *A Short History of the Movies*, 3rd ed., 1971; rpt. Indianapolis: Bobbs-Merrill, 1981.

———. "The Gold Rush and the General." *Cinema Journal*, Spring 1970, 24–30.

Monaco, James. "The Importance of Being Funny: Comics and Comedians." Chapter in *American Film Now*. New York: New American Library, 1979.

Montgomery, John. *Comedy Films: 1894–1954*, 2nd ed., 1954; rpt. London: George Allen and Unwin, 1968.

Robinson, David. *The Great Funnies: A History of Film Comedy*. New York: E. P. Dutton, 1969.

Robinson, Jeffrey. *Teamwork: The Cinema's Greatest Comedy Teams*. New York: Proteus, 1982.

Sarris, Andrew. "Make Way for the Clowns!" Chapter 10 in *The American Cinema: Directors and Directions, 1929–1968*. New York: E. P. Dutton, 1968.

———. "The Sex Comedy Without Sex." *American Film*, March 1978, 8–15.

Sennett, Ted. *Lunatics and Lovers*. New Rochelle, N.Y.: Arlington House, 1971.

Smurthwaite, Nick and Paul Gelder. *Mel Brooks and the Spoof Movie*. New York: Proteus Books, 1982.

◆ *5* ◆

Broadcast Humor

Lawrence E. Mintz

OVERVIEW

Broadcast entertainment—particularly television—and comedy meet at the very center of American popular culture.[1] Television is surely, to use Horace Newcomb's phrase, "the most popular art," and most observers of the medium would support Gilbert Seldes' oft-quoted observation that "comedy is the axis on which broadcasting revolves."[2] From the early days of radio to the TV tube's powerful present, various formats of comedy programming have dominated the airwaves. David Marc, one of the most perceptive analysts of the cultural significance of television, suggests that the prevalence of comedy on television may serve as a kind of disguise, hiding the vast power of the medium under a motely of the constantly stated disclaimer, "just kidding folks."[3] Such prominence of humor in an entertainment medium is not unique to broadcasting, of course; film, for another instance, exhibits a similar tendency, and the same claim might be made for comic strips as well. But in no other medium does humor play as large a role, and certainly in no other one does it play to as large an audience.

Broadcasting has become the repository of many different forms of popular entertainment, including many of those traditionally associated with American humor. The variety show, for instance, takes over for theatrical popular entertainments such as the minstrel theater, vaudeville, burlesque show, tent show, and the variety theater of the Earl Carroll's vanities/Ziegfeld Follies genre. The format provides opportunities for standup comedians, both as masters of ceremony and as separate acts on the bill (as in the theatrical versions as well), and for short comic skits and humorous jugglers, magicians, and other artists. The situation comedy, a format that will be discussed more fully later in this chapter, has to a considerable extent replaced the comic drama of the live theater, though the latter survives in the work of such artists as Neil Simon, among others, and of course in the medium of film. Sitcom is indeed a new form of comedy, rather than merely a broadcasted version of comedy drama that precedes it, but its contextual role is similar to that of the humorous popular theater of an earlier era.[4] There are other shows that are properly understood as made-for-broadcasting humor: one might find parallels for radio's Allen's Alley and for such TV comedy as Ernie Kovacs', *Laugh-In's*, or that of such contemporary shows as *Saturday Night Live* and the other late-night offerings, but there are enough broadcasting-connected features to make a good case for considering them to be new formats developed essentially by the broadcast media.

Moreover, humor in broadcasting is by no means limited entirely to formats that are specifically indicated as comedy shows. Joanne Cantor makes this point dramatically in a content analysis of television programming undertaken a decade ago. Cantor found that while comedy programs per se manifested humor as only a small percentage of their total expressive content, humor was to be found just about everywhere else in the medium's repertory as well.[5] There are, of course, talk shows that are hosted by comedians, such as *The Johnny Carson Show*, and the appearances by budding standup comics in these showcases as well as, more recently, on cable TV programs designed exclusively for standup comedy performance. Quiz shows and game shows are often as appealing for their comedy as they are for their ostensible gimmicks, for instance in the case of such shows as Groucho Marx's *You Bet Your Life* or *Hollywood Squares*, and in the case of some "gimmick" formats, e.g., *The Dating Game*, *The Newlywed Game*, *The Gong Show*, or *Real People*, the humor is just about all of whatever substance that might be found. Television, of course, is a significant purveyor of comedy film, both original to the medium and borrowed from the theater, and children's programming is largely comic from the cartoons (also borrowed from the movie theater) to the Muppets of *Sesame Street* as well as of their own *The Muppet Show*.

But even the roll call of all of the various comedy formats available in the broadcast media does not begin to cover all of the miscellaneous humorous expression constantly manifested over the airwaves. Radio disc jockeys are nearly always as conscious of their comedy as they are of their musical expertise, and as often as not they either borrow the radio comedy technique of Bob and Ray and the traditions of the two-person comedy teams from other media as well, to engage in comic dialogue banter, or they develop a satirical, aggressive comic persona (e.g., Don Imus, Howard Stern, DC's Greaseman), which parallels the abusive standup comedy of a Jackie Leonard or Don Rickels and the controversial comic stances of such comedians as Lenny Bruce and Mort Sahl, among others. Sportscasters in both radio and television employ humor as a central aspect of their craft, and in the case of such color commentators as Joe Garagiola, John Madden, Alex Karras, or particularly the two-act team of Howard Cosell and

Don Meredith, the comedy is as carefully developed and nurtured as is the athletic expertise. Some sports—for instance professional wrestling and roller derby—are essentially media dramas that can be appreciated as slapstick humor as well as on a more primitive level. Even the more serious realm of news reporting has been vitally affected by the prevalence of humor in broadcasting. Humorous weather reporters and sportscasters have been around from the earliest days, but in recent years they have been joined by a huge cast of theater and film critics, consumer and health reporters, cooking and eating experts, and "human interest" reporters whose feature presentations are often primarily in the comic vein. A more serious development has been the evolution of the "happy news format," in which the actual reporters and anchorpersons rely significantly on friendly banter, kidding, joking, and other humorous expression, primarily in between stories as a kind of comic lightening or sometimes in connection with a light or frivolous story, but occasionally spilling over into a more serious piece of reporting (some of the more excessive examples of this format have been curtailed in recent years). Even advertising, the commercial lifeblood of the broadcasting industry, relies heavily on humorous expression. Individual ads use just about every comic technique to be found in American popular culture, and campaigns such as the Lite Beer battle between the two groups of retired jocks and media celebrities over the relative merits of the product's taste and lightness insure that the regular viewer and listener will be continuously bombarded with humor. From the *Today Show*'s Willard Scott and Gene Shalit to late at night with David Letterman and company, humor is omnipresent in television, the major broadcasting medium today.

HISTORICAL DEVELOPMENT

A look at the historical development of broadcast humor properly begins with radio comedy, not just because of a strict chronology but because most of the forms that have become more familiar through television were already in place when that newer medium emerged. Arthur Frank Wertheim's excellent study, *Radio Comedy*, chronicles the growth of radio comedy as broadcasting began to shift its emphasis from a largely information medium to an entertainment arena.[6] By the middle of the decade of the 1920s, radio comedy provided a venue for vaudeville comics and for humorists from the popular theater and other media as well. Radio demanded some changes in both the structure and content of the familiar popular comedy traditions, however. The most obvious difference is, of course, the missing element of the visual, but as the aficionados of radio comedy are quick to point out, the imagination went a long way in compensating for what might seem to be a serious handicap. There *are* sight gags in radio comedy—Fibber McGhee's famous closet, for instance—but the listener provides the imagery. A perhaps more significant difference is the need to appeal to all of the various segments of a national audience simultaneously. By the mid-twenties, popular entertainment was a national phenomenon anyway, with the careful professional development of the vaudeville and popular theater circuits and with the growing availability of movies. The wise comedian would develop material that could play in all of the different regions of the country and across urban-rural, male-female, and even to some extent class lines, but in live performance the material could be edited for the specific audience. Parts of a routine could be deleted, other parts expanded, special material could be developed to appeal to a particular audience and to enhance the humorist's reception.[7] Radio continued, furthered, what was already a trend toward a national comedy, but interestingly enough it did so without immediately abandoning humor based on racial, ethnic, and regional stereotypes. Many of the early radio humorists—e.g., Will Rogers, Webber and Fields, Jack Pearl, and many others—merely moved their successful acts from the popular theater to the radio studio, and the radio variety hour, like its television offspring, was little different in either form or content for more than a decade into the medium's mature era. Even the "new" form of the situation comedy (the scholarly and critical controversy over just how original it was will be discussed in detail below) acknowledged the powerful appeal of racial, ethnic, and regional stereotypes as a source of humor.

Amos and Andy, of course, provides both the first and perhaps the most significant example. Born as *Sam and Henry* in 1926 and reincarnated in its more familiar persona in 1928, the characters created by Freeman Gosden and Charles Correll were holdovers from minstrel theater comedy and more modern versions from the variety stage. But the black stereotype was by no means unique; *The Goldbergs* provided Jewish comedy, *Vic and Sade* a rural humor, and a host of other characters from various shows combined to make this kind of comedy central during the period. This is not the place to discuss the social and cultural meaning of the centrality of racial, ethnic, and regional comedy, in radio as well as the other entertainment media including film and comic strips as well as the above-mentioned popular theater, but it is an important part of our cultural history that has justifiably received considerable attention. The manifestation of such character comedy did not disappear from the radio comedy of the 1930s and 40s, and for that matter it was a part of early television and is still significant today, in media comedy as well as in serendipitous joking, but it begins to be toned down as the national nature of broadcast comedy becomes realized, and it also begins to take a backseat to other characterizations and motifs.

The repertory comedy of the Jack Benny shows and of Fred Allen's *Allen's Alley* is a good case in point. Both shows have elements that are clear holdovers from vaudeville and the preradio stage, including racial, ethnic, and regional character-types, but both shows transcend that kind of comedy in two significant ways: their central characters (Benny and Allen, of course, but also Mary Livingston and Portland) are consciously not "placeable," though they could have been presented as such quite easily, and they began to develop a new kind of variety comedy, dependent upon running gags, recurrent "schtick," and familiar aspects of the character's personalities, idiosyncrasies, and situations rather than stock types. This point should not be exaggerated, perhaps, especially at this point. The observer who is knowledgeable in the history of comedy will note in the Benny and Allen versions of radio humor more that is familiar than is unique or surprising. Indeed it isn't hard to trace all of the characters on both shows back to familiar archetypes from the commedia dell'arte, for that matter. Later on when we discuss Ernie Kovacs, *Rowan and Martin's Laugh-In*, and *Saturday Night Live*, among other examples of programming that is widely acknowledged to be "innovative," we should be reminded that a careful look— or rather a careful listen—to the "golden age" of radio comedy also evidences a humor that is conscious of the medium and that departs from tradition and evolves to serve the expressive needs of the artists and the cultural needs of the audience.

Following a strict chronological structure in this account of the historical development of broadcast comedy, we would return to radio from time to time during our discussion of the fifties, sixties, seventies, and eighties since it never completely disappears from the medium. But the major comedy genres—variety humor and situation comedy—are virtually completely usurped by television, and all that remains to be said of radio comedy is on the periphery both of the older medium and of the history of American humor. This is not to belittle the individual importance of particular performers, of course. Bob and Ray fans would be rightfully outraged if their heroes were not awarded prominent places alongside Benny and Allen; indeed the continuing popularity of Bob and Ray revivals both on and off the airwaves suggests that such attention is warranted. Various repertory groups and improvisational groups have also sought to revive radio comedy, often on public radio, and their successes are not to be ignored despite the fact that they have not reversed any mainstream trends. Recently, for example, Garrison Keillor's *Prairie Home Companion* has sprung from Minnesota Public Radio to national attention, which includes marketing record albums, t-shirts, and two best-selling books as well as to the spawning of imitators from West Virginia and other regions. Radio music formats are increasingly conscious of the marketability of humorous disc jockeys, two-acts, and other comic gimmicks. The insult comedy of Don Imus and Howard Stern has even succeeded to the point of national syndication, and the ratings of local "kamikaze comics" such as DC's Greaseman (Douglas Tracht, like the author of this chapter, a product of the Bronx's DeWitt Clinton High School, though that institution would probably not want to claim either of us, even if we mentioned that Robert Klein also went there) and WAVA's "Zoo" duo (who successfully incorporate some of the Letterman ethos on radio) are comfortably ensconced in most major markets.

Arthur Wertheim notes that by the time television was sufficiently developed and available to become the major purveyor of mass-market humor, radio comedy was probably already in decline.[7] However, despite frequent critical warnings that the radio humor formats were in themselves stale and were certainly inappropriate to the demands and circumstances of the visual medium, early television comedy begins with the simple transference of the familiar formats and person-

alities from the existing media of the popular arts to the home screens. Ed
Sullivan's *The Toast of the Town* brought the vaudeville show almost intact to
television, in 1948, and his package of standup comedy, song and dance, production numbers, celebrities, and both traditional entertainment and gimmick
acts not only established the potential for such a mix on TV, it remained successful itself for more than two decades (until 1971). Performers from vaudeville,
burlesque, and the popular theater became wildly popular doing what came
naturally and familiarly. In 1948 Milton Berle's *Texaco Star Theater* swallowed
Tuesday night, and according to the famous aprocraphal story, the nation's
plumbing systems evidenced the strain of accommodating the medium's ability
to regulate nature's call according to the dictates of commercial breaks. "Uncle
Miltie's" or "Mr. Television's" broad comedy—slapstick, drag, insults, and
the like—is rarely cited by today's critics as worthy of nostalgic, much less
scholarly, attention, but it was a nicely molded example of its type, and its type
appealed to America's viewers for some as yet unexplained reason. The medium
could accommodate quality fare at the same time, however, as witnessed by the
emergence in 1950 of *Your Show of Shows*, hosted by Sid Ceasar, a less simplistic
Berle with much more range, but written by a crew of widely acknowledged
(now if not then) comedy geniuses including Mel Brooks, Woody Allen, Larry
Gelbart, and Neil Simon, to list just the ones more familiar to today's American
humor students. Jackie Gleason's television success between 1952 and 1970
raises an interesting case in that it reflects a qualitative evolution that spans the
burlesque roots, which Gleason shares with Berle, and the creativity of the *Your
Show of Shows* team. The brilliant Gleason is celebrated today for his genius in
The Honeymooners, which transcended its roots as a skit feature of the variety
show to become one of the great sitcoms of television history, but his variety
characters such as Reggie Van Gleason, The Poor Soul, Joe the Bartender, and
others also attest that such "lowbrow" popular arts as the variety theater and
television can offer opportunities for comic geniuses to develop as well as the
more celebrated media such as film, for instance. Other variety shows were, for
the most part, less memorable during the early years of television, but it is
interesting and important to note that they are not much less popular. Red Buttons,
George Gobel, and Jerry Lewis (the latter, leaving aside the creative arguments
concerning his comedy films) were comets on television, and this phenomenon
of sudden, red-hot, and massive presence in the medium for performers who
seem to have little in their pre-TV and postfame careers to suggest such prominence continues well into the present with such bursts as Flip Wilson, Sonny
and Cher, and the Smothers Brothers, among others.

    The structure and motifs of the situation comedy will be explored more fully
below, but looking at sitcom chronologically is also interesting, reflecting
changes over the decades, not surprisingly, but also both continuities and even
revivals that provoke analysis. The 1950s set the tone of the sitcom as domestic
comedy, with such families as the Aldriches, the Goldbergs, the Rileys, the
Nelsons, and the Ricardos capturing the attention of the American comedy

audience. To be sure, there is a considerable difference among the individual shows, and lumping ethnic and racial shows such as *Amos and Andy* and *The Goldbergs* with the blue-collar Rileys and the middle-American archetypes of *My Little Margie*, *Ozzie and Harriet*, and *Father Knows Best* simply will not do. Perceptive observers such as John Bryant, Rick Mitz, Horace Newcomb, and David Grote (see the checklist at the end of this chapter) have offered valuable distinctions between domestic comedies that center around resolving family problems or parent-child relationships; shows with racial, ethnic, or regional motifs; programs with locales such as school (e.g., *Our Miss Brooks*), the military (*You'll Never Get Rich/Sgt. Bilko*), or even the desert island of Gilligan and company. Certainly a show such as *I Love Lucy* must be studied independently rather than suffering categorization of *any* sort, for its innovations of televising, its basic premise with its implications for the role of women in post–World War II America, its characterizations, and its particular themes and recurring orientations. But a roll-call view of the sitcoms of the 1950s, and early 1960s does provoke one to generalizations despite the warnings of well-wrought studies by John Bryant and David Marc. The programs seem too benign, for one thing; their structure (as we will note again) restoring familiar harmony after the mildly disturbing interruption of petty problems, their characters basically familiar and likeable, sometimes stereotypical, sometimes archetypes of ideal national character-types, sometimes celebrities made household-familiar (Jack Benny, George Burns and Gracie Allen), and their mood or tone blending into a nostalgic haze of pleasantness and affectionate bemusement that only dissipates when one stares at it long and hard enough, as indeed one must.

Before we move on, however, into television's third and fourth decades, a few notable shows and trends should be noted in passing, at the very least. In 1951 a unique talent, Ernie Kovacs, moved beyond the various regional and ephemeral formats in which he had experimented for years, and for five years he created a television comedy unlike any that had gone before. Kovacs' use of blackouts and slapstick recalls the zany comedy of the popular theater and of both radio and film humor, but his brand was always aware of the potential of the camera, and his metacomedic, satiric references to other aspects of his own medium such as commercials and variety entertainment were unparalled until *Rowan and Martin's Laugh-In* and even more recent shows such as *Saturday Night Live*, *SCTV*, and *The David Letterman Show*. As mentioned above, Gleason's *The Honeymooners* and the Ball/Arnaz *I Love Lucy* are still receiving both attention and admiration bordering on veneration, in part because they helped establish the boundaries of the genre of situation comedy and to guarantee its continuing centrality, but in a larger part because they brought a very high quality of performance to the new medium. Gleason, Carney, Meadows, Ball, and their supporters, regular and guest, are today treated with critical respect, though in their own time it was a rare critic (Gilbert Seldes, for one) who joined the viewing fans in expressing enthusiasm for the new art form. More recent critics such as David Marc are providing reevaluations of other popular fare, e.g., *The*

Beverly Hillbillies or John Bryant's reassessment of the 1960s domestic comedy fare, arguing that the audience appeal of these shows is not indicative of the low level of intelligence of the TV viewer and that the "vast wasteland" thesis is at least simplistic and overstated. Even programs such as *Candid Camera* are gaining new respect since Norman Cousins discovered its life-saving qualities! Supporters of *The Smothers Brothers Comedy Hour* (1967–1969) add martyrdom to the accolades, proudly affirming that the show's political satire and topical pertinence was sufficiently on target to force its cancellation (a debatable contention). One wonders how far such praise and celebration should be carried, of course, and the term "genius" is perhaps stretched a little too far by the time it fits Carol Burnett and Tim Conway, but the argument that the 1950s and 1960s are a "golden age" of television comedy is not merely fanzine hype; there is at least some critical merit to the case.

The 1970s are marked primarily by the complete dominance of the sitcom. Shows such as Carol Burnett's, Flip Wilson's, Sonny and Cher's and a couple of others provide a not-insignificant holdover of the variety format. The previously mentioned *Laugh-In*, a product of George Schlatter, deserves particular notice, though its originality is vastly overstated by its enthusiasts in light of many parallels in pre-TV comedy, the work of Ernie Kovacs, the contribution of the Smothers Brothers, and a program called *That Was the Week that Was*, or TW3, an adaptation of a British satirical, topical review that was quite successful in its American manifestation until it burned itself out (1964–1965). But *Laugh-In* was a good comedy show, mixing the topical humor skillfully among a barrage of blackout jokes, recurring character-gags, physical "schtick," and guest appearances such as Richard Nixon's famous "Sock it to *me*?" one-liner. *Laugh-In* is also notable for giving us such stars as Goldie Hawn, Arte Johnson, and the brilliant Lily Tomlin.

The decade, however, belongs to the "relevant" situation comedies of Norman Lear, to "*M*A*S*H*", and to Mary Tyler Moore. Lear took a British sitcom about a blue-collar worker and made *All in the Family*, a program that revolutionized the genre. Lear's bigot, Archie Bunker, was portrayed more sympathetically—almost as a wise fool—and the political contrasts became secondary to the social comedy of resolving the family's conflicts, but the trend of topical comedy was established. *All in the Family* did not "tackle" all of the big issues of the decade, as its fans maintain, but it did mention them in public. Racism, sexism, abortion, menopause, homosexuality, and dozens of other topics were approached much as the vagaries of embarrassment and opportunity were handled in the fifties; i.e. they caused confusions and minor problems that could be put to rest without much action or significant change so that normal domestic life could go on as before. But if, for instance, the spin-off shows and imitators such as *The Jeffersons, Maude, Sanford and Son, Chico and the Man*, et al., failed to provide profound social commentary, we must be reminded that they were, after all, comedies and mass media entertainment, and they did reflect, indirectly perhaps, a growing realization of American pluralism and of the complex realities that were a part of daily American life as well as grist for the news media mill. Similarly *The Mary Tyler Moore Show* and *M*A*S*H* mixed the standard conventions of the genre with more complicated topical, social, and moral introspection. Structurally they still vaporized problems and restored "family" harmony in each episode, but the characters faced more serious conflicts than did Lucy, Ralph, and Riley, and consequently they were more interesting intellectually if not funnier or more satisfying viscerally.

By the mid-seventies there seemed to be a departure from the "relevant" sitcoms, a reaction or return to the "happy days" of the fifties and sixties comedies. But if *Happy Days*, *Laverne and Shirley*, and *Three's Company* suggest an ethos of uncomplicated embarrassment-comedy, such shows as *Alice*, *Soap*, *Mork and Mindy*, *Taxi*, *Welcome Back Kotter*, and *One Day at a Time* seem to be more of a compromise, a mixture of warm comedy, simplistic laugh-chasing, moralism, and social-topical referencing. The sitcoms of the late-seventies and eighties combine elements of both the simple domestic, problem-solving comedies of the first generation and the topicality of the second group. *Cheers*, *Kate and Allie*, *The Golden Girls*, *WKRP*, and the other survivors of what seemed to be a brief dip in the popularity of the genre during the early years of the eighties decade clearly exhibit that hybrid quality, but the best example of it is also the far-ahead winner of the recent popularity derby: *The Cosby Show*. Is *Cosby* so enormously popular in the mid-eighties because of the brilliant comedy of its star, Bill Cosby? Or is it because audiences are ready for a return to a show that emphasizes family unity, parent-child communication, morality, and conservative social if not political principles (cf. the show's successful trailer, *Family Ties*)? What is the significance of the portrayal of an upper-middle class, professional *black* family in which race is never ignored but also never a source of stereotype humor? *Cosby* deals with both kinds of problems like how to handle a child's grief over the death of a goldfish (cf. the shows of the fifties and sixties) and, by implication as well as directly, questions of sex, sex roles, race, and so forth. And it plays to both critical and popular acclaim.

A comprehensive history of television comedy would explore these and other shows not mentioned more fully, and it would note minitrends such as the cross-racial adoptions of *Webster* and *Different Strokes* or the nonfamily/families of *Mary Tyler Moore*, *Taxi*, *The Bob Newhart Show*, *WKRP*, and of course *Cheers* as demanding more attention and analysis. Content analysis would break program types into topical as well as premise groups, and the issues would be related to their manifestations in other media and in the real world. There would also be a place to discuss humor in the talk shows, particularly the enormous talent of Johnny Carson who is equally at home with standup comedy, in his monologue, ad lib joking with the audience and guests, and skit comedy with his "Mighty Carson Art Players." Carson's tremendous popularity has survived a quarter of a century of nearly nightly performance, and the show seems stronger for the familiarity of its formula. Johnny has outlasted, defeated essentially, numerous challengers to his late night talk-show throne, including the recent defection of his frequent guest-host Joan Rivers—a short-lived rival—and even the strong youth-appeal of a David Letterman is wisely scheduled after the king. The game of musical chairs played on the competing shows on other networks seems unlikely to end in the near future.

In 1975 a program entitled *Saturday Night Live* scored a major hit on late-night television, achieving almost cult-status with a younger audience and transcending that to some extent with broader attention. The repertory company featuring John Belushi, Chevy Chase, Gilda Radner, Jane Curtin, Larraine Newman, and Garrett Morris, and a talented staff of writers and producer/directors reminded observers of the glory days of *Your Show of Shows*, and the subsequent success of most of the members of the SNL team constitutes a major part of the young-audience comedy of the era in several media. The second- and third-generation *SNL* programs have been less successful, both in terms of popularity and critical significance, but they have given us Joe Piscopo and Eddie Murphy, among others, and they reflect the reality that variety comedy's small foothold at least holds on today. Another promising arena for standup and variety comedy in the medium is cable television. While cable has produced only a few situation and dramatic comedies, it has provided numerous opportunities for standup comics and improvisational groups. In the updated, 1985 edition of his study of standup comedy, *The Last Laugh*, Phil Berger goes so far as to state that cable TV "busted standup comedy out of the neat and neutered format it had been on network telly."[8] HBO comedy specials and such shows as *Evening at the Improv* have certainly provided showcases for younger comics and have allowed some of the latitude of language, topic, and wildness that has promoted the national craze for small comedy nightclubs over the past fifteen years or so to be transfered to the screen, and comics such as Robert Klein, for one, can finally find a home on television to supplement club and recording careers.[9]

Before leaving the historical section, we must also at least call attention to humor in the game and quiz shows, particularly with such shows as *The Gong Show*, *The Dating Game*, and *The Newlywed Game*, where comedy is more significant than the game/quiz challenge, in the "blooper genre" programs, and in such shows as *Real People*, which are essentially a kind of serendipitous public comedy ritual. These programs receive very little critical and scholarly attention, particularly from this perspective, and that is unfortunate since their use of nonprofessionals as the source and target for laughter is unique in the medium—or, for that matter, in our popular culture humor (though not, of course, to our folk humor). As we have suggested above, following Joanne Cantor's lead, a thorough overview of broadcast comedy would also trace its development in news formats, advertising, sports coverage, and elsewhere across the full range of broadcast programming; perhaps one of the primary purposes of an essay such as this is to call for and to support such more focused efforts.

THEMES AND ISSUES

The study of popular culture, of broadcasting media, and of humor is increasingly respected and sponsored, but it is still really at the beginning. Most of what has been written about radio and television comedy is appreciative, qualitative criticism in the popular press. There have been a few truly excellent books and articles, which we will note more fully in the bibliographical survey, but there are very few careful, analytic cultural analyses of specific formats, genres, thematic tendencies, and particular programs; and there is a serious paucity of useful theoretically grounded examinations. Over the next several years, students of humor and media need to address a few key concerns, to develop contacts, networks, and institutional bases in the universities and professional associations, in order to advance the quality and quantity of work done in this field.

There is a profound need for better archiving and organizing of information concerning the availability of primary sources. More than a decade ago I tried to begin a newsletter, *Popular Culture Airwaves Bulletin*, to coordinate and disseminate information concerning the holdings of various libraries, archives, and collections, but not only was the gathering of information a task that proved beyond the grasp of a single individual, there was little support or even cooperation for the endeavor and the newsletter folded after one issue was published. Since then the archiving of radio and television materials—tapes, scripts, film, and documents—has expanded dramatically, but the task of finding out what exists, who has it where, and how one can get ahold of it is necessarily haphazard. More than any other single activity, the development of primary source research services is key to further study of broadcast comedy.

The understanding of program formats, structures, and conventions is another area that promises notable yields for further work. Horace Newcomb's *TV: The Most Popular Art* should have been a seminal work, but the harvests have not been plentiful yet. David Grote's study of the structure of the situation comedy, in *The End of Comedy*, provides a good example of the value of such an approach.[10] Grote's description of the way in which sitcom structure, unlike the progressive evolution of previous dramatic comedy and film comedy, returns inevitably to the normality of the opening scenes suggests a crucial aspect of interpreting the significance and popularity of the genre. When the situation comedy opens, everything is in its familiar, comfortable, if mundane place (this is often established by a stock opening shot, scene, and or theme). An intrusion into these conditions of normality occurs—either a mild, slightly threatening problem or a chance for advancement, achievement, or gain of some sort. The characters take actions that invariably make things worse, complicate the simple problems, create new, more serious problems, or cause character conflicts that are more disturbing than can be justified by the original intentions for the actions. There is an unpredictable, miraculous "deus ex machina" resolution that resolves the problem and/or conflict, but does not really "solve it," i.e., there is no favorable change or advance. Everything returns to normal (established by a closing scene or shot). There can, of course, be change over a long-term run of a show, as actors leave or writers feel the need for a shaking up of a tiring premise. But the structure of the episodes is static. Sitcom opposes change; it neutralizes both threat and opportunity, indeed equating them as disturbing a status quo acceptance of middle-class serenity. Much of the communication of the situation comedy may be covert and completely independent of elements of premise, characterization, plot/theme, dialogue, physical action, or setting, and its message may be antithetical to the so-called American Dream's delineation of vertical mobility, of growth as a defining characteristic.[11] Similar investigations of the nature of the many other broadcast humor genres may also have interesting lessons.

Studies of the thematic content of broadcast comedy are called for as well. The routines of standup comedians, the comic personae of television personalities, the skits of variety comedy, and the plots of the sitcoms all provide models of behavior and belief that are held up for public review. What are we laughing at? What are we laughing with? What is the relationship of the humorous presentation of character models and of pronouncements of opinion and our culture, our ideology? How does the depiction of society in humor compare and contrast with nonhumorous analogues—for instance, in the treatment of war and the military, or sex roles, sexual conduct, or family relationships.

I have discussed some of the significant themes confronted in the contemporary situation comedy, both in my chapter on sitcom in Brian Rose's anthology and in my article "Ideology in the American Situation Comedy," but two examples should be included here as illustration.[12] In *One Day at a Time*, Ann Romano counsels her young daughter who is facing pressure from a boyfriend to engage in premarital sexual relations. Romano provides the overt thematic message, offering the now-standard (perhaps) American situation ethics repose: *you* have to be the one who makes the decisions. No one—parent, teacher, religious leader, friend—can tell you what to do, and the decision is not based on "morality" but on what is best for you as an individual. Covertly Romano undercuts the message by worrying frantically and expressing angry, hostile sentiments while the daughter is out with the boyfriend and equally dramatic (and comic) relief when it turns out that the daughter says "no" for all of the right reasons. In an episode of *Different Strokes*, a young teenage girl believes that she is pregnant. To make a long half-hour short, it turns out that she is not and the overt themes are: children, trust your parents, be open and honest with them, and they will help you solve your problems; and parents, stay calm, nonjudgmental and supportive and your kids will not hide anything from you (the need for "communication" is, perhaps, ultimately the "mono-theme" of the sitcom). The covert message is, perhaps, that "nice girls do" since no one seems at all disturbed by the behavior that led to the (false) threat in the first place. So what? What can learn about our attitudes toward teenage sex, toward "morality," from these and similar programs dealing with the theme? What can we learn from a content analysis of the representation of homosexuals in TV comedy, or from a study of any of the many recurring themes? No doubt quite a lot.

However, we must go beyond studying these issues from the texts only and examine the relationship between the text and the culture and society in which the texts have been produced, distributed, sponsored, and consumed. Ben Stein, in *The View from Sunset Boulevard* and Newcomb and Alley in *The Producer's Medium* tell us a little about the people who make TV shows,[13] but we need to know a lot more about the industry that creates, chooses, judges, and promotes shows and the motivating criteria. Similarly we need to know more about the audience and its reactions. There have been a plethora of studies about the effects of TV violence and TV on children's consumer behavior, but there is very little known about why an audience finds a particular image or set of images funny and what effect, beyond laughter, such a response might have.

It is no longer necessary to justify close and thorough study of broadcast humor. The growth of institutional interest in humor, in popular culture, and in broadcast communication has paved the way for the serious research for which we have called. It is important that researchers in the field break out of narrow disciplinary boundaries and communicate with each other across the field. The models, the historical overviews, and the research handbooks are now in place and the work that will be emerging in the future will indeed be exciting.

NOTES

1. The relationship between popular culture and humor is discussed more fully in my chapter, "Humor and Popular Culture," in *Handbook of Humor Research*, ed. Paul McGhee and Jeffrey Goldstein (New York: Springer Verlag, 1983), pp. 129–42.

2. Horace Newcomb, *TV: The Most Popular Art* (Garden City, N.Y.: Anchor, 1974), and Gilbert Seldes, *The Public Arts* (New York: Simon & Schuster, 1956), p. 133.

3. David Marc, *Demographic Vistas: Television in American Culture* (Philadelphia: University of Pennsylvania, 1984).

4. David Grote, *The End of Comedy: The Sit-Com and the Comedic Tradition* (Hamden, Conn.: Archon Books, 1983).

5. Joanne Cantor, "Humor on Television: A Content Analysis," *Journal of Broadcasting* 20 (Fall 1976):501–10.

6. Arthur Frank Wertheim, *Radio Comedy* (New York: Oxford, 1979).

7. Ibid., pp. 380ff.

8. Phil Berger, *The Last Laugh* (New York: Limelight Editions, 1985), p. 381.

9. Stephanie Koziski Olson discusses how comedians develop their relationship with the audience through specifically tailored material in Chapter 6 on standup comedy in this volume and in her article on the genre in the *Journal of Popular Culture*. It is also explored in my study, "The Standup Comedian as Social and Cultural Mediator," *American Quarterly* 37, 1 (Spring, 1985): 71–80.

10. Grote, *The End of Comedy*. Similar analysis is offered by David Marc, Horace Newcomb, John Bryant, and myself.

11. These issues are discussed more fully in my chapter on situation comedy in Brian

Rose's *TV Genres: A Handbook and Reference Guide* (Westport, Conn.: Greenwood Press, 1985), pp. 105–29, and in my article "Ideology in the American Situation Comedy," *Studies in Popular Culture* 8,2 (1985): 42–51.

12. Mintz in Rose, *TV Genres*, and in "Ideology in the American Situation Comedy."

13. Ben Stein, *The View from Sunset Boulevard: America as Brought to You by the People Who Make Television* (New York: Basic Books, 1979), and Horace Newcomb and Robert S. Alley, *The Producer's Medium: Conversations with the Creators of American TV* (New York: Oxford, 1983).

BIBLIOGRAPHICAL SURVEY

The literature devoted to the study of humor and to overviews of American humor rarely mentions broadcast comedy directly, except in a few passing references. But it is useful to begin with a look at recent anthologies that reflect the broad ranges of modern humor theories and the methodologies that have been applied to the study of humor from numerous disciplinary perspectives. The best place to start such a survey is with the two collections edited by Tony Chapman and Hugh Foot and the two, including the indispensible two-volume *Handbook of Humor Studies*, edited by Paul McGhee and Jeff Goldstein. The bibliography in the *Handbook* includes all the further references to journals, conference abstracts, books, and articles that one might need up to this point. The serious student will want to keep up with the activities of the international scholars who study humor and meet periodically to share their knowledge. Until recently one way to do that was to subscribe to a newsletter entitled *American Humor: An Interdisciplinary Newsletter* edited by Tom Inge and Lawrence Mintz from 1974 to 1977 and by Mintz until 1985. There are plans to revive *AH:IN* as a part of a journal called *Studies in American Humor*, but the journal itself has been sporadic over its decade or so of existence. Perhaps the best advice is to pursue personal contact with Jeff Goldstein at Temple University (Psychology), Lawrence Mintz at the University of Maryland (American Studies), Tony Chapman at Leeds University (Psychology), Avner Ziv at Tel Aviv University (Education), Harvey Mindess at Antioch University West (Psychology), or Don Nilsen at Arizona State University (English; convenor of the WHIM conferences). These people can help "network" scholars effectively within the varied areas of humor studies.

Overviews of American humor that are required reading for their indirect implications for broadcast comedy if not their direct usefulness include a wonderful essay by Louis Rubin, Jr. entitled "The Great American Joke," which was originally published in Rubin's book *The Comic Imagination in American Humor* and which is also available in the anthology *Humor in America* edited by Enid Veron. Walter Blair's writing on native humor, Blair and Hamlin Hill's history, *America's Humor*, and Jesse Bier's *The Rise and Fall of American Humor* are also recommended. Of course the other nine chapters in this volume are useful parallels for this one, and they introduce significant introductory and historical material as well.

Arthur Wertheim's *Radio Comedy* is not only the best book on its subject; its American studies perspective, connecting the media texts with the cultural and social milieu in which they were found originally and to larger issues of American history and sociology, makes it a model for media studies. There really should be a comparable book for television comedy; David Grote's *The End of Comedy* is a good study of the situation comedy genre but it is far from a definitive study of broadcast humor. Rick Mitz's trade paperback, *The Great TV Sitcom Book*, is aimed at aficionados and trivia buffs in style, but its substance is really much better than that. Mitz's categories are useful and intelligently thought out, his observations are usually accurate, and the total amount of information he gives us is laudable. Several chapters in Brian Rose's *TV Genres: A Handbook and Reference Guide*, particularly Mintz's on sitcom, Rose's on the talk show, and Timothy Scheuer's on variety shows, are helpful beginnings, as is Horace New-comb's writing in *TV: The Most Popular Art*. Newcomb's collection of essays in *Television: The Critical View* and his co-authored study with Robert Alley, *The Producer's Medium*, also deserve mention here. David Marc's *Demographic Vistas: Television in American Culture* is one of the very best books that has been written about American television, and it has many fine insights concerning television comedy (it is perhaps the closest thing we have at present to the kind of book Wertheim gave us for radio comedy), and the writings of Arthur Asa Berger, Todd Gitlin, Raymond Williams, and Ben Stein are to be cited for their provocative value.

There are a number of articles and chapters that deserve separate mention in this essay. Dan Brown and Jennings Bryant's "Humor in the Mass Media" and my own "Humor in Popular Culture" are to be found in the Goldstein and McGhee *Handbook*, and my article "The Ideology of American Situation Comedy" was published in *Studies in Popular Culture*. John Bryant is one of the most interesting writers dealing with comedy on American television. His article "Emma, Lucy, and the American Situation Comedy of Manners" appeared in the *Journal of Popular Culture*, and his manuscript, "Situation Comedy of the Sixties: The Evolution of a Popular Genre," has been of great help to me in my own thinking about broadcast comedy. Several chapters in Chapman and Foot's second collection *Its a Funny Thing, Humour* merit being singled out, including those by Joanne Cantor, Dolf Zillman, and Gary Alan Fine. Robert Sklar's work on sitcom is thoughtful, and an article by Douglas Kellner, "TV, Ideology, and Emancipatory Popular Culture," in Newcomb's *Television: The Critical View* is also recommended.

Articles appearing in popular magazines and newspapers are sometimes very important; unfortunately more often they are merely descriptive or idiosyncratically judgmental. It is still a good idea to keep up with current media criticism, with the technical studies in the communications and broadcasting press, and with the information about the media industries in such publications as *Variety* and other trade papers. It is not hard, all in all, to find thought-provoking writing on broadcast comedy and on the many related subjects; it's just that there is so much need for more that it sometimes seems like it is the literature devoted to the study of television that is "the vast wasteland" after all.

CHECKLIST AND ADDITIONAL SOURCES

Ackerman, Harry. "Program Poker: The Half-Hour Forum." *Television Quarterly* 6, 4 (Fall 1976):63–66.

Adler, Richard P., ed. *All in the Family: A Critical Appraisal.* New York: Praeger, 1979.

Alley, Robert S. *Television: Ethics for Hire.* Nashville: Abington, 1977.

Arlen, Michael J. "The Media Dramas of Norman Lear." Reprinted in *Television: The Critical View,* edited by Horace Newcomb. New York: Oxford, 1976.

Berger, Arthur Asa. *The TV Guided American.* New York: Walker, 1976.

Berger, Phil. *The Last Laugh,* updated ed. New York: Limelight Editions, 1985.

Brown, Dan and Jennings Bryant. "Humor in the Mass Media." In *Handbook of Humor Research,* edited by Paul McGhee and Jeffrey Goldstein. New York: Springer Verlag, 1983.

Bryant, John. "A Checklist of American Situation Comedy." *American Humor: An Interdisciplinary Newsletter* 5, 2 (Fall 1978): 14–31.

———. "Emma, Lucy, and the American Situation Comedy of Manners." *Journal of Popular Culture* 13, 2 (Fall 1979): 248–56.

———. "Situation Comedy of the Sixties: The Evolution of a Popular Genre." Forthcoming in *Studies in American Humor.*

Cantor, Joanne. "Humor on Television: A Content Analysis." *Journal of Broadcasting* 20 (Fall 1976): 501–10.

———. "Tendentious Humor in the Mass Media." In *Its a Funny Thing, Humour,* edited by Antony Chapman and Hugh Foot. London: Pergamon, 1977, pp. 303–10.

Cater, Douglas and Richard Adler, eds. *Television as a Cultural Force.* New York: Praeger, 1976.

———. *Television as a Social Force.* New York: Praeger, 1975.

Chesbro, James W. "Communication, Values, and Popular Television Series—A Four Year Assessment." Reprinted in *Television: The Critical View,* edited by Horace Newcomb. 3rd ed. New York: Oxford, 1982, pp. 8–46.

Eaton, Mick. "Happy Days are Here Again." In *Popular Film and Television,* edited by Tony Bennett et al. London: British Film Institute, 1981, pp. 64–76.

Fine, Gary Alan. "Humour and Communication: Discussion." In *Its a Funny Thing, Humour,* edited by Antony Chapman and Hugh Foot. London: Pergamon, 1977.

Gitlin, Todd. *Inside Prime Time.* New York: Pantheon, 1983.

Goodlad, Sinclair. "On the Social Significance of Television Comedy." In *Approaches to Popular Culture,* edited by C. W. E. Bigsby. Bowling Green, Ohio: The Popular Press, 1976.

Grote, David. *The End of Comedy: The Sit-Com and the Comedic Tradition.* Hamden, Conn.: Archon Books, 1983.

Hansen, Arlen. "Entropy and Transformation: Two Types of American Humor." *American Scholar* 43, 3 (Summer 1974): 405–21.

Joslyn, James and John Pendleton. "The Adventures of Ozzie and Harriet." *Journal of Popular Culture* 7 (Summer 1973): 23–31.

Kellner, Douglas. "TV, Ideology, and Emancipatory Popular Culture." In *Television: The Critical View*, edited by Horace Newcomb. 3rd ed. New York: Oxford, 1982, pp. 382–421.

Kirkpatrick, John T. "Homes and Homemakers on American TV." In *The American Dimension*, edited by W. Arens and Susan P. Montague. Port Washington, N.Y.: Alfred, 1976, pp. 69–79.

Leonard, Sheldon. "Why Do You Laugh?" In *Television: A Selection of Readings from TV Guide Magazine*, edited by Barry G. Cole. Glencoe, Ill.: Free Press, 1970.

Leonard, Sheldon and Carl Reiner. "Comedy on Television: A Dialogue." *Television Quarterly*, Summer 1963.

McGhee, Paul and Jeffrey Goldstein, eds. *Handbook of Humor Research*. 2 vols. New York: Springer Verlag, 1983.

McNeil, Alex. *Total Television: A Comprehensive Guide to Programming from 1948 to 1980*. New York: Penguin, 1980.

Malone, Michael. "And Gracie Begat Lucy Who Begat Laverne. . . ." *Channels of Communication*, October 1981.

Marc, David. *Demographic Vistas: Television in American Culture*. Philadelphia: University of Pennsylvania, 1984.

Mintz, Lawrence E., "Humor and Popular Culture." In *Handbook of Humor Research*, edited by Paul McGhee and Jeffrey Goldstein. New York: Springer Verlag, 1983, pp. 129–42.

———. "Ideology in the American Situation Comedy." *Studies in Popular Culture* 8, 2 (1985): 42–51.

———. "Situation Comedy." In *TV Genres: A Handbook and Reference Guide*, edited by Brian Rose. Westport, Conn.: Greenwood Press, 1985, pp. 105–29.

———. "The Standup Comedian as Social and Cultural Mediator." *American Quarterly* 37, 1 (Spring, 1985): 71–80.

Mitz, Rick. *The Great TV Sitcom Book*. New York: Perigree Books, 1983.

Moss, Sylvia. "The New Comedy." *Television Quarterly*. 4, 1 (Winter 1965): 42–45.

Newcomb, Horace. "The Television Artistry of Norman Lear." *Prospects* 2, edited by Jack Salzman. New York: Burt Franklin, 1976, pp. 109–26.

———. *Television: The Critical View*. New York: Oxford, 1st ed., 1976; 2nd ed., 1979; 3rd ed., 1982 (note content changes).

———. *TV: The Most Popular Art*. Garden City, N.Y.: Anchor, 1974.

Newcomb, Horace and Robert S. Alley. *The Producer's Medium: Conversations with the Creators of American TV*. New York: Oxford, 1983.

Primeau, Ronald. *The Rhetoric of Television*. New York: Longman, 1979.

Rollin, Roger B. "In the Family: Television's Re-Formation of Comedy." *The Psychocultural Review* 2, 4 (Fall 1978).

Rose, Brian G. *TV Genres: A Handbook and Reference Guide*. Westport, Conn.: Greenwood Press, 1985. Note, too, Rose's chapter in the volume, "The Talk Show," pp. 329–52.

Scheurer, Timothy. "The Variety Show." In *TV Genres*, edited by Brian Rose. Westport, Conn.: Greenwood Press, 1985, pp. 307–27.

Seldes, Gilbert. *The Public Arts*. New York: Simon and Schuster, 1956, 1964.

Sklar, Robert. *Prime Time America: Life on and Behind the Television Screen*. New York: Oxford, 1980.

Stein, Ben. *The View from Sunset Boulevard: America as Brought to You by the People Who Make Television*. New York: Basic Books, 1979.

Waters, Harry F. "TV Comedy: What it's Teaching the Kids." *Newsweek*, May 7, 1979, 64–72.

———. "TV: Laughing all the Way." *Newsweek* January 21, 1974, 62–69.

Wertheim, Arthur Frank. *Radio Comedy*. New York: Oxford, 1979.

Williams, Martin. *TV: The Casual Art*. New York: Oxford, 1982.

Williams, Raymond. *Television, Technology and Cultural Form*. New York: Schocken, 1974.

Winick, Charles. "The Social Contexts of Humor." *Journal of Communication* 26, 3 (Summer 1976): 124–28.

Zillmann, Dolf. "Humour and Communication: Introduction to Symposium." In *Its a Funny Thing, Humour*, edited by Antony Chapman and Hugh Foot. London: Pergamon, 1977.

♦ *6* ♦

Standup Comedy

Stephanie Koziski Olson

OVERVIEW

An understanding of standup comedy performance involves an examination of the artist-comedian, the content of a performance routine, the audience response, and the structure of the American entertainment industry that markets popular culture to consumers. Some elements of standup comedy performance seem mysterious and illusive while other aspects are more accessible to direct study and understanding.

Standup comedy performance is more than a performer's ability to hold people's attention and generate laughs every thirty or forty seconds (which, in itself, is no small task). In the hands of the most gifted and skillful comedians, the ability to generate laughs while presenting thought-provoking material can touch a profound and universal human chord in audience members. Such gifted comedians validate comic writer Abe Burrows' claim that "with comedy we make much more serious points than we do with anything . . . serious. A laugh is one of the most profound things that can happen to a human being. When you make a man laugh, you have evidently hit him right where he lives—deep. You've done something universal. You've moved him. . . . "[1] Less-gifted performers can generate a kind of automatic laughter—a nervous or mechanical response to such subjects as sex, drugs, or relationship problems—subjects that are sure to stimulate some kind of audience response and do not depend on the comedian's skill with an audience.

The power and authority with which some comedians hold their audiences' attention and gain agreement with their points of view seem almost shamanistic in the hands of such artists as the late Lenny Bruce, Mort Sahl, or Bill Cosby. A charismatic comedian at his best can catalyze new awarenesses in his or her audience when humor illuminates new possibilities or puts old prejudices in a new light. Within the unique compact between performer and audience (whether directly via the live performance or indirectly on television or a record), the audience, temporarily suspending its defenses, can receive the artist's view of one or another fragment of reality. In this moment of trust and communal laughter, the larger world seems more manageable and less threatening.

In this regard, the standup comedian

serves two apparently universal functions: as a licensed spokesman he is permitted to say things about society that we want and need to have uttered publicly [sic], but would be too dangerous and too volatile if done without the mediation of humor; and as a comic character, he can represent, through caricature, those negative traits which we wish to hold up to ridicule, to feel superior to, and to renounce through laughter.[2]

Standup comedians with such abilities perform an important role by providing an arena where an array of volatile and tension-provoking subjects can be publicly scrutinized.

Standup comedy is a "vitally important social and cultural phenomenon that reveals a culture's values, attitudes, dispositions, and concerns . . . the oldest, most universal, most basic, and most deeply significant form of humorous expression."[3] The performers themselves, their audiences, and the cultural artifacts they create—records, written texts, radio tapes, videotapes, and live performances, as discrete events in time,—are worthy of study by the critical investigator of American humor.

Lawrence Mintz defines standup comedy as an encounter between a single, standing performer who behaves comically and says humorous things to an audience without much use of costume, props, or setting. Mintz emphasizes the importance of the direct communication between artist and audience and the high proportion of comic behavior and comic dialogue to the development of plot and situation. Mintz's definition excludes much of the comedy that occurs in theater and in other media.[4]

HISTORICAL DEVELOPMENT

This popular culture form so familiar to us today on television, records, and in live performances has ancient roots, not only in America, but in Europe, Asia, Africa, South and Central America. Predecessors to the standup comedian— clowns, jesters, tricksters, and fools—have appeared throughout the world in so-called primitive cultures as well as in technologically advanced societies. They appeared in ancient times as fools or buffoons, male and sometimes female, in solo roles or in comedy teams. For example, Greek stage plays featured humorous dialogues between a pretender or imposter and a straight man whose cunning exposed the imposter. A third actor humorously explained the action to the audience in an interlocutor role.[5] Earlier incarnations can also be found in the spirit of unrestrained merrymaking allowed revelers during the kalends and Saturnalia of ancient Rome and in the comedic roles and repertoire of humorous conventions enacted by fools in the royal courts of Egyptian, Chinese, Greek, Roman, and Aztec emperors. Traces of standup comedy performance can be recognized in the itinerant clown troupes of ancient Greece, which distilled scenes of everyday life, important social issues, and characters from those times into entertaining farces. Fools entertained Moslem and Hindu potentates and kings and popes of medieval Europe. This noble history of merrymakers in their many forms and in their cultural context is described by John Towsen in his book, *Clowns*.[6]

The forerunners of today's standup comedians can also be seen on our own continent in the indigenous clown societies or clans of so-called primitive cultures. These societies in American Indian tribes were formed exclusively to clown during public ceremonies, especially sacred ones. These clowns are officially sanctioned by their culture to perform important functions within their society having to do with reality maintenance and social control. For example, Hopi clowns parody sacred aspects of the calendrical renewal ceremonies by dancing out of step alongside sacred dancers, by chanting irreverent parodies of the holy kochina songs sung by the sacred dancers, by randomly teasing audience participants with sexually obscene and other irreverent humor, and by acting out socially disapproved behavior such as drunkenness, which may be a community problem. These clowns may also single out a particular individual for public ridicule to curb antisocial behavior which that particular individual seems to typify. At another juncture in the ceremony, the clowns may step out of their irreverent behavior and behave in a sacred manner, such as when they sprinkle cornmeal on the kachina dancers, an act considered sacred in the Hopi culture. Towsen perceptively analyzes the role of the clown in Indian cultures in *Clowns*, noting the interesting paradox that the role of clowns in many earlier cultures is to burlesque the sacred while at the same time supporting it.[7]

One of the roles of the clown is to display human foibles in such a way as to connect an audience to its humanness and to act out chaotic behavior that contrasts with behavior supportive of social cohesiveness. This is especially true in primitive groups' struggles to survive against intrusions of an alien culture. The clown's act also provides comic relief during the solemnity of religious activities. By providing a pressure valve to participants, the clown also acts as an agent to ensure social control during the highly charged atmosphere of public events.

Another aspect of the clown is that of being the "trickster" spirit. We see this, for example, when tribal members portray and "become" the trickster during sacred and other occasions.

The trickster figure exists in the folklore of many cultures, incarnated in such animal characters as Coyote the Mischief Maker in Navajo tales. Through the examples of the trickster's disobedience to accepted codes of behavior, the storyteller can clarify the behaviors expected from a culture's members in every-day social existence. As Towsen writes,

the fool represents the free spirit . . . whose example encourages others to view the world in new and extraordinary ways. Most cultures recognize, consciously or unconsciously, the value of the fool's perceptions. Often he is seen as an inspired madman or even as a spiritual prophet. . . . the performer who can present the fool's perceptions in a socially acceptable manner often proves quite popular—even if everything he stands for runs counter to prevailing beliefs.[8]

Many medieval jesters and members of fool societies were not only skilled entertainers but possessed a keen understanding of human psychology and the structure of their cultures. These medieval performers satirized the injustices of despotic monarchs and other social behavior meriting censure, using clever repartee and topical skits in which all humanity was shown as foolish. The great power exercised by the Catholic Church in medieval Europe was questioned during church-sanctioned clown festivals where priests donned masks, engaged in irreverent status inversions of the reigning religious potentates, and mimicked sacred events in the Feast of Fools and the Feast of the Ass. When the church no longer sanctioned these potentially subversive activities, these comedy forms moved into a secular arena. In improvisational street theater, members of the sixteenth-century Italian commedia dell'arte portrayed stock characters of their day in a format of social satire. In eighteenth-century England, unemployed actors performed humorous sketches and pantomime acts on the street. By 1837 a theater was opened in London's East End specifically to present such comedy acts with music and each act was introduced by a comedian.[9]

Humor scholar Joe Franklin tells us in his book, *Joe Franklin's Encyclopedia of Comedians*, that comedy in the United States got off to a slow start because the puritanical value system of most settlers did not allow them to enjoy public displays of gaiety and fun.[10] Franklin points out that in 1774 the Continental Congress closed by decree all places of public amusement. Still, the young nation had its traveling variety entertainments, and America's first standup comedians and clowns traveled with medicine shows and circuses and blended imported and indigeneous comedy elements into their acts.

In the American one-ring circus of the late eighteenth century, clowns used conventions similar to those in the acts of standup comedians. While clowns mainly excel in acrobatics and other physical comedy forms, it is in their use of stylized comic dialogue, joke tellings, comic songs, parodies of political and religious rhetoric, witty repartee, puns, malapropisms, double entendres, topical commentary, funny costumes, ridiculous props, slapstick, buffoonery, and magic tricks that they resemble the performance style and structure of standup comedians' acts. The comic interplay of buffoon clowns and the more refined brunt of the clown's jokes, the ringmaster, mirror the dynamics that enlivened the acts of comedy teams in minstrelsy, vaudeville, burlesque, and later standup comedy teams in other show business formats.

Beyond the circus arena, nineteenth-century clown Dan Rice, in his persona as philosophical jester and licensed spokesman on a lecture circuit, commented with sharp insight and pungent wit on the major causes of his day and on corrupt behavior by "respectable" figures. Dan Rice was a "totally self-educated man . . . sufficiently confident in his own native intellect to give his comic effusions the aura, if not the substance, of profound thought. He was a self-proclaimed rationalist, philosopher, and moralist, and at the same time a superb showman who prided himself on knowing how best to reach the 'plain people.' "[11] Dan Rice's definition of the qualities necessary to be a clown include "intellect, ability, and originality. . . . He must be a crack mimic, an elocutionist, a satirist, and so ready witted that he, to the ringmaster, is a stupid fool, a buffoon; to the audience a wise man whose every remark is impregnated with philosophy as well as humor."[12]

The nineteenth-century lecture circuit also brought to Victorian audiences such famous comic-spokesmen as Mark Twain, Josh Billings, and Artemus Ward whose original stories had roots in America's tall tale. As social observers and comic spokesmen, these lecturers ridiculed the beliefs and behaviors of their day and drew approving laughter from their audiences.

There were many similarities between the standup comedy featured in the circus and in the minstrel theater of nineteenth-century America. In minstrelsy, the witty repartee between the two comic endmen, Tambo and Bones, in blackface makeup, and the more dignified master of ceremonies called the interlocutor, anticipated the comic interchange between later standup comedy teams. As wise fools and comic spokesmen, Tambo and Bones criticized prevailing social opinion of the day in topical satire. Sexually suggestive material was also included in the minstrel shows. Men played female roles. "Behind his black face, the actor could acquire the whimsical detachment from the real world which the clown needs to perform his psychic magic."[13]

Scholar Albert McLean, Jr., points out that in America,

prior to 1860 there had been no massive amusement enterprises involving hundreds of persons, chains of theaters, and capital investments of millions of dollars. The public demand for entertainment was satisfied by traveling menageries, circuses, minstrel shows, independent repertory theaters, road shows, and show boats. . . . Various kinds of musical entertainment, including musical comedy, appealed to scattered audiences of quality, while the less cultivated enjoyed the musical and humorous festivities of taverns, saloons, and brothels.[14]

Comic dialogues and farcical and satiric songs were a part of some of these entertainment forms.

Burlesque became popular in the late nineteenth century. This entertainment form offered stage shows featuring slapstick humor and striptease acts. Burlesque became a training ground for comedians who wanted to enter vaudeville, the Follies, and musical comedy shows. In between striptease acts, standup comedians engaged in "zany behavior, eccentric characterizations, insult and joke comedy.[15] Until the twenties, burlesque was considered family entertainment and the jokes told by standup comedians were relatively clean. With the introduction of less-modest striptease in the late twenties, comedians told jokes characterized by sexually suggestive material. Kaye Ballard was one of the first women on the burlesque stage to achieve the status of comedy partner to a male comedian, rather than stripper, like most female entertainers in burlesque.

To accommodate this new popular entertainment, vaudeville theaters sprang up in downtown areas of cities, reaching all but the most remote rural areas of America. Vaudeville offered audiences conventions from earlier variety shows such as comic monologues, songs, dances, and skits, along with elements of minstrel show humor and circus staples—animals and acrobatic acts. By 1900, vaudeville eclipsed the circus, minstrel shows, and musical comedies in popularity even though "its most evident sources were . . . the minstrel show, the circus, troupes of traveling players who accommodated themselves to tents, show boats, opera houses, or town halls, whatever the particular stopping place provided."[16]

Variety theaters like the Ziegfeld Follies offered such comedy acts as Eddie Cantor, Will Rogers, Fanny Brice, and Bert Williams and brought the personas of ethnic stereotypes to the stage with a more "refined brand of topical banter, social satire, and clever song-and-dance."[17]

In vaudeville, hard-hitting, often ethnic-based and sexually suggestive humor and attacks on the polite society of the day were delivered with aggressiveness and physical energy. These standup comedians were "practioners of the 'new humor,' the crass, unsentimental humor of the city streets, which comes to its punch line quickly and dispenses with the refinements of storytelling technique. . . . Their ritual consists of a rapid cross-fire of jokes, puns, riddles, and insults which brings the audience to a pitch of amusement."[18] Scholar Albert McLean tells us that the accepted topics of the day, such as politics, marriage, streetcars, and local weather, were addressed in the vaudeville monologue, "a humorous talk spoken by one person, which possesses unity of character, is not combined with another entertainment form, is marked by compression, follows a definite form of construction and usually requires from ten to fifteen minutes of delivery."[19] "Changes in American humor, the growing literacy of Americans, the nationalization of immigrant groups, a developing sophistication in regard to city ways, and a revised estimate of American family life were all expressed upon the vaudeville stage."[20]

McLean theorizes that vaudeville was a response to powerful and unprecedented forces running through American culture at the turn of the century. In McLean's view, vaudeville expressed in symbols and images the need of Americans to have perspective on the new industrialism and urbanization that was changing their country. Showmen entrepreneurs directed audience members to these cultural and sociological changes to encourage a belief in social progress and personal success as a virtue on the vaudeville stage.

As the vaudeville entertainment form was a response to the mass technology changing American culture, so were the media forms created by this new technology to offer standup comedians new ways to disseminate their humor to larger audiences. A portent of vaudeville's future was indicated in 1896 when "large-screen motion pictures were introduced to the United States . . . before the audience of a New York vaudeville house. As a novel filler for a bill of live entertainment, silent pictures posed no great threat to the world of stage."[21] By 1912, "small-time vaudeville—a combination of film features and live presentation—had attracted a diverse patronage. Competing with the legitimate houses and nickelodeons of urban entertainment districts, the small-time vaudeville format set the stage for the critical transition that produced . . . several thousand . . . million-dollar movie palaces," Valerio and Friedman tell us.[22]

In the vaudeville of the late nineteenth and early twentieth centuries, a great many comedians found a lucrative showcase in which to practice their comedy. Some of the best known were Eddie Cantor, Leon Errol, Bob Hope, Lou Holtz, Eddie Foy, Frank Tinney, Frank Fay, Lew Dockstader, Joe Cook, comedy teams like Collins and Harlan, Harrigan and Hart, McIntyre and Heath, Smith and Dale, Weber and Fields, Clark and McCullough, George Burns and Gracie Allen, Van and Schenck, Gallagher and Shean, Wheeler and Woolsey, Miller and Lyles, and comediennes Eva Tanguay, Lotta Crabtree, May Irwin, Nora Bayes, Belle Baker, Marie Dresslow, Joan Davis, The Duncan Sisters, May West, and Sophie Tucker. Gifted black comedians such as Mantan Moreland, Step 'n Fetchit (Lincoln Theodore Perry), and Moms Mabley played the black vaudeville circuit, Harlem nightclubs, and revues, while other black comedians such as Bert Williams and comedy team Miller and Lyles made their way to the white vaudeville circuit and to the variety theater stages.

At the turn of the century, standup comedians also gained entertainment experience at the resort hotels, summer camps, and tourist bungalow colonies in New York's Adirondack Mountains, the Pocono Mountains in Pennsylvania, and in the Berkshires in New England, called the "Borscht Belt." As "social directors" or "toomlers" (a tumult maker is one who could keep the guests entertained), comedians were called upon to be "producer, director, writer, actor, song-and-dance man, emcee, comedian, scenic designer, electrician, stage manager, stagehand and sometimes waiter. After the show he had to mingle with the guests, dance with the fat old women and romance the 'dogs.' "[23] The Borscht Belt was basically a male comedian's world. As vaudeville and burlesque declined in popularity by the late 1930s, the Borscht Belt continued to be an important place for standup comedians to break into the entertainment business. The Borscht Belt was a training ground for such famous comedians as Jerry Lewis, Danny Kaye, Joey Adams, Red Buttons, Jan Murray, Buddy Hackett, Mel Brooks, and Sid Caesar.

Joey Adams says that as the Borscht Belt grew from humble summer resorts to a sophisticated and expensive tourist area of plush hotels and night clubs, professional, rather than amateur, comedians were booked.[24] The training ground vacuum for amateur standup comedians was filled by nightclubs in urban bohemian sectors such as Greenwich Village in New York City or in areas such as Las Vegas and Miami Beach, where it became fashionable to feature standup comedians on the entertainment bill of fare.

Some comedians made the transition from vaudeville and/or burlesque and the Follies to the new media of film, records, radio, and television. The list includes such comedians as Jack Benny, W. C. Fields, Eddie Cantor, Al Jolson, Step 'n Fetchit, Wheeler and Woolsey, Bob Hope, George Jessel, Moran and Mack, Mantan Moreland, Morey Amsterdam, Milton Berle, Cliff Arquette, Abbott and Costello, Red Buttons, Joey Faye, Kaye Ballard, Belle Baker, Joan Davis, George Burns and Gracie Allen.

In the early twentieth century, Max Sennett opened a Hollywood movie studio and hired comedians from vaudeville for his films. From 1915 to 1925, comedy in silent film was in its zenith with such stars as Buster Keaton, Charlie Chaplin, Fatty Arbuckle, Harold Lloyd, Ben Turpin, and Laurel and Hardy. Talking pictures became available by 1927 and "production and screenplays were tailored to support a new type of movie star . . . who could sing, dance, and talk. . . . More significantly, the concept of augmented entertainment—live stage shows, organs, and orchestras—faced a near-total eclipse."[25] As the movie palaces that showcased silent films faded from the entertainment scene, comedians no longer found employment in the live stage productions that accompanied the silent films. Then vaudeville's popularity crested in 1930 in the face of the new medias of radio, records, and motion pictures with sound. Again, standup comedians had to adjust their performing spaces and media to the changing economics and technologies that affected the art world and the consuming public.

Prior to the development of radio, film, and television, it was possible for standup comedians to build a whole act on a single routine as in vaudeville, where the same form and content of an act could be presented over many years to new audiences every day. In comparison, the instant dissemination of a comedy routine through radio, film, or television, instantly communicating the act to millions of people, required fresh material from established comedians and demanded new comedy personalities. This paved the way for the profession of the comedy writer. While many comedians continued to write their own material, many hired professionals to create a constant supply of new jokes.

By the late 1920s, the radio was a common fixture in many American homes; by the early 1930s, it was the most popular medium.[26] Among the vaudeville comedians who successfully made the transition to radio were Eddie Cantor, Jack Haley, Julius Tannen, Joe Laurie, Jr., Morey Amsterdam, W. C. Fields, George Burns and Gracie Allen, Joan Davis, Henny Youngman, Cliff Arquette, Joe Penner, Edgar Bergen (with dummy Charlie McCarthy), Fred Allen, and Bob Hope. The Happiness Boys were the first comic duo to perform on radio in 1921 on WJZ in Newark, New Jersey, one of the first radio stations in America.[27] They preceded such popular comedy teams as Coon and Sanders, Lum and Abner, Amos 'n' Andy, and Bob and Ray. During the 1930s, Joe

Penner on Rudy Vallee's program, Jack Benny with Rochester (Eddie Anderson), Goodman Ace, Richy Craign, Jr., Ed Wynn, Henry Morgan, Lum and Abner, and Fibber McGee and Molly delighted radio audiences with their comic commentary and free-wheeling humor. Ed Gardner in Duffy's Tavern, Henry Morgan, Goodman Ace, Morey Amsterdam, and Henny Youngman on Kate Smith's radio program proved popular in the 1940s. Steve Allen, Stan Freeberg, and Alan Young were popular in the 1950s.

Novelty records with funny songs were popular with Americans when they first became available. Bert Williams, who did wry social commentary, was possibly, Joe Franklin tells us, the first black comedian to be preserved on early Victor recordings;[28] Weber and Fields' records offered humorous dialogues on etiquette, baseball, and other familiar subjects. With the invention of the long-playing record in the early 1950s, however, standup comedians could develop more than three- to four-minute routines that the early records allowed. "Party records" featuring sexually explicit material by such comedians as Redd Foxx or Rusty Warren achieved an underground popularity. Tom Lehrer's humorous songs and Bob Newhart's comic monologues from the 1950s and 1960s helped to popularize the comedy record album with the American public. In the 1950s, Shelley Berman's "Inside Shelly" record album was at the top of the LP bestseller's list for two months, a rarity for a nonmusic record. Mort Sahl, Nichols and May, Allan Sherman, and Buddy Hackett were also popular. Foxx's "blue" albums or the Firesign Theater popular in the 1960s could present sexually explicit or politically biting material to their record audiences, not possible with a radio audience. The 1960s saw the popularity of political satire in such albums as Vaughn Meader's "The First Family" or David Frye's "I Am the President" albums. Counterculture comedians such as Cheech and Chong parodied the drug culture. The gifted vaudeville comedian Moms Mabley became popular with nonblack audiences during the 1960s as did Flip Wilson, Bill Cosby, and Richard Pryor. In the 1970s, standup comedians such as Bill Cosby and George Carlin enjoyed the success of gold records and Grammy Award-winning albums.

Film comedies were another media showcase for comedians. Clark and McCullough, Wheeler and Woolsey from vaudeville, along with the Marx Brothers, were popular in film comedies of the 1920s. Laurel and Hardy, Abbott and Costello, the Marx Brothers, Wheeler and Woolsey, W. C. Fields, Leon Errol, Jack Haley, and Mantan Moreland were also popular form the 1930s through the 1950s. Comedy team Dean Martin and Jerry Lewis came to the movie public's attention in the 1940s. A different kind of comedian like Woody Allen, Don Adams, or Buddy Hackett could be seen in the comedy movies of the 1960s and 1970s. In the 1970s and 1980s, standup comedians like Steve Martin, Richard Pryor, Lily Tomlin, Martin Mull, Goldie Hawn, and Eddie Murphy have definitely moved to the big time of movie success.

As identifiers of their comic status, styles of comedians' costumes and comedy props changed, going from the blackface makeup, clown, or formal servant attire of minstrelsy, to the variety of theatrical outfits worn by vaudeville stars to reflect their comic personae; the exaggerated face makeup, wigs and flashy costumes worn by America's talking clowns; the oversized polo coats with padded shoulders and suede shoes that typified 1950s comedians; the counterculture uniform of longer hair, jeans, t-shirts and beads worn by some 1960s comedians; and to the late 1960s designer suits, dark ties, and dress shirts that most male comedians wear today. Comediennes like Phyllis Diller adopted either flamboyant dress to mask feminine sexuality, or, like Lily Tomlin, wore neutrally styled and colored clothes with little jewelry so audiences would focus on their comic message rather than their womanly anatomy.

A new crop of comedians who postdated vaudeville began their performing careers exclusively in the new media and with live audiences in clubs. Coffeehouses and small night clubs called "chichi" rooms came into being in the 1950s and 1960s. They were places where the acts of standup comedians were showcased along with folk and jazz musicians and poets.[29] During this time, comedians also reached their audiences on the college comedy circuit and through record albums. Since the 1960s, comedy clubs like The Bitter End in New York and The Hungry I in San Francisco and The Improvisation in Los Angeles have become popular in most American cities. Established comedians are featured along with local professionals and amateur standup comedians. Many of these clubs feature amateur nights, which give beginners a chance for audience exposure and experience.

Some humor theorists date a marked change in standup comedy styles to the late 1950s and 1960s. The "traditional" style of comedy up to the 1950s, as practiced by such comedians as Red Skelton, Morey Amsterdam, Joey Adams, Milton Berle, Red Buttons, and Henny Youngman, was characterized by "formal, glib, structured routines." In the 1970s came "new wave" humor which was "irreverent, iconoclastic, shocking, combative, cynical, bitter, bizarre, sophisticated, intellectual, and complicated." Practitioners of the New Wave, such as Mort Sahl, Lenny Bruce, Jonathan Winters, and Richard "Lord" Buckley, delivered their monologues in an "informal, relaxed and spontaneous" manner to create an "atmosphere of a conversational off-handed discussion of the subject at hand."[30] Their humor involved highly political, sexually explicit and satiric social commentary. Other humor scholars argue that the so-called new wave humor had earlier precedents and the group of "new wave" comedians in no way constituted a homogeneous, identifiable group.

Some critics and historians characterize 1950s humor as "sick" since many comedians of that time irreverently lambasted life in general, from its sacred to its mundane aspects. As one *Time* reviewer wrote, "what the sickniks dispense is partly social criticism liberally laced with cyanide, partly a Charles Addams kind of jolly ghoulness, and partly a persona and highly disturbing hostility toward all the world."[31] If earlier American traditional humor was "the wisecrack, the tall tale, the deadpan japes, the shaggy-dog story,"[32] there was a turn in the comic sensibility of the 1960s to seriousness and "ghastly-funny" subjects such as nuclear annihilation and the Vietnam War.[33] Folklorist Barre Toelken offers the hypothesis that joke topics, particularly about politics, sex, religion, and ethnicity, indicate the emotional concerns of a society.[34]

Dick Gregory, Mort Sahl, Lenny Bruce, and other social-commentary comics dominated the standup comedian scene in the 1960s. Some theater and popular culture historians feel that Second City, a comedy troupe organized in Chicago in 1959 with a focus on satiric comedy and skillful improvisation, "pioneered the fast, smart, topical improvisational theater that rose to prominence in the sixties."[35] This comedy troupe was a training ground for such comics as Dan Aykroyd, Gilda Radner, Bill Murray, and John Belushi, who satirized news events and parodied entertainment personalities on television's *Saturday Night Live*. Rowan and Martin's *Laugh-In* also typified fast comedy sketches revolving around political and social satire and other topical humor. Although many standup comedians were introduced to the television public through shows like *Laugh-In* or *Saturday Night Live*, their special pinnacle on television became the role of host or guest-host on *The Tonight Show*. Steve Allen hosted *The Tonight Show* from 1948 to 1950, giving television exposure to comedians Louis Nye, Don Knotts, Tom Posten, Bill Dana, Pat Harrington, and Dayton Allen. He was the first talk-show host with a major late-night following, followed by Jack Paar in the 1950s and 1960s, and Johnny Carson from 1961 to the present. Comedians such as Robert Klein, Joan Rivers, George Carlin, Alan King, and Bill Cosby have guest-hosted *The Tonight Show* over the years. "The comedian who can make it on television is the one who can preside over the talk show landscape. He's the comedian who can keep things going and react to the traffic of guests sitting down on and leaving a couch; he's the comedian who represents security and durability to a network. . . . he can react and act with the flow of the society, and because of that he's worth more than any eight sitcoms."[36]

In 1951, Johnny Carson had his own TV show prior to *The Tonight Show* role, called "Carson's Cellar" where comedians like Red Skelton and Groucho Marx made guest appearances. Other 1940s and 1950s television variety shows of Jackie Gleason, Arthur Godfrey, Ed Sullivan, Perry Como, Garry Moore, George Gobel, and Ernie Kovacs featured such comedians as Alan Young, Orson Bean, Joey Bishop, Al Kelly, Jack Benny, and Red Skelton. Comedians Buddy Hackett and Sid Caesar had their own television shows in the 1950s. Comedians who had their own shows in the 1960s included the Smothers Brothers, Bill Cosby, Flip Wilson, and Carol Burnett. Standup comedians continued to capture moments in the television spotlight on the variety programs of Mike Douglas, Merv Griffin, and Dean Martin.

Talent scouts for Jack Paar and Johnny Carson and such network situation comedy producers as Norman Lear would often sit in the audiences of comedy clubs to discover new talent for television. These comedy clubs came into being since 1974 specifically to showcase standup comedy acts—established performers and amateurs. Since the 1970s, there has been a greater demand for new personalities to star in television sitcoms. From comedy clubs such comedians as David Frye, Dick Cavett, Lily Tomlin, Robert Klein, Clifton Davis, Richard

Pryor, Anne Meara and Jerry Stiller, Rodney Dangerfield, David Brenner, Gabe Kaplan, Jimmie Walker, Elayne Boosler, and Freddy Prinze made their way into the college comedy-concert circuit, to *The Tonight Show*, and, sometimes, to their own television sitcom series (Gabe Kaplan's *Welcome Back, Kotter*, Jimmie Walker's *Good Times* and the late Freddie Prinze's *Chico and the Man*) or to television specials or recording contracts.

If 1960s comedians were didactic and politically serious, many 1970s comedians adopted a light-hearted irreverence and an "arrogance . . . a way of pretending to know it all—that's the joke."[37] *Newsweek*'s Tony Schwartz characterized the prevailing comedy style of 1970s humor as

less political, but it retains an ethnic edge and an outsider's perspective. Woody Allen mines a mother lode of anxiety and insecurity, pleading the case for the little guy. Lily Tomlin urges that attention be paid to society's outcasts. Richard Pryor spins complex tales of survival in the ghetto. All Steve Martin asks is that everyone have a good time. His approach is a throw back to vaudeville, slapstick and the comedy of his childhood idols, Red Skelton and Jerry Lewis, but it is inflected with a '70s penchant for self-parody.[38]

Until recently, the world of standup comedy has basically been a male domain. During the 1970s, comediennes were able to break into the entertainment business in greater numbers. Phyllis Diller, Joan Rivers—*The Tonight Show*'s frequent guest hostess in the 1980s—the late Totie Fields, Jessica James, Lily Tomlin (the list excludes sketch comics such as Carol Burnett or Imogene Coca and comic actress Lucille Ball) were some of the performers who led the way for other comediennes in nightclubs and television. In 1977 Tomlin made her Broadway debut in *Appearing Nitely*. Her second Broadway show, *The Search for Signs of Intelligent Life in the Universe*, was a Broadway smash. The show was described by theater critic David Richards as "a compendium of pop history, a living anthropological exhibit of the relics of a society that subscribes to disposable life styles. . . . " Richards heralds Tomlin as a superb monologuist, mime, and actress who "has always had an acute awareness of mankind as a species that lives on bread, water and fads. The zest and accuracy with which she identifies—then skewers—cultural and sociological trends is exhilarating."[39] In her show she portrays a mixed group of American characters from a radical feminist, a mad punker, a bored matron, a hip hooker, a crazy baglady, and a contemporary California housewife.

During the 1980s, comediennes Maureen Murphy, Sandra Bernhard, Gilda Radner, Andrea Martin, and Victoria Jackson appeared on *The Tonight Show*. In the growing number of comedy showcases across America, a whole new group of comediennes, including Sandra Bernhard, Carol Siskind, Rita Rudner, Margaret Smith, Joy Behar, Emily Levine, Cathy Ladman, Elayne Boosler, Marjorie Gross, and Paula Poundstone are earning their livings as standup comediennes.

The 1970s and 1980s were the years in which many standup comedians made it big in the movies and on television. Martin Mull is representative of these performers. A star on Norman Lear's sitcom, *Mary Hartman, Mary Hartman*, he received a 1972 recording contract, toured in a show called "Martin Mull and His Fabulous Furniture," and was asked to write and star in a movie of his own. Steve Martin enjoyed tremendous success as a headliner in Las Vegas clubs, appeared as guest host on *Saturday Night Live*, won Grammy Awards for some of his records, and starred in television specials and movies. Richard Pryor's comedy writing for a Lily Tomlin TV special won him an Emmy award. With Gene Wilder he formed the first successful interracial comedy team whose movies *Silver Streak* in 1976 and *Stir Crazy* in 1980 grossed approximately $200 million according to *Newsweek*.[40] *Newsweek* says of Pryor: "Even on records he can paint a vivid picture of the skewed reality created by poverty or racism, a reality that has its own paradoxical beauty. Pryor has plenty of anger, but he also has plenty of love, plenty of delight in his own creative power. . . . "[41]

Richard Corliss, in a *Time* review of the new wave comedians, noted that the standup comedics of the 1970s and 1980s tend to base their humor on a radical examination of the comic's relationship to society. "What began as a defiant form of anti-shtik has become a dominant mode in the funny-peculiar 1980s. It is saturating the big screen with the films of Albert Brooks, Steve Martin, Murray Langston, Martin Mull, Andy Kaufman, Lily Tomlin and now ready-for-prime-time cutups of NBC's Saturday Night Live," Corliss noted.[42] These comics

do not spin whimsical stories of urban childhoods, like Bill Cosby and George Carlin. They do not deal in analysis and self-hatred, like Woody Allen and Rodney Dangerfield. They do not refract their rage in race-and-reefer jokes, like Lenny Bruce and Richard Pryor. They do not tell topical or political jokes, like Johnny Carson. Indeed, they rarely tell jokes or satires at all. They do not talk about their mothers, their wives, their egos. Their past is a mystery; their presence is perplexing. They may be the first generation of comics to forgo the funnyman's implicit plea: love me by laughing at me. The post-funny comics can do without both.[43]

These comedians ridicule stereotypes of the entertainment industry. Or as co-median and humor scholar Steve Allen deftly puts it, the "new" comedians "imitate jerks."[44] Within this group, Steve Martin has become a kind of spokes-man for the everyman of the 1980s.

Bill Cosby has been described in *Newsweek* as a "one-man multimedia phe-nomenon. Actor, comedian, pitchman nonpareil, he has made himself into the most ubiquitous presence in American pop culture."[45] *The Cosby Show* in 1985 is the number-one rated series on television with Cosby as "lead player, co-creator, co-producer, executive consultant and co-writer of the theme song." The authenticity of the Huxtable family in Cosby's sitcom is reviewed by Harvard Medical School psychologist Dr. Alvin Poussaint, who believes "the singular universality of the Huxtables may be having a potent subliminal impact . . .

changing the white community's perspective of black Americans''; Coretta Scott
King hails the Huxtable sitcom as "certainly the most positive portrayal of black
family life that has ever been broadcast."[46]

At this point—the 1980s—standup comedy is alive and doing very well. Live
performances of standup comedy in the comedy clubs that came into being in
the 1970s are very popular. These comedy clubs give audience experience to
newcomers in "open mike" sessions or amateur nights and feature established
comedians. There is no lack of rising young comics, male or female, making
their way from unpaid amateur nights at these types of clubs to being paid
performers.

A cast of characters from American life has been humorously recreated in
Broadway shows by such comediennes as Lily Tomlin's *The Search for Signs
of Intelligent Life in the Universe* and by Whoopie Goldberg, who prefers not
to be typecast as a standup comedienne nor an actress but as a versatile innovator
of many entertainment forms. Goldberg's *The Spook Show* toured the United
States and Europe. She also performed in a one-person show, *MOMS*, based on
the life of comedienne Moms Mabley, before Goldberg starred in her movie hit,
The Color Purple.

Comedians, male and female, are appearing as guest hosts or hostesses or in
spots on *The Tonight Show*, the *David Letterman Show*, *Saturday Night Live*,
or in their own sitcoms. Television programming such as an *Evening at the
Improv* showcases the talents of upcoming standup comedians. Amateur talent
shows on television such as *Star Search* also give public exposure to hopefuls.

Standup comedians such as Steve Martin, Richard Pryor, Lily Tomlin, Goldie
Hawn, and Robin Williams have gone on to successful movie careers in the
1980s.

Standup comedians also find a lucrative market for their humor on comedy
record albums. Some of these records offer routines from the greats in the
business that have historical value. Excerpts from the golden age of radio comedy
featuring some classic comedy routines are also available on tape cassettes.

Comedians such as Steve Allen, David Brenner, Sid Caesar, George Carlin,
Redd Foxx, Buster Keaton, Jerry Lewis, Groucho Marx, Mort Sahl, and Henny
Youngman have written books about their lives or the subject of humor. Comedians are also getting feature-article coverage in magazines such as *Life* or in
newspapers. For example, Steve Wright was hailed recently in *The Christian Science Monitor* as "the fastest-rising young comic in America, with a new style, a
unique delivery, and material that will make you think rather than smirk." The
article says that Wright draws his material from the "rich comic mother lode of
'everyday' life" and "uses a reverse type of humor, turning the truth inside out,
helping us to see other angles, other ways of feeling. He makes you think."[47]

Along with all the positive popular media coverage of standup comedy performance, the time is ripe for serious scholarship on the subject.

THEMES AND ISSUES

Key issues requiring research for a fuller understanding of standup comedy performance are the relationship between standup comedians and their audiences; standup comedians' roles as spokespersons for special topical areas and particular population segments; the performance experience; standup comedy's relationship to other genres; and content-analysis of standup comedy routines.

Standup comedy performance does not typically generate written records of audience perception or demographic information about audience composition for a researcher to study. The fields of anthropology, folklore, and sociology may offer some fruitful tools for researching this relationship.

Taking an ethnographic perspective from the field of anthropology, audience members would be regarded as "authorities about their own culture."[48] The cultural scene of the live or recorded performance as it is being experienced by an audience or by the comedian as he or she is relating to an audience would be the focus of the research. It would be the task of the researcher to collect data from audience members and comedians by administering structured interviews, questionnaires, and psychological tests, compiling life histories, and acting as a participant observer prior, to, during, and after a performance. On the basis of this data, audience members' and artists' interpretations of the performance could be described by the researcher.

I have found it fruitful to examine certain comedians' relationships to their audience through their role as protoanthropologists. Certain standup comedians such as the late Lenny Bruce, Mort Sahl, Bill Cosby, George Carlin, Dick Gregory, Hal Holbrook, Steve Martin, Bob Newhart, Richard Pryor, Flip Wilson, Lily Tomlin, Mel Brooks, Carl Reiner, Rusty Warren, and Steve Wright do not just entertain, but offer critical perspectives on American culture, much like anthropologists. One comedian was quoted as proclaiming; "I am like an anthropologist. My job is to watch people and notice all of the quaint, strange things they do. I will not take anything for granted about people. I will study them patiently and sooner or later I will uncover absurdities."[49] Researchers Seymour and Rhoda Fisher noted in their psychological analyses of comedians that "the average comedian moves among his fellows like an anthropologist visiting a new culture. He is a relativist. Nothing seems natural or 'given.' He is constantly taking mental notes. . . . Instead of publishing his findings in a scientific journal, he immediately acts them out in the broad metaphors of comedy."[50]

As protoanthropologists, comedians discuss everyday reality in their routines, interwoven with humorous distortion. Select comedians highlight aspects of human life that are the focus of anthropologists' research—beliefs, values, meanings, associations, customs, social structure, institutions, behavior, artifacts, language, and other elements they feel merit examination, analysis, and discussion. The more sensitive and critical comedians not only highlight these aspects of life, but keep playing with their material until novel interconnections are seen in the seemingly unrelated. They may account for the discrepancies found in their observations of how things should operate in the culture, but don't.

One aspect of comedians' relationships with their audiences is their role as licensed spokespersons who identify and talk about contradictions in society that other persons may be unaware of or reluctant to acknowledge openly. Even though the comedian and audience share the same culture, part of the cultural knowledge within which they operate is tacit, that is, unspoken or unseen. In a routine, an audience may hear its own behavior described as if it is an alien culture in the sense that they knew the information all along but no one ever described the components. As an anthropologist examines a foreign culture against which American institutions, values, and behaviors are contrasted—thereby throwing a spotlight on American society—so some comedians cause their audiences to take stock by highlighting the ordinary and hidden patterns, alienations, injustices, incongruities, and immoralities in American life. Through the comedian's revelations, people can stand back from their lives and become aware of their human situation. Cross-cultural studies of humor, not just themes and techniques of American humor, are important topics for further research.

A researcher can examine comedians' explanations of American society using analytical concepts from anthropology. Textual analysis of comedians' routines and audiences' perceptions of the routines could include looking for discussions of marriage, new life-styles, received notions of male and female nature, qualities attributed to particular age groups, artifacts, authority, wealth, status, rules for behavior, privacy definitions and rights, the ordering of physical space, property distribution, ownership rules, the structure of social institutions, education practices, food preparation and rules, clothing design, home design and activities, work and leisure activities, sexual expression, religious expression, and other categories within which Americans order their experience.

The field of folklore offers some research strategies for studying the relationship of standup comedians to their audiences. Beyond the pleasure of entertainment, folklorist Barre Toelken sees joke telling in a group as an important form of human communication that helps people learn, reinforce, and maintain the central values, daily logic, and worldview of their group. Jokes can be a way for a comedian to share culturally acceptable philosophies with an audience. This information is communicated through references to an inherited system of culture-based knowledge, language, and decorum, phrased in the joke form. Further, joke telling gives advice about the cultural landmarks of a group by reference to common places, stock figures, and stock systems of organizing the society. Jokes identify outsiders by defining who belongs in the group and who does not belong. Jokes also introduce new ideas before they are more widely accepted by a society's members.

Toelken sees the meaning stemming from joke telling as "connotative, for it resides not in the item or situation or in the denotation of the words, but in the feelings people have about the items, situations, and words. These attitudes are culture-specific, the deepest meanings seldom arise automatically from the text but need to be extrapolated from ethnographic evidence.''[51] Toelken discusses jokes that depend upon a basic set of absurdities for their effect, asking what the telling of jokes symbolized for a particular group at a particular time when many other absurdities were available for comments. He notes:

If we were to list the most common jokes told in our culture, I believe we could relate most of them to anxieties, threats, and concerns felt by different groups at different, noticeable periods of time in our history. Probably the bulk of American jokes concern sex, politics, religion, and ethnicity—just the very subjects that cause us continual malaise in conversation, the topics our mothers told us never to discuss in public. I think it is too much to lay on the shoulders of coincidence that all these joke topics continue to parallel the ongoing emotional concerns of society.[52]

Toelken notes that when questioned intellectually about their responses to jokes, most people give intellectual answers regarding their feelings about other groups. But if one collected jokes told by the group questioned, an entirely different cultural answer may be gathered about the dimensions of intergroup feelings and tensions directed to other groups.

In the hands of certain comedians, joke telling is an expressive event that reflects a learning process. Using analytical concepts from folklore, standup comedians' joke telling and their audience's response might be analyzed in terms of common elements in jokes and songs from the past and present, recurrent forms of expression in American standup comedy, changed audience perceptions and learning that resulted from hearing a comedian's routine, and joke telling as a form of communication.

Perspectives from sociology offer some areas of standup comedy needing research: the social context of standup comedy performance, the social class of comedians and their audiences, group behavior in audiences viewing a live standup comedy performance versus home viewing of a recorded event, the social class and social network of comedy writers who create humorous material for standup comedians, and the people who shape the entertainment industry that employs standup comedians. Humor response as a way groups handle the problems are handled by a society's members has much to do with social maintenance and social change. The comedian's revelations to an audience can communicate some important information about the values and material conditions of life thought necessary to sustain a given social system. A routine can pinpoint areas where social change or tension may be occurring. In their ludicrous explanations of a causal chain of events, many comedians may come close to truth in suggesting factors responsible for changes in particular patterns of thought and behavior in their society. The importance of standup comedy as an entertainment form during leisure time in a technological society is another way to consider standup comedy performance.

Sociological forces at work in a comedian's routine can be glimpsed in textual analysis through character portrayal. Distinct character types may be embodiments of the artist's perceived place as a participant or alienated being in society or his or her general awareness of social class. Stylized and formal language modes also reflect perceptions about social roles. An artist's association of a particular regionalism with a type of cultural inferiority or superiority may bracket deeply held mental constructs in his or her thinking or may serve to represent the view of the audience to whom the comedian is gauging his or her material. Modes of expression and attitudes embedded in dialogue, notions of male and female nature, and laudable or punishable behavior can be analyzed for the comedian's individually held images of society or widely held preoccupations held by a large segment of Americans. Researchers can also look for expressions of principles of order, explanations of anomalies, reward and punishment modes, definitions of self and society, strategies of reassurance, persuasion or allegiance and descriptions of social types worthy of emulation or criticism—that is, the body of knowledge deemed essential for group maintenance.

More personality profiles such as those done by Seymour and Rhoda Fisher and Samuel Janus are needed. The field of psychology offers analytical tools for studying the motivations and behavior of standup comedians and their audiences. Many standup comedians come from disadvantaged formative experiences. As Larry Wilde notes in his book, *The Great Comedians*,

in America, a predominantly Protestant country, the great majority of nationally known comedians are of a minority or religious faith—Catholic or Jewish. With the emergence of Negroes Bill Cosby, Nipsey Russell, Godfrey Cambridge, Scoey Mitchell, Richard Pryor, Stu Gilliam, Flip Wilson et al., it would appear that persecution, poverty, and prejudice are still the breeding grounds for most of America's laugh-makers.[53]

Comedians' early life events can be examined for clues as to why they became entertainers and how these experiences may have shaped the philosophy expressed in their routines. Some theorists explain the humor response of standup comedians as a kind of self-therapy used to overcome their insecurities, channel their anger at society's injustices, and win acceptance from their audiences. In this light, humor can be viewed as an enabling device that allows comedians to compensate for their own feelings of isolation from mainstream society and a bridge to bring them into closer fellowship with their audiences.

Standup comedy has also been described as an aggressive act. Comedians' use of humor might be seen as a defense mechanism to ward off the hostility and aggression of others. Humor can also be used as a bonding experience through the shared experience of laughter. Humor has a healing power when used to dissect and ease fearful and tension-provoking issues by bringing these subjects into a public arena for analysis and laughs.

Psychologist Samuel Janus spent a year as a standup comedian and ten years traveling around the country to interview top comedians. He administered psychological tests and found most comedians "had been in psychotherapy and almost all had major traumas in early childhood . . . they live for acceptance.

They are always working for it, always worrying and insecure.''[54] A *Time* review of his research in 1978 noted that Janus found most comedians he interviewed to be bright, sensitive people and ''although Jews constitute only 3% of the U.S. population, 80% of the nation's professional comedians are Jewish.'' Further in the same review, Janus accounted for the great number of Jewish comedians with an explanation that ''Jewish humor is one born of depression and alienation from the general culture.''[55] Because a comedian's personality—even charisma— is such an important factor in capturing an audience's interest, more psychological profiles and other biographical data about the earlier standup comedians, while they are still alive, and the newcomers in the business need to be added to research on this subject.

Standup comedians' roles as spokespersons for special topics and particular populations is another area offering topics for research. Certain comedians advocate a particular point of view such as racial equality, feminism, or liberal politics, and their following may be a select group rather than a broad public. In addition to entertainment, some comedians picture conflicting strains of thought or baffling human behavior occurring in society through the artistic constructions of their routines. These patterns can become visible symbolically in a performance. An audience may come to understand something about what it means to be handicapped by society's sexual rules or by minority status through examples of those situations enacted by standup comedians. Perspectives from women's or black studies may offer some ways of examining standup comedians' role in promoting new views of racial equality or feminist viewpoints. For example, women's studies might offer perspectives for studying the first comediennes to break into the standup comedy business, as well as the new crop entering in increasing numbers. Because standup comedy has until recently been basically a male domain, women's opportunities in the standup comedy world, expressions of male and female nature expressed in routines, and the structure of the entertainment industry that employs standup comedians can be studied as to how these images and social structures reflect the place of women in the culture at large or specifically in the entertainment industry.

Different bonding experiences will happen with different groups, depending upon which segment of the population the comedian is aiming his or her message. Comedians can play routines with a broad appeal to diverse audiences or esoteric messages to a select group. The act of being in an audience can reinforce a special feeling of membership. For example, when Bob Hope brought his comedy to troops in war situations, his humor helped soldiers cope with less-than-ideal life conditions. By naming some of the horrifying and unpleasant ingredients of war in humorous reconstructions of the daily reality soldiers were experiencing, Hope was helping soldiers, in moments of shared laughter with their comrades, keep up their courage and envision feelings of identification and achievement. In contrast, a counterculture comedian like George Carlin or Dick Gregory performing before a liberal college audience during the 1960s might broadcast values in opposition to the values of dominant society, reinforcing a special feeling of membership among audience members who share political and social values.

Comedy performance is an art form and humor is a specialized form of communication that provides a framework in a high-energy setting for people to reflect about the complexity of the world around them. Perspectives from the fields of theater arts and communication can offer some analytic tools for researching this subject.

The comedy performance can be regarded as a system in which the elements of gesture, dialogue, voice tone, timing, rhythm, style, props, lighting, sound effects, pauses, and other ingredients are interwoven by the comedian into an artistic construction. How these different elements contribute to the overall effect of a performance can be a focus of the research.

Along with viewing the act as a coordinated system of elements, performance can be viewed as preritual, ritual, and postritual states of awareness or as the rehearsal or warm up, the act, and the cool-down or reentry into the nonperformance mode. Audience and artist preperformance , performance, and post-performance states of mind and behavior topics for research.

Taking another view of the performance, the individual comedian or comedy writer can be viewed as opereating for a media industry and audience made up of people whose tastes and responses condition and occasion the performance. The researcher can question to what extent the taste of the producers or audience encouraged or modified elements of the performance.

The design of the performance space is also an appropriate research topic. In clubs, the audience is seated closely together so when one person laughs, others close around will also laugh in a chain reaction of communal laughter. The communication equipment, acoustics of the room, and stage design are important so the comic's message can be delivered and heard with clarity. Reciprocal relations between people and the built environment might be one avenue through which audience perceptions of a standup comedy performance can be assessed.

The researcher should be aware that a standup comedy performance is different when a comedian is taping in a television or radio studio or performing live in a club. For example, in a club the seasoned comedian is aware of the audience's composition and of subtle elements of information operating in the performance setting. Comedians and their emcees mingle with their audiences before a performance to discover audience characteristics. This information gathering allows comedians to assess their audience's interest and comprehension level. They discard issues and explanation forms that meet little audience response and utilize ideas and strategies that command attention. Within their arsenal of techniques are also ways of handling hecklers.

The relationship between standup comedy performance and other popular culture genres is another area needing research. Standup comedians are practitioners of popular culture, and the records of their performances are popular culture artifacts. Strategies for researching standup comedy performance from popular culture methodologies involve examing the production, distribution, and consumption of popular culture forms, as well as the historical roots and fusions of these entertainment expressions.

Standup comedy performance as "most popular culture has, as its primary motive and function, commercial success, popularity, and entertainment, but it also reveals many significant themes and cultural statements . . . [which can be examined through] formula, conventions, structure, imagery, symbols, language, setting, and many other features of a popular culture entity."[56]

Content analysis of comedy routines and critics' commentary on comedians' works may give insights into the artist, the meaning of his or her performance, the audience to whom the comedian aims material, and current interests and concerns felt by the public for whom he or she speaks.

The investigator can regard the imaginative material of the standup comedian—texts, transcripts, videotapes, records, and revelations expressed during a live performance—as a body of social opinion, valuable to the researcher of American culture for what is expressive and revealing about the content of adult minds. This body of social opinion offers insights into widely accepted, selectively experienced, or rarely acknowledged social and personal values, beliefs, and behaviors. These artistic responses can pinpoint from their unique way of perceiving and presenting reality, subjective intentions, social and mental concepts, values, fears, anxieties, doubts, and behaviors. These may be obvious or exist at subconscious levels.

Trying to understand the subjective phenomena lying behind the comedian's routine, the researcher must recognize covert themes and values so pervasive, basic, and internalized that people have difficulty describing them.

A textual analysis would involve examining recurrent themes, image patterns, word and phrase repetitions, canons of propriety, character portrayal, dialogue, regional associations, images with wide currency in the culture, and other such elements. A comedian may aim his or her message to a select audience or a broad public. In dealing with written materials from such a highly differentiated culture in terms of race, class, region, religion, and ethnicity, the researcher may be confronted with the dilemma of which groups' values, norms, themes, philosophies, sentiments, characteristic and novel behaviors are being addressed by the standup comedian. Clues to the group for whom he or she speaks may be indicated in an examination of the comedian's biographical data. Here may be found evidence of the artist's attitude toward society by his or her perceived place, family background, career stage, and significant other influences that shaped them as an artist.

Levels of meanings intended by the standup comedian and others discovered by a particular audience can be discovered by attention to textual analysis, a comedian's explanations of his or her message, the social context of the performance, the historical time in which the performance occurs, and audience response.

Standup comedians have delighted and instructed diverse audiences by their portrayal of the ridiculous and the incongruous; connected people to their common humanity through the comedic response to life; broken ground with new concepts, definitions, and interpretations; and discharged some of their audiences' fears, anxieties, and other preoccupations in moments of shared laughter. This unique entertainment form and cultural expression is an important subject that deserves careful research and offers many fruitful topics for futher study.

NOTES

1. Larry Wilde, *How the Great Comedy Writers Create Laughter* (Chicago: Nelson-Hall, 1976), p. 6.

2. Lawrence E. Mintz, "The 'New Wave' of Standup Comedians: An Introduction," *American Humor: An Interdisciplinary Newsletter* 4,2 (Fall 1977): 1–3.

3. Lawrence E. Mintz, "Standup Comedy As Social and Cultural Mediation," *American Quarterly* 37, 1 (Spring 1985): 71.

4. Ibid., pp. 71–72.

5. Joe Franklin, *Joe Franklin's Encyclopedia of Comedians* (Secaucus, N.J.: The Citadel Press, 1979), p. 14.

6. John H. Towsen, *Clowns* (New York: Hawthorn Books, 1976).

7. Ibid., pp. 3–30.

8. Ibid., p. 6.

9. Franklin, *Joe Franklin's Encyclopedia of Comedians*, p. 15.

10. Ibid., p. 16.

11. Towsen, *Clowns*, p. 130.

12. Ibid.

13. Albert F. McLean, Jr., *American Vaudeville As Ritual* (Lexington: University of Kentucky Press, 1975), p. 26.

14. Ibid., p. 17.

15. Mintz, "Standup Comedy," p. 9.

16. McLean, *American Vaudeville As Ritual*, p. 16.

17. Mintz, "Standup Comedy," p. 9.

18. McLean, *American Vaudeville As Ritual*, p. 98.

19. Ibid., pp. 111–12.

20. Ibid., p. 23.

21. Joseph M. Valerio and Daniel Friedman, *Movie Palaces: Renaissance and Reuse*, (Worcester, Mass.: Mercantile Printing Company, 1982), p. 16.

22. Ibid., p. 17.

23. Joey Adams with Henry Tobias, *The Borscht Belt* (New York: Bobbs-Merrill, 1966), p. 3.

24. Ibid., p. 202.

25. Valerio and Friedman, *Movie Palaces*, p. 28.

26. Overview of new media dates and their impact on the American public in this section given in an interview with Don Drucker, Media Specialist, National Endowment for the Arts, Media Arts Program, October 1985.

27. Franklin, *Joe Franklin's Encyclopedia of Comedians*, p. 160.

28. Ibid., p. 337.

29. Mintz, "Standup Comedy," p. 9.

30. Mintz, "The 'New Wave' of Standup Comedianes," pp. 1–3.

31. "Nightclubs: The Sickniks," *Time*, July 13, 1959, p. 42.

32. Melvin Maddocks, "We Are Not Amused and Why," *Time*, July 20, 1970, p. 30.

33. Barre Toelken, *The Dynamics of Folklore* (Boston: Houghton Mifflin, 1979), p. 270.

34. Maddocks, "We Are Not Amused and Why," p. 30.

35. John Morthland, "Comedy Roots," *New Times* 10, 1 (January 9, 1978): 42.

36. Peter W. Kaplan, "David Letterman, the Vice-President of Comedy," *Esquire*, December 1981, p. 65.

37. Tony Schwartz, "The Good Humor Men," *Newsweek*, April 3, 1978, p. 70.

38. Ibid., p. 61.

39. David Richards, "Tomlin, the One-Woman Wonder," *The Washington Post*, October 1, 1985, p. E4.

40. Jack Kroll with David T. Friendly, "Richard Pryor, Bustin' Loose," *Newsweek* (Entertainment), May 3, 1982, p. 48.

41. Ibid., p. 50.

42. Richard Corliss, "Comedy's Post-Funny School," *Time*, May 25, 1981, p. 86.

43. Ibid.

44. Ibid.

45. Harry F. Walters, "Cosby: He's No. 1," *Newsweek*, September 2, 1985, p. 1.

46. Ibid.

47. Daniel B. Wood, "Steve Wright's G-Rated Humor Is Comic Relief," *The Christian Science Monitor*, February 3, 1986, pp. 1, 36, and 38.

48. James P. Spradley and David W. McCurdy, *The Cultural Experience: Ethnography in Complex Society* (Chicago: Science Research Association, 1972).

49. Seymour Fisher and Rhoda Fisher, *Pretend the World Is Funny and Forever: A Psychological Analysis of Comedians, Clowns, and Actors* (Hillsdale, N.J.: Lawrence Erlbaum Associates, 1981), pp. 8–9.

50. Ibid.

51. Toelken, *The Dynamics of Folklore*, p. 205.

52. Ibid.

53. Wilde, *The Great Comedians*, p. 17.

54. "Analyzing Jewish Comics," *Time*, October 2, 1978, p. 76.

55. Ibid.

56. Lawrence Mintz, "Notes Toward the Compilation of a Popular Culture Studies Methodology," *Studies in Popular Culture*, April 1982.

BIBLIOGRAPHICAL SURVEY

A definitive and chronological history of standup comedy as an art form has yet to be written, particularly a history of the genre in America since World War II. This history needs to be written now while many comedians who started in vaudeville and earlier entertainment formats are still alive to be interviewed.

Most books about standup comedians, especially biographies or autobiographies, are impressionistic and anecdotal, rather than analytic of standup comedy from historical, aesthetic, cultural, psychological, or other perspectives. A few good scholarly studies of standup comedy are found in academic journals and in the popular press. Although other books on aspects of standup comedy or predecessors of standup comedians have been written, such as treatments of circus clowns, comics in minstrelsy, vaudeville, burlesque, radio and other media, this subject is ripe for more comprehensive and scholarly research. One factor that has contributed to the lack of scholarly research on standup comedy is the lack of serious consideration given the subject by researchers in traditional disciplines.

A definitive history needs to include biographic sketches of comedians with illustrative photographs, samples of their jokes and routines, data on the content and location of performances, the audiences to whom they played, economic data on the comedian's earnings, and an interview by a skilled researcher that allows the right questions to be asked and the comedian to describe his or her particular style of humor and unique qualities in his or her own words. *Joe Franklin's Encyclopedia of Comedians* is a good example of the format such a history could take and a valuable reference. His biographic sketches are richly illustrated with photographs, many rare, of the artists, with excerpts from the routines that made these comedians famous. The book is valuable in giving an overview of the various entertainment formats that have showcased standup comedians from minstrelsy, vaudeville, burlesque, musicals, to the newer medias of silent and sound films, radio, records, and television. Many comedians featured in this history began their careers in one format such as vaudeville and made a successful transition into the newer media of radio, movies, and television.

In the same format as Franklin's *Encyclopedia* is Larry Wilde's *The Great Comedians* and *How the Great Comedy Writers Create Laughter* and William Fry and Melanie Allen's *Make 'Em Laugh: Life Studies of Comedy Writers*. Wilde is an experienced standup comedian who has played many clubs across America, appeared in prime-time TV shows, and teaches a comedy class at UCLA. In describing humor and the people who write and perform comedically in front of an audience, he realizes that he deals with an elusive and hard-to-pin-down subject. His methodology is to do in-depth interviews with a smaller sample of comedians and comedy writers than is covered in Franklin's *Encyclopedia*. He selects some of the best comedians and comedy writers in the business for his sample and allows these practitioners of humor to speak for themselves in these two important books. The results of his interviews are presented with an insider's knowledge and expertise about which questions to ask fellow comedians and comediennes and how to come to grips with this elusive subject. While comedians as a group are a diverse lot, Wilde discovered common characteristics such as great intelligence, energy, self-awareness, warmth, and a talent for getting along with people.

Phil Berger refers to his book, *The Last Laugh*, as a history of the standup comedy genre. While it is not a systematic history but more a selective look at many comedians, it does recreate for the reader a picture of the world of standup comedians with excerpts from their routines. Berger has just published an updated (October 1985) edition of *The Last Laugh* with a chapter entitled, "And Since Then," which covers standup comedy from 1975 through 1985.

Seymour and Rhoda Fisher's book, *Pretend the World Is Funny and Forever: A Psychological Analysis of Comedians, Clowns and Actors*, offers insights into standup comedians from a psychological perspective. The authors interviewed and administered various psychological tests to forty comedians such as Sid Caesar, Jimmie Walker, and Tommy Smothers, entertainers who are involved in standup comedy as a full-time profession, to learn about their life patterns. They supplemented data gathered from interviews and tests with data in published autobiographies and biographies of humorists. Their interview questions are shared with the reader. The study offers some helpful insights into the origins, motivations, and personalities of comedians and factors that shape public entertainers. The authors also studied children and college students who engaged in humor for insights into people who are humorous in ordinary situations. One interesting finding in the book is the author's disagreement with those who pin a higher incidence of psychological disturbance on comedians. The authors found the comedians in their sample to be resilient and psychologically tough, given their often-disadvantaged formative experiences and the variable audiences to whom comedians must prove their worth every performance. A useful profile of the professional comedian emerges from this study.

Also worthy of mention is John H. Towsen's book, *Clowns*. A trained clown and Ph.D. in theater, Towsen describes delight-makers in many historical times and cultures, giving the reader a sense of the range of comedians throughout history. These glimpses into the predecessors of today's standup comedians help the researcher understand the honorable tradition and historical roots and fusions of standup comedy through the ages. The author describes comics in ancient and modern, Western and non-Western, American and European cultures and examines clowning within anthropological, social, historical, and psychological perspectives.

From these various treatments of standup comedy performance the researcher can consider models for additional contributions to sophisticated humor studies.

CHECKLIST AND ADDITIONAL SOURCES

Allen, Steve. *Funny People*. Briarcliff Manor, N.Y.: Stein and Day, 1982.

Apte, Mahadev. *Humor and Laughter: An Anthropological Approach*. Ithaca, N.Y.: Cornell University Press, 1985.

Bacon, James. *How Sweet It Is: The Jackie Gleason Story*. New York: St. Martin's Press, 1985.

Berger, Philip. *The Last Laugh: The World of the Standup Comics*. New York: William Morrow, 1975.

Berryhill, Ken. *Funny Business: A Professional Guide to Becoming a Comic*. Englewood Cliffs, N.J.: Prentice-Hall, 1985.

Blair, Walter. *Native American Humor*. New York: Chandler, Harper and Row Publishers, 1960.

Blair, Walter and Raven I. McDavid, Jr., eds. *The Mirth of a Nation: America's Great Dialect Humor*. Minneapolis: University of Minnesota Press, 1983.

Brenner, David. *Soft Pretzels with Mustard*. New York: Arbor House, 1983.

Brodwin, Stanley. "Strategies of Humor: The Case of Benjamin Franklin." *Prospects* 9 (1979): 121–67.

Byron, Stuart and Elizabeth Weis. *Movie Comedy*. New York: Penguin Books, 1977.

Caesar, Sid and Bill Davidson. *Where Have I Been?* New York: Crown Publishers, 1982.

Cahn, William. *A Pictorial History of the Great Comedians*. New York: Grosset and Dunlap, New York: 1970.

Carlin, George. *Carlin: Sometimes A Little Brain Damage Can Help*. Philadelphia: Running Press, 1984.

Chaim, B., ed. *Films of Charles Chase*. New York: Revisionist Press, 1979.

Chapman, Antony and Hugh Foot, eds. *It's a Funny Thing, Humour*. London: Pergamon Press, 1977.

———, eds., *Humour and Laughter: Theory, Research, and Applications*. New York: John Wiley, 1976.

Colby, Elbridge. *Early American Humor*. Darby, Penn.: Folcroft Library Editions. 1919.

Douglas, Mary. "Jokes." In *Implicit Meanings: Essays in Anthropology*. Boston: Routledge and Kegan Paul, 1978, p. 93.

Eisner, Joel and David Krinsky. *Television Comedy Series: An Episode Guide to 153 TV Sitcoms in Syndication*. Jefferson, N.C.: McFarland and Company, Inc., 1984.

Fisher, Seymour and Rhoda Fisher. *Pretend the World Is Funny and Forever: A Psychological Analysis of Comedians, Clowns and Actors*. Hillsdale: N.J.: Lawrence Earlbaum Associates, 1981.

Foxx, Redd and Norman Miller. *The Redd Foxx of Black Humor*. Pasadena: Ward Ritchie Press, 1977.

Franklin, Joe. *Joe Franklin's Encyclopedia of Comedians*. Secaucus, N.J.: Citadel Press, 1979.

Freud, Sigmund. *Jokes and Their Relation to the Unconscious*. New York: W. W. Norton, 1960.

Fry, William and Melanie Allen. *Make 'Em Laugh: Life Studies of Comedy Writers*. Palo Alto, Calif: Science and Behavior, 1975.

Goldman, Albert. *Freakshow*. New York: Atheneum, 1971.

———. *Ladies and Gentlemen, Lenny Bruce*. New York: Ballantine, 1974.

Goldstein, Jeffrey and Paul McGhee. *The Psychology of Humor*. New York: Academic Press, 1972.

Gordon, Mel. "Lazzi: The Comic Routines of Commedia Del Arte." In *Performing Arts Resources*, edited by Ginnie Cocuzza and Barbara Cohen-Stratyner. New York: Theater Library, 1981.

Grawe, Paul H. *Comedy in Space, Time and Imagination*. Chicago: Nelson-Hall, 1983.

Green, Stanley. *The Great Clowns of Broadway*. New York: Oxford University Press, 1984.

Griffiths, Trevor. *Comedians*. New York: Grove Press, 1976.

Grote, David G. *The End of Comedy: Sit-Com and the Comedic Tradition*. Hamden, Conn.: Shoe String Publishers, 1983.

Gurewitch, Morton. *Comedy: The Irrational Vision*. Ithaca, N.Y.: Cornell University Press, 1975.

Haining, Peter. *The Legend of Charlie Chaplin*. Secaucus, N.J.: Castle, 1982.

Haskins, Jim. *Richard Pryor: A Man and His Madness: A Biography*. New York: Beaufort Books, 1984.

Heilman, Robert B. *The Ways of the World: Comedy and Society*. Pullman: University of Washington Press, 1978.

Helitzer, Melvin. *Comedy Techniques for Writers and Performers: The Hearts Theory of Humor Writing*. Athens, Ohio: Lawhead Press, 1984.

Hill, Hamlin and Walter Blair. *America's Humor*. New York: Oxford University Press, 1978.

Hugill, Beryl. *Bring on the Clowns*. Secaucus, N.J.: Chartwell Books, 1980.

Jacobs, Linda. *Gabe Kaplan: A Spirit of Laughter*. New York: EMC Publishing, 1978.

Keaton, Buster and Charles Samuels. *Buster Keaton: My Wonderful World of Slapstick*. New York: Quality Paperbacks, 1982.

Kern, Edith. *The Absolute Comic*. New York: Columbia University Press, 1980.

Kerr, Walter. *The Silent Clowns*. New York: Alfred A. Knopf, 1975.

Kirby, E. T. "The Shamanistic Origins of Popular Entertainments." *The Drama Review* 18, 1 (March 1974): 5–15.

Klapp, Orrin E. *Heroes, Villains, and Fools: The Changing American Character*. Englewood Cliffs, N.J.: Prentice-Hall, 1962.

Koenig, Teresa and Rivian Bell. *Eddie Murphy*. Minneapolis: Lerner Publications, 1985.

Koziski, Stephanie. "The Standup Comedian As Anthropologist." *Journal of Popular Culture* 18 (Fall 1984): 57–76.

Lahue, Kalton C. *World of Laughter: The Motion Picture Comedy Short 1910–1930*. Stillwater: University of Oklahoma Press, 1972.

Lax, Eric. *On Being Funny: Woody Allen and Company*. New York: Charterhouse, 1979.

Lewis, Jerry and Herb Gluck. *Jerry Lewis in Person*. New York: Pinnacle Books, 1983.

Maltin, Leonard. *Great Movie Comedians from Charlie Chaplin to Woody Allen*. New York: Crown, 1982.

Martin, Robert B. *The Triumph of Wit: A Study of Victorian Comic Theory*. New York: Oxford University Press, 1974.

Mason, Jackie. *Jackie Mason's America*. Secaucus, N.J.: Lyle Stuart, 1983.

Mast, Gerald. *The Comic Mind: Comedy and the Movies*. Chicago: University of Chicago Press, 1979.

Marx, Groucho. *The Groucho Letters*. New York: Woodhill Press, 1978.

———. *Memoirs of a Mangy Lover*. New York: Woodhill Press, 1978.

McFadden, George. *Discovering the Comic*. Princeton, N.J.: Princeton University Press, 1982.

McLean, Albert F., Jr. *American Vaudeville As Ritual*. Lexington: University of Kentucky Press, 1975.

McNamara, Brooks. *Step Right Up*. Garden City, N.Y.: Doubleday, 1976.

Mintz, Lawrence E. "Brother Jonathan's City Cousin: The Wise Fool in Urban American Social and Political Satire." Ph.D. Diss. Michigan State University, 1969.

———. "The 'New Wave' of Standup Comedians: An Introduction." *American Humor: An Interdisciplinary Newsletter*. 4, 2 (Fall 1977): 1–3.

———. "Standup Comedy As Social and Cultural Mediation." *American Quarterly* 37, 1 (Spring 1985): 71–80.

Morella, Joe. *The Amazing Careers of Bob Hope*. Moore Haven, Fla.: Rainbow Books, 1978.

Morthland, John. "Comedy Roots," *New Times* 10, 1 (January 9, 1978): 42.

Nazel, Joseph. *Richard Pryor*. Los Angeles: Holloway House, 1980.

Perry, George. *The Life of Python: And Now for Something Completely Different*. Boston: Little, Brown, 1984.

Pollio, Howard R. and John W. Edgerly. "Comedians and Comic Style." *Humour and Laughter: Theory, Research, and Applications*, edited by Antony Chapman and Hugh Foot. New York: John Wiley, 1976.

Pool, Gary. *TV Comedians*. New York: Ace Books, 1979.

Rubin, Louis D., Jr. "The Great American Joke." *Humor in America*, edited by Enid Veron. New York: Harcourt, Brace, Jovanovich, 1976, pp. 255–65.

Ruth, Marianne. *Eddie: Eddie Murphy from A to Z*. Los Angeles: Holloway House, 1985.

Sahl, Mort. *Heartland*. New York: Harcourt, Brace, Jovanovich, 1976.

Saks, Sol. *The Craft of Comedy Writing*. Dubuque: William C. Brown, Publishers, 1985.

Sandback, F. H. *The Comic Theatre of Greece and Rome*. New York: W. W. Norton, 1977.

Schaeffer, Neil. *The Art of Laughter*. New York: Columbia University Press, 1981.

Seidman, Steve. *Comedian Comedy: A Tradition in Hollywood Film*. Ann Arbor: University of Michigan Press, 1981.

Shifreen, Lawrence J. "Standup-Comedy: A Discography." *American Humor: An Interdisciplinary Newsletter* 4, 2 (Fall 1977): 19–47.

Shore, Sammy. *The Warmup: Life As a Warmup Comic*. New York: William Morrow, 1984.

Simon, Neil. *Comedy of Neil Simon*. New York: Random House, 1971.

Smith, Ronald L. *The Comedian's Encyclopedia: One Hundred Stars of Stand-Up*. New York: Garland Publishers, 1985.

Toll, Robert. *Blacking Up: The Minstrel Show in Nineteenth Century America*. New York: Oxford University Press, 1977.

———. *The Entertainment Machine: American Show Business in the Twentieth Century*. New York: Oxford University Press, 1982.

———. *On With the Show: The First Century of Show Business in America*. New York: Oxford University Press, 1976.

Towsen, John H. *Clowns*. New York: Hawthorn Books, 1976.

Veron, Enid., ed. *Humor in America*. New York: Harcourt, Brace, Jovanovich, 1976.

Wertheim, Arthur F. *Radio Comedy*. New York: Oxford University Press, 1979.

White, E. B. and Katherine S. White, eds. *A Subtreasury of American Humor*. New York: Perigee Books, 1980.

White, Kenneth S. *Savage Comedy since King Ubu: A Tangent to "The Absurd."* Lanham, Md.: University Press of America, 1977.

———. *Savage Comedy: Structure of Humor*. Lanham, Md.: University Press of America, 1978.

Wilde, Larry. *The Great Comedians*. Secaucus, N.J.: Citadel Press, 1973.

———. *How the Great Comedy Writers Create Laughter*. Chicago: Nelson-Hall, 1976.

Wilmut, Roger. *From Fringe to Flying Circus: Celebrating a Unique Generation of Comedy, 1960–1980*. New York: Methuen, 1985.

Wolcott, James. "The Young Comedians: But Seriously Folks." *Village Voice* 19, 52 (December 30, 1974): 8.

Woodward, Bob. *Wired: The Short Life and Fast Times of John Belushi*. Austin: S&S Press, 1984.

Youngman, Henny. *Take My Jokes, Please*. New York: Simon and Schuster, 1983.

◆ 7 ◆

Women's Humor

Zita Dresner

OVERVIEW

If American humor, in general, has been slighted by historians and literacy critics, the work of American women humorists has doubly suffered from a lack of scholarly consideration. Omitted, by and large, from the major anthologies, pioneer studies, and modern analyses, which have served to advance a canon and theoretical framework for a male tradition in American humor,[1] women's humorous writing has also received relatively little attention from those feminist critics who have been working to reclaim, reevaluate, and reconstruct the work and significance of American women novelists, poets, journalists, diarists, and essayists. While a tendency to view humor as too topical, too elusive, or too unimportant a genre of literature may account, in part, for its overall dearth of critical treatment,[2] other reasons exist as well for the particular neglect of women humorists.

The position of women, historically and culturally, in American society is obviously one factor in both the lack of recognition of women's humor and the kind of humor women have created. Recent studies by feminist scholars, in particular, have documented many of the legal, economic, political, social, and cultural factors that have operated, from the Puritan era through the twentieth century, to limit women's lives. Such factors as women's subordinate status as citizens, their lack of access to education, to the vote, and to a public voice, their relegation to the domestic sphere and to legal and economic dependence upon men, their exclusion from professions, careers, and positions of power or decision making in both the political and corporate arenas, their castigation by men for attempts to usurp what were defined in different periods as masculine roles and prerogatives, and their treatment, as both negative stereotypes and minor authors, by the male literary establishment have all been cited as constraints on women's participation in American society and, especially, on women writers—determining what, how, and to whom they have written.[3]

In the field of humor, women have faced additional obstacles related to the nature and functions of humor and to the appropriation by men of the role of the joker. Among these obstacles (which will be discussed in more detail later) has been the generally acknowledged antifeminine bias in what has been labeled "native" American humor. Defined by Jesse Bier, in *The Rise and Fall of American Humor*, as a "rampant misogyny" in male humorists from Billings to Thurber, this bias has been evident not only in the relative absence of women as primary humorous characters, but also in their functions as negative stereotypes in masculine humor. Undoubtedly, it has contributed as well to perpetuating the assumption that women lack, or ought to lack, a capacity for humor and wit—an assumption that feminists and female humorists felt compelled to argue against as late as a decade ago.[4] Other barriers to the recognition and acceptance of women humorists have been the masculine control of the media and the concomitant conditioning of both sexes to laugh at what men have defined as humorous, the socialization of women to be submissive rather than aggressive, the contradictions between male and female perceptions of incongruity, resulting from their different cultural experiences, and the cultivation by women of a humorous style that, both by choice and necessity, has been considered less political, less iconoclastic, less dynamic, and, therefore, less significant than the male variety.

Nevertheless, although American women's humor still needs to be retrieved and assessed, there is ample evidence that women have overtly and covertly been employing the tools and techniques of humor in their writing since the beginning of American letters and that their work, in addition to contributing to humor's importance in American culture, establishes a tradition of its own.

HISTORICAL DEVELOPMENT

Studies of early American humor tend to identify two general modes of humorous expression: the formal, consciously satiric, derived from British models, and the informal, sometimes unconsciously ironic or sardonic, found in diaries, journals, and letters. The first category includes works from Nathaniel Ward's 1647 satire of Puritan society, *The Simple Cobbler of Agawam*, to the patriotic satires of the "Connecticut Wits" and the political essays of Benjamin Franklin; whereas the sceond is usually illustrated by reference to Captain John Smith's narrations of his explorations and experiences in the New World, Samuel Sewall's diaries, William Byrd's accounts of his travels in Virginia and North Carolina, and even Franklin's *Autobiography*.[5] The latter works variously display some of the traits associated with the development of native American humor: the use of vivid, concrete detail for humorous effect, of exaggeration, of a comic persona

whose irony is directed both at himself and at those around him, and of a narrative
style that expresses a taste for the earthy and physical aspects of life. Women's
writing in the seventeenth and eighteenth centuries also reflects these two strains,
but with differences in focus, style, and tone from that of their male counterparts.

Anne Bradstreet (1612–1672), the first poet to be published in America, has
been considered a meditative rather than satirical writer, although her work has
been noted for its use of the devices of wit, derived from Elizabethan and
Metaphysical poetry, to express the poet's thoughts on marriage, motherhood,
creativity, and religion. In addition, recent studies by feminist critics have seen
in Bradstreet's work an ironic treatment of woman's subordinate place in a Puritan
order that chastised her intellectual ambition, attributed the fall of mankind to
her moral weakness, and denied her more than marginal participation in political,
social, and religious affairs.[6] However, in contrast to the somber, caustic satire
of Ward's excoriation of Puritan transgressions in manners, fashions, and religious practices, particularly those of women, Bradstreet adopted a gentler irony
to speak of more personal concerns. Conscious of her vulnerable position as a
woman writer in a culture hostile to "literary ladies," and aware of the penalties
meted out to women, like her sister Sarah Keane, who were excommunicated
and expelled from communities for daring to preach, Bradstreet used a double-
edged irony in poems like "To Her Book" (which introduced the second edition
of *The Tenth Muse*) both to mock—and, thereby, defuse criticism of—her pre-
sumption to write and publish poetry and to challenge "Each carping tongue/
Who says my hand a needle better fits," sardonically adding that "if what I do
prove well, it won't advance? They'll say it's stolen, or else it was by chance."
In other poems—such as "In Reference to Her Children," "A Letter to Her
Husband, Absent upon Public Employment," "The Flesh and the Spirit," and
Meditations Divine and Moral—Bradstreet's irony, as well as her puns, conceits,
and witty aphorisms, help to depict positive relationships between mother and
child, husband and wife, individual and Nature, and individual and God. What
characterizes these relationships are the same qualities that Wendy Martin finds
in Bradstreet's view of the ordering principles of the universe in *The Four
Elements*: balance, mutuality, and cooperation replacing hierarchy, the patriar-
chal ordering system.[7] These values, in part, make up what Martin calls the
"female aesthetic-ethic" in women's writing.

The second mode of early American humor is evident in the diary kept by
Sarah Kemble Knight (1666–1727) of a five-month journey she began in October
1704 from Boston to New Haven to New York City and back to Boston. Published
in 1825 as *The Journal of Madam Knight*, her account contains many of the
elements of humor found in John Smith and William Byrd: satiric portraits of
backwoods settlers, a keen eye and ear for local color and idiom, anecdotes
about regional customs and manners, self-parody, and even humorous verse and
scatological references. As a Puritan woman imbued with a notion of proper
"housewifery," Knight made a prime target of her humor the landladies who
provided uncomfortable lodgings and unappetizing food at the inns on her route,

such as the woman who greeted her "with her hair about her ears, and hands at full pay scratching," and who served such an inedible meal that "we left it, and paid sixpence a piece for our Dinners, which was only smell." Her wit was also directed against others who lacked her Puritan ideas of appropriate conduct, such as the rowdy drinkers who kept her awake at an inn and the farmers of Fairfield, Connecticut, who "have aboundance of sheep, whose very Dung brings them great gain, with part which they pay their Parsons salary. And they Grudg that, prefering their Dung before their minister." For Knight, as for other Puritans, as W. Howland Kenney remarks, satire directed toward those outside their community "helped them order their world and protect their identity."[8]

In the eighteenth century, the most recognized female exponent of the satiric mode was Mercy Otis Warren (1728–1814), whose political dramas and poems have earned her a position as one of the most important of the Revolutionary satirists. Undoubtedly because she was the sister of Boston patriot James Otis, wife of General James Warren, and intimate friend of Abigail and John Adams, she was encouraged to develop a political conscience and to employ her wit to further the Patriot cause, despite the general criticism to which women were subject if they addressed themselves to politics.[9] While there is some question of her authorship of *The Blockheads* (1776) and *The Motley Assembly* (1779), the three Revolutionary-era pamphlet plays attributed to her—*The Adulateur* (1773), *The Defeat* (1773), and *The Group* (1775)—were similar to those of her male contemporaries in attacking the Tories and the British for both personal and political villainy, and in lauding the Patriots for virtue and integrity. However, two distinguishing features of Warren's plays, noted by Benjamin Franklin V, in his introduction to her work, were her use of nature imagery to reinforce the corruption of the Tories and the purity of the Patriots, and her concern with the lot of women.[10] In *The Group*, for example, Warren depicted the abusive and callous treatment suffered by three women from their Tory husbands and concluded the play with a monologue recited by a female Patriot who predicts that Nature will remain out of balance until the Patriots destroy the British and restore Freedom, thus ending on a note of "hope for the Patriots, for women, and for nature, all of which have been violated by the government's men."[11]

In her two five-act tragedies, written between 1783 and 1785, *The Sack of Rome* and *The Ladies of Castile*, Warren again dealt with the sufferings of women in political upheavals over which they have no control, as well as illustrated the tragic consequences that occur when the moral and humane qualities, represented by the women, are defeated by male tyranny and corruption.

Discussions of Warren's satiric poetry have generally focused on her political pieces: "The Squabble of the Sea Nymphs," written at John Adams' request, which parodies the Boston Tea Party; "The Genius of America," which chastizes the frivolous behavior of some Americans while others are still fighting and dying for freedom; and "to the Hon. J. Winthrop, Esq.," which satirizes women who were more concerned with obtaining British finery than supporting America's cessation of trade with Britain. However, her use of irony and wit are also evident in other poems that show her, like Bradstreet, at odds with prevailing masculine views in her rejection of Deism ("To Torrismond"), of fatalism ("To Mr.—"), and of sexual laxity in "To a Young Lady," a parody of the *carpe diem* mode in its exhortation to women to "Snatch every moment time shall give,/ And uniformly virtuous live."

While Warren's consciousness about issues affecting the rights of women in the new republic were more openly expressed in her private correspondance than in her published work, Susanna Haswell Rowson (1762–1824) and Judith Sargent Murray (1751–1820) used satire and wit to address questions raised and hotly debated in the wake of the publication of Mary Wollstonecraft's *A Vindication of the Rights of Women* (1792), concerning women's place in the new society. Rowson, whose *Charlotte, a Tale of Truth* (London, 1791; Philadelphia, 1794) was a bestseller in both England and America, wrote two plays for a Philadelphia theater company in which she acted for a time. *Slaves in Algiers* (1795), a comedy about the capture and enslavement of Americans by Barbary pirates, was calculated to rouse audiences to action to free the Americans held in Algiers. In addition, as Eve Kornfeld argues, Rowson used the play to assert a woman's right to deal with political, as well as moral, issues and to show a connection between civic virtue (illustrated by the female American characters in the play) and the preservation of liberty.[12] In avowing that "a woman can face danger with as much spirit, and as little fear, as the bravest man amongst you," the heroine suggests that women have a complementary but equal moral role, with men's military role, to play in maintaining America's political integrity and independence.

Murray, in her essays, articles, comedies, and fiction, also expressed a connection between women's moral behavior and the political functioning of the Republic, responding in large part to male assumptions about woman's physical, mental, and moral weakness that were used to justify woman's exclusion from political participation in the Republic. Representing what Nancy Cott calls "the equalitarian feminist view" of the late eighteenth century,[13] Murray's work (much of which was originally published in the *Massachusetts Magazine*, 1792–1794 and collected in *The Gleaner*, 1798) attacked the idea that women were inferior to men and protested the continued restrictions on women's training, education, and political activity in a society that had her two comedies of manners, *Virtue Triumphant* (1795) and *The Traveller Returned* (1796), Murray employed many of the conventions of the genre—comic stereotypes of drawing-room figures and conniving servants, mistaken identities, and unexpected happy reunions—both to provide positive models for republican women and to demonstrate that a proper social order is achieved when political and personal virtue, reason and sentiment, domestic and civic behavior, and the moral values of men and women in marriage are balanced. In *Virtue Triumphant*, for example, Murray depicted two contrasting relationships between men and women that are out of balance and, therefore, unfulfilling. The lovers of the first possess equal virtues, but the woman, Eliza Clairville, lacks the social and economic equality with her lover that she believes would make them suitable marriage partners. Mr. and

Mrs. Bloomville, the husband and wife of the second, are equal in upbringing and social class but have become alienated by Mrs. Bloomville's loss of sight of her responsibilities as a wife and her indulgence in the frivolities of fashion. In *The Traveller Returned*, Murray's use of a political subplot develops an analogy (similar to Rowson's) between civic and personal virtue in which disloyalty for personal pleasure or gain threatens the stability of both a marriage and the state and in which loyalty to a spouse and a government that reason shows to be deserving of that loyalty lead to order and felicity. The targets of satire in both plays are those who value outward trappings of social fashion more than inner qualities of character, who permit sentiment to override reason, and who put personal indulgence before moral commitment. Both are also notable of Murray's insistence that mutual friendship and respect between men and women—rather than sentimental feelings of love and passion—are the basis for a stable and happy marriage.

In other essays and articles, Murray employed her wit to demonstrate women's capabilities in all areas of human endeavor and to promote the education and training of women for occupations that would make them financially independent, thereby freeing them from the *necessity* to marry and granting them the opportunity for self-reliance. Self-sufficiency, Murray believed, would enhance women's self-esteem, provide them with a source of livelihood if they remained unmarried or were widowed, develop moral character by directing their energies toward self-improvement rather than snaring a husband, and better prepare them to execute their duties as wife and mother if and when they chose to marry. These duties included running their households efficiently, educating their children to be virtuous and loyal citizens, and contributing to their husbands' well-being through their domestic industry, moral support, and intellectual companionship.

Murray's advocacy of a proper education for women, at least in part as an antidote to the sentimentalism espoused in the popular literature of the late eighteenth century, was echoed during the nineteenth century, as the sentimental novel proliferated, in the work of women humorists. The earliest of these portraits of women infected with sentimental delusions appears in Tabitha Tenney's satirical novel, *Female Quixotism* (1801), which recounts the romantic misadventures of Dorcasina Sheldon, from young womanhood to old age. Having accepted the romantic claptrap promulgated by the novels to which she is addicted, Dorcasina rejects a perfectly suitable young man because his proposal of marriage lacks the passionate effusions of fictional lovers. She then falls victim to a series of adventurers and connivers who prey on her romantic delusions while eyeing her money. Although presented as a ridiculous figure because of her blindness to the men's motivations and to her own behavior and vanity, Dorcasina is also made sympathetic to the reader, not just because of her victimization but because Tenney endows her with virtues of kindness, candor, and generosity. When, at the end of the novel, Dorcasina recognizes the corrupting influence of novels on her life and repents having wasted her life in pursuit of illusions of happiness, she reinforces Tenney's message that women need to be taught life "as it really is . . . chequered with good and evil,'' and to learn that marriage is not all "transport, joy, and felicity,'' but attended with "cares and anxieties.''

Presenting life as it really is was Caroline Kirkland's intent in *A New Home— Who'll Follow?* (1839), which describes the life and manners of settlers in the then remote parts of Michigan. Like Knight, Kirkland had a sharp eye and ear for the language and behavior of the people who became the subjects of her satirical sketches and whom she viewed from the point of view of a woman from the East (her persona Mary Clavers) unprepared for the roughness of backwoods life. In her depiction of Miss Eloise Fidler, a poet who comes to Michigan to find a husband, Kirkland ridiculed both the effusiveness of sentimental poetry and the pretensions of Miss Fidler, who seeks in a lover a French surname that she can adopt in marriage and who dresses in inappropriately fancy shoes and gowns that prevent her from venturing outdoors and communing with the Nature she claims as her poetic inspiration. The treatment of Miss Fidler is just one example of the "strong antiromance sentiment" that Josephine Donovan observes in the book and that is also reflected in Mrs. Danforth and Cleory Jenkins, whose language and deportment give the lie to the "cult of true womanhood."[14] While Kirkland's work, like that of later male frontier humorists, helped to dispel some of the romantic fantasies of life in the West, her focus on the difficulties of women's existence on the outskirts of civilization lacked the nostalgia, evident in male humorists, for the male camaraderie and the freedom from social constraints (imposed, in their view, by female notions of gentility) that the frontier afforded.[15]

Women humorists were also concerned about the effects of gentility, urbanization, and industrialization on society, but, more particularly, on women's lives. Like the male humorists, they often satirized the genteel pretensions and frivolous behavior of women, but their purpose was not simply ridicule per se. They also offered positive role models and exposed the social and political conditions that limited women's sphere and reinforced negative female behavior, including the masculine attitudes that encouraged it. Anna Cora Mowatt's popular comedy *Fashion* (1850), for example, dealt with the clash between urban and rural values and ways of life, an important concern of both male and female writers, by juxtaposing the Tiffanys, a socially aspiring New York City family, with Adam Truemen and his daughter Gertrude, whose honesty, integrity, and forthrightness save the Tiffanys from the blackmail and ruin to which their pursuit of fashion has led them. Although Mrs. Tiffany and her daughter are mainly responsible for the situation, the corrupting influence of city life is also blamed, as is the absence of any productive occupations for women, other than striving for social position through marriage and through the acquisition of material trappings deemed marks of fashion. In addition, the character of Gertrude, as much as that of her father, provides a model of republican virtue and demonstrates that a proper upbringing and education will produce an admirably moral, industrious, self-reliant woman. A more extensive satire of urban artificiality appeared in Ann Stephens' *High Life in New York* (1854), which utilized a New

England Yankee "wise-fool" figure to expose, in a series of letters, the sham and affectations of New York society, in the same manner as Seba Smith created Yankee Major Jack Downing to comment on the political corruption in Washington. Adopting the persona of Jonathan Slick, whose naiveté and incredulous tone underscore the satire, Stephens targeted men as well as women for their fashions in dress, the hypocrisy of their drawing-room behavior, their obsession with money and status, their courting of foreigners—especially those affecting titles—and their general falsity in morals and manners.

While country virtues were being idealized by some, Frances Whicher, whose *The Widow Bedott Papers* (1856) was one of the most popular midcentury works of humor, used rustic settings and narrators to attack the pretentiousness, narrow-mindedness, and vicious gossip that she found rampant in small-town life. In particular, she ridiculed the excesses endemic to gentility, using women as both subjects and objects of her humor. *Widow Spriggins*, her earliest work, is narrated by a young country woman, Permilly Spriggins, who, like Tenney's Dorcasina, models herself on the life of a heroine of a sentimental novel and serves as a burlesque of the sentimental female. In *The Widow Bedott Papers*, Whicher turned from the foolishness of a girl to the affectations of a garrulous, middle-aged widow, obsessed with finding a new husband. Although Whicher expressed some sympathy for Bedott's motivation—the loss of status and lack of purpose and place experienced by a widow, especially in a small town—she lampooned both Bedott, a stereotypical busybody and gossip, and the townswomen who formed her circle for rudeness, self-righteousness, pretentiousness, and mean self-interest. In her *Aunt Maguire Letters*, Whicher shifted from narrators like Spriggins and Bedott, who were the objects of most of the humor, to a common-sense country woman, whose tone of curiosity and befuddlement at the behavior of those around her, especially of the women of her sewing circle, again reveals the small-mindedness and smug self-interest that Whicher deplored. Though male characters are also satirized by Whicher, her main concern was with the ways in which women betray their nature, themselves, and each other by falling prey to meanness and vanity, by ignoring the needs of others, and by acceding to the materialistic values of the male marketplace.

As the women's rights movement, which began with the Seneca Falls convention of 1848, gained momentum in the latter third of the century, Marietta Holley promoted the cause of women's equality in twenty-one volumes of humor, published between 1873 and 1914. Using the vernacular mode, Holley adopted the persona of Samantha Allen, a farm wife who, like Aunt Maguire, represents reason and moderation, to address "the great subject of Wimmin's Rites" in practical, down-to-earth terms. In her first book, *My Opinions and Betsey Bobbett's*, Holley reversed the popular, established images of the sexes by making Samantha physically larger and stronger than her husband, Josiah, as well as more logical, less susceptible to fads and fashions, and less dependent. Like Whicher, she derided the gossiping, social apathy, and genteel pretensions of small-town women, but she also attacked masculine attitudes supporting women's inequality by arguing that women's rights were congruent with women's nature, whereas the genteel ideal of passivity corrupted it by promoting idleness and vanity. Through Samantha's discussions of her domestic responsibilities with Betsey Bobbett, another caricature of a husband-hunting spinster given to sentimental versifying and effusions about women's need for a man to cling to, and through her depiction of women who suffered degrading marriages to weak and abusive husbands, Holley offered a realistic view of marriage that countered the sentimental ideal. In other books that take Samantha traveling to fashionable spas, World's Fairs, and Europe, Holley extended her range of subjects to include racial prejudice, political ethics, social attitudes, and regional manners both in America and abroad. Throughout her work, as Nancy Walker notes, "Samantha's implacable logic is the source of much of the humor, contrasted as it is with the illogicality of sentiment or prejudice, and the homely metaphor serves . . . to reinforce common sense."[16]

Three of the most popular women humorists who did not write in the vernacular mode also focused, in different ways, on women's lives and women's place. Phoebe Cary typifies the kinds of humorous verse that appear in Kate Sanborn's *The Wit of Women* (1885). Directed in part against the excesses of sentimentalism, Cary's *Poems and Parodies* (1854) exhibits a polished wit in her parodies of well-known works of literature and anticipates Dorothy Parker in the tone of her poems that humorously address relationships between the sexes and the socialization of women to view marriage as their only acceptable goal. These characteristics are evident in even a brief excerpt from "A Psalm of Life":

> Tell me not, in idle jungle,
>   Marriage is an empty dream,
> For the girls is dead that's single
>   And things are not what they seem.

Sara Willis Parton, a newspaper columnist who published two volumes of articles, *Fern Leaves From Fanny's Portfolio* (1853 and 1854), under the pseudonym of Fanny Fern, is best known as a sentimental writer. However, she also produced numerous pieces of satire on the behavior and attitudes of the fashionable and on prevailing notions of the women's sphere. For example, she mocked the idea that married women were necessarily happy or happier than single women, and, like Murray, she attributed much of the unhappiness in marriage to imbalances—but of power rather than virtue. An advocate of female education and independence, she argued that, if the height of ambition in women was to have diamonds, as some men claimed, that was because men valued women of wealth more than women of character.

Another journalist and popular social commentator, Mary Abigail Dodge, who used the pseudonym of Gail Hamilton, combined a subtle wit and sense of the incongruous in discussing a range of topics in essays and articles published in magazines and newspapers and collected in books that appeared mostly in the

1860s and 1870s. One of her recurrent subjects was the constraints on women, fostered by the cult of true womanhood and the glorification of the self-sacrificing mother. In *Wool-Gathering* (1867), an account of her travels in America, and in *Twelve Miles from a Lemon* (1874), a description of country living, she recalls Kirkland and Knight in her point of view, style of description, and ability to see some of her own behavior and attitudes, as well as those of others, in a humorous light.

Throughout the nineteenth century, women humorists spoke to the conditions of women's lives, delineating the incongruities between the realities and the illusions fostered by sentimental or genteel images of the "true" woman, encouraging an enlargement of woman's sphere, and protesting the restrictions that, in barring women from utilizing their talents and abilities in the public arena, countenanced their dissipating their energies in the pursuit of husbands, social status, and fashion.

By the turn of the century, a shift in humor began to appear, reflecting the increase in urban over rural population, the growth of new publications for humor that appealed to the values and concerns of a more sophisticated metropolitan culture, the influx of journalists into the field of humor, and the changes brought about by advances in technology, new theories in psychology (especially those of Freud) and in the social sciences, and the emergence of the New Woman.[17] Although dialect humor continued, the locale changed from country to city, from rustic to immigrant, and the "crackerbox philosopher" of vernacular humor evolved into what Norris Yates labeled the "Little Man": an average male who feels less independent economically, less secure psychologically, and less important and in control both socially and in his own home.[18] Feelings of anxiety, confusion, and resentment over men's sense of loss in stature and control were often expressed by male humorists, from Ade to Thurber, in attacks on women who rebelled against traditional roles or usurped "masculine" positions, as well as what H. L. Mencken called the "Boobus Americanus," who mindlessly accepted the shallow values of middle-class culture and ambition. Women humorists responded to these changes, particularly as they affected women's lives, by entering into the "war between the sexes" and by dealing with the ramifications of increased freedom in dress and social deportment and of greater opportunities in education, employment, and political involvement.

Before the passage of the suffrage amendment in 1920, writers like Josephine Daskam, in *Fables for the Fair: Cautionary Tales for Damsels Not Yet in Distress* (1901), and Helen Rowland, in *The Sayings of Mrs. Solomon* (1913), worked both with and against established stereotypes of men and women in giving advice to women on how to deal with men, while Alice Duer Miller, in *Are Women People?* (1915) and *Women Are People!* (1917), employed a caustic wit to parody in verse both antisuffrage arguments and those who advanced them. Also reacting against negative stereotypes and to changes in woman's opportunities, Mary Roberts Rinehart produced, between 1910 and 1937, a series of stories that challenged the traditional image of the man-hungry old maid by featuring an independent spinster, Letitia ("Tish") Carberry who, content with her unmarried status, employs her time and energy in adventures that involve her in racing, flying, camping, catching crooks, and even liberating a town from the enemy in World War I.

In the 1920s, Dorothy Parker and Anita Loos were the best-known female humorists who entered the war between the sexes. Like the men, they explored the feelings of suspicion, distrust, and betrayal that had begun to dominate relationships between the sexes, but rather than blaming women's "emancipation" or desire to "wear the pants," they attributed the changing values and modes of behavior of the society as a whole to the alteration in men's and women's expectations of and commitments to each other. They also recognized that the "new morality" was, in many ways, a double-edged sword, demanding more accountability of women while granting them more freedom. In Parkers's poems, for example, the speaker is often caught between the romantic illusions of the nineteenth century and the antiromantic or antisentimental attitudes fashionable among the "smart set" of the 1920s. The cynicism with which she treats the themes of permanence and fidelity in love and the pose of indifference she assumes toward the pain of rejection suffered or inflicted in the pursuit of love are defenses against despair over the absence in her life of the grand passion that she craves, fears, and, consequently, mocks as antithetical to a culture that celebrated carefree and casual relationships between men and women. In her stories, Parker created a type of "little woman," as bewildered and victimized by shifting mores and roles as men. The conflicts depicted, moreover, suggest that, for all the pretense made of sexual equality in the twenties, the average woman was still ultimately dependent upon men—emotionally, as well as socially and economically.

In *Gentlemen Prefer Blondes* (1925), Anita Loos focused more on the connection between sexual manipulation and changing socioeconomic values than on emotional manipulation. Influenced by Mencken, Loos attempted to create in Lorelei Lee a female American "boob," in order to attack the opportunism that Loos saw dominating all aspects of American life. Although Lorelei was a prime target of Loos' satire, she also served as a vehicle for social satire through her ability to manipulate to her advantage masculine illusions and expectations about the nature of heterosexual attachments and to adapt the strategies of capitalism to her dealings with men.

During the 1930s, the sardonic tone and style of Parker's stories appeared in Mary McCarthy's *The Company She Keeps* (1942), while the Lorelei type was perpetuated in Hollywood films about gold diggers and in the characters of Mae West, who also incorporated the traits of the tough, independent, wise-cracking female adopted by the heroines of thirties comedies. However, the psychological and economic dislocations produced by the Great Depression and World War II resulted in a reversal in women's status after the war, as women were compelled to relinquish their wartime jobs to returning soldiers and admonished to return to the home as a first step in the process of "normalization." As the old shibboleths about women's primary duties to home and family were dusted off and a campaign to refeminize the American woman got off the ground, a new trend in women's humor began to develop and eventually dominate in the decades of the fifties and sixties. This "domestic" humor concerned the trials and tribulations of middle-class housewives who, in increasing numbers, lived in the suburbs from which their husbands commuted to work, and associated primarily with other women, children, and unscrupulous repairmen.

Two of the most popular transitional writers were Cornelia Otis Skinner, who began publishing humorous sketches in the thirties, and Betty MacDonald (pseudonym of Ann Elizabeth Campbell Bard), whose *The Egg and I* (1945) recalled the work of Kirkland and the local colorists of the late nineteenth century in its intent to provide a realistic portrayal of rural life. It also created a model of the harried, incompetent housewife found in later domestic humorists. Although Skinner wrote pieces about her experiences as an actress, speaker, and traveller, many of her sketches are written from the viewpoint of a wife and mother who must soothe her husband's ruffled feathers, endure the vicissitudes of pregnancy, and suffer the condescension and intimidation of salespeople, servants, and other mothers when she takes her son shopping or to parties. Intimidation is a major theme in Skinner's work, whose persona seems perpetually in a state of anxiety and embarrassment over her inability to measure up to what she perceives as other people's standards of appearance and performance. Betty MacDonald's persona is also intimidated: by her husband, who takes her off to live in a remote section of the Olympic Mountains and expects her to perform her housekeeping duties perfectly with primitive equipment, and by female neighbors, like Mrs. Hicks, who glories in drudgery and expects the same from others. However, both Skinner and MacDonald, in evoking laughter at their personae's insecurities, also call into question the values and attitudes that make them feel inadequate.

Later domestic humorists also appear to have had a dual purpose in describing women's lives as homemakers. Shirley Jackson, in *Life Among the Savages* (1953) and *Raising Demons* (1957), presents on the surface the image of a harried housewife who, nevertheless, enjoys the responsibilities of raising energetic if, sometimes, alien-seeming children and of trying to establish order in a chaotic household. She is akin to MacDonald, however, in the undertone of depression that emerges from her sense of isolation in a Vermont town where she is treated like an outsider and in the anger that surfaces at her husband's domineering posture, as well as his dependency and childishness in certain situations. Jean Kerr, a successful playwright, was closer to Skinner in style and tone. The pieces collected in her books, from *Please Don't Eat the Daisies* (1957) to *Penny Candy* (1970), cover a range of topics: parodies of popular literature, descriptions of child-rearing and homemaking tasks that overwhelm her, accounts of some of the frailties and foibles of men, theater talk, and discussions of her never-ending battle to conform to images of women promoted in the media. Although Phyllis McGinley tended to present an idyllic picture of suburban life and to glorify the roles of wife and mother, even some of her verses reveal the emptiness and idleness of women's lives in the suburbs—a theme central to Margaret Halsey's *This Demi-Paradise: A Westchester Diary* (1960).

In the late sixties and early seventies, encouraged by Betty Friedan's analysis in *The Feminine Mystique* (1963) of the discontent of middle-class housewives and by the rebirth of the women's movement, a spate of women's novels appeared, beginning with Sue Kaufman's *Diary of a Mad Houswife* (1967), which documented, with satirical bite, the stultification of women's lives as full-time homemakers and, with the publication of Erica Jong's *Fear of Flying* (1975), which challenged masculine attitudes about woman's nature and place in every area, including the sexual. However, for women not willing, ready, or able to throw in the towel, burn their bras, and leave the security of their homes for the challenges of a "liberated" life, domestic humor retained its popularity as a kind of safety valve for the expression of confusion and resentment about the housewife's role and status. At the same time, the tone of this humor began to change as writers like Erma Bombeck and Judith Viorst (and comediennes like Joan Rivers and Phyllis Diller) challenged the notion that being a model housewife was a fulfilling full-time occupation. By detailing the daily drudgery, problems of child-rearing, lack of intellectual stimulation, and unrealistic, often conflicting demands of what constituted the housewife's existence, Bombeck underscored the incongruities between the reality and glorified media image of being a housewife, encouraging covert rebellion against the role. Like Diller and Rivers, who revelled in their bad cooking and poor housekeeping, Bombeck made fun of "supermoms" and their obsessions, presenting the incompetence of her persona as a refusal to take seriously what she saw as absurd and vacuous activities and, thus, urging women to reassess their behavior and attitudes in order to make choices congruent with their individual needs rather than with the models promoted by advertisers and self-proclaimed experts. Judith Viorst appealed to a better-educated, more urban-oriented and politically liberal group of women who, like her persona, agonize over discrepancies between their social conscience and middle-class life-style, their positions as housewives and their fantasies about glamorous careers, the mundane reality of who they are and their romantic illusions of who they could or should be. Her verse suggests that no one can have it all and that contentment comes from making choices based on a frank and rational evaluation of oneself and then taking responsibility for those choices.

Alongside domestic humor, a feminist humor began to emerge in the late sixties, abetted by the Women's Liberation Movement. As demonstrated in Gloria Kaufman and Mary Kay Blakely's collection *Pulling Our Own Strings* (1980), feminist humor reinforced the validity of women's perceptions about their oppression and subordinate status, undermined the bases of male chauvinism, and supported the legitimacy of women's demands for political, social, and economic equality. In contrast to domestic humor, which satirized popular images of the ideal housewife by creating representative personae who failed to conform to the ideal, feminist humor was more overtly and aggressively directed against repressive male attitudes and institutions, as Gloria Steinem's "If Men Could Menstruate" illustrates. A new aggressiveness and iconoclasm was also apparent in *Titters* (1976), a collection of humor by women, edited by Deanna Stillman and Anne Beatts, that purported to prove not only that women were at least as funny as men, but also that, if not censored by men, women's humor could be as caustic, nihilistic, and irreverent as the male humor that had marked the previous decade.

The refusal to be limited to "female" subject matter, genteel language, a self-deprecating style, and a passive or accommodating stance has been the hallmark of new women humorists of the last decade—especially of performers and media writers, sometimes to the detriment of their careers.[19] These traits are observable in the characters of Lily Tomlin, whose telephone operator, Ernestine, for example, uses corporate power and intimidation to cow her callers; in the aggressive stance and sexual subject matter of recent standup comediennes; in the self-reliance and independence of the Jamaican woman or the street jargon and irreverence of the junkie dude created by Whoopi Goldberg. The iconoclasm and hip tone of Fran Liebowitz's satiric essays in *Metropolitan Life* (1978) and *Social Studies* (1980); Cyra McFadden's lampoon of the hedonism and pretentiousness represented by the California life-style in *The Serial* (1977); the ironic treatment of political and social behavior by columnists like Ellen Goodman and Joan Didion; and the attacks on white society's values and attitudes, as well as on those aspects of black culture that oppress women in the work of black writers like Ntozake Shange, Toni Cade Bambara, Toni Morrison, and Alice Walker also attest to women's confidence in their right and ability to speak without constraint about any topic that concerns them both as women and human beings.

Whether or not these trends continue in a conservative era, dominated by an administration hostile to women's equality, remains to be seen. But it is unlikely that women in the future, any more than in the past, will cease using humor to expose the flaws and failings they perceive in the values, mores, attitudes, and institutions of the society in which they live.

THEMES AND ISSUES

Anyone undertaking research in American women's humor will probably experience both the excitement and the obstacles involved in the exploration of any relatively uncharted territory. Some of the difficulties stem from the problem of finding primary sources, and others, from the lack of a body of critical theory and extensive scholarly analysis.

Prior to the nineteenth century, the caveats against women writing and against the public expression of female opinion on the administration of public affairs resulted in an absence of a complete published record of women's experiences. The diaries, journals, and private correspondence used by recent historians to reconstruct women's lives and thinking in the early years of American history reveal women's use of the devices of humor but have yet to be studied and analyzed by humor researchers. In addition, more thorough studies of known figures are needed. For example, although Warren has been discussed as a political satirist within the context of the work produced during the same period by men, there has been little analysis of her total output as a reflection of her position as a woman during the Revolutionary War and establishment of the Republic. Also, Bradstreet, Rowson, and Murray have received attention from literary scholars and historians more in terms of their view on women's roles and status than of their use of the devices of wit and humor to express their ideas. The proliferation of women's writing in the nineteenth century encouraged the publication of women humorists, but the tasks of searching, recovering, and assessing their work still need to be done.

In addition, the ramifications of the notion that humor is a masculine prerogative, either lacking or best suppressed in a "true" woman, require further study. A debate aired in two 1884 issues of *The Critic*[20] over whether or not women were capable of humor motivated Kate Sanborn to publish *The Wit of Women* (1885) specifically to prove that women could and did produce humor in a variety of forms. Although her collection failed to end the debate, it did reveal some of the reasons why women's humor was (and continued to be) unrecognized or considered subordinate to men's humor by male anthologists and critics, and why, therefore, it has not been easily accessible. First, Sanborn suggested that the best women's humor was expressed on an impromptu basis within groups exclusively female. Second, many women published in magazines directed to women and children instead of in humor publications, like Porter's *The Spirit of the Times*, which were essentially restricted to men. Other women, like Fanny Fern and Phoebe Carey, published their humorous work along with the "genteel" poetry or "sentimental" stories for which they were more commonly read by female readers. Moreover, given their primary audience of women and, frequently, young people, women humorists wrote about the experiences of women's lives—which generally took place in the domestic or circumscribed social sphere of drawing room, parlor, churchwomen's meeting, sewing circle, or shop—in language and tone considered appropriate for such an audience. During the same period, on the other hand, male humorists were abandoning the formal, English model of social satire and developing what has been called a "native" brand of humor that focused on masculine activities in the "unfeminized" locales of the backwoods, frontier town, and mining camp, and that featured comic heroes like lumberjacks, tricksters, mountain men, and other frontier types. At the same time, they developed a style characterized, particularly after the Civil War, by an irreverence, wise-cracking ribaldry, physicality, and ridicule of women that served to mock the gentility of a society becoming increasingly middle class and, to male humorists, feminized.[21] The prohibitions against women adopting masculine modes of expression and the differences between men's and women's experiences, concerns, and audience produced differences in their humor that continued into the twentieth century. These differences need to be assessed in relationship to at least two questions: Are they qualitative, as male critics have implied, and, if so, how and why? Do they indicate differences in male and female sensibility or in social conditioning?

In the 1920s and 1930s, the debate over women's humor continued to be voiced in articles and in Martha Bensley Bruère and Mary Ritter Beard's 1934 collection, *Laughing Their Way: Women's Humor in America*. Following Sanborn's lead, women attributed their overshadowing in the humor field to social pressure on women to repress their own humorous instincts and to approve male humor as part of their role in maintaining harmony between the sexes.[22] More recent articles, expanding on the assumption that women's humorous nature has been molded by social conditioning, have argued that women who have challenged the male role of joke-teller have risked being odd woman out, or not being taken seriously by men, or alienating men (and women) by threatening the stereotype of the passive, accepting female, or, if their humor is considered too aggressive and "unfeminine," not being hired for work in the male-controlled media.[23]

In evaluating women's humor and its differences from men's, therefore, it is important to explore the effects on women's style and tone of the restrictions on the ways in which they could express themselves. These effects may be what Habegger addresses in criticizing Sanborn's collection of humor for its "strident" tone at the same time that he denigrates it for being bland.[24] Similar terms have been used by male critics to dismiss or downgrade twentieth-century women's humor, placing it in a double bind: if it employs ridicule, it is abrasive; if it relies on wit, it is insipid. Female critics, on the other hand, beginning with Sanborn, who applauded the self-confident tone of the humor she collects, respond differently and more warmly to content and style in women's humor.

A more thorough and objective approach to the issue may be achieved in part by looking at and accounting for earlier notions of what constitutes a female tradition of humor. Sanborn, for example, found female humor more subtle than male. Elizabeth Stanley Trotter asserted, in "Humor with a Gender" (1922), that "women have a quick perception of absurdity, the ability . . . to accord a narrative its due of imaginative embellishments, and to carry on the give-and-take of conversation with amusing raillery," but are not attracted to the mockery, ridicule, and physical joking that men enjoy.[25] Mary Roberts Rinehart made a similar point in "Isn't That Just Like a Man" (1920), arguing that women do not take themselves as seriously as men do and, therefore, can view themselves with irony, while men love a joke only if it is on someone else. Indeed, the whole question of how irony is used and how it functions in women's humor demands study, since a brand of double-edged irony has been a primary tool of women humorists, from Bradstreet's use of the deferential pose to the self-mocking stance of domestic humorists and even the more aggressive posture of feminist humor.

Related to the question of irony is women's perception and expression of incongruity. If, as Elizabeth Janeway observed, the female role has been at odds with the cultural ethos, women would tend to perceive as normal for them behavior that is incongruous in the dominant (male) culture and to perceive as incongruous for them behavior that is applauded in the culture.[26] These contradictions and double binds would affect the ways in which incongruity is exploited in women's work and, since incongruity is considered to be a major element of humor, would also affect the ability of the reader or audience to respond to the humorous intent. An extension of Morris' work on differences between male and female usage, diction, and manipulation of linguistic devices would not only help clarify issues of irony and incongruity but also add to a general understanding of how humor operates.

Another key issue for research into the nature of women's humor concerns the relationship between the humorist and her audience and the effects of that relationship on her perspective. Habegger suggests that nineteenth-century women's humor, stemming from the genteel culture maintained by women, weighted the humorous clash between the genteel and vernacular modes of apprehending reality in favor of the former, whereas native American (i.e., masculine) humor weighted the outcome of the clash in the other direction. While Habegger overgeneralizes, he also touches on a point made by Morris who, in differentiating between male and female vernacular humor, stated that, unlike the male, the female humorists "understood that women were particularly oppressed by the genteel code" and, therefore, used their humor not just "to condemn luxurious idleness and social pretentiousness" but to call "attention to the social abuses and injustices suffered by women."[27] This dual purpose of women humorists affected not only how they dealt with social issues—which values they reinforced and which they derided—but also how they handled negative female stereotypes also depicted in male humor. Similarly, in the twentieth century, while male humorists have developed black humor, humor of cruelty, pornographic and scatalogical humor, sick jokes, and ethnic slurring as modes of response to feelings of alienation and importance, women's humor has been more circumscribed and seen, therefore, as more conservative. Perhaps because women have been the child-bearers and homemakers, assumed or been prevailed upon to accept the role of civilizers and stabilizers of society, and barred from public positions of power, they have generally been more concerned with private issues, or with public issues as they affected their domestic lives and social position, than with political events and technological developments over which they have had no influence. Perhaps because women have had a history of coping with powerlessness, lowering their sights, modifying their needs, and compromising their desires, their humor has been less volatile and nihilistic than men's. These connections also need to be considered by humor researchers.

In addition, in twentieth-century, as in nineteenth-century, humor, the relationship between women's perspective on social issues and their treatment of female stereotypes requires closer scrutiny. As has already been suggested, the negative stereotypes of sentimental women, social climbers, frivolous flirts, garrulous busybodies, and frustrated old maids in women's humor through the early twentieth century were not intended as indictments of women per se, but as examples of the ways in which women's nature was perverted and lives trivialized by the limitations and false values of the culture. In twentieth-century women's humor, negative stereotypes, particularly the incompetent housewife, have also been used not simply to portray women as pathetic or ludicrous but to attack prevailing assumptions about women's roles and places. How these stereotypes are used and how they function for a predominantly female audience needs to be more carefully examined, especially as they relate to the major concerns of women's humor: the quality of women's lives and the ideology of women's place in American culture.

It is impossible in a brief survey of this kind, covering four centuries of material that is relatively unknown and unexamined, to include, let alone anticipate, all of the issues and themes open to investigation. Recent work in humor theory by sociologists, cultural historians, anthropologists, and psychologists indicates that increased application of their approaches to women's humor would yield important data.[28] The use of feminist critical theory to analyze themes, images, and linguistic devices employed by women humorists would also be fruitful.[29] Studies by media specialists of women humorists in radio, television, and film are similarly needed, as are analyses of the work of women cartoonists, journalists, and standup comics—especially those whose work has been confined to clubs.[30] Finally, much work must be done to discover, as well as to assess, the humor of women who are neither white nor middle class before any generalizations about American women's humor can be considered valid. For better or worse, then, the field of women's humor is wide open, and the potential for rich and rewarding exploration is unlimited.

NOTES

1. Compare Walter Blair's *Native American Humor, 1800–1900* (New York: American Book Co., 1937) and *Horse Sense in American Humor* (Chicago: University of Chicago Press, 1942); also, Norris W. Yates, *The American Humorist: Conscience of the Twentieth Century* (Ames: Iowa State University Press, 1964); Willard Thorp, *American Humorists* (Minneapolis: University of Minnesota Press, 1964); Jesse Bier, *The Rise and Fall of American Humor* (New York: Holt, Rinehart and Winston, 1968); Louis D. Rubin, Jr., ed., *The Comic Imagination in American Literature* (New Brunswick, N.J.: Rutgers University Press, 1973).

2. Arthur Power Dudden, "American Humor," *American Quarterly* 37, 1 (Spring 1985): 7.

3. A good summation of these factors appears in the introductory essays by Sandra M. Gilbert and Susan Gubar in *The Norton Anthology of Literature by Women: The Tradition in English* (New York: W. W. Norton, 1985).

4. Compare, for example, Sharon Weinstein, "Don't Women Have a Sense of Comedy They Can Call Their Own?" *American Humor: An Interdisciplinary Newsletter* 2, 1 (Fall 1975), pp. 9–12; Naomi Weisstein, "Why We Aren't Laughing . . . Anymore," *Ms.*, November 1973, pp. 50–54; and Anne Beatts, "Can a Woman Get a Laugh and a Man, Too?" *Mademoiselle*, November 1975, pp. 140ff.

5. Louis B. Wright, "Human Comedy in Early America," and Lewis P. Simpson, "The Satiric Mode: The Early National Wits," both in Rubin, *The Comic Imagination in American Literature*. Also, Peter M. Briggs, "English Satire and Connecticut Wit," *American Quarterly* 37, 1 (Spring 1985): 13–29.

6. Jacqueline Hornstein, "Comic Vision in the Literature of New England Women Before 1800," *Regionalism and the Female Imagination* 3, 2 & 3 (Fall 1977/Winter 1977–1978): 11–13; Wendy Martin, *An American Triptych: Anne Bradstreet, Emily Dickinson, Adrienne Rich* (Chapel Hill: University of North Carolina Press, 1984); Adrienne Rich, "The Tensions of Anne Bradstreet," *On Lies, Secrets, and Silence* (New York: W. W. Norton, 1979), pp. 21–32; Gilbert and Gubar, "Anne Bradstreet," in *The Norton Anthology*, pp. 58–61.

7. Martin, *An American Triptych*, pp. 43–45.

8. W. Howland Kenney, ed., *Laughter in the Wilderness: Early American Humor to 1783* (Kent, Ohio: Kent State University Press, 1976), pp. 11–12.

9. This point is developed by both Linda Kerber, in *Women of the Republic: Intellect and Ideology in Revolutionary America* (Chapel Hill: University of North Carolina Press, 1980), and Mary S. Benson, in her landmark *Women in Eighteenth Century America* (New York: Columbia University Press, 1935).

10. Benjamin Franklin V, *The Plays and Poems of Mercy Otis Warren* (New York: Scholars Facsimiles and Reprints, 1980), pp. vii–xxviii.

11. Ibid., p. xvi.

12. Eve Kornfeld, "Women in Post-Revolutionary American Culture: Susanna Haswell Rowson's American Career 1793–1824," *Journal of American Culture* 6, 4 (Winter 1983): 58.

13. Nancy F. Cott, *The Bonds of Womanhood: "Woman's Sphere" in New England, 1780–1835* (New Haven, Conn.: Yale University Press, 1977), p. 202.

14. Josephine Donovan, *New England Local Color Literature* (New York: Frederick Ungar, 1982), p. 26.

15. Compare Blair, *Native American Humor*, and Alfred Habegger, Chapters 12 and 13 in *Gender, Fantasy, and Realism in American Literature* (New York: Columbia University Press, 1982).

16. Nancy Walker, "Wit, Sentimentality and the Image of Women in the Nineteenth Century," *American Studies* 22, 2 (Fall 1981): 18.

17. Yates, *The American Humorist*, pp. 38–47; Thorp, *American Humorists*, pp.30–40.

18. Yates, *The American Humorist*, p. 38.

19. Compare interviews with Zora Rasmussen, Anne Beatts, and Lynn Roth in *Spare Ribs: Women in the Humor Biz*, by Denise Collier and Kathleen Beckett (New York: St. Martin's Press, 1980); also Fred Ferretti, " 'Women in Humor' Confer: Is It a Man's World?" *New York Times*, May 1, 1983, "Style," p. 70; and Phil Berger, "The New Comediennes," *New York Times Magazine*, July 29, 1984, pp. 27ff. Of particular interest in Berger's article are Johnny Carson's comments about aggressive comediennes on p. 51.

20. Alice Wellington Rollins, "Woman's Sense of Humor," *The Critic and Good Literature* 1, 13 (March 29, 1884): 145–46, and "The Humor of Women," 1, 26 (June 28, 1884): 301–2.

21. Blair, *Native American Humor*, Chapters 4 and 5; Habegger, *Gender, Fantasy*, Chapters 12 and 13.

22. Compare, for example, Elizabeth Stanley Trotter, "Humor With a Gender,"

Atlantic Monthly, December 1922, pp. 184–787, and Marietta Newel, "Are Women Humorous?" *Outlook*, October 14, 1931, pp. 206ff.

23. Compare note 19; also Weinstein "Don't Women Have a Sense of Comedy," and Weisstein, "Why Aren't We Laughing."

24. Habegger, *Gender, Fantasy*, pp. 169–170.

25. Trotter, "Humor with a Gender," pp. 784–86.

26. Elizabeth Janeway, *Man's World, Woman's Place* (New York: Delta, 1971), pp. 104–5.

27. Habegger, *Gender, Fantasy*, p. 2.

28. Compare, for example, Jeffrey H. Goldstein and Paul E. McGhee, eds., *The Psychology of Humor* (New York: Academic Press, 1972), and Antony J. Chapman and Hugh C. Foot, eds., *Humor and Laughter: Theory, Research, and Applications* (New York: John Wiley, 1976).

29. A good overview of trends and methods in feminist critical theory is *Feminist Criticism: Essays on Women, Literature and Theory*, ed. Elaine Showalter (New York: Pantheon Books, 1985).

30. Two important articles on stand-up comics are Lawrence E. Mintz, "Standup Comedy as Social and Cultural Mediation," *American Quarterly* 37, 1 (Spring 1985): 71–80, and Karen M. Stoddard, " 'Women Have No Sense of Humor' and Other Myths: A Consideration of Female Stand-Up Comics, 1960–1976," *American Humor: An Interdisciplinary Newsletter* 4, 2 (Fall 1977): 11–14.

BIBLIOGRAPHICAL SURVEY

Although all areas of women's humor are wanting attention, work has been done, especially within the last two decades, and sources do exist that provide direction for new researchers.

For the early period, W. Howland Kenney's *Laughter in the Wilderness: Early American Humor to 1783* is valuable, particularly for its introduction, which helps to set a context for Knight's journal. Louis B. Wright's "Human Comedy in Early America," in *The Comic Imagination in American Literature*, edited by Louis D. Rubin, Jr., is similarly helpful. Focusing exclusively on women, Jacqueline Hornstein's "Comic Vision in the Literature of New England Women Before 1800," in *Regionalism and the Female Imagination*, though sketchy, is important in offering a theoretical framework for analyzing the work of Bradstreet, Knight, Warren, Rowson, and Murray. For these same figures, work by feminist literary critics and historians helps to clarify these writers' themes, images, and perspectives as women responding to the events and ideologies of the times in which they lived. Wendy Martin's *An American Triptych: Anne Bradstreet, Emily Dickinson, Adrienne Rich*, Linda K. Kerber's *Women of the Republic: Intellect and Ideology in Revolutionary America*, and Eve Kornfeld's "Women in Post-Revolutionary American Culture: Susanna Haswell Rowson's American Career 1793–1824," in *Journal of American Culture*, Nancy F. Cott's *The Bonds of Womanhood: "Woman's Sphere" in New England, 1780–1835*, and Laurel Thatcher Ulrich's *Good Wives* are particularly helpful in this regard. In addition, books and articles on early political satire—Bruce I. Granger's

Political Satire in the American Revolution, 1763–1783, Lewis P. Simpson's "The Satiric Mode: The Early National Wits," in Rubin's collection, and Peter M. Briggs' "English Satire and Connecticut Wit," in *American Quarterly* (1985)—generally treat Warren as a satirist, as well as provide a humor context in which to look at her work and that of her contemporaries. Benjamin Franklin V's introduction to *The Plays and Poems of Mercy Otis Warren* offers more extensive discussion of her work and suggests some elements of it that reflect her concerns as a woman writer of the period.

Numerous books and articles have treated nineteenth-century humor, but almost exclusively in terms of a masculine tradition. Walter Blair's landmark study, *Native American Humor*, and his later *Horse Sense in American Humor* trace the development of themes and techniques, focusing on various modes of vernacular humor from Down East humorists to literary comedians. Although Blair's work slights women humorists, it suggests approaches for assessing women's vernacular humor and its differences from men's. Alfred Habegger, in *Gender, Fantasy, and Realism in American Literature*, includes chapters on women in his discussion of nineteenth-century humor; however, his conclusions about women's humor seem skewed by his preference for masculine humor. A counterperspective is offered by Linda A. F. Morris in her unpublished dissertation, "Women Vernacular Humorists in Nineteenth-Century America: Ann Stephens, Frances Whicher, and Marietta Holley." A significant piece of research that deserves publication, Morris' work sets the humorists discussed within a social and cultural context, as well as differentiates their work from similar work by men in terms of themes, images of women, and linguistic devices. Kate Sanborn's collection, *The Wit of Women*, is an invaluable resource for identifying nineteenth-century women humorists and experiencing the range and variety of their work. Its usefulness is marred, however, by an absence of biographical and bibliographic material, including a tendency to use only "Mrs." and a last name to refer to some writers. For understanding women's humor within the larger context of nineteenth-century women's writing, Nina Baym's *Woman's Fiction: A Guide to Novels by and about Women in America, 1820–1870* is indispensable, especially since a number of nineteenth-century women humorists also wrote "sentimental" fiction. Josephine Donovan, in *New England Local Color Literature*, performs a similar service in suggesting connections between humorists and local color realists. The relationship between wit and sentimentality is explicitly explored by Nancy Walker, in "Wit, Sentimentality and the Image of Women in the Nineteenth Century," in *American Studies*. Among recent books in cultural history that enlarge our understanding of women's changing images and roles in the nineteenth century are Lois W. Banner's *American Beauty* and Karen Haltunen's *Confidence Men and Painted Women*.

An excellent source on the evolution of nineteenth-century humorous modes and styles into twentieth-century humor trends is Norris Yates *The American Humorist*, which has a useful chapter on Dorothy Parker and a brief treatment of Anita Loos. A good analytical overview of nineteenth- and twentieth-century women's literary humor appears in Nancy Walker's *The Tradition of Women's Humor in America*. In addition, Walker's work complements studies like Willard Thorp's *American Humorists* and Jesse Bier's *The Rise and Fall of American Humor*, which tend to neglect women's work.

For names and examples of late nineteenth- and early twentieth-century women humorists, Bruère and Beard's *Laughing Their Way* is invaluable but, like Sanborn's collection, lack biographical and bibliographical information and also fails to provide a clear context for short excerpts. Not until *Titters*, edited by Deanne Stillman and Ann Beatts, and *Pulling Our Own Strings*, edited by Gloria Kaufman and Mary Kay Blakely, have new collections of women's humor been available. Both, however, have limitations similar to those of Sanborn's and Bruère and Beard's collections. Nevertheless, *Titters*, in its focus on newer, hip humor by women working in various media, and *Pulling Our Own Strings*, in its discussion and examples of feminist humor, are important contributions to women's humor, adding to our awareness of new trends and styles in women's content and expression. Other work that deals with specific aspects of twentieth-century women's humor includes Nancy Walker's "Humor and Gender Roles: The Funny Feminism of the Post-World War II Suburbs," in *American Quarterly* and my own work on domestic humor in "The Housewife as Humorists" (*Regionalism and the Female Imagination*) and in "Delineating the Norm: Allies and Enemies in the Humor of Judith Viorst and Erma Bombeck." In addition, the collection of essays devoted to women's humor in the Fall 1977/Winter 1977–1978 issue of *Regionalism and the Female Imagination*, edited by Emily Toth, offers a variety of approaches to a range of topics, from early American to contemporary lesbian humor, while Sarah Blacher Cohen's introduction to *Comic Relief: Humor in Contemporary American Literature* and her chapter on "Jewish Literary Comedians" help to offset the other chapters in the book that focus on male humor.

Nonliterary approaches to women's humor have also produced interesting results. In addition to articles previously cited on the nature of women's humor, work by sociologists and psychologists, in particular, have significant direct or indirect application to women's humor. Valuable overviews of work in recent humor theory, humor references, social functions of humor, and humor perception and response are available in *The Psychology of Humor*, edited by Jeffrey H. Goldstein and Paul E. McGhee, and in *Humour and Laughter: Theory, Research, and Applications*, edited by Antony J. Chapman and Hugh C. Foot. In addition, articles by Alice Sheppard, Joanne R. Cantor, and Carol A. Mitchell on gender-related preferences and styles deal specifically with women's humor. A number of articles in popular magazines during the last decade and a half (some of which are cited in the bibliography) have also focused on the nature, effects, and styles of women's humor, particularly as revealed in the work of standup comics. An excellent discussion of the social functions of standup comedy appears in Lawrence E. Mintz's "Standup Comedy as Social and Cultural Mediation," which analyzes, in terms applicable to female as well as male comics, different ways in which the relationship between humorist and audience is manipulated to reinforce or challenge cultural values and social behavior. More specific treatment of commediennes is offered by Karen M. Stoddard in " 'Women Have No Sense of Humor' and Other Myths: A Consideration of Female Stand-Up Comics," and by Joan B. Levine in "The Feminine Routine." Another source for female comics, as well as for women working with humor in other media, is *Spare Ribs: Women in the Humor Biz,* edited by Denise Collier and Kathleen Beckett, a collection of interviews with writers, actresses, standup comics, producers, and cartoonists concerning their work, aspirations, and difficulties as women in the humor field.

Whatever a particular individual's interest in women's humor may be, studies exist, and continue to appear, that point to paths and open up issues for research and analysis.

CHECKLIST AND ADDITIONAL SOURCES

Banner, Lois W. *American Beauty.* New York: Alfred A. Knopf, 1983.

Baym, Nina. *Woman's Fiction: A Guide to Novels by and about Women in America, 1820–1870.* Ithaca, N.Y.: Cornell University Press, 1978.

Beatts, Anne. "Can a Woman Get a Laugh and a Man, Too?" *Mademoiselle,* November 1975, pp. 140ff.

———. "Why More Women Aren't Funny." *Mademoiselle,* March-April 1976, pp. 22–28.

Benson, Mary S. *Women in Eighteenth Century America.* New York: Columbia University Press, 1935.

Berger, Phil. "The New Comediennes." *New York Times Magazine,* July 29, 1984, pp. 27ff.

Bier, Jesse. *The Rise and Fall of American Humor.* New York: Holt, Rinehard and Winston, 1968.

Blair, Walter. *Horse Sense in American Humor.* Chicago: University of Chicago Press, 1942.

———. *Native American Humor, 1800–1900.* New York: American Book Co., 1937.

Briggs, Peter M. "English Satire and Connecticut Wit." *American Quarterly* 37, 1 (1985): 13–29.

Bruère, Martha Bensley and Mary Ritter Beard, eds. *Laughing Their Way: Women's Humor in America.* New York: Macmillan, 1934.

Cantor, Joanne R. "What Is Funny To Whom?" *Journal of Communication* 26 (1976): 164–72.

Chafe, William H. *The American Woman: Her Changing Social, Economic, and Political Role, 1920–1970.* New York: Oxford University Press, 1972.

Chapman, Antony J. and Hugh C. Foot, eds. *Humour and Laughter: Theory, Research, and Applications.* New York: John Wiley, 1976.

———. *It's a Funny Thing, Humour.* New York: Pergamon, 1977.

Cohen, Sarah Blacher, ed. *Comic Relief: Humor in Contemporary American Literature.* Urbana: University of Illinois Press, 1978.

Collier, Denise and Kathleen Beckett. *Spare Ribs: Women in the Humor Biz*. New York: St. Martin's Press, 1980.

Cott, Nancy F. *The Bonds of Womanhood: "Women's Sphere" in New England, 1780–1835*. New Haven, Conn.: Yale University Press, 1977.

Curry, Jane, ed. *Samantha Rastles the Woman Question*. Urbana: University of Illinois Press, 1983.

Donovan, Josephine. *New England Local Color Literature*. New York: Frederick Ungar, 1982.

Dresner, Zita Z. "Delineating the Norm: Allies and Enemies in the Humor of Judith Viorst and Erma Bombeck." *Thalia*, 7 (1984): 28–34.

———. "The Housewife as Humorist." *Regionalism and the Female Imagination* 3, 2–3 (1977/1978): 29–38.

Dudden, Arthur Power. "American Humor." *American Quarterly* 37, 1 (1985): 7–12.

Ferretti, Fred. " 'Women in Humor' Confer: Is It a Man's World?" *New York Times*, May 1, 1983, "Style," p. 70.

Franklin, Benjamin V. "Introduction." *The Plays and Poems of Mercy Otis Warren*. New York: Scholars Facsimiles and Reprints, 1980.

Friedan, Betty. *The Feminine Mystique*. New York: Dell, 1974.

Fury, Kathleen. "Okay Ladies, What's the Joke?" *Redbook*, June 1980, pp. 163–66.

Gilbert, Sandra M. and Susan Gubar, eds. *The Norton Anthology of Literature by Women: The Tradition in English*. New York: W. W. Norton, 1985.

Gilligan, Carol. *In a Different Voice*. Cambridge, Mass.: Harvard University Press, 1982.

Goldstein, Jeffrey H. and Paul E. McGhee, eds. *The Psychology of Humor*. New York: Academic Press, 1972.

Granger, Bruce I. *Political Satire in the American Revolution, 1763–1783*. Ithaca, N.Y.: Cornell University Press, 1960.

Habegger, Alfred. *Gender, Fantasy, and Realism in American Literature*. New York: Columbia University Press, 1982.

Haltunen, Karen. *Confidence Men and Painted Women: A Study of Middle-Class Culture in America, 1830–1870*. New Haven, Conn.: Yale University Press, 1982.

Hornstein, Jacqueline. "Comic Vision in the Literature of New England Women Before 1800." *Regionalism and the Female Imagination* 3, 2 & 3 (Fall 1977/Winter 1978): 11–19.

Janeway, Elizabeth. *Man's World, Woman's Place*. New York: Delta, 1971.

Kaufman, Gloria and Mary Kay Blakely, eds. *Pulling Our Own Strings: Feminist Humor and Satire*. Bloomington: Indiana University Press, 1980.

Kenney, W. Howland, ed. *Laughter in the Wilderness: Early American Humor to 1783*. Kent, Ohio: Kent State University Press, 1976.

Kerber, Linda K. *Women of the Republic: Intellect and Ideology in Revolutionary America*. Chapel Hill: University of North Carolina Press, 1980.

Kornfeld, Eve. "Women in Post-Revolutionary American Culture: Susanna Haswell Rowson's American Career 1793–1824." *Journal of American Culture* 6, 4 (1983): 56–62.

Levine, Joan B. "The Feminine Routine." *Journal of Communication* 26 (1976): 173–75.

Martin, Wendy. *An American Triptych: Anne Bradstreet, Emily Dickinson, Adrienne Rich*. Chapel Hill: University of North Carolina Press, 1984.

Mintz, Lawrence E. "Standup Comedy as Social and Cultural Mediation." *American Quarterly* 37, 1 (1985): 71–80.

Mitchell, Carol A. "The Sexual Perspective in the Appreciation and Interpretation of Jokes." *Western Folklore* 36 (1977): 303–29.

Morris, Linda A. F. "Women Vernacular Humorists in Nineteenth-Century America: Ann Stephens, Frances Whicher, and Marietta Holley." Ph.D. Diss. University of California, Berkeley, 1978.

Newell, Marietta. "Are Women Humorous?" *Outlook*, October 14, 1931, pp. 206ff.

Rich, Adrienne. "The Tensions of Anne Bradstreet." *On Lies, Secrets, and Silences.* New York: W. W. Norton, 1979, pp. 21–32.

Rinehart, Mary Roberts. *Isn't That Just Like A Man.* New York: George H. Doran, 1920.

Rogers, Katherine M. *The Troublesome Helpmate: A History of Misogyny in Literature.* Ann Arbor: University of Michigan Press, 1961.

Rosen, Marjorie. *Popcorn Venus.* New York: Coward, McCann & Geoghegan, 1973.

Rubin, Louis D., Jr., ed. *The Comic Imagination in American Literature.* New Brunswick, N.J.: Rutgers University Press, 1973.

Sanborn, Kate. *The Wit of Women.* New York: Funk and Wagnalls, 1885.

Sheppard, Alice. "Funny Women: Social Change and Audience Response to Female Comedians." *Empirical Studies in the Arts* 3, 2 (1985): 179–95.

Sheppard, R. Z. "She Wits and Funny Persons." *Time*, May 29, 1978, pp. 92–96.

Showalter, Elaine, ed. *Feminist Criticism: Essays on Women, Literature and Theory.* New York: Pantheon Books, 1985.

Stillman, Deanne and Anne Beatts, eds. *Titters: The First Collection of Humor by Women.* New York: Collier, 1976.

Stoddard, Karen M. " 'Women Have No Sense of Humor' and Other Myths: A Consideration of Female Stand-Up Comics, 1960–1976." *American Humor: An Interdisciplinary Newsletter* 4, 2 (Fall 1977): 11–14.

Thorp, Willard. *American Humorists.* Minneapolis: University of Minnesota Press, 1964.

Toth, Emily. "Female Wits." *Massachusetts Review* 22 (1981): 183–93.

Trotter, Elizabeth Stanley. "Humor With a Gender." *Atlantic Monthly*, December 1922, pp. 784–87.

Ulrich, Laurel Thatcher. *Good Wives.* New York: Alfred A. Knopf, 1982.

Walker, Nancy. "Humor and Gender Roles: The Funny Feminism of the Post–World War II Suburbs." *American Quarterly* 37, 1 (1985): 98–113.

———. *The Tradition of Women's Humor in America.* Huntington Beach, Calif.: American Studies Publishing Co., 1984.

———. "Wit, Sentimentality and the Image of Women in the Nineteenth Century." *American Studies* 22, 2 (Fall 1981): 5–22.

Weibel, Kathryn. *Mirror, Mirror: Images of Women Reflected in Popular Literature.* New York: Doubleday/Anchor, 1977.

Weinstein, Sharon. "Don't Women Have a Sense of Humor They Can Call Their Own?" *American Humor: An Interdisciplinary Newsletter* 2, 1 (Fall 1975): 9–12.

Weisstein, Naomi. "Why We Aren't Laughing . . . Anymore." *Ms.* November 1973, pp. 50–54.

Weston, Jesse. *Making Do: How Women Survived the 30's.* Chicago: Follett, 1976.

Yates, Norris. *The American Humorist: Conscience of the Twentieth Century.* Ames: Iowa State University Press, 1964.

◆ 8 ◆

Racial and Ethnic Humor

Joseph Dorinson and Joseph Boskin

OVERVIEW

"The essential American soul," D. H. Lawrence wrote harshly in the 1920s, "is hard, isolate, stoic and a killer. It has never yet melted." Of all the aspects of American culture that corroborates Lawrence's tough prescription, ethnic humor stands out as among the most unifying and oppressive. Ethnic slurs, or *blasons populaires*, have been continually spun through joke cycles and will impact upon American culture into the next century at the very least. Active and resurgent, intently cruel and demeaning, the humor of oppression has had a lengthy past characterized by qualities both resilient and adaptive.

There can be little doubt that humor is one of the most effective and vicious weapons in the repertory of the human mind. It was for this reason that Thomas Hobbes perceived laughter in relation to power. In his naturalistic account of the origins and purposes of laughter, Hobbes offered an explanation of social rivalry. The passion of laughter, he sensed, was nothing more than the realization of "some eminency in ourselves by comparison with the infirmity of others" or with our own former position.[1]

One of the primary forms that humor assumes revolves around the stereotype. Stereotypes are a highly developed type of image that may have their origin in an aspect of social reality but that are often embellished and extended to include other features of a predetermined or expected attitude. As Gordon W. Allport has aptly noted. "some stereotypes are totally unsupported by facts; others develop from a sharpening and overgeneralization of facts."[2] Yet, once formed, they assume a circular structure within which all behavior is assumed to conform to the inner message of the conceptualized image.

From the earliest colonization in the seventeenth century to the present, many groups have been the object of humor stereotyping. While usually directed against the powerless—the politically ineffective and economically deprived—the humor stereotype has also been employed against upwardly mobile minority groups. Humor stereotypes share some significant similarities—class, sex, race, and religious stratifications—but also contain several pointed distinctions as well. Historical circumstances have flowed in and out of the development of group images, thus producing a peculiar amalgam.

While ethnic humor demonstrates aggressive intent, at the same time there is a considerable body of evidence to conclude that it possesses a salutary side as well. Several observers, Lawrence LaFave and Roger Mannell, for example, argue that some jokes of this genre actually compliment the maligned group.[3] In this instance, the disparaged group appreciates and disseminates the barbs. Thus, the humor of ridicule may well provide heat for the melting pot, thereby fostering upward social mobility. In Buffalo, for instance, Polish Americans relate the following quips.

Why doesn't the Pope let any dogs into the Vatican?
Because they pee on poles.

The New Pope wanted to call himself John Paul John Paul until his advisors suggested John Paul II.

The new Pope bought fifty pounds of birdseed to feed the cardinals.[4]

Polish jokes have sparked controversy. Add to this combustible mix, a recent current of light bulb riddles:

How many poles does it take to change a light bulb?
Six. One to hold the bulb and five to rotate the ladder.

How many WASPs does it take to change a light bulb?
Two. One to call the electrician and one to fix the martinis.

How many Jewish children does it take to change a light bulb?
None. "I'll sit in the dark!" the mother *kvetches* (whines).[5]

In this chapter, however, we maintain (in concert with Alan Dundes) that all joke cycles are rooted in social contexts and shaped by historical forces. Clearly, the women's revolution coupled with diminished energy sources sparked the light bulb cycle. Fear of sexual impotence and failure to match Japanese "high tech" stimulate these jokes. The message is no longer subliminal. If we are unable to screw in or turn on, we shall kvetch in the dark with our Jewish mother bereft of sexual energy and stripped of political power.[6]

Since anomie fosters frustration and stokes rage, civilization's discontents turn to aggression. Disguised by a "smile through one's teeth," aggressive humor or wit employs two salient functions: conflict and control. The latter keeps the lid on our rage thereby preventing suicidal raids into enemy territory: the PLO (Push Leon Overboard) notwithstanding. Conversely, conflict vehicles in the form of irony, sarcasm, caricature, parody, and burlesque reinforce the in-group and weaken the out-group. Most conflict humor can be traced to stereotypes. These guided missiles of verbal aggression shape our thought processes from a preliterate age. As difficult to dislodge as underground silos, these images are deeply rooted in collective folklore and firmly fixed in individual memory. Humor, launched from stereotype, can enfeeble, scapegoat, and emasculate a group.[7] Directed against the upwardly mobile and aimed at the powerless, such humor triggers projection and spurs displacement.

HISTORICAL CONTEXT

Ethnic slurs must be examined in historical context. As the Irish streamed into America, for example, they became targets of *blasons populaires*. The English had viewed the Irishman as a "bundle of Celtic contradictions: a creature both happy and melancholy, drunk on whiskey and drunk on dreams, violent and gentle . . . ignorant and cunning."[8] From the 1850s on, Americans regarded the Irish in comparable terms. Irishmen brawled constantly, drank excessively, and spoke nonsense. "Irish confetti" designated bricks; "Paddy wagons," police vans; "Irish banjo," a shovel. In black folklore, the Irishman looms large as incompetent, stupid, and lazy. A visitor in hell saw all kinds of ethnics burning in torment. "Where are the Irish?" he asked. Escorting him to a room filled with Irish, the Devil remarked: "We are just drying them here; they are too green to burn now." Walking through the woods, goes another anecdote, an Irishman encounters a [black?] panther and proceeds to kill him with a club. An onlooker wants to know why the Irishman continues to beat the already dead animal. Pat responds: "I want to show him there's punishment after death."[9]

The Irish carved out a distinctive image on stage. Vaudeville teams—Needham and Kelly, Rooney and Rogers, the Shamrocks—engaged in bluster and blarney. They conjure up a vivid portrait: "a figure in a derby hat and dudden pipe, a melodic if not sentimental songster having a belligerent attitude, a love for the bottle, a penchant for politics, . . . a quizzical look." In the comics, Irish folks inhabited shanties where the chimney, a patched stovepipe, pitched crazily. One needed a ladder to get into the house filled with children and dominated by a hot-headed washer-woman wife.[10]

This kind of caricature flourished precisely when the nation confronted a large wave of immigrants who could not—or would not—assimilate rapidly. As one method of promoting cultural conformity, jokes influenced the behavior of these newcomers. The response yielded an aggressive humor of social control. If indeed they represented alien corn, the Irish would employ wit in criticizing American values and peculiar institutions. In a decade—the 1890s—seething with anti-

Catholicism, Finley Peter Dunne took up humor's cudgels through his comic creation, Martin Dooley. Mr. Dooley's wit and wisdom fail to reach a large audience in our time; fortunately, several scholars have rescued him from oblivion. Arthur Dudden observes that "Dooley's Irishness was fundamental to all issues. . . . He was merely employing his insider's insight into politics together with an outsider's grasp of the democratic pretentions and nativist contradictions of American society." Dudden cites some of Dooley's gems on the Supreme Court, which "follows th' iliction returns"; the vice presidency: "it isn't a crime exactly"; and senatorial courtesy, which Dooley insisted rules the Senate in the absence of other rules.[11]

Jewish humor builds on folk sources. Living in the margins of Christian Europe, Jews found a comic voice. During the medieval wedding ceremonies, *badchonim* and *marshallikim* enjoyed license—well before Howard Cosell—to "tell it like it is." At wedding banquets, while guests broke bread, these ceremonial figures cracked jokes. On other occasions, rabbis engaged in *sihat hullin*, or "light talk," as they expounded the law. Rabbi Dovidl of Dinov, for example, defended this tradition against critics on the grounds that all humorous stories contained God's truth.[12] Today, *mohels* (ritual circumcizers) furnish humor as they remove foreskins.

Before coming to America, a tradition of folk humor sprouted in Europe, primarily in the eastern part, featuring arcane characters and droll types. Some— Hershl Ostropolier and Motke Chabad—were real people, unlike ersatz Paul Bunyans. Born in the Ukraine around 1750 to impoverished parents, Hershl had neither education nor calling. So he turned to wit, which paid off with *parnosseh* (livelihood). As court jester, he entertained a melancholy rabbi. Hershl laughed all the way to the *keyver* (grave). When the rabbi, his boss, rebuked him for spending so little time at prayer, Hershl responded: "You have so much to be grateful for! Your carriage and your fine horses, your gold and silver, your fancy dishes. But look at me, I have a nagging wife, my six children and a skinny goat. And so my prayers are very simple: 'Wife, children, goat'—and I'm done." As he lay dying, Hershl advised members of the Burial Society: "Remember, my friends, when you lift me up to lay me in the coffin, be sure not to hold me under the armpits. I've always been ticklish there " So he died with a smile on his lips. Like fellow imps, Hershl played the wise fool. He unmasked the rich who pretended to be righteous and the ignorant who pretended to be learned.[13]

Other humor forms flowered in the *shtetl* (small town). Chelm stories parodied the Jewish preoccupation with scholarship devoid of common sense. They poked fun at sages fixed on millenial concerns at the expense of mundane matters. The village elders of Chelm, for example, refuse to grant a raise in salary to the Messiah-watcher because, though the pay is low, the work is steady.[14] Still another type featured rabbi-priest stories with verbal jousts. As trickster, the rabbi often wins. Here are two examples:

Priest: "When will you give up those silly dietary laws?"
Rabbi: "At your wedding, excellency."

Priest: "Have you ever sinned, rabbi?"

Rabbi: "Yes, father, I once ate a ham sandwich. And you, father?"

Priest: "I once had a woman."

Rabbi: "Beats a ham sandwich, no?"[15]

After centuries of massacres and indignities, emancipation created another comedic possibility: the humor of marginality. Caught between two worlds— "one dead, the other powerless to be born"—Jews responded with irony. Sig Altman chronicled this transformation from *badchen* humor to stand-up comedy.[16] "For the Jew," wrote Albert Goldman, "a highly developed wit serves as both shield and salvation."[17] If ghetto life led to self-deprecation, indeed psychic masochism, in humor, how did emancipation and integration shape the Jewish comic spirit? Irony, several scholars contend, is the response of people who find themselves in the twilight zone of two cultures. The humor of irony is gentler than that of Hobbesian superiority and more cogent than Schlemieldom's self-derogation. Indeed, it summons us to fun, truth , and dignity. In this process, hostility actually plays second fiddle.[18]

To understand what happened to Jewish humor as it crossed the Atlantic Ocean, we turn to a fine model fashioned by Lawrence Mintz, who isolated four developmental stages. The first features critical, humor which targets the outgroup; the second, self-deprecatory humor; the third, realism; and the fourth reverses stage one as the oppressed minority gains revenge in assaulting the majority culture.[19]

Stage one can be found in nineteenth-century caricature. *Puck*, *Judge*, *Life*, and *Leslie's Weekly* identified Jews with greed, bargain hunting, and fraud (principally arson). For example, *Puck* employed cartoons to pillory Jews.[20] Two hooked-nosed dandies converse: "Ah, Jacob, I fear I hafe not many tays to live." "Nonsense, Fader, you have as much as t'irty years yet before you." "Non, Jacob, no! The Lord isn't going to take me at 100 when he can get me at 70." Although somewhat altered, such stereotypes carry over into current oral tradition. Jews are still identified with the money obsession. How do the Israelis take a census? "They roll a nickel down the street." What is their favorite football cheer? "Get the quarter back!" Station KVY, Tel Aviv, signals: "1400 on your dial, but for you, 1395!" Why did Moses accept the Ten Commandments? "Because they were free." Status joins money as a favorite pursuit. What did Mr. Mink give Mrs. Mink for Christmas? "A full length Jew." What is a CPA? "It's a Jewish boy who can't stand the sight of blood and one who stutters." Sorrow and pleasure fuse when a father discovers that his son is a homosexual but that he's going with a doctor. Finally, stage-one folklore retains physical caricature coupled with stage-two mockery. The Jewish nose is so big because the air is free. When Little Red Riding Hood calls on her bubby, she exclaims: "Bubby, what a big nose you have!" The wolf replies: "You should talk!"[21]

By 1965, Jewish humor had traversed the intervening stages and in the antics of several exemplary stand-up comics had staked out a firm position in stage four. Wallace Markfield celebrated the "Yiddishization of American humor" and Sam Janus analyzed it.[22] Only 3 percent of our nation's population, Jews account for 80 percent of its foremost professional comedians. As Abe Burrows explained, "humor is a way to keep from killing yourself . . . it removes anxiety. Other kids threw rocks, I make jokes." Making jokes, Stephen Whitfield maintains, is designed to defy the *Malach Hamoves* (Angel of Death).[23] As *unzer shtick* (our thing), it helps to define our place in an amorphous, anxiety-driven America. A distillation of group experience fusing oppression, poverty, pain, and put-downs, this humor enabled Jews to enter mainstream America laughing.

Pulsing with coarse vitality, Jewish comedians sharpened their skills in street encounters. They mimicked "hoity-toity" teachers, snarling rabbis, fat cops. Since their ethnic *landsleit* (fellow travelers) owned or operated many theaters, they plunged into "show biz" as careers in comedy opened to talk and *chutspe* (impudence). Old folks found renewed expression on stage:

"Have I got a girl for you!" the *shadchan* (matchmaker) insists. On cue, as rehearsed, the *shadchan's* apprentice embellishes. *Shadchan*: "A pretty girl." *Apprentice*: "A beauty! Queen Esther." "Intelligent!" "Brilliant. She knows six languages." "She's from a good family." "The highest *yichus* (status). Her grandfather was a famous scholar." "She's rich." "Her uncle is a Rothschild." "She has only one fault. She has a little hump." "A hump!" cries the apprentice, "a regular Mt. Sinai!"[24]

With a gift for colorful pastiche, Jewish comedians engaged in "ethnic acts." Weber and Fields, Smith and Dale, Gallagher and Shean emerged. Other Jewish entertainers put on burnt cork. Behind the Irish names or black masks, many forces—aggression, nostalgia, guilt, anxiety, and anger—coalesced. Al Jolson, for example, pandered to wish fulfillment. Jolson had inherited a Jewish blue note, whcih he used to conjure up a magnolia-scented South teeming with *Gemeinshaft* (communal togetherness). Fusing a somber, cantorial strain with vibrant, demonic energy, Jolson captivated audiences. Other Jewish entertainers learned how to mix *schmaltzy* sentiment and aggressive humor safely.[25]

The Marx Brothers carried on this vaudeville tradition minus the minstrel masks. Fortified with S. J. Perelman scripts, they plunged into gleeful nihilism. Listen to Groucho, the *schnorrer* as explorer or the egomaniac as Napoleon. To the strains of the Marseillaise, dressed as the great dictator, he says: "Ah, the Mayonnaise. The Army must be dressing." Groucho and his brothers trampled on every American ideal or institution: romantic love, fair play, college athletics, higher education, lower classes, business, law, medicine, and the martial spirit. Theirs is preeminently the Jewish comedy of deflation. Groucho quips: "When I came to this country, I didn't have a nickel in my pocket. Now, I have a nickel in my pocket." Zappo goes the Horatio Alger myth. To a priest who confesses that Groucho is his mother's favorite comedian, Mr. Marx replies: "I didn't know that you guys were allowed to have mothers." When another priest thanks Groucho for bringing so much joy into life, Groucho reciprocates. "Thanks for taking so much joy out of life." Resigning from the Friars, he explains: "I do not care to belong to a club that accepts people like me as members." Self-deprecation to be sure; Jewish to boot. But there were many more kicks for Margaret Dumont, that pillar of piety and monument to WASP stolidity. Groucho assaults mindless Margaret: "That remark covers a lot of territory. As a matter of fact, you cover a lot of territory. Is there any truth to the fact that they're going to tear you down and put up an office building?"[26] No one remained safe from Marx's demolition derby. Whatever it is, Groucho is against it.

Since radio furthered a blander style of comedy, a trend already established in vaudeville, Benny Kubelski became Jack Benny and his wife, née Sadie Marks, metamorphosed—new nose, new name—into Mary Livingston. Eddie "Rochester" Anderson, Dennis Day, Messrs. Kitsel and Schlepperman provided comic relief ethnically, but the main victim, more often than not, was the miserly, vain, slightly pompous Benny. Only his violin and his preoccupation with money conveyed a Jewish connection. Benny's image was WASPy, recalled Edgar Bergen. Later in his career, Benny poked fun at his own tribe. When, for example, General Motors recalled 72,000 Cadillacs on the eve of Yom Kippur, the thirty-nine year old miser quipped: "I've never seen so many Jews walking to synagogue in my life." When in Israel, a tour guide offered to take Benny across the sea for ten dollars, he erupted: "Ten dollars! Now I know why Jesus walked on water."[27]

The Hitler years were marked by a curious period in relative desemitization, contends Harry Popkin. Silence during World War II was broken by the advent of television. On this new medium, Jewish comedians, now solo and standup, came out of the cultural closet. Sid Caesar and Jack E. Leonard sent messages declaring in effect: *mir zeinen doh* (we are here). Mort Sahl and Lenny Bruce, strongly tinctured with Jewish iodine, cleaned up old acts and injected fresh doses of comic realism.[28] Both stood up as authentic performers, pop culture *mayvns* (experts), *maggadim* (preacher-teachers), and medicine men. Both dramatically departed from their predecessors' constricting formulas. As children of depression, war, movies, comic books, and radio, they mined a vast lode of funny stuff. Sahl took the high ground vacated by Will Rogers minus the rope and the bumpkin mask. This casually attired graduate school dropout peppered the Republican establishment with the democratic deflation of Jewish humor.

Lenny Bruce stumbled into success around 1958. While Sahl hacked at politicos primarily, Bruce blitzed hustlers, especially those who wore collar and cloth. The only Jewish kid in a German-American community, Lenny grew up thoroughly assimilated. Radio and movies shaped his comic style. Radio, Philip Roth avers, celebrated Jack Armstrong, the "All-American Goy." Movies promoted the dream girl, a blonde *shikse* "nestling under your arm whispering love,

love, love!'' Bruce's acute sense of alienation may have contributed to his compulsive use—and misuse—of Yiddish phrases. Consummately nasty, Bruce relished put-downs pickled in Jewish brine.

Shelly Berman is the goyishe Sam Levinson. Alexander King is the junkie Mark Twain. Nichols and May are the Vic and Sade of younger comics. Jackie Kennedy. A chick like that could hitchhike from coast to coast and not be molested.[29]

Like other Jewish comics, Bruce aspired to higher things. Unlike them, however, he regarded his role as that of moralist. He used dirty words and ethnic phrases to shock white Christians and fellow-Jews into self-awareness. A latter-day Jonathan Edwards, he located our demons and invited us to exorcise them. Unfortunately, Bruce could not purge his own *dybbuk* (demon). Earlier in his career, Lenny had maintained a delicate balance: he could express contempt, yet escape punishment. Haunted by his own corruption—drugs, deceit, vocation, *shund* (vulgarity)—Lenny found himself forced into a ''glass enclosure'' from which, as in Jean Paul Sartre's universe, there is no exit. A chronic optimist in the tradition of Manachem Mendel, Bruce tried to break loose and lead his minions to some fantasy island free of societal constraints and cultural ''no-nos.'' ''A disease of America'' in Kenneth Tynan's judgment, that marginal comic and double alien, Lenny Bruce plunged the ultimate needle into his vulnerable body and self-destructed on a toilet in 1966.[30]

Most Jews and some comics are survivors. Woody Allen is two in one. Representing *dos kleine mentschele*, cum laude graduate from Chelm University for *schlemiels*, Woody Allen né Alan Stewart Konigsberg, confronts the cosmos. Born of a neurotic *ménage à trois* embracing Sigmund Freud, Franz Kafka, and Sholem Aleichem, he embodies the comedic antihero. In one bit, he is hired as a token Jew. Desperately trying to look the part, he reads a memo from right to left. For taking off on too many Jewish holidays, he is fired. According to movie critic Richard Schickel, Woody's style—verbal as well as visual—combines understatement and parody.[31] For a little guy, he packs a devastating punch. At the end of the film, *The Front*, Woody refuses to answer the questions put by HUAC grand inquisitors and speaks defiantly for the good guys: ''You can all go fuck yourselves!''

Prior to Sahl, comedians were essentially visual clowns dressed in tuxedos who put down their mothers-in-law while supported by chorus girls (''tits and ass'' in Lenny Bruce's argot) in big dance numbers. Following in Sahl's wake, Woody decided to come on as the sad-faced, alienated, urban Jew. One can trace his progress as a comic pilgrim through one liners.

I was breast fed through falsies. My parents worshipped old-world values: God and carpeting. We were too poor to own a dog; so my parents went to a damaged pet store and bought me an ant. My neighborhood was so tough that the kids stole hubcaps from moving cars. They broke my violin and left it embedded in my body. I stole second when playing softball. Guilty, I returned to first. I went with a girl who had a child by a future marriage. My first wife was so immature: she sank my boats in the bathtub. My cousin was very successful, a lawyer. He insured his wife with Mutual of Omaha for orgasms. If he failed to deliver, she collected. I spent $1,000 to have my nose fixed. Now, my brain won't work. My apartment was robbed so often, I put up a sign: "We gave already." I moved to a safer apartment with a doorman. Two weeks later I was mugged—by the doorman. Not only is there no God, but try getting a plumber on weekends.[32]

Laughter provides distance from pain and protection against an oppressive world. In the wacked-out world of Woody Allen, wit functions as a defense mechanism as well as a cry of defiance.

Preoccupied with death, obsessed with dignity, concerned with artistry, Woody tries to transcend his role of Jewish humorist. He does not quite succeed. In whatever mask or pose, Woody Allen remains a character whom Yacowar describes as

essentially Jewish. The performer stands alone and without a prop before a crowd of strangers. By his wit he attempts to forge a sense of community with them. By his brain and humor he tries to gain their acceptance, the laughter that denotes approval. . . . Despite his strangeness and alienation, he must persuade them that he is one of them. . . . So he stands alone in front of a silent and alien audience, spinning out his line of self-deprecating patter or charming cheek (*chutzpah*). The stand-up comedian is the eternal outsider, the wandering Jew.[33]

Allen's humor—indeed, all Jewish humor—issued from pain. Although conditions improved measurably, the tradition crossed the Atlantic. Mort Sahl's deflationary monologues owe more to ancestral tradition than to Will Rogers. Lenny Bruce fiercely distilled prophetic wisdom into social outrage. The self-parody in Woody Allen is both a mechanism for survival and a plea for love. "If your enemy is laughing," jokes Mel Brooks, "how can he bludgeon you to death?" As a coping device for "high anxiety," he advised that "every small Jew should have a tall *goy* for a friend." As the 2000-year-old man, Brooks pontificated that "death is more of an enemy than a German soldier."[34]

Unzer shtick, kosher nostra, the Jewish comic perspective promotes endurance. A view from the bottom, not the bridge, it helps to restore balance and to shore up dignity. Occasionally a weapon for open combat, Jewish humor carries clout as Adolf Hitler must have sensed when he banned cabaret humor, liberally spiced with Jewish ingredients, in Germany. Jewish comedians later helped to topple Richard Nixon with their acid commentary on Watergate. Sahl, Frye, Mason, Steinberg, Klein, and Roth all helped to dethrone, or at least disrobe, the man who would be emperor. Is there a secret formula to oust a sanctimonious crook? It takes a large dose of aggression coupled with a pinch of deflation. Jack Mason advises: "Never spit into a man's face unless his mustache is on fire." Saul Bellow warns: "Lead me not into Penn Station . . . " [especially with a killer on the loose].[35] From high to low culture, one finds ample evidence of Jewish humor throughout American culture: in gossip columns, in syndicated advice to the lovelorn by sisters Lederer (Dear Abby and Ann Landers), in cartoons by David Levine and Jules Feiffer, in plays by Neil Simon and Herb Gardner, in fantasies by S. J. Perelman and Mel Brooks, in novels by Bernard Malamud, Philip Roth, and Saul Bellow.

Is it true, as Salcia Landmann asserts, that "Jewish humor is more profound, more varied and altogether richer than that of other peoples?" To a people allegedly chosen—and frequently reviled—such hyperbole is doing what comes naturally. Through mass communication, Paul Buhle observes, it serves as an "anodyne against pain and antidote against futility."[36] Where once religion reconciled us to death, pain, and evil, now humor—especially Jewish humor—performs this vital function. Jewish comedians have travelled far from the *shtetl chupeh* (small town wedding) and Berlin cabaret. In the main, Jews are accepted, acculturated, affluent. So, why do they still *kvetsch* (complain) and joke compulsively? Because terrorists strike, presidential candidates use epithets like "Hymie;" because *tsores ba leitn*—that host of real as well as imagined problems—continues to rain on their parade. In "making it" with Norman Podhoretz and Irving Kristol, some have become caught up in materialism and power in opposition to their spiritual heritage. Jewish comedy provides armor in the ultimate confrontation with the Angel of Death. To the rescue, Woody Allen would have our days lettered instead of numbered. He prefers to run through the valley of the shadow of death.[37]

Black humor sprang from sources not dissimilar from Jewish but it developed its own idiosyncratic form and style in response to unique circumstances in American culture. Slavery and segregation forged a stereotype of Afro-Americans so tenacious that, as novelist Ralph Ellison symbolically wrote in the title of his powerful work (*The Invisible Man*), blacks were perforce "invisible." Sustenance derived from the ability of blacks to develop their own separate and distinct culture, a culture that few whites realized and even fewer touched.

"When the country was not looking at Negroes," Ellsion exclaimed in a dialogue with Robert Penn Warren in the mid-sixties, "when we were restrained in certain of our activities by the interpretation of the law of the land, something was present in our lives to sustain us. This is evident when we go back and look at our cultural expression, when we look at the folklore in a truly questioning way, when we scrutinize and listen before passing judgment. Listen to those tales which are told by Negroes themselves."[38]

Before the activities of the Civil Rights movement in the late fifties and early sixties had reached deep into the inner recesses of the outside world, few whites had even heard those tales told by blacks. Occasionally, folklorists, writers, musicians, and others were privy to the language and lore of the black community but they were few in number and in communicating power. Occasionally, a Caucasian writer or entertainer utilized black materials and expressions—Joel Chandler Harris and Al Jolson share this historic distinction—but they came to black society with an outsider's presumptuousness. Yet, by the time Stokley Carmichael uttered those prophetic rallying words before a group of Mississippi sharecroppers in 1966—"We want Black Power! We want Black Power!"— whites were being thrust into the arena of black struggle by acts of verbal uprisings, spontaneous outbursts, printed works and, most significantly, humorous stories and satirical jibes. *The Invisible Man*, Ellison's title that had trenchantly capsulated a historic past, was no longer applicable to the generation of the late sixties.

Whether they realized it or not, the militant actions that confronted Caucasians in the past few decades were made possible by a folk tradition of incredible power and latitude. Distinguished by a literary quality, imaginative expressiveness, breadth of experience, and psychological flexibility, the Afro-American patterns of folklore extend deep into the past. Although its roots can be traced back to African culture, the slave period reinforced and altered its uses and patterns. The concerted attempt of the colonists to obliterate African culture, to split up tribes ostensibly to prevent uprisings and to prohibit reading and writing, forced the slave to develop subtle means of communication in order to transmit values, attitudes, history, and existential affirmations to other slaves and to younger generations.

Survival with a caste system that forbade many of the normal expressions of intercourse was an added pervasive factor in determining oral patterns. The ability to circumvent the system was crucial to the black man. Hence blacks devised many ways to communicate with one another even while under the wary eyes of whites. Dance, songs, voice and body inflections were methods by which Afro-Americans "talked" to each other. Communication became a primary mode of aggression. Unable physically to strike back at his oppressors, the black man sheathed his fist in humor.

As with most areas of black life, the world of black humor was obscured until the protest decade of the sixties. Part of the obscurity resulted from the stereotypical images developed by the white to maintain the slave and caste systems. To the Caucasian, the Negro was "Sambo," "Rastus," "Uncle Tom," "Aunt Jemima," "Boy": a lazy, shiftless, shuffling, singing, dancing, exaggerated being. To perpetuate the image, it was essential to deny the African and his descendants a range of social and intellectual capacities, among them the ability to translate life experiences into humor. The psychology of the slave and caste systems reinforced the situation. By refusing to recognize the complexity and depth of black humor, society was thus able to maintain its imbalance and ignorance and to portray the black as a comic being.

Segregation in almost all areas of life, but particularly in the fields of entertainment and mass communication, compounded the situation by preventing the emergence of humorists who could have corrected the picture. Afro-American storytellers and comedians in the past have played mainly to black audiences. Few persons outside the black community prior to the contemporary period could have identified such able humorists as "Moms" Mabley, "Slapsey" White,

"Pigmeat" Markham, Redd Foxx, George Kirby, Timmy Rogers, and others. The humor was practically unknown to the majority of Caucasians. Even the sophisticated writer Ogden Nash expressed astonishment about the reach of black humor. In his review of Langston Hughes' work, *The Book of Negro Humor*, Nash wrote: "The range of humor here collected is a surprise. One would not have expected so many kinds, from so many sources. There are jokes having to do with jive and the blues. There are anecdotes from the pulpit. There are stories from New Orleans and Harlem."[39]

Perhaps one of the most vital changes in American culture in the 1960s, then, was the rise to national prominence of black humorists and comedians of several generations. The recognized stature of Godfrey Cambridge, Dick Gregory, Bill Cosby, Nipsey Russell, Richard Pryor, Flip Wilson, and other reflected the growing acceptance of the Afro-American insistent ethnic challenge to the social structure through a humor that is the mark of a group struggling fiercely to achieve a desired status. The routines and acts seen in coffeehouses, television programs, night clubs, college appearances, and on records—in short, the dissemination of the humor through the mass media—made whites aware of black attitudes for the first time. Although many of the humorists' acts reflected their own personal concerns, a considerable body of folk humor was contained with their materials.

On the surface, blacks and Jews share in the humor of oppression. Inwardly masochistic, indeed tragic, externally aggressive, even acrimonious, their humor exemplifies several distinctive forms: gallows humor, the ironic curse, double entendre, trickster tales, and retaliatory jokes. Theirs is the connection between subserviency and humor and the use of humor to overturn roles and position.

Yet, black humor has developed along its own historical paths. The outstanding traits of Afro-American humor are its play qualities that ward off punishment, a style that offers quick retaliation, and a type of control humor vital for the maintenance of a highly sensitized community.[40] Springing from its own folk sources, black humor has proceeded along two main tracks. Externally, it represented an accommodation to white society and therefore functioned as a mechanism for survival. To shore up their psychic defenses, for example, slaves employed veiled language to vent their anger, just as they used coded expressions to mask their true feelings.

The John-Master stories illuminate this process. John cusses out his massa whenever he pleases—whenever the massa is up at the big house and John is down in the field. John steals food and lies his way out of trouble by turning a pig into a baby and, when caught, reversing the magic. Slave stories featured outwardly docile subjects paying homage to their master as in this deathbed scene: "Farewell massa! Pleasant journey! You soon be dere, massa—[it's] all de way down hill!" Some slaves refused to be buried in the same gravesite with their masters for fear the Devil, "old Sam," might take the wrong body. Blacks chortled as they slipped past white scrutiny:

I fooled old Master seven years,
Fooled the overseer three.
Hand me down my banjo,
And I'll tickle your bel - lee.

John represented both the rewards as well as the hazards of the "trickster."
Even in the circumstances, verbal facility and skill in role-play were often not
enough. In one tale, John's absolute faith in prayer betrays him as the massa's
cruel children prey on his gullibility and pelt him with "God's stones." To track
the inner feelings of the Afro-American in servility, one has to turn to the animal
trickster. Rabbit is correctly identified with the slave; yet he also mirrors the
oppressor's cruelty. As Lawrence Levine noted, the trickster tales were profound
parodies of white society. Because whites wielded awesome power, their chattels
preferred to seek revenge with guile and indirection. Even if the meek fail to
inherit the earth, they might enjoy a last laugh. Slaves laughed "to keep down
the trouble and to keep our hearts from being broken . . . ," as John Little put
it, "I have cut capers in chains."[41]

Vulnerability played an important role in the development of the black humor
response. The power of the majority's reach—indeed, their racist attitude and behavior—led to a type of gallows humor similar to that devised in Jewish quarters.
A post-World War II story about a black soldier who was decorated for valor in
Europe and also married a French woman succinctly makes the point:

The soldier decided to bring the woman of his dreams back to his hometown in Mississippi.
He wrote to his U.S. Senator, the vitriolic Theodore Bilbo, of his plans. A few weeks
later, he received a reply from the Senator's office: 'Have hung your letter in my office.
Am waiting on you.'

Perhaps the sharpest jibe indicating the previous state of tenuousness in white
society was contained in the old quip: "A black hen laid a white egg and they
hung her." That the white world was overpowering in all areas, whether real
or imagined, was the basis for twisting an old fairy tale: "Mirror, mirror on the
wall," asks a black girl as she stands before the magical reflecting glass, "who
is the fairest one of all?" "Snow White, you black bitch," answers the mirror,
"and don't you forget it."

When elements of black humor became part of American culture in the early
decades of the nineteenth century, a ritual sacrifice occurred. At that time the
black as comic figure loomed into white fantasy as the smiling descendant of
Pan. He lusts after chicken, watermelon, pig's feet, white women. He fears
ghosts (particularly in white sheets) and speaks in malapropisms. White performers Thomas Rice and Dan Emmett swooped down South to cannibalize
black culture. Two blatant stereotypes surfaced, Jim Crow and Jim Dandy: the
former, a rural, slow-witted buffoon; the latter, an urbane, effeminate city-

slicker. Prodded by the upper-class whitefaced interlocutor who played it straight, Dandy and Coon created havoc on the stage. These types, contends Robert Bone, triggered laughter as audiences perceived the gap between affectation and reality. The travesty aimed "to keep the pretender in his place."[42]

Sambo, Crow's cousin, a Darwinian loser and preindustrial primitive, became the nation's demeaned alter ego or, in Bone's formulation, antiself. To whites he was

slow-witted, loosely-shuffling, buttock-scratching, benignly-optimistic, superstitiously-freightened, childishly lazy, irresponsibly-carefree, rhythmically-gaited, pretentiously-intelligent, sexually-animated. His physical characteristics added to the jester's appearance: toothy-grinned, thick-lipped, nappy-haired, slack-jawed, round-eyed.[43]

Unlike Lear's fool, Ahab's Pip, Bergen's McCarthy, our Sambo lacked wisdom. He was, in short, a buffoon.

For the white performer, putting on the blackface minstrel mask constituted a rite of exorcism, a safety valve for repressed emotions. Indolent, inept, indulgent, the black persona embodied the antiself and objectified the distance between social norms and man's instincts. Imparting a sense of freedom and inviting a return to childhood, minstrelsy answered deep psychic needs: "the mammy for security and comfort; . . . the Negro male for ridicule and jest."[44] For blacks themselves, the laughter of ridicule forged psychic chains: a bag for Uncle Tom, a joke for Rastus, a pancake restaurant for Sambo.

To survive, the black had to perpetuate a self-caricature. To succeed, he had to perpetuate vile stereotypes. Billy Kersands juggled a cup and saucer in his mouth. Ernest Hogan, Ma Rainey, and Bert Williams donned the mask to conceal, as well as to express, true feelings. Williams, in fact, used two sets of jokes: one for whites, the other for black folks. As "Jonah Man" Williams, helped and comforted by "Nobody," successfully pulled laughter from pain. Most of his peers, however, deflected, if not defeated, painful indignities with derisive laughter. Minstrelsy no doubt ministered to a society beset with problems wrought by industrialization. But this art form heaped great indignities on black people.[45]

Until recently, the humor of accommodation was the only one to which whites were exposed. To laugh openly at the "Man," "Mr. Charley," "Miss Ann," "pig," "honkey," "vanilla," was to invite certain punishment. Blacks, therefore, developed a gaming stance stoically laughing on the outside to cope with their pain inside. In its broader range, black humor has served many important functions, namely, group survival, escape into pride and dignity, self-criticism, and the promotion of conflict.[46] Getting past society's censors, internal and external, Freud maintained, brings pleasure because a joke saves energy normally expended on inhibition and disguised aggression. Such jokes function as mini-rebellions. In Daryl Dance's anthology of materials, which often pit the poor against those with power, one set targets the Negro preacher in order to expose vanity, ignorance, hypocrisy, lechery, alcoholism, gluttony, and materialism.

The church people were having a party at which they served some punch, but the punch was so weak that, every time they got a chance, some of the men would sneak in a bottle and pour some whiskey into the punch. The Preacher enjoyed it so much, he just kept nipping. Later, when he was called to pray, he said: "God bless the cow that gave this milk."[47]

When another minister and his son encounter a bear in the woods, the son urges, "Let us pray!" The minister responds: "Let us run. Son, prayers is all right in a prayer meetin' but they ain't no good in a bear meetin'!"[48]

The elephant-joke riddles of the 1960s were a crude disguise for white stereotypes. One type explicitly depicted the elephant as sexually superior:

Why does the elephant have four feet?
It's better than six inches.

How do elephants make love in the water?
They take their trunks down.

In another cycle, the elephant is castrated:

How do you keep an elephant from charging?
Take away his credit card.

The elephant, of course, represents the Negro. Coincidental with "elephantasy and elephanticide," color-riddles appeared:

What's black and has a red cape?
Super Nigger.

What is black and white and rolls in the grass?
Integrated sex.

Black liberation evidently spurred anxiety; this in turn triggered regression. Abrahams and Dundes contend that the elephant can represent an adult sexual rival or a Negro sexual competitor.[49]

Why did white audiences respond so favorably to ethnic comedians in this period? Perhaps the answer lies in the role that standup comics play as cultural anthropologists. Lawrence Mintz offers a crucial insight:

as a licensed spokesman he is permitted to say things about our society that we want and need to have uttered publicly but which would be too dangerous and too volatile if done so without the mediation of humor; and as a comic character he can represent through caricature, those negative traits which we wish to hold up to ridicule, to feel superior to, and to renounce through laughter. Thus, for example, the blackfaced minstrels can be the objects of racist hostility and in defining socially-undesirable behavior, yet at the same time they can function as positive, likeable spokesmen for topical satire. . . . Similarly the ethnic comedians could represent "greenhorns" to be laughed at for their ignorance, gullibility, poverty, and vulnerability, but laughed with for their street-wise insistance on survival and their ironic exposure of injustice. . . . [50]

Building on folk sources and in-group banter ("the dozens") black comedians joined their Jewish counterparts in imparting cultural commentary and anthropological insight. Dick Gregory carried the comic ball directly into enemy territory in the early 1960s. As a civil rights activist-commentator, he scored:

Restauranteur: "We don't serve Nigras!"
That's cool. I don't eat them.

I sat in so long at lunch counters. It took me ten years to discover that they didn't have what I wanted.

It's kinda sad, but my little girl doesn't believe in Santa Claus. She sees that white cat with the whiskers and even at two years old she know damn well that no whiteman coming to our neighborhood at midnight.

Just my luck, bought a suit with two pair of pants today . . . burnt a hole in the jacket.

Makes you wonder . . . when I left St. Louis I was making $500 a week for saying the same thing loud that I used to say under my breath.

Wouldn't it be a hell of a thing if all this was burnt cork and you people were being tolerant for nothing?[51]

Godfrey Cambridge laughed at his wife's "Back to Africa" kick. "She did the bedroom in brown, the whole thing, drapes ceiling, carpet, spread, pillow. One day she took a bath, came into the room and it took me three hours to find her." Cambridge barbed whites, too, with his "How to Hail a Taxi" routine and their concern over property values. "Do you realize," he asked, "the amount of havoc a Negro couple can cause just by walking down the street on Sunday morning with a copy of the *New York Times* real estate section under the man's arm?"[52]

Redd Foxx furnished an array of weapons. He once threatened a less than enthusiastic audience with "Why should I be wasting time with you here when I could be knifing you in an alley?" Reverting to gallows humor, he observed that the first black to receive an athletic scholarship from "Old' Miss" was a javelin catcher. He parodied *Tarzan* and called Long Beach, California, blacks the "ugliest Negroes that I have ever seen." Foxx confessed the ambivalences inherent in mulattodom: "You wake up in the morning with a taste for . . . filet mignon with biscuits." Unmasking Sambo, Foxx revealed that " 'Boss' spelled backwards is double SOB."[53]

Both Jackie "Moms" Mabley and, more recently, Richard Pryor found rich veins of humor in folk sources. Mabley's appearance, her references to soul food, and her earthy wit established the appropriate image and tightened the bonds of kinship with black audiences. Spouting comic reversals, she addressed powerful white men as "boy" and called prestigious white women "girl." She related an account of a major United Nations conference:

Aw, everybody was there. They had a ball. Yeah. All of them men from the Congo, some of 'em was late getting there 'cause they had plane troubles, and they had to be grounded in Arkansas, Little Rock. One of them Congo men walked up to the desk in Little Rock and said, "I'd like to reserve a room, please." The man said, "We don't cater to your kind." He said, "No, you misunderstand me. I don't want it for myself. I want it for my wife. She's your kind."[54]

Humor, Dwight MacDonald once observed, is like guerilla warfare. Success depends on travelling light, striking unexpectedly and getting away fast.[55]

But ethnic humor reveals a constant intent to return to the action, never to escape into fatalism, and always to skirt on the edge of gallows laughter. Thus, in the quest for control over events and lives, ethnic behavior demonstrates that both oppressors and their adversaries use humor but for strikingly different ends. The oppressors employ ridicule to maintain conformity to the status quo and to forge an iron-bound stereotype. In their response, ethnics have created a world of internal joking where, in Langston Hughes' observation, "certain aspects of the humor of minority groups are so often inbred that they are not palatable for outside consumption.[56] Moreover, they often role-reverse and turn the tables on their adversaries by striving for a language of self-acceptance. Poet Marianne Moore perceptively noted that "one's sense of humor is a clue to the most serious part of one's nature." Mocking features ascribed to them by outsiders has been one of the more prominent infusions into national humor, particularly by Afro-Americans and Jews. Nevertheless, in the laughter of oppression and its response is to be found that continued reflection of D. H. Lawrence's indictment of American culture. Minority laughter is insight into the constant and often cruel struggle to achieve definition and place in a society buttressed by the ideology of Social Darwinism. That minority groups have been able to cope with and rise above the derisive images directed against them attests to their resiliency through the imaginative devices of humor.

ISSUES

Humor study, a still relatively virgin field, beckons to the modern researcher. So many stimulating questions invite deeper probes. Why the recent rash of Polish and light bulb jokes? How does one explain other current trends such as the popularity of truly tasteless ethnic humor? What accounts for the vogue of *Maledicta*, Reinhold Aman's cultish journal that sparkles with witty *schmutz* (dirt) and ethnic caricature? Why haven't the NAACP and B'nai B'rith protested?

What happened to Irish humor in America? Why didn't Jewish humor follow the Irish suit? Is Jewish humor really masochistic? What conceptual models best explain our protean subject? Although these questions are intriguing, indeed, seductive, they yield no easy answers.

Our approach is to sample various interpretations. The coupling of Polish and light bulb jokes constitutes a marriage not of convenience but of contemporary conflict and scholarly debate. Alan Dundes has devoted much effort to this inquiry. A truly perceptive observer, Dundes points out that in transferring heat from one group to another, ethnic jokes are both aggressive and demeaning. Lydia Fish disagrees. When Polish American students poke fun at their Pope, they are not engaged in character assassination. Actually, in the joking process, they affirm ethnic pride. From another perch, theology expert Harvey Cox expresses lofty distaste for this genre. Nevertheless, Cox concedes that in targeting mindless bureaucracies and blitzing dehumanized societies, these jokes possess redemptive value. Do they "mask the unconscious admiration we harbor for the good Soldier Schweiks of the modern world?" Scholars show no inclination to establish a consensus. In a prior publication authors Boskin and Dorinson were persuaded to delete several jokes alleged to be offensive by cautious editors. Although we strongly maintained our identification with oppressed groups, we prudently submitted to critical surgery. The editors believed that we had crossed the pale into enemy territory.

Should we have lit a candle or cursed the darkness? Analysis of ethnic humor, properly grounded in solid research, will prove more illuminating than denunciating. If the lines of civility seem murky at best, researchers should take comfort. As pioneers of intercultural as well as interdisciplinary study, we are the cutting edge. To discover the limits, we turn to an arresting study by Christie Davies. A British sociologist, Davies argues that we need clearer boundaries. In our postindustrial society, wherein values clash, goals are cloudy, impersonal systems dominate, and Big Brother observes everything, ethnic jokes serve a vital purpose. They help us draw clearer boundaries: social, geographical, and moral. In highly anomic societies, individuals require both guidance and escape. Davies demonstrates how ethnic humor helps to restore balance as well as to elucidate values. It provides an international police force to patrol these ambiguous boundaries.

Humor is now almost a cottage industry. The search for an all-embracing motor force or catholic theory has accelerated. Thanks to a spurt of activity by experimental psychologists, empirical sociologists, pop culture buffs, and broadminded historians, the literature on laughter grows exponentially. Faced with a plethora of information, students of humor need conceptual models. Of the many schema proposed, three have proved most useful. The above-mentioned Mintz model applies with special force to Jewish humor. With regard to black humor, we rely on the Arnez-Anthony paradigm and C. Erik Lincoln's "triple A" response to oppression. Arnez and Anthony contend that throughout slavery, blacks employed privately coded in-group humor. Later this form evolved into public expressions of either self-parody or racist caricature, shades of the minstrel show. Finally blacks emerged from the halcyon 1960s with openly aggressive humor that affirmed racial pride and cultural dignity. Although Lincoln's model was designed to illuminate the process of black nationalism, it can be applied, heuristically, to the strategies of humor. An oppressed group, he maintains, has three options: acceptance, avoidance, aggression. Clearly, the jokes cited in this chapter reflect all three with noticeable overlap on occasion. This model also illuminates the demise of Irish humor.

Irish types once dominated the Anglo-American literary scene as rustic clowns, rogues, stage Irishmen, and comic heroes. The rustic clown, easily duped like the Yiddish *schlemiel*, with a born loser. He was superceded by the witty rogue, a "broth of a bhoy" who talks his way out of all predicaments. An outlaw, he lives beyond the fringe of community and invites comparison with his American cousin, Teague O'Reagan. The merry, bibulous, pugnacious, clown-like stage Irishmen followed. A creature of Dion Boucicault, his lazy, lovable, devil-may-care persona served as the antithesis of Victorian respectability, a role he shared with America's Sambo. Finally, we encounter Synge's Christy Mahon, a full-fledged comic here who gained ascendency with poetry and punch. When Christy's right cross put his roguish father down for the count, the Playboy of the Western World struck a blow for comic freedom and scored a victory over stultifying tradition.

In America, Finley Peter Dunne also boxed with authority figures. He jabbed the powerful and punched the pompous. After World War I, he essentially retired from the ring of political satire. Since his departure, Irish humor has almost vanished. With the exception of radio's Fred Allen, television's Anne Meara, literature's Flannery O'Connor and John O'Hara—the Irish comic sensibility did not shed its grace on America for very long. It survives perhaps in the folk songs of Tommy Makem and the Clancy Boys. The rest are silent. Why? Father Andrew Greeley offers a key insight. He argues that the wild Irish have been tamed through acculturation. They "have become dreadfully civilized." As in Lincoln's paradigm, acceptance lured the Irish-Americans. Once, they laughed at sex and death, especially during wakes. Now, seriousness and respectability prevail. Before becoming New York's Cardinal, John O'Connor had a well-deserved reputation for wit. Since his great advent, however, humor takes a back pew. Priesthood and politics, William Shannon, a prominent Irish author suggested, eclipse the vocation of humor. Success evidently dulls the comic needle.

Scholars continue to debate the essence of Jewish humor. Is this a *nechtikn tog* (lost cause)? Still the best analysis of Jewish jokelore, as Elliot Oring confirms, is Doctor Sigmund Freud's. In his diagnosis, Jewish humor exemplified the "tendency wit" of skepticism, democratic thought (deflation), social principles, and social criticism. His disciple, Theodore Reik, loved this genre's intimacy, dialectical process, and release of unmerry laughter at a moment of subjective truth or profound insight. Although doctors of lower *yichus* (status) and lesser judgment have labeled it "psychic masochism," folklorists and sociologists have found evidence to the contrary. The rabbi has resurfaced as a "trickster." Jewish jokes often propel aggression outward. Therefore, identity crises, that issue from cultural marginality bear more relevance than self-hatred. As America tries to cope with recurrent, perhaps insoluble problems, Jewish humor becomes germane, indeed therapeutic.

Why are there so many Jewish humorists in various cultures? Why not? Is it genetic by way of Genesis? How accurate are the models of Mintz, Arnez-Anthony, and Lincoln? These questions invite further study. Jewish humor, Novak and Waldoks conclude, is substantive—combining moral fiber with didactic flavor. Essentially democratic, it targets authority and punctures pomposity. In the contest of wit, little people (Mendele's *kleine mentschelech*) frequently win. *Shpritsing* (attacking) dogmas, institutions, celebrities, and enemies, Jewish humor does not even spare God. When bloated with daily *tsores* (trouble), the Jewish joke purges with the suddenness and effectiveness of seltzer. Relief!

Where did Jewish humor originate? Is the Jewish joke still alive and kicking? Salcia Landmann, a German Jewish scholar, has engendered controversy on this subject. Landmann contended that Jewish humor died because three preconditions for its existence no longer applied. These included a break with religious orthodoxy and all that it entailed; a move to assimilate that the gentile world rejected; and a difficult but not desperate lot. Nobel Laureate I. B. Singer emphatically disagreed. After paying tribute to her erudition, he refuted Landmann's thesis point by point. Even during the Holocaust, Singer argued, at the gas chambers, Jews continued to joke. Ironically, Jewish culture has survived American affluence. The refusal to die, Singer quipped, was a form of Jewish humor. Support for his position can be found in Holocaust literature, namely, the Ringelbaum diaries and the writings of Viktor Frankel.

Did blacks also slip the yoke, as Ralph Ellison maintained, when they changed the joke? Arising from an African base, slave humor reversed, psychologically at least, abominable conditions. The comedy of avoidance worked effectively. Afro-American humor, until recently, resided underground. The messages were dressed in the medium of animal tales and in other forms of in-group humor: word-play, self-deprecation, aggression against the man, and insult-swapping. The "dirty dozens" as well as the clean ones are verbal jousts that have sparked scholarly controversy. A. R. Radcliffe-Brown was the first to explain "the joking relationship as an institution by which a person is expected, sometimes required to make fun of another who, in turn, is required to take no offense." Radcliffe-Brown found these joking relationships among tribal societies throughout the globe. They arise when people are in ambiguous relationships to each other. John Dollard was the first social scientist to examine the "dozens" per se. He concluded that they functioned as a "valve for aggression in a depressed group." The "dozens" therefore provide a safe substitute for physical violence. Venturing into the urban jungle of South Philadelphia, Roger Abrahams discovered a different interpretation. He viewed the "dozens" or "sounding" or "cracking" or "joining" as a ritual designed to liberate black adolescents from their mommas as a means of resolving acute Oedipal and identity problems. Does God bless the male-child who copes as Shine, the hard man of Titanic Toasts, or as Brer Rabbit, the guileful get-over artist of black folklore? Lawrence Levine, on whose brilliant book we rely heavily, rejected all single-cause interpretations. He noted two principal functions in the ritual of insult: training in verbal facility and training in self-discipline.

What price glory for the black entertainer? Did he strike a Faustian bargain to succeed in show business? How destructive was the minstrel mask? Robert Toll has documented the degrading racism inherent in Tambo and Bones. To be sure, the laughter of ridicule forged psychic chains but William Stowe and David Grimstead and Lawrence Mintz argue for a more positive view of minstrelsy. Further research is needed to resolve this debate. Minstrelsey's principal legacy, however, remains—shades of Nat King Cole's "Mona Lisa, Mona Lisa"—that enigmatic grin.

Humor, in the final analysis, is no laughing matter. Among the Irish, blacks, and Jews, ethnic humor served to bind their groups with the strands of communal laughter, cathartic release, and retaliation against oppressors. For the host society or power elite, this kind of humor also provided a triple A option, to wit; aggression (slurs), avoidance (caste consciousness), and acceptance (pluralism). From subtle barb to gratuitous insult, ethnic jokelore offered enormous range and safely concealed malice. But it also continues to keep social bridges in good repair. Getting past both internal and external censors, Freud maintained, brings pleasure because a good joke saves energy normally expended on inhibition and disguised aggression. If ethnic jokes are minirebellions against authority, they also constitute a device for social control—sometimes to impede, sometimes to accelerate, absorption in the host society. In this process, humor resonates within and among groups to sound a consensus. As a cultural force, ethnic comics have imparted renewed vitality to a slumping America. Through their humor, lubricating as well as abrasive, they have recharged our nation's machinery. Tuned in and turned on, we hear their electric hum of talent.

In this chapter, we have raised some salient issues. We urge scholars to join us in charting new areas of research. Our field of inquiry is unique. Few academicians share our synthesis of Max Weber's Protestant Ethic with Johann Huizinga's *Homo Ludens*. Ours is genuinely a labor of love wherein business joins pleasure, and play informs works.

NOTES

1. Thomas Hobbes, "Human Nature, or the Fundamental Elements of Policy," in *The English Works of Thomas Hobbes*, ed. Sir William Molesworth (London: John Bohn, 1840), Vol. IV, p. 46. For examples of blasons populaires, see Alan Dundes and Carl R. Pagler, eds., *Urban Folklore from the Paperwork Empire* (Austin: Publications of the American Folklore Society, 1975), pp. 174–79; and Sterling Eisiminger, "Ethnic and

National Stereotypes and Slurs," *American Humor: An Interdisciplinary Newsletter* 7 (Fall 1980): 9–13.

2. Gordon W. Allport, *The Nature of Prejudice* (Garden City, N.Y.: Doubleday Anchor, 1958), p. 186.

3. Lawrence LaFave and Roger Manell, "Does Ethnic Humor Serve Prejudice?" *Journal of Communication* 26 (1976): 116–17, 122.

4. Lydia Fish, "Is the Pope Polish?" Some Notes on the Polack Joke in Transition," *Journal of American Folklore* [JAF hereafter] 93 (1980): 450–54.

5. The "power" jokes are found in Judith B. Kerman, "The Light Bulb Jokes: Americans Look at Social Action Processes," *JAF* 93 (1980): 454–55, 457–58; for additional enlightenment, see Alan Dundes, "Many Hands Make Light Work: or Caught in the Act of Screwing in Lightbulbs," *Western Folklore* 40 (1981): 266; Joseph Boskin, "Obscure Humor: Comments on Contemporary Laughter, Circa. 1980s," paper presented at the Third International Conference on Humor, August 1982, Washington, D.C., pp. 9–10.

6. Dundes, "Many Hands," p. 266; Boskin, "Obscure Humor," pp. 9–10.

7. Joseph Boskin, *Humor and Social Change in Twentieth-Century America* (Boston: Boston Public Library, 1979), pp. 28–31; Richard Stephenson, "Conflict and Control Functions of Humor," *American Journal of Sociology* 56 (May 1951): 569.

8. Perry L. Curtis, Jr., *Apes and Angels: The Irishmen in Victorian Caricature* (Washington, D.C.: Smithsonian Institution, 1971), pp. 94–95, as cited in Eisiminger, "Ethnic and National Stereotypes," p. 10.

9. Eisiminger, "Ethnic and National Stereotypes," p. 10. The Irish anecdotes are found in several sources: Ray Ginger, *Ray Ginger's Jokebook about American History* (New York: Franklin Watts/New Viewpoints, 1974), p. 31; Isaac Asimov, *Isaac Asimov's Treasury of Humor* (Boston: Houghton Mifflin, 1971), pp. 287, 289; Lawrence W. Levine, *Black Culture and Black Consciousness: Afro-American Folk Thought from Slavery to Freedom* (New York: Oxford University Press, 1977), pp. 302–3.

10. William R. Linneman, "Immigrant Stereotypes: 1880–1900," *Journal of American Humor* 1 (April 1974): 29.

11. Arthur P. Dudden, "The Record of Political Humor," *American Quarterly* 37 (1985): 55, 56.

12. Nathan Ausubel, ed., *A Treasury of Jewish Folklore* (New York: Crown Publishers, 1948), p. 264; Mark Zborowski and Elizabeth Herzog, *Life Is with the People: The Culture of the Shtetl* (New York: Schocken Books, 1978), pp. 279–80; Israel Abrahams, *Jewish Life in the Middle Ages* (New York: Atheneum, 1969), pp. 133, 198.

13. Ausubel, *Treasury*, pp. 304–19; William Novak and Moshe Waldoks, eds., *The Big Book of Jewish Humor* (New York: Harper & Row, 1981), pp. 26–27.

14. Allen Guttmann, "Jewish Humor," in *The Comic Imagination in American Literature*, ed. Louis D. Rubin, Jr. (New Brunswick, N.J.: Rutgers University Press, 1973), p. 331.

15. Ed Cray, "The Rabbi Trickster," *JAF* 77 (1964): 341–42.

16. Sig Altman, *The Comic Image of the Jew: Explorations of a Pop Culture Phenomenon* (Rutherford, N.J.: Fairleigh Dickinson University Press, 1971), p. 144, 163–67. For this apposite phrase from the author of "Dover Beach," see Matthew Arnold, "Stanzas from the Grande Chartreuse," in *The Norton Anthology of English Literature*, ed. M. H. Abrams et al. (New York: W. W. Norton, 1979), p. 1381.

17. Albert Goldman, "Boy-Man Schlemiel: The Jewish Element in American Humor," in *Freakshow* (New York: Atheneum, 1971), p. 175.

18. Bernard Rosenberg and Gilbert Shapiro, "Marginality and Jewish Humor," *Midstream* 4 (1958): 70–80; Israel Knox, "The Traditional Roots of Jewish Humor," *Judaism* 12 (1963): 329.

19. Lawrence E. Mintz, "Jewish Humor: A Continuum of Sources, Motives and Functions," *American Humor* 4 (Spring 1977): 4.

20. The *Puck* cartoon is cited and reproduced in Rudolph Glanz, *The Jew in Early American Wit and Graphic Humor* (New York: Ktav, 1973), pp. 114–15; John J. Appel, "Jews in American Caricature: 1820–1914," *American Jewish History* 71 (1981): 103–18. Glanz and Appel agree that Americans caricatured Jews less viciously than Europeans did. For a markedly different view, see Michael N. Dobkowski, *The Tarnished Dream: The Basis of American Anti-Semitism* (Westport, Conn.: Greenwood Press, 1979), pp. 60–63.

21. Alan Dundes, "A Study of Ethnic Slurs," *JAF* 84 (1971): pp. 189, 184–95.

22. Wallace Markfield, "The Yiddishization of American Humor," *Esquire* 64 (October 1965): 114; Samuel Janus, "The Great Comedians: Personality and Other Factors," *The American Journal of Psychoanalysis* 35 (1975): 169–74; "Analyzing Jewish Comics," *Time* 112 (October 2, 1978): 76. Also consult Anthony Lewis, "The Jew in Stand-Up Comedy," in *From Hester Street to Hollywood: The Jewish-American Stage and Screen*, ed. Sarah Blacher Cohen (Bloomington: Indiana University Press, 1983), pp. 58–68.

23. Larry Wilde, *How the Great Comedy Writers Create Laughter* (Chicago: Nelson-Hall, 1976), p. 89; Stephen J. Whitfield, "Laughter in the Dark: Notes on American Jewish Humor," *Midstream* 24 (February 1978): 48, 51. On the subject of mortality, Mel Brooks confessed: "My liveliness is based on an incredible fear of death. In order to keep death at bay, I do a lot of 'Yah! Yah! Yah!' . . . Most people are afraid of death, but I really hate it! My humor is a scream and a protest against goodbye. . . . I suspect you can launch a little better artillery against death with humor." See Mel Brooks, "Interview," *Playboy*, February 1975, p. 233.

24. Nahma Sandrow, " 'A Little Letter to Mamma': Traditions in Yiddish Vaudeville," in *American Popular Entertainment*, ed. Myron Matlaw (Westport, Conn.: Greenwood Press, 1979), p. 90.

25. Paul Antonie Distler, "Ethnic Comedy in Vaudeville and Burlesque," in ibid., pp. 33–41; Ronald Sanders, "The American Popular Song," in *Next Year in Jerusalem: Portraits of the Jew in the Twentieth Century*, ed. Douglas Villiers (New York: Viking Press, 1976), pp. 197–98; Lewis A. Erenberg, *Steppin' Out: New York Night Life and the Transformation of American Culture 1890–1930* (Westport, Conn.: Greenwood Press, 1981), pp. 190–95; Stanley White, "The Burnt Cork Illusion of the 1920's in America: A Study in Nostalgia," *Journal of Popular Culture* 5 (1971): 543.

26. Charles Michener, "Comedy's King Leer," *Newsweek* 90 (August 29, 1977): 78–79; Jesse Bier, *The Rise and Fall of American Humor* (New York: Holt, Rinehart and Winston, 1968) pp. 3, 270–71; Altman, *Comic Image*, pp. 188–89; James K. Feibelman, *In Praise of Comedy: A Study in Its Theory and Practice* (New York: Horizon Press, 1970), pp. 223–25.

27. Harry Golden, *The Golden Book of Jewish Humor* (New York: G. P. Putnam's Sons, 1972), pp. 232–33; Nathan Hurwitz, "Blacks and Jews in American Folklore," *Western Folklore* 33 (October 1974): 309, contains the Benny quip on the Cadillac recall.

Also see Steve Allen, *The Funny Men* (New York: Simon & Schuster, 1956), pp. 65, 66–69, 71.

28. Henry Popkin, "The Vanishing Jew of Our Popular Culture," *Commentary* 14, 1 (July 1952): 45–55; Irving Howe, *World of Our Fathers* (New York: Harcourt, Brace, Jovanovich, 1976), pp. 568–73; Markfield, "Yiddishization," p. 114.

29. Philip Roth, *Portnoy's Complaint* (New York: Bantam, 1969), 164–65; Nat Hentoff, "Where Liberals Fear to Tread," *Reporter* 22 (June 23, 1960): 51; John Cohen, ed., *The Essential Lenny Bruce* (New York: Ballantine Books, 1968), pp. 47–48; Joseph Dorinson, "Lenny Bruce: A Jewish Humorist in Babylon," *Jewish Currents* 35 (February 1981): 14–19, 31–32.

30. The "glass enclosure" metaphor comes from jazz great Bud Powell as quoted in "Talk of the Town," *The New Yorker* 42 (August 20, 1966): 25; Kenneth Tynan, intro. to Lenny Bruce's *How to Talk Dirty and Influence People* (Chicago: Playboy Press, 1966), pp. vi–xi. Several sources illuminate Lenny's dark humor. Gilbert Milstein, "Man, It's Like Satire," *New York Times Magazine*, June 27, 1971, pp. 16, 18, 19, 20, 22; Robert Alter, "Defaming the Jews," *Commentary* 55 (1973): 80–81; Pauline Kael, *Reeling* (Boston: Little Brown/Atlantic Monthly Press Book, 1976), pp. 373–76. There are many fine records of Bruce in action but the best in our judgment is "Lenny Bruce at Carnegie Hall," United Artists UA 9800.

31. Richard Schickel, "The Basic Woody Allen Joke . . . ", *New York Times Magazine*, January 7, 1973, pp. 33, 35, 36, 37; Whitfield, "Laughter in the Dark," p. 57; Philip Berger, *The Last Laugh: The World of the Standup Comics* (New York: Ballantine Books, 1975), pp. 108–12.

32. Earl Wilson, *Show Business Laid Bare* (New York: New American Library, 1974), pp. 246–47; Maurice Yacowar, *Loser Take All: The Comic Art of Woody Allen* (New York: Frederick Ungar, 1979), p. 20; Schickel, "Basic Woody," p. 33. Many of these jokes were culled from a wonderful two-record set: "Woody Allen: Standup Comic, 1964–1968," United Artists LA849-J2.

33. Yacowar, *Loser Take All*, p. 213.

34. Kenneth Tynan, *Show People: Profiles in Entertainment* (New York: Simon & Schuster, 1979), pp. 213–14. *Tsores* (trouble) as the motor force of Jewish humor is canvassed in a variety of sources: Allen, *Funny Men*, pp. 212–18; Wilde, *How the Great Comedy Writer*, pp. 67, 106–7, 125; Albert Memmi, *The Liberation of a Jew*, trans. Judy Hyun (New York: Orion Press, 1966), pp. 43–54; Whitfield, "Laughter in the Dark," p. 53.

35. Bier, *Rise and Fall*, pp. 335–36, 346, 447.

36. Salcia Landmann, "On Jewish Humor," *Jewish Journal of Sociology* 4 (1962): 204; Paul Buhle, "Jewish Humor: An Interpretation," *Shmate* 6 (1983): 2.

37. Yacowar, *Loser Take All*, p. 215; Eric Lax, *On Being Funny: Woody Allen and Comedy* (New York: Charterhouse, 1975), pp. 224–25.

38. Robert Penn Warren and Ralph Ellison, "A Dialogue," *Reporter*, (March 25, 1965) p. 43.

39. *Los Angeles Times*, March 13, 1966, p. 33.

40. Afro-American humor's twin tracks are charted in Joseph Boskin, "Goodbye, Mr. Bones," *New York Times Magazine*, May 1, 1966, p. 31. The roguish John stories are conveyed in a variety of sources: Daryl Cumber Dance, *Shuckin' and Jivin': Folklore from Contemporary Black Americans* (Bloomington: Indiana University Press, 1978), pp. 189–90; Richard Dorson, *American Folklore* (Chicago: University of Chicago Press,

1959), pp. 186–90; Norine Dresser, "The Metamorphosis of the Humor of the Black Man," *New York Folklore Quarterly* 26 (September 1970): 216–19; Gil Osofsky, ed., *Puttin' on Ole Massa: The Slave Narratives of Henry Bibb, William Wells Brown, and Solomon Northrup* (New York: Harper & Row, 1969), pp. 21–23; Harry Oster, "Negro Humor: John & Old Marster," in *Mother Wit from the Laughing Barrel: Readings in the Interpretation of Afro-American Folklore*, ed. Alan Dundes (Englewood Cliffs, N.J.: Prentice-Hall, 1973), pp. 550–55. The "getting over" song is cited in Levine, *Black Culture*, p. 125. Also see Nancy Levi Arnez and Clara B. Anthony, "Contemporary Negro Humor as Social Satire," *Phylon* 29 (Winter 1968): 339–40.

41. Osofsky, *Puttin' on Ole Massa*, pp. 39–40; Levine, *Black Culture*, pp. 118–19.

42. Robert Bone, *Down Home: A History of Afro-American Short Fiction from Its Beginning to the End of the Harlem Renaissance* (New York: G. P. Putnam's Sons, 1975), pp. 59, 60–61; Arnez and Anthony, "Contemporary Negro Humor," pp. 339–40; Nathan I. Huggins, *Harlem Renaissance* (New York: Oxford University Press, 1971), pp. 261–83.

43. Joseph Boskin, "The Life and Death of Sambo: Overview of an Historical Hang-Up," *Journal of Popular Culture* 4 (Winter 1971): 649.

44. White, "Burnt Cork," p. 543; Albert F. McLean, Jr., *American Vaudeville as Ritual* (Lexington: University of Kentucky Press, 1965), pp. 24–26; Robert Toll, *Blacking Up: The Minstrel Show in Nineteenth Century America* (New York: Oxford University Press, 1974), p. 29; Huggins, *Harlem Renaissance*, pp. 260–74, offers a brilliant analysis of travesty.

45. Toll, *Blacking Up*, pp. 245–48, 254–59, 262, 274; Robert Toll, *On with the Show: The First Century of Show Business in America* (New York: Oxford University Press, 1976), p. 123; Morris Goldman, "The Sociology of Negro Humor," unpublished dissertation, New School for Social Research, 1960, p. iv refers to dual set of jokes used by Bert Williams.

46. Boskin, *Humor and Social Change*, p. 57; Robert Brake, "The Lion Act is Over: Passive/Aggressive Patterns of Communication in American Negro Humor," *Journal of Popular Culture* 9 (Winter 1975): 551–53.

47. Dance, *Shuckin' and Jivin'*, pp. 41–76; Levine, *Black Culture*, p. 321.

48. For the bear meetin' joke, see Mary Frances Berry and John Blassingame, *Long Memory: The Black Experience in America* (New York: Oxford University Press, 1982), p. 102.

49. Roger D. Abrahams and Alan Dundes, "On Elephantasy and Elephanticide," *Psychoanalytic Review*, 56 (1969): 230, 231, 233, 237, 238–39.

50. Lawrence E. Mintz, "The 'New Wave' of Standup Comedians: An Introduction," *American Humor* 4 (Fall 1977): 1. The comedian who made the biggest waves is still mired in myth. See Joseph Dorinson, "Lenny Bruce, A Jewish Humorist in Babylon," *Jewish Currents* 35 (February 1981): 14–19, 31–32.

51. Dick Gregory, *Nigger: An Autobiography* with Robert Lipsyte (New York: Pocket Books, 1970), p. 132; Dresser, "Metamorphosis," pp. 226–27; William Schechter, *The History of Negro Humor* (New York: Fleet Press Corp., 1970), pp. 186–88, 189.

52. Schecter, *History of Negro Humor*, pp. 105–6, 192–94; Levine, *Black Culture*, p. 362; Mel Gussow, "Laugh at this Negro but Darkly," *Esquire* 62 (November 1964): 94–95.

53. Redd Foxxisms are found in Boskin, *Humor and Social Change*, p. 50–51; Levine, *Black Culture*, pp. 361, 365; Schechter, *History*, p. 196; Redd Foxx and Norma Miller,

The Redd Foxx Encyclopedia of Black Humor (Pasadena: Ward Ritchie Press, 1977), pp. 234–56.

54. Arnez and Anthony, "Contemporary Negro Humor," p. 342; Levine, *Black Culture*, pp. 363–66.

55. Dwight MacDonald, *On Movies* (Englewood Cliffs, N.J.: Prentice-Hall, 1969), pp. 160–61.

56. Langston Hughes, "Jokes Negroes Tell on Themselves," *Negro Digest* 9 (June 1951): 25.

BIBLIOGRAPHICAL SURVEY

It is a curious fact that while there is an extensive literature devoted to racial and ethnic humor, no single book or major collection of essays approaches the subject definitively. A recent article in *American Quarterly* by John Lowe, "Theories of Ethnic Humor: How to Enter Laughing," provides a good overview of the subject, as does an earlier Boskin-Dorinson essay dealing with racial and ethnic humor in America, also in *American Quarterly* (1985). Most of the general studies of humor, as well as the handbooks and collections of essays on humor, deal with the topic extensively. *Its a Funny Thing, Humour*, edited by Antony Chapman and Hugh Foot, devotes a whole section to ethnic joking, largely as a forum for Lawrence LaFave's theories and work that follows from them, but the volume also contains several essays on humor and communication, humor and small group interaction, which have relevance here. *The Handbook of Humor Research*, edited by Paul McGhee and Jeffrey Goldstein, presents several useful chapters, as does their earlier collection, *The Psychology of Humor* (1972), notably the essay by William H. Martineau entitled "A Model of the Social Functions of Humor." Other general studies that deserve mention include Christie Davies' "Ethnic Jokes, Moral Values, and Social Boundaries," Harvey Cox's "... and Polish Jokes," Alvin Schwartz's *Witcracks: Jokes and Jests from American Folklore*, and the rarely cited treasure, *Jokes: Form, Content, Use and Function*, by Christopher P. Wilson. Lawrence E. Mintz has constructed a continuum model of the motives and functions of racial, sexist, and ethnic humor, but the work has yet to appear in print except for abstracts of a presentation at the Second International Conference on Humor and of an application to Jewish humor presented at the Modern Language Association convention in 1976. There are also many useful collections of jokes published as mass market paperbacks, but the collecting activity of Larry Wilde and the dozen-or-so volumes on racial and ethnic humor that have resulted from it deserve special attention.

Afro-American Humor

There are many fine studies of Afro-American humor, some of which are virtually paradigmatic for ethnic, racial humor research. Nancy Arnez and Clara B. Anthony published an article, in 1968, which anticipates the complex appreciation of the motives and functions of humor that became more commonplace a decade later (''Contemporary Negro Humor as Social Satire''), Joseph Boskin's *Sambo: The Rise and Demise of an American Jester* is a model study of comic stereotyping, and Lawrence W. Levine's sections on humor in *Black Culture and Consciousness* open numerous important issues for further attention. Joseph Boskin's ''Goodbye, Mr. Bones,'' Norine Dresser's ''The Metamorphosis of the Black Man,'' Robert Brake's ''The Lion Act is Over: Passive/Aggressive Patterns of Communication in American Negro Humor,'' and Robert Toll's study of the minstrel theater, *Blacking Up*, are also indispensible. Critical studies of ''the dozens'' and of oral Black folklore are instructive concerning the motives and functions of joking and they offer useful insights into the importance of tradition and local custom. John Dollard's ''The Dozens: The Dialect of Insults,'' Roger Abraham's *Deep Down in the Jungle*, and Daryl Cumber Dance's *Shuckin' and Jivin': Folklore from Contemporary Black Americans* provide important reference. Anthologies of primary source material are abundant: notable collections include Richard Dorson's *American Negro Folktales*, Langston Hughes' *The Book of Negro Humor*, Henry Spaulding's *Encyclopedia of Black Folklore and Humor*, Philip Sterling's *Laughing on the Outside*, Gilbert Osofsky's *Puttin' on Ole Massa*, and the *Redd Foxx Encyclopedia of Black Humor*.

Jewish Humor

It is probably best to start looking at Jewish humor by reading Freud's *Jokes and Their Relation to the Unconscious*, followed closely by Theodore Reik's *Jewish Wit* and Elliott Oring's *The Jokes of Sigmund Freud: A Study in Jewish Humor and Identity*. Martin Grotjahn clearly articulates the case against Jewish humor as masochistic and destructive in his ''Jewish Jokes and Their Relation to Masochism,'' and dozens of articles take up the debate from there; perhaps the best ''answer'' to the position advanced by Grotjahn et al. is Dan Ben-Amos' excellent ''The 'Myth' of Jewish Humor.'' Other articles, cited in the checklist, worthy of attention include those by Irving Kristol, Ed Cray, Leslie Fiedler, Nathan Hurwitz, Howard Erlich, Stephen Whitfield, Earl Rovit, I. B. Singer, Marion Magid, Emanuel Ringelbaum, and H. R. Rabinowitz. Major overviews include Harvey Mindess' *The Chosen People?*, Avner Ziv's *Personality and the Sense of Humor*, and Joseph Dorinson's ''The Gold Dust Twins of Marginal Humor: Blacks and Jews.'' Collections of primary sources include Henry Spaulding's *A Treasure Trove of Jewish Humor*, Nathan Ausubel's *A Treasury of Jewish Humor*, Leo Rosten's *Hooray for Yiddish*, and the interesting and enjoyable *Big Book of Jewish Humor* edited by William Novak and Moshe Waldoks.

Other Groups, Other Issues

The joke book anthologies mentioned above make it abundantly clear that while Jews and blacks account for a very significant percentage of the ethnic joking in America, they are by no means the only targeted groups. Indeed when one thinks of ethnic joking in America, perhaps the first group that comes to mind is the Polish-American. Alan Dundes has compared the Jewish joke and the Polish joke in a 1971 article and Roger L. Welsh has written "American Numbskull Tales: The Polack Joke." A useful historical perspective is suggested by William R. Linneman in "Immigrant Stereotypes: 1800–1900," and by Robert Sklar in "Humor in America." Sources on Irish humor include those cited in the checklist by Vivian Mercier, Charles Fanning, Maureen Waters, and Andrew Greeley. While much has been done in the field, as is suggested by this bibliographical survey and the checklist, a great deal more remains for the scholars who are approaching racial and ethnic humor from so many theoretical, methodological, and disciplinary perspectives.

CHECKLIST AND ADDITIONAL SOURCES

Abrahams, Roger. *Deep Down in the Jungle*. Hatbro, Penn.: Folklore Associates, 1964.

Aman, Reinhold. *Maledicta: The International Journal of Verbal Aggression*. Waukesha, Wis.: published annually.

Apte, Mahadev L. "Ethnic Humor Versus 'Sense of Humor': An American Sociocultural Dilemma." *American Behavioral Scientist* 30; 1 (January/February 1987): 27–41.

———. *Humor and Laughter: An Anthropological Perspective*, Ithaca, N.Y.: Cornell University Press, 1985.

Arnez, Nancy Levi and Clara B. Anthony. "Contemporary Negro Humor as Social Satire." *Phylon* 29 (Winter 1968): 339–46.

Ausubel, Nathan, ed. *A Treasury of Jewish Humor*. Garden City, N.Y.: Doubleday, 1951.

Ben-Amos, Dan. "The 'Myth' of Jewish Humor." *Western Folklore*, 32 (1973): 112–31.

Bergler, Edmund. *Laughter and the Sense of Humor*. New York: International Medical Book, 1956.

Bier, Jesse. *The Rise and Fall of American Humor*. New York: Holt, Rinehart and Winston, 1968.

Boskin, Joseph. "Goodbye, Mr. Bones." *New York Times Magazine*, May 1, 1966, pp. 31, 84–92.

———. *Humor and Social Change in Twentieth-Century America*. Boston: Trustees of the Public Library of the City of Boston, 1979.

———. *Sambo: The Rise and Demise of an American Jester*. New York: Oxford University Press, 1986.

Boskin, Joseph and Joseph Dorinson. "Ethnic Humor: Subversion and Survival." *American Quarterly* 37; 1 (Spring, 1985): 81–97.

Brake, Robert. "The Lion Act is Over: Passive/Aggressive Patterns of Communication in American Negro Humor." *Journal of Popular Culture* 9 (Winter 1975): 549–60.

Brandes, Stanley. "Jewish American Dialect Jokes and Jewish American Identity." *Jewish Social Studies* 45 (1983): 233–40.

Burma, John. "Humor as a Technique in Race Conflict." *American Sociological Review* 11 (December 1946): 710–12.

Chapman, Antony J. and Hugh Foot, eds. *Humour and Laughter: Theory, Research, and Applications*. New York: John Wiley, 1976.

———. *Its a Funny Thing, Humour*. London: Pergamon Press, 1977.

Cox, Harvey. " . . . and Polish Jokes." *Commonweal* 105 (1978): 754–55.

Cray, Ed. "The Rabbi Trickster." *The Journal of American Folklore* 77 (1964): 331–45.

Dance, Daryl Cumber. *Shuckin' and Jivin': Folklore from Contemporary Black Americans*. Bloomington: Indiana University Press, 1978.

Davies, Christie. "Ethnic Jokes, Moral Values, and Social Boundaries." *British Journal of Sociology* 33 (1982): 383–403.

DeLoria, Vine. "Indian Humor." In *Literature of the American Indians*, edited by Abraham Chapman. New York: New American Library, 1975.

Dollard, John. "The Dozens: The Dialect of Insults." *American Imago* 1 (1939).

Dorinson, Joseph. "The Gold-Dust Twins of Marginal Humor: Blacks and Jews." *Maledicta* 8 (1984–1985): 163–92.

Dorson, Richard. *American Negro Folktales*. New York: Fawcett Publications, 1967.

Dresser, Norine. "The Metamorphosis of the Black Man." *New York Folklore Quarterly* 26 (September 1970): 216–28.

Dundes, Alan. "A Study of Ethnic Slurs: The Jew and the Polack in the United States." *Journal of American Folklore* 84 (1971): 187–202.

Erlich, Howard J. "Observations on Ethnic and Intergroup Humor." *Ethnicity* 6 (1979): 383–98.

Fanning, Charles. "The Short Sad Career of Mr. Dooley in Chicago." *Ethnicity* 8 (1981): 169–88.

Fiedler, Leslie. "The Jew as Mythic American." *Ramparts* 2 (August 1963): 34–45.

Foxx, Redd and Norma Miller. *The Redd Foxx Encyclopedia of Black Humor*. Pasadena: Ward Ritchie Press, 1977.

Freud, Sigmund. *Jokes and Their Relation to the Unconscious*, translated and edited by James Strachey. New York: W. W. Norton, 1963.

Goldman, Albert. "Boy-Man Schliemel: The Jewish Element in American Humor." *Commonweal*, rpt., along with additional material dealing with Lennie Bruce, in *Freakshow*. New York: Atheneum, 1971, pp. 169–221.

Goldstein, Jeffrey and Paul McGhee, eds. *The Psychology of Humor: Theoretical Perspectives and Empirical Issues*. New York: Academic Press, 1972.

Greeley, Andrew M. *That Most Distressful Nation: The Taming of the American Irish*. Chicago: Quadrangle Books, 1972, esp. pp. 48–61.

Grotjahn, Martin. "Jewish Jokes and Their Relation to Masochism." In *A Celebration of Laughter*, edited by Werner M. Mendel. Los Angeles: Mars Books, 1970, pp. 135–42.

Hughes, Langston. *The Book of Negro Humor*. New York: Dodd, Mead, 1981.

Hurwitz, Nathan. "Blacks and Jews in American Folklore." *Western Folklore*, 33 (October 1974): 301–25.

Kristol, Irving. "Is Jewish Humor Dead? The Rise and Fall of the Jewish Joke." *Commentary* 12 (November 1951): 431–36.

Levine, Lawrence W. *Black Culture and Consciousness: Afro-American Folk Thought from Slavery to Freedom*. New York: Oxford University Press, 1977.

Lincoln, C. Eric. *The Black Muslims in America*. Boston: Beacon Press, 1961.

Linneman, William R. "Immigrant Stereotypes: 1800–1900." *Journal of American Humor* 1 (April 1974): 29ff.

Lowe, John. "Theories of Ethnic Humor: How to Enter Laughing." *American Quarterly* 38, 3 (1986): 439–60.

Magid, Marion. "Jewish Wit Psychoanalyzed." *Commentary* 34 (September 1962): 265–66.

Martineau, William H. "A Model of the Social Functions of Humor." In *The Psychology of Humor*, edited by Jeffrey Goldstein and Paul McGhee. New York: Academic Press, 1972.

McGhee, Paul and Jeffrey Goldstein, eds. *The Handbook of Humor Research*. 2 vols. New York: Springer Verlag, 1983.

McLean, Albert F., Jr. *American Vaudeville as Ritual*. Lexington: University of Kentucky Press, 1965.

Mercier, Vivian. *The Irish Comic Tradition*. New York: Oxford University Press, 1972.

Mindess, Harvey. *The Chosen People?* Los Angeles: Nash Publications, 1972.

Mintz, Lawrence E. "A Continuum Description of the Motives and Functions of Racial, Sexist, and Ethnic Humor." Paper presented at the Second International Conference on Humor, Los Angeles, 1979. Abstracted in conference abstracts. A version applying the description exclusively to Jewish humor was presented at the Modern Language Association Conference in 1976 and abstracted in *American Humor: An Interdisciplinary Newsletter* 4 (Spring 1977).

Novak, William and Moshe Waldoks, eds. *The Big Book of Jewish Humor*. New York: Harper & Row, 1981.

Oring, Elliott. *The Jokes of Sigmund Freud: A Study in Humor and Jewish Identity*. Philadelphia: University of Pennsylvania, 1984.

Osofsky, Gilbert. *Puttin' on Ole Massa: The Slave Narratives of Henry Bibb, William Wells Brown, and Solomon Northrup*. New York: Harper & Row, 1969.

Rabinowitz, H. R. *Kosher Humor*. Jerusalem: R. H. Hochen, 1977.

Radcliffe-Brown, A. R. "On Joking Relationships." *Africa* 13 (1940): 195–210.

Reik, Theodore. *Jewish Wit*. New York: Gamut Press, 1962.

Ringelbaum, Emanuel. *Notes from the Warsaw Ghetto*, edited and translated by Jacob Sloan. New York: McGraw-Hill, 1958.

Rosten, Leo. *The Joys of Yiddish*. New York: McGraw-Hill, 1968.

———. *Hooray For Yiddish!* New York: Simon & Schuster, 1982.

Rovit, Earl. "Jewish Humor and American Life." *American Scholar* 36 (Spring 1967): 237–45.

Schwartz, Alvin. *Witcracks: Jokes and Jests from American Folklore*. Philadelphia: J. B. Lippincott, 1973.

Signorelli, Nancy. *Portrayal and Stereotyping on Television: An Annotated Bibliography of Studies Relating to Women, Minorities, Aging, Sexual Behavior, Health and Handicaps*. Westport, Conn.: Greenwood Press, 1985.

Singer, I. B. "Everlasting Joke." *Commentary* 35 (November 1961): 458–60.

Sklar, Robert. "Humor in America." In *A Celebration of Laughter*, edited by Werner Mendel. Los Angeles: Mara Books, 1970.

Spaulding, Henry. *Encyclopedia of Black Folklore and Humor*. Middle Village, N.Y.: Jonathan David, 1972.

———. *Encyclopedia of Jewish Humor*. New York: Jonathan David, 1969.

————. *A Treasure Trove of Jewish Humor*. New York: Jonathan David, 1985.

Stephenson, Richard M. "Conflict and Control Functions of Humor." *American Journal of Sociology* 56 (May 1951): 569–74.

Sterling, Philip. *Laughing on the Outside*. New York: Grosset and Dunlap, 1965.

Stowe, William and David Grimstead. "Review Essay: Black-White Humor." *Journal of Ethnic History* 3 (1975): 78–96.

Toll, Robert. *Blacking Up: The Minstrel Show in Nineteenth Century America*. New York: Oxford University Press, 1974.

Waters, Maureen. *The Comic Irishman*. Albany: State University of New York Press, 1984.

Welsh, Roger L. "American Numbskull Tales: The Polack Joke." *Western Folklore* 26 (1967): 183–86.

Whitfield, Stephen J. "The Distinctiveness of American Jewish Humor." *Modern Judaism*, Fall 1986.

————. "Laughter in the Dark: Notes on American Jewish Humor." *Midstream* 24 (February 1978): 48–57.

————. *Voices of Jacob, Hands of Esau: Jews in American Life and Thought*, esp. Chapters 7 and 8. Hamden, Conn.: Archon Books, 1984.

Wilde, Larry. *The Complete Book of Ethnic Humor*. Los Angeles: Pinnacle Books, 1978.

Wilson, Christopher P. *Jokes: Form, Content, Use, and Function*. London: Academic Press, 1979.

Winick, Charles. "The Social Contexts of Humor." *Journal of Communication* 26 (1976): 124–28.

Ziv, Avner, ed. *Jewish Humor*. Tel Aviv: Papyrus Publishing, 1986 (published in English and in Hebrew editions).

————. *Personality and the Sense of Humor*. New York: Springer, 1984.

Political Humor

Stephen J. Whitfield

OVERVIEW

A nation whose political independence was justified according to ''a decent respect for the opinions of mankind'' has long been especially sensitive to the political attitudes that its citizens have nurtured. A polity founded according to the ideal of popular sovereignty is likely to tilt in the direction of indulgence toward ordinary people. Their relationship to authority cannot easily be ignored. Since the responsibility of self-government is at once intimate and intricate, necessary and sometimes even nonsensical, the comic spirit has been an inextricable part of political attitudes. Humor expresses a supremely democratic temperament. In free societies political satire expresses popular beliefs, assumptions, and prejudices with relatively unalloyed fidelity. Humor, though not necessarily wit, is more accessible and more participatory then the civic obligation to wrestle with dilemmas of policy, with articulations of first principles, or with ingredients of ideology. It is therefore an index, though hardly the most significant or even reliable one, of popular will and opinion. It can even flourish under autocratic regimes, where it often serves as a psychically urgent safety valve, though sometimes with unintended subversive effects. That is why such humor is among the residual deposits of the past that political historians must sift through—and neglect at their peril—if the *histoire des mentalités* is to be faithfully reconstructed.

Political humor can have consequences. One of the most honored of recent immigrants to the United States, Aleksandr I. Solzhenitsyn, had been sentenced in 1945 to eight years in the Gulag Archipelago, plus three years in exile, because of his joke about Stalin in a private letter that was intercepted. Dictatorships are notoriously grim, and the cruelty of the conditions they impose is incompatable with a mellow appreciation of human folly. That suggests a certain intimacy between the democratic ethos and the comic spirit. In the United States, where the novelist William Dean Howells defined realism in terms of "the smiling aspects of life,"[1] the stakes are much lower. In recent years, both Secretary of Agriculture Earl Butts and Secretary of the Interior James Watt were forced to resign from the cabinets of Presidents Ford and Reagan, respectively, because of jokes that were deemed insensitive and insulting to minorities. Ford himself was the only Republican candidate to lose a presidential election since 1964, and perhaps one factor in his narrow loss in 1976 was a reputation for clumsiness (and incompetence) that television comedian Chevy Chase effectively skewered.

Sometimes pivotal to meditations on power, humor can nevertheless be so unexpected and subtle in its techniques that the already treacherous terrain of politics can be littered with maps of misreading. Consider George Orwell's *Animal Farm* (1946), a fable that indelibly summarizes the fate of the Bolshevik revolution. Though its author never repudiated his own democratic socialism, *Animal Farm* enlists the repertoire of comic incongruities to condemn the Soviet endeavor to use corrupt and immoral means in extinguishing oppression and exploitation. The power of Orwell's vision was magnified by a 1954 animated cartoon, which suggests an accessibility to political satire that polemicists and propagandists might well envy. Yet the American publisher nevertheless missed the point, and during World War II turned down Orwell's manuscript because of too small a prospective market for "animal stories." As the distinguished Renaissance historian Garrett Mattingly has argued, Machiavelli's *The Prince* was not at all a handbook for the cynical autocrat but itself a satire, written from a republican perspective.[2] It presents the model of Cesare Borgia only with "mordant irony" and was designed to heap scorn on the newly minted tyrants, like the Medici, who are so fulsomely praised. Centuries of readers have nevertheless responded to *The Prince* with shock and anger, oblivious to the possibility that the Machiavellian moment may well have been detonated with what became the last laugh. Such are among the imaginative uses to which political humor can be put.

In its American context, however, this form of gall should be divided into three parts. Perhaps the least consequential and interesting has been humor *by* politicians, who have sometimes deployed it as natural expressions of their own personality and sensibility. More often they have injected humor to burnish their own reputations for folksiness or humanity, or to please their constituencies. John Randolph's description of an adversary ("He shines and stinks like rotten mackerel by moonlight")[3] is often quoted; and in recent American history, Adlai Stevenson and John F. Kennedy have made the most generous contributions to the treasury of American humor. But no statesman exceeded the putative source of such mid-nineteenth century volumes as *Honest Abe's Jokes* and *Old Abe's Jokes*. Lincoln's favorite story about himself underscores the centrality of this feature of his personality. During the Civil War two Quakers sitting in a train were overheard in conversation. "I think Jefferson (Davis) will succeed." "Why does thee think so?" "Because Jefferson is a praying man." "And so is Abraham a praying man." "Yes," the first Quaker replies, "but the Lord will think that Abraham is joking."[4]

An historically more important category has been humor directed *at* politicians. This has functioned as a way of getting even, converting public servants into figures of ridicule, making of them heightened exemplars of folly or special incarnations of greed and corruption. Probably the best-known novel to tap that particular vein is Samuel Clemens and Charle Dudley Warner's *The Gilded Age* (1873). Though its most famous character is Colonel Beriah Sellers, a stock buffoon who incarnated the definition of the public realm as a welcome mat for private interests, its most preposterous politician is Senator Abner Dilworthy, whose resemblance to Senator Samuel C. Pomeroy (GOP-Kansas) was certainly not purely coincidental. The Pulitzer Prize-winning musical by George and Ira Gershwin, *Of Thee I Sing* (1931), is a more modern instance, satirizing a national administration honeycombed by fools who simply cannot be trusted.

The most ambitious, daring, and artistically rich form of political humor slashes directly at the heart of the democratic polity itself. Such derision is not directed at politicans but more fundamentally at politics as such. Here political humor allies itself with a searing comic vision for which remedies cannot be found through rotation in office or an improved civil service or the Australian ballot or institutional tinkering. It is, in other words, radical—striking at the root. Unlike the soporific articles that editors of radical magazines in the twentieth century seem to have encouraged, the socialist cartoons that appeared in *The Masses* used black humor to excoriate militarism, capitalism, imperialism, racism, and the exploitation of labor. In the 1960s the solemn Students for a Democratic Society, with slogans like the vow to "Screw the ass of the ruling class," could be contrasted with Abbie Hoffman, who wanted to goose it instead. This erstwhile leader of the Youth International Party (Yippies) remains the only radical in American history notably subject to the influence of a professional comedian (Lenny Bruce). A cinematic example of systematic satire is Stanley Kubrick's *Dr. Strangelove* (1964), which takes on the grisly—the ultimate— topic of nuclear war. The film shows that, in the shadow of the mushroom cloud, profiles of more conventional forms of madness cannot readily be identified. The early standup comedy of Dick Gregory, himself a presidential candidate in 1968 (Write Me In!), and the often raunchy monthly, the *National Lampoon*, have also probed well beyond the foibles of seekers or holders of elective office.

However, American political humor has generally been most characteristic and authentic in its middle range. It has preferred to work the room by poking fun at politicians. Because the system itself has been so stable (always allowing for the great exception of the Civil War), because political participation has been comparatively widespread and democracy has faced few determined opponents, savage antagonism to the American experiment in self-government has found only a limited audience here. Critics who have been most tenacious in their opposition to the normal operations of American politics have rarely seen or exposed the humor behind their own grievances. Unlike the tragic fatalism and lethal circumstances in which politics elsewhere has commonly been enmeshed, politics here has usually resembled professional wrestling, a body contact sport that bristles with its Gorgeous Georges and Killer Kowalskis who shriek and thump and threaten and never inflict any serious damage—except perhaps to the dignity of the spectators. The United States has harbored no Swifts or Voltaire or Daumiers, no poems like Brecht's satire, "The Jew a Misfortune for the People" (1938) or his anti-Ulbricht "The Solution" (1953). Even our counterpart to George Bernard Shaw—H.L. Mencken—could not completely stifle his own delight in the rogues whose pious bombast his newspaper columns so regularly barbequed. Thus, to recount the development of American political humor, it is not necessary to keep track of any depth charges.

HISTORICAL DEVELOPMENT

Humor is one facet of American history that need not begin with the Puritans, whose gift of levity was not conspicuous; and even the rehabilitation of their reputation that scholars inaugurated two or three generations ago has not advanced a case for the Puritans' comic vision. The subject properly begins with the first important ideological dissident from the Puritan *Weltanschauung*, Benjamin Franklin (1706–1790), whose ironic wit and flair for hoaxes were often directed at political targets. In 1754, in conjunction with the Albany Plan of Union, he devised the first political cartoon ever to appear in an American newspaper (a severed snake above the slogan, "Join, or Die"). Franklin also became a virtuoso of the pointed parable that aimed at American unity and—eventually—independence, as in his essays, "Rules by which a Great Empire May Be Reduced to a Small One" and "An Edict by the King of Prussia" (both 1773). Perhaps the most startling piece, much indebted to Swift's "A Modest Proposal," was Franklin's "On Humbling Our Rebellious Rebels," which appeared in the London *Public Advertiser* (1774). To eliminate the threat of revolution, the emasculation of His Majesty's colonial Americans was proposed. So drastic a policy, the author pretended to suggest, would also cancel the need to import *castrati* from Italy, thriftily promoting the cultivation of home-grown musical talent. But Franklin could also reach for the high notes himself, as in "A Parable Against Persecution" (1775), an apocryphal 51st Chapter of Genesis that adopts Biblical cadences to champion a more open and tolerant society.

Verse was the preferred mode with which the wits of the Revolutionary era jousted, though the fiendish cleverness once imputed to lines like the following— an invective against the Tory spokesman Joseph Galloway of Pennsylvania— are unlikely to provoke the mirth of the modern reader:

> Gall'way has fled, and join'd the venal [General] Howe;
> To prove his baseness, see him cringe and bow;

A traitor to his country, and its laws,
A friend to tyrants, and their cursed cause . . . [5]

The culmination of this tradition of political satire was undoubtedly *The Anarchiad* (1786–1787), the work of Federalist conservatives known as the Connecticut Wits or Hartford Wits. Their suspicion of the triumphant excesses of popular sovereignty can be gauged by their warning of "the certain woe that waits

The giddy rage of democratic States,
Whose pop'lar breath, high-blown in restless tide,
No laws can temper, and no reason guide . . . ''[6]

The first genuinely American accent can be detected only with the advent of Jacksonian democracy, when a Main journalist named Seba Smith (1792–1868) invented a Yankee farmer named Major Jack Downing of Downingville, Away Down East. Applying the test of common sense to the oddities of representative government, whether in the state legislature of Maine or in the cabinet of President Jackson, Downing became the comic prototype of the democratic tradition, a naif whose wry perceptions unmask the insolence of officeholders. This tradition was enriched by James Russell Lowell (1819–1891), whose *Bigelow Papers* drew upon the comic possibilities of the New England dialect to sheathe the anger directed at the aggressive war with Mexico and at the slavocracy that made bloodshed necessary. But perhaps the exemplars of this genre were Charles Farrar Browne (1834–1867), who created a rustic travelling showman named Artemus Ward, and David Ross Locke (1833–1888), whose Petroleum V. Nasby sought to pour some oil on the troubled waves of fratricide that engulfed the mid-nineteenth century. Such wise simpletons, with their own notions about spelling and their unassuming folksiness, established the standard forms of American satire during an era that exalted the virtuous yeomen and dismissed sophistication as mere snobbery.

An entirely different tradition was inaugurated with Ambrose Bierce (1842–1914?), who interrupted the cracker-barrel style of conversation with some of the most bleak and corrosive quips ever targeted at national sancta. Bierce is rare among American humorists in that he refused to be constructive or affirmative or genial; he foresaw no possibilities of redemption. In this sense he was more uncompromising in his blackness even than his admirer—and first heir—Mencken. It is possible to extract from his *Devil's Dictionary* (1906) the outlines of a reasonably consistent and coherent philosophy. It is more tempting, however, to quote this lexicographer's lethal denotations and detonations. For instead of praising the *polis* as the forum of civilized dialogue and noble aspirations, Bierce dismissed politics itself as "a strife of interests masquerading as a contest of principles. The conduct of public affairs for private advantage." He knew enough about diplomacy to define a consul as "a person who having failed to secure an office from the people is given one by the Administration on condition that he leave the country.'' Bierce knew enough about war to define gunpowder as ''an agency employed by civilized nations for the settlement of disputes which might become troublesome if left unadjusted.'' And as a severely wounded Union army veteran, he was able to define an insurrection as ''an unsuccessful revolution. Disaffection's failure to substitute misrule for bad government.''[7]

Samuel L. Clemens (1835–1910) was far less consistent in his political beliefs, and much more ambivalent about the revolt of the masses that had begun in the Jacksonian era, if not sooner. Although he adopted—especially in his later years—some stances that resembled Bierce's acrid cynicism, Mark Twain continued to exude the homespun sagacity that implied ultimate sanction for the democratic prospect itself. Within Twain's poignantly divided self, an unexcelled gift for humor was coiled with the profoundest melancholy. The wildly popular raconteur could entertain practicing politicians, while the estranged rebel could expose the horrors of racism, imperialism, warfare, and lynching—all without breaking stride. He could denounce the shocking defects of American democracy, such as its hypocrisy, its ignorance, its greed and venality, its mob spirit. And yet ''the Lincoln of our literature'' could resist the logic of his own pessimism, putting in the comic perspective of European feudalism and obscurantism the native grounds from which he so frequently exiled himself.

Perhaps the sagest and sanest of political satirists was Finley Peter Dunne (1867–1936), who drew upon the dialect jokes and odd orthography of the phunny phellows, shared in the urban sophistication of Chicago journalists like George Ade, and then established his own original creation: a bartender named Martin Dooley of Archey Road. Probably no literary humorist before or after Dunne has been so exclusively preoccupied with politics. His skepticism and detachment remain fresh, minimizing the need to explain or identify the historical episodes and characters that triggered Mr. Dooley's more than seven hundred disquisitions (mostly to a customer named Hennessy, a very good listener). Thus, after George Baer, the president of the Reading Railroad, claimed in 1902 that property rights had been conferred upon the nation's business elite by a wise Deity, Mr. Hennessy asked about ''the man down in Pennsylvania who said the Lord and him is partners in a coal mine.'' Mr. Dooley responded: ''Has he divided the profits?'' His observation that ''whether the Constitution follows the flag or not, the Supreme Court follows the illiction returns'' has become a truism of Constitutional history. Imperialism drew particular scorn. Theodore Roosevelt's egocentric account of the Spanish-American War, Mr. Dooley wickedly suggested, should have been called *Alone in Cubia*. Hennessy's jingoist boast that ''we're a gr-great people'' brought this jibe: ''We ar-re that. An' th' best iv it is, we know we ar-re.''[8] But so essentially benign was the criticism that issued from Archey Road that Dunne's pieces were regularly read aloud at cabinet meetings, and he had no difficulty striking up a friendship with the putative author of *Alone in Cubia*. Dunne could join the editorial staff of a Progressive organ like the

American magazine while still dismissing the outcries for reform as the sound of the electorate "beatin' the rug."

H. L. Mencken (1880–1956) presents a rather special case, for though his iconoclasm was genuine and sincere, it was constantly undercut by the bon vivant's lip-smacking praise of folly. A trail-blazing critic and champion of avant-garde literature, a precocious explainer and adapter of Nietzsche, an innovative scholar of *The American Language*, a valiant foe of most of what was meretricious and stultifying in American politics and culture, Mencken was an adornment of American letters quite apart from his contribution to the mirth of a nation. He simply could not help finding something funny about American mores and behavior, or indulging in baroque (but never cluttered) prose to express his raucous delight. Mencken rarely missed a nominating convention, and an excerpt from one of his reports to the *Baltimore Evening Sun* in 1924 compresses his animus toward politicians and registers as well the gusto of his own voice:

"There is something about a national convention that makes it as fascinating as a revival or a hanging. It is vulgar, it is stupid, it is tedious, it is hard upon both the higher cerebral centers and the *gluteus maximus*, and yet it is somehow charming. One sits through long sessions wishing heartily that all the delegates and alternates were dead and in hell—and then suddenly there comes a show so gaudy and hilarious, so melodramatic and obscene, so unimaginably exhilarating and preposterous that one lives a gorgeous year in an hour.[9]

Maybe that is why, unlike so many other literati in the 1920s, Mencken chose to fire off his bastinadoes from Baltimore, to remain among the booboisie, rather than escape to the Left Bank. Expecting the electorate to send in the clowns, Mencken the patriot found the American scene—especially the political scene— the greatest show on earth. And the cheapest as well, for he reminded readers of "On Being an American" (1922) how low taxes were: "My private share of the expense of maintaining the Hon. Mr. Harding in the White House this year will work out to less than 80 cents." Because, as a journalist, he received a free subscription to the *Congressional Record*, Mencken was "thus entertained as Solomon never was by his hooch dancers." Among professional humorists Mencken appears to have inspired few imitators, perhaps because the style that was so integral to his stance could fizzle in lesser hands to merely grotesque and predictable exaggeration, perhaps because the sources of Mencken's drollery were fundamentally philosophical. But he undoubtedly influenced the way that presidential nominating conventions have been covered, in particular by Norman Mailer, who was stimulated to exploit an otherwise dormant talent for satiric invective. Fainter echoes—or derision for the benighted custodians of presumably outmoded beliefs—can also be found in (of all places) the economic writings of Thurman Arnold and John Kenneth Galbraith, who have pressed a job buzzer to the invisible hand that conservatives claimed was guiding American capitalism. More recent commentators—up to Mort Sahl and Art Buchwald—have often rounded up Mencken's usual suspects, but without his amazing energy for hatred coated with mellow tolerance.

The last in the line of the cracker-barrel sages to enjoy widespread popularity as a political commentator was Will Rogers (1879–1935), a Democrat whose good-natured ribbing of both parties and of normative political practice gave audiences the impression of horse sense and folk wisdom. With his reassuring midwestern twang came allusions to part-Indian ancestry, so that Rogers could boast that, even though his own forebears had not come over on the *Mayflower*, they had met the boat. Rogers' actual judgments were too feeble to last, his quips too superficial to spice subsequent conceptions of politics; but he was dextrous enough to make the transition to the urban ambience of vaudeville (Ziegfield's Follies) and to the new technology of radio, which he mastered. (Only Fred Allen, on *Town Hall Tonight*, was as adroit in pressing the medium into the service of political ridicule, though his more barbed wit was only intermittently applied to the enterprise of self-government.) Rogers' harmless amiability and aw-shucks ease charmed audiences more fully than any subsequent standup political comedian has achieved, and his facility in getting Americans to laugh away part of their troubles during the Great Depression is not to be disparaged. Because he aimed at the funny bones without also going for the jugular—or hearts and minds—Rogers has been honored with statues and postage stamps more than any sort of literary or political legacy.

The prestige of Rogers' brand of political humor and the eclipse of Mencken (first into sour tirades against the New Deal, then into silence) coincided with the rise of newer writers who, however gifted, ignored the follies of representative government. James Thurber, Dorothy Parker, Ring Lardner, and S. J. Perelman belong on any chronicler's short list of the Paganinis of American humor; yet their major work, which peaked in the interwar years, almost entirely excluded political commentary. Then the junior Senator from Wisconsin, who became an eponym for the domestic Cold War, has sometimes been blamed for the decline of American political and social satire in the post-World War II era. However, Joseph R. McCarthy did enough actual harm not to need censure for the withering of American political humor as well, which was already close to expiring. In 1962 Professor Arthur P. Dudden could describe it as "a suspended if not vanished art,"[10] finding the literary landscape barren of figures equal to Seba Smith, Charles Farrar Browne, David Ross Locke, Ambrose Bierce, Finley Peter Dunne, H. L. Mencken, and Will Rogers.

Yet ironically, at the very moment of Professor Dudden's lament, political humor was beginning once again to pulsate with life. During the presidential campaign two years earlier, the Republicans issued a leaflet directed at workers ("Jack Kennedy Wants Your Job"), warning of the consequences of Democratic economic policies. An indignant Kennedy assured factory employees that "the only job I want is Mr. Eisenhower's"; and when he got it, an ironist with an irrepressible natural wit was installed in the White House. The ingenious and indefatigable Art Buchwald had moved from Paris to Washington, and the *New*

York Times' Russell Baker was inside the Beltway as well. Walking on stage with a newspaper (which Rogers had earlier boasted was his only source of knowledge), Mort Sahl was unleashing some of the most piquant, slashing, and pungent commentary any practicing politicians had ever experienced. Two years after the publication of Dudden's landmark anthology came *Dr. Strangelove*, still the most savagely effective political comedy ever to come from Hollywood. Political cartooning was at perihelion: Jules Feiffer ws already extending the form through the *Village Voice,* the brilliantly acidulous caricatures of David Levine obviated the need for fighting words, and *Doonesbury* soon became more than a gleam in the eye of a Yale undergraduate named Garry Trudeau. A decade after Dudden complained that "many of the conditions so fruitful for political humor in the past no longer exist. It is probably useless to wish for their return," Democratic Party headquarters in the Watergate complex were subjected to a bungled burglary attempt that ignited the most sustained political hilarity in American history.

The definition of American political humor is too elastic to be confined to commentary at its most explicit and *au courant*. It crops up almost everywhere. So arch is the gloom that permeates *The Education of Henry Adams* (1907, 1918) that some readers are apt to miss its sly and ample wit. Adams' chapter on the Grant administration, for example, deftly yields to ancestor worship by inserting science into political science: "That, two thousand years after Alexander the Great and Julius Caesar, a man like Grant should be called—and should actually and truly be—the highest product of the most advanced evolution, made evolution ludicrous. . . . The progress of evolution from President Washington to President Grant, was alone evidence enough to upset Darwin."[11] Among the best novels ever dedicated to the illumination of American politics is *The Last Hurrah* (1956). Primarily a fond character study of a raffish party-machine pol, Edwin O'Connor's book does not allow its Boston Irish sentimentality to keep humor—often vengeful—from percolating frequently to the surface. Though scholars have certainly given William Faulkner his due as a humorist, the works that earned him a speaking engagement in Stockholm (at the Nobel prize ceremonies) are not in a comic mode; and only his most disparaged novel, *A Fable,* could be designated political. Yet notice how in *The Mansion* (1959), the culmination of the Snopes trilogy, V. K. Ratliff destroys the congressional candidacy of Clarence E. Snopes by having the trousers of the office-seeker doused with canine urine, causing the dogs of the district to be so eager to relieve themselves on the candidate's legs that he is forced out of the race. Snopes is ineligible, according to Yoknapatawpha king-maker Will Varner, because "I aint going to have Beat Two and Frenchman's Bend respresented by nobody that ere a son-a-bitching dog that happens by cant tell from a fence post."[12]

Just as the most formidable and complex of modernist American novelists could deploy political humor (barnyard variety), the detritus of popular culture could also include political humor that ought to engage scholarly interest. Mass communications in the twentieth century have expanded the possibilities for entertainers whose earlier counterparts might have been confined to the ephemera of journalism or the vagaries of the lecture circuit. Comedy albums have often been devoted to political subjects, from Stan Freberg's spoof of Senator Mc-Carthy, the 45 r.p.m. "Point of Order," to Vaughn Meader's dissection of the Kennedy clan in *The First Family,* to Tom Lehrer's *That Was the Year That Was,* a liberal songfest assaulting Hubert Humphrey, Werner Von Braun, NA-TO's Multilateral Force, and the revised Roman Catholic mass. Though pitched toward adolescents and devoted primarily to parodying the other artifacts of mass culture, *Mad* magazine has often taken political stands. The cover of a 1985 issue, for example, features President Ronald Reagan looking quite distinctly like Alfred E. Newman (the magazine's equivalent of the *New Yorker's* Eustace Tilley), showing Rambo (Sylvester Stallone) a map on which Nicaragua is located.

Ever since Benjamin Franklin's "Join, or Die," cartoons have long been a staple of political humor. The pinnacle was quite possibly reached after the Civil War with Thomas Nast (1840–1902), whose drawing and quartering of New York City's Tweed Ring is a civic achievement that every schoolchild knows—or used to. Sending those thieves to jail or into exile remains the standard against which all editorial cartoonists have subsequently measured themselves. But some of the finest graphic humorists have appeared in American newspapers only during the past couple of decades. Herblock's caricatures of Richard M. Nixon in the *Washington Post* were so definitive that they may have affected the effort of his political consultants (and cosmeticians) to distance himself from the scruf-finess and shadiness that the staunchly liberal critic had emphasized. Younger cartoonists of comparable luster have included Tony Auth of the *Philadelphia Inquirer*, Paul Conrad of the *Los Angeles Times*, Jeff MacNelly of the *Richmond News Leader*, Pat Oliphant of the *Denver Post* and later the *Washington Star*, Mike Peters of the *Dayton Daily News*, Paul Szep of the *Boston Globe*, and Don Wright of the *Miami News*. These curmudgeons make no attempt to court popularity, and some of them might be disappointed if more than three cars were to show up at their funerals. Yet their work comprises the diadems of daily journalism—and of political criticism as well.

Two others have been especially innovative in advancing the art of graphic political humor. Jules Feiffer of the *Village Voice* has endowed the six or eight panels to which he has confined himself with exceptional deadpan wit, literacy, political acumen, and psychological sensitivity. David Levine, the staff artist of the *New York Review of Books*, has specialized in literary as well as political caricatures, a genre at which he ranks with the very greatest who have ever lived. His portraits of political figures, conceived within a radical political matrix, are noteworthy for their high acid content, especially during the Vietnam War and the presidencies of Johnson and Nixon.

The recent status of American political humor ought to be considered healthy. No major society has allowed its writers and artists such latitude to express themselves, to mock its leaders, and to traduce its values. With the untrammeled production of Barbara Garson's *MacBird* (1966), a parody of *Macbeth* that accused President Johnson of assassinating his predecessor, it became apparent that freedom of political expression was, perhaps for the first time in the history of civilization, unlimited. Obscenity—which etymologically meant that which could not be staged—had by the end of the 1960s virtually become an essential accoutrement of theatrical productions. The drug abuse and scatological language of the late Lenny Bruce, whose standup comedy included a cynical derision of liberals as well as conservatives, had prevented him from appearing in cities where audiences soon thereafter flocked to the Bob Fosse film biography, *Lenny* (1974), which downplayed his satiric savagery. So legitimate had relentless political satire become that, in Robert Coover's novel, *The Public Burning* (1977), the execution of the atomic spies, Julius and Ethel Rosenberg, could be treated as show biz and Nixon sodomized by the figure of Uncle Sam. Philip Roth's utterly unsparing parody of Nixon's rhetorical and political style, *Our Gang (Starring Tricky and His Friends)* (1971), which includes a scene in Hell, made the best-seller list.

Political humorists have also used their freedom in imaginative ways. If a capital fellow named Art Buchwald does not dominate the field of humorous political commentary as incontrovertibly as, say, Will Rogers did, the reason may be increased competition. Political satire has appeared on television (from *The Smothers Brothers* to *Laugh-In* to *Saturday Night Live*) and another Potomac prankster named Mark Russell remains at large. The cartoons on the editorial pages of many newspapers continue to glisten with swing-for-the-fences satire. Garry Trudeau's *Doonesbury* has become something akin to essential reading among politicos and political aficionados, as much as the editorials next to which the saga of Walden Commune and its offshoots commonly appears. When Trudeau received a Pulitzer Prize in 1975 for editorial cartooning, *Doonesbury* became the first comic strip to be so honored. Even before the Watergate scandals generated a comic extravaganza, Feiffer was speaking for his fellow cartoonists when he wrote of the Johnson administration: "These are the best days since Boss Tweed."[13] Even though Mort Sahl went into a tailspin and Tom Lehrer did not fulfill the high promise of *That Was the Year That Was*, even though filmmaker Woody Allen has gone from this side of parodies to increasingly mordant morality tales rather than political lampooning, even though black humorists like Kubrick and novelist Joseph Heller have focused most of their attention on targets other than politics, there is reason to believe that satire won't close next Saturday night. For so long as the United States remains considerably east of Eden and less than perfect, its political actors and arrangements will provide adult entertainment rather than replicate a junior high civics textbook. They will still elicit words and deeds too humorous to mention.

KEY ISSUES FOR RESEARCH

Despite the impressive historical fund of American political humor, much work remains to be done to explicate and interpret it. It is a natural topic for interdisciplinary approaches, since it ought to challenge the talents of historians, political scientists, literary critics, students of popular culture, paladins of American Studies, and rank amateurs who can appreciate all the absurdities of self-government.

One issue that could be addressed in future research is the receptivity of the marketplace for political humor. Humor *by* politicians poses no heuristic problems, since most presidents have been rather deficient in this gift. President Reagan, who has tended to memorize risible excerpts from *Reader's Digest*, is in this respect quite typical. Some of his predecessors, however, have felt obliged to rein in their own flair for the ludicrous. For example, Lyndon Johnson's humor was so rooted in the scatological underground of frontier folklore that it was deemed too tasteless for public consumption, as when the president disparaged the competence of a Cabinet member: "He couldn't pour piss from a boot if the instructions were written on the heel." Others, like Kansas Senator Robert Dole, have been so acerbic in their wit that they have tried to sheathe it as something of a political liability. In 1952 candidate Eisenhower was able to turn his own lack of humor against the irrepressibly witty Stevenson, by insisting that international circumstances were too critically serious for levity, an assault that seems to have worked. But generally humor in a politician is a bit of an asset, though its form and directness are subject to change and to the vagaries of taste. How these fluctuations have affected political style is worthy of some historical investigation. Very shrewd remarks in this respect can be found in Jeff Greenfield's *Playing to Win* (1980), a handbook for the contemporary politico that is *not* (*pace* Mattingly) a satire. Otherwise no major research issues on humor *by* politicians belong on the agenda.

That is not the case with humor *about* politics. Some questions might be posed as follows: Is the effect of such humor to promote derision and therefore contempt for politics in general, promoting withdrawal or political quiescence, thus in effect affirming (however unintentionally) the status quo? Or does such humor, because of its very adroitness and vitality and pungency, make the political process more interesting? Is it an ancilla of political interest? Does such humor find more effective or vulnerable targets on any particular part of the political spectrum, and are the creators or custodians of such humor more likely to come from the liberal or progressive element (as is commonly the case, with some important exceptions) than on the right, and if so, why? Is political humor commonly associated with any sort of program or policy, or does that tend to undermine the nature of comedy itself? Is the satiric imagination itself an extension of a certain manner or habit that can have a political content or context?

Researchers might also investigate the forms and genres that political humor has assumed. Surely it makes a difference that Twain wrote fiction, which can summon the most ample resources for the full play of human emotion, folly, and psychological and social depth, whereas Herbert Block surveys the political scene as a cartoonist (however incisive the commentary that he provides in the chapters of collections of his cartoons). Feiffer has engaged in political satire both as a cartoonist and as a playwright (*The White House Murder Mystery*). Have Art Buchwald and Russell Baker been limited in their political commentary by the restrictions of a columnist's space, thus preventing them from the sort of amplitude that Twain's genius enabled him to attain? Have there been innovative formal breakthroughs? It has undoubtedly mattered that David Levine's caricatures (by no means confined to political figures) were enlarged in the pages of the *New York Review of Books*, rather than in the smaller confines of the magazines where his portraits initially appeared.

Has political humor on television been decisively limited by the character of the medium itself—its need to appeal to the largest imaginable audience, its commercial requirements, its sensitivity to the expectations of audiences and sponsors and producers, its awareness that network affiliates are regulated by an agency of the federal government? Some political comedies deserve to be ranked among the best films ever to emerge from Hollywood, such as *Ninotchka* (1939), *The Great Dictator* (1940), and *Dr. Strangelove* (1964). Other films have poked fun at the obsession with anticommunism, such as *One, Two, Three* (1961) and *The Russians are Coming, the Russians are Coming* (1966). But oddly enough the classic films about the practice of American politics, from *Mr. Smith Goes to Washington* to their fainter echoes, such as *Advise and Consent*, have not been comedies. Why serious cinematic satire has generally been directed abroad—to communism and to fascism—deserves further speculation. Some of the most charged political commentary has been provided by standup comedians, either in night clubs or "concerts" or through studio albums. Their work has generally been preserved—if at all—on records (where the most comprehensive collection can be found in the Library of Congress, in the Recorded Sound Division). What difference does it make that their satire must achieve its effects entirely through verbal and aural means?

Finally, all such questions can be placed within a comparative perspective. How has American political humor differed from or resembled political humor in other countries, such as Canada, or Great Britain, or France, or the Soviet Union? Where are the American equivalents of Britain's *Punch*, G. K. Chesterton and George Bernard Shaw, or the political satire of Gilbert and Sullivan; or France's newspaper, *Le Canard Enchainé* or of the Soviet Union's newspaper *Krokodil*? What functions do these media or figures perform in other countries for which there is no precise American counterpart—and if not, why not? There are highly suggestive comparative remarks in Chapter IX ("American and Foreign Humor") of Jesse Bier's *The Rise and Fall of American Humor* (1968), but its political manifestations constitute another entree into national and cultural differences that still need exploration.

In her classic introduction to the subject of *American Humor* (1931), Constance Rourke observed: "In the nation, as comedy moves from a passing effervescence into the broad stream of common possession, its bearings become singularly wide. There is scarcely an aspect of the American character to which humor is not related, few which in some sense it has not governed."[14] Oddly enough her own book virtually ignored political satire as such, while finding space for the sorts of writers—from Hawthorne to Henry James—whose comic zingers would have gotten them few bookings in the Catskills or anywhere else (a reminder of how annoyingly impossible it is to reach a consensus on the definition of humor). But Rourke's volume can be cited to certify that questions of humor ultimately coalesce into questions of national character, into that process of incessant self-interrogation that has done so much to define America itself.

NOTES

1. William Dean Howells quoted in Alfred Kazin, *On Native Grounds: An Interpretation of Modern American Prose Literature* (Garden City, N.Y.: Doubleday Anchor, 1956 [1942]), p. 17.

2. Garrett Mattingly, "Machiavelli's *Prince*: Political Science or Political Satire?" in Hiram Haydn and Betsy Saunders, eds., *The American Scholar Reader* (New York: Atheneum, 1960), pp. 447–62.

3. John Randolph quoted in Leon A. Harris, *The Fine Art of Political Wit* (New York: E. P. Dutton, 1966), p. 53.

4. Carl Sandburg, *Abraham Lincoln: The Prairie Years and the War Years* (New York: Harcourt, Brace, 1954), p. 573.

5. Joseph Galloway quoted in Bruce Ingham Granger, *Political Satire in the American Revolution, 1763–1783* (Ithaca, N.Y.: Cornell University Press, 1960), pp. 288–89, 304–5.

6. Ibid.

7. Ambrose Bierce, *The Devil's Dictionary* (New York: Hill and Wang, 1957).

8. Finley Peter Dunne, *Mr. Dooley on Ivrything and Ivrybody*, ed. Robert Hutchinson (New York: Dover, 1963), pp. 5, 106, 160, 200, 244.

9. H. L. Mencken, *A Carnival of Buncombe*, ed. Malcolm Moos (Baltimore: Johns Hopkins University Press, 1956), p. 79.

10. Arthur P. Dudden, *The Assault of Laughter: A Treasury of American Political Humor* (New York: A. S. Barnes–Thomas Yoseloff, 1962), p. 34.

11. Henry Adams, *The Education of Henry Adams*, ed. Ernest Samuels (Boston: Houghton Mifflin, 1973 [1918]), p. 266.

12. William Faulkner, *The Mansion* (New York: Random House, 1959), pp. 317–19.

13. Jules Feiffer, Introduction to Sig Rosenblum and Charles Antin, eds., *LBJ Lampooned* (New York: Cobble Hill Press, 1968), p. 15.

14. Constance Rourke, *American Humor: A Study of the National Character* (Garden City, N.Y.: Doubleday Anchor, 1953 [1931]), p. 9.

BIBLIOGRAPHICAL SURVEY

No overall interpretive history of American political history is extant; it remains to be written. But as prolegomena to such a history, the invaluable introductions to Arthur Dudden's anthologies and to that of Leonard C. Lewin should be consulted. Dudden's essay in the special issue of *American Quarterly* (vol. 37, Spring 1985) on "The Record of Political Humor" updates his earlier views.

Though it is neither interpretive nor confined to the United States, Leon Harris' *The Fine Art of Political Wit* also includes much relevant material.

No single volume is devoted to a particular period in the history of American political humor, apart from Bruce Ingham Granger's study of satire in the American Revolutionary era. Nor is there a book-length study of a particular magazine or journal devoted to political and social satire. Proceeding at their own risk, interested students must therefore consult more general studies of American humor, from Rourke's *American Humor* through Blair and Hill's *America's Humor*, as well as the biographies of particular contributors to the treasury of political humor. These more specialized studies are also listed in the checklist that follows.

CHECKLIST AND ADDITIONAL SOURCES

Adler, Bill, ed. *The Kennedy Wit*. New York: Citadel, 1964.

Becker, Stephen. *Comic Art in America*. New York: Simon & Schuster, 1959.

Bier, Jesse. *The Rise and Fall of American Humor*. New York: Holt, Rinehart and Winston, 1968.

Bierce, Ambrose. *The Devil's Dictionary*. New York: Hill and Wang, 1957.

Blair, Walter, and Hamlin Hill. *America's Humor: From Poor Richard to Doonesbury*. New York: Oxford University Press, 1978.

Bode, Carl. *Mencken*. Carbondale: Southern Illinois University Press, 1969.

Boller, Paul. *Presidential Anecdotes*. New York: Oxford University Press, 1981.

Boskin, Joseph. *Humor and Social Change in Twentieth-Century America*. Boston: Trustees of the Public Library of the City of Boston, 1979.

Brooks, Charles, ed. *Best Editorial Cartoons of the Year*. Gretna, La.: Pelican, 1973 on. Published annually.

Brown, William Richard. *Imagemaker: Will Rogers and the American Dream*. Columbia: University of Missouri Press, 1970.

Buchwald, Art. *Up the Seine and Down the Potomac*. New York: G. P. Putnam's Sons, 1977.

Budd, Louis J. *Mark Twain: Social Philosopher*. Bloomington: Indiana University Press, 1962.

A Cartoon History of United States Foreign Policy, 1776–1976, edited by The Foreign Policy Association. New York: William Morrow, 1975.

Chapel, Gage William. "Humor in the White House: An Interview with Presidential Speechwriter Robert Orben." *Communication Quarterly* 25 (Winter 1978): 44–49.

Cox, Samuel S. *Why We Laugh*. New York: Harper and Brothers, 1876.

Dennis, Everette E. "The Regeneration of Political Cartooning." *Journalism Quarterly* 51 (Winter 1974): 664–69.

Dennis, Everette E., and Melvin Dennis. "One Hundred Years of Political Cartooning." *Journalism History* 51 (Spring 1974): 6–10.

Duberman, Martin. *James Russell Lowell*. Boston: Beacon, 1966.

Dudden, Arthur P. *The Assault of Laughter: A Treasury of American Political Humor*. New York: A. S. Barnes–Thomas Yoseloff, 1962.

————. *Pardon Us, Mr. President! American Humor on Politics*. South Brunswick, N.J.: A. S. Barnes, 1975.

————. "The Record of Political Humor." *American Quarterly* 37 (Spring 1985): 50–70.

Dunne, Finley Peter. *Mr. Dooley on Ivrything and Ivrybody*. New York: Dover, 1963.

Fanning, Charles. *Finley Peter Dunne and Mr. Dooley: The Chicago Years*. Lexington: University of Kentucky Press, 1978.

Feiffer, Jules. *Feiffer: Jules Feiffer's America from Eisenhower to Reagan*. New York: Alfred A. Knopf, 1982.

Fitzgerald, Richard. *Art and Politics: Cartoonists of the MASSES and LIBERATOR*. Westport, Conn.: Greenwood Press, 1973.

French, Bryant Morey. *Mark Twain and THE GILDED AGE: The Book that Named an Era*. Dallas: Southern Methodist University Press, 1965.

Fry, William F. "The Power of Political Humor." *Journal of Popular Culture* 10 (Summer 1976): 227–31.

Gibson, William M. *Theodore Roosevelt Among the Humorists: W. D. Howells, Mark Twain, and Mr. Dooley*. Knoxville: University of Tennessee Press, 1980.

Granger, Bruce Ingham. *Political Satire in the American Revolution, 1763–1783*. Ithaca, N.Y.: Cornell University Press, 1960.

Harris, Leon A. *The Fine Art of Political Wit*. New York: Bell, 1964.

Hess, Stephen and Milton Kaplan. *The Ungentlemanly Art: A History of American Political Cartoons*. New York: Macmillan, 1968, 1975.

Hoffman, Abbie. *Soon to be a Major Motion Picture*. New York: G. P. Putnam's Sons, 1980.

Holden, Joan. "Satire and Politics in America." *Theater* 10 (Spring 1979): 104–7.

Kaplan, Justin. *Mr. Clemens and Mark Twain: A Biography*. New York: Simon & Schuster, 1966.

Keller, Morton. *The Art and Politics of Thomas Nast*. New York: Oxford University Press, 1968.

Levine, David. *The Arts of David Levine*. New York: Alfred A. Knopf, 1978.

Lewin, Leonard C., ed. *A Treasury of American Political Humor*. New York: Dial, 1964.

Macdonald, Dwight, ed. *Parodies: An Anthology from Chaucer to Beerbohm—and After*. New York: Modern Library, 1960.

Maland, Charles. "*Dr. Strangelove* (1964): Nightmare Comedy and the Ideology of Liberal Consensus." In *Hollywood as Historian: American Film in a Cultural Context*, edited by Peter C. Rollins. Lexington: University of Kentucky Press, 1983, pp. 190–210.

Mattingly, Garrett. "Machiavelli's *Prince*: Political Science or Political Satire?" In *The American Scholar Reader*, edited by Hiram Haydn and Betsy Saunders. New York: Atheneum, 1960, pp. 447–62.

Mintz, Lawrence E. (chairman), Art Buchwald, Jeff MacNelly, Robert Orben, and Mark Russell. "Perspectives on American Political Humor." *American Humor: An Interdisciplinary Newsletter* 5 (Fall 1978): 1–13.

Morrison, Donald, and Stefan Kanfer. "Doonesbury: Drawing and Quartering for Fun and Profit." *Time* 107 (February 9, 1976): 57–60, 65–66.

Ninotchka. Screenplay by Charles Brackett, Billy Wilder, and Walter Reisch. New York: Viking, 1972.

Petersen, Svend, ed. *Mark Twain and the Government*. Caldwell, Idaho: Caxton, 1960.

Press, Charles. *The Political Cartoon*. Rutherford, N.J.: Fairleigh Dickinson University Press, 1981.

Robinson, Jerry, ed. *The 1970's: Best Political Cartoons of the Decade*. New York: McGraw-Hill, 1981.

Roth, Philip. *Our Gang (Starring Tricky and His Friends)*. New York: Random House, 1971.

Rourke, Constance. *American Humor: A Study of the National Character*. New York: Harcourt, Brace, 1931.

Rubin, Louis D., ed. *The Comic Imagination in American Literature*. New Brunswick, N.J.: Rutgers University Press, 1983.

Sandburg, Carl. *Abraham Lincoln: The War Years*. New York: Harcourt, Brace, 1939, Vol. 3, Chapter 56.

Schutz, Charles E. *Political Humor: From Aristophanes to Sam Ervin*. Cranbury, N.J.: Associated University Presses, 1977.

Tighe, M. A. 'The Caricature of David Levine." *New Republic* 174 (March 20, 1976): 19–21.

Trachtenberg, Stanley, ed. *American Humorists, 1800–1950*. 2 vols. Detroit: Gale, 1982.

Waters, Harry F., and Jane Whitmore. ''Poison Penmanship.'' *Newsweek* 93 (January 22, 1979): 73–74.

Wertheim, Arthur Frank. *Radio Comedy*. New York: Oxford University Press, 1979, esp. Chapter 8.

Westin, Alan, ed. *Getting Angry Six Times a Week*. Boston: Beacon, 1979.

Whitfield, Stephen J. ''Richard Nixon as a Comic Figure.'' *American Quarterly* 37 (Spring 1985): 114–32.

Yates, Norris W. *The American Humorist: Conscience of the Twentieth Century*. Ames: Iowa State University Press, 1964.

Zall, Paul M., ed. *Abe Lincoln Laughing*. Berkeley: University of California Press, 1982.
———. *Ben Franklin Laughing*. Berkeley: University of California Press, 1980.

DISCOGRAPHY

Frye, David. *I am the President*. Elektra EKS 75006 (1970).

Gregory, Dick. *The Two Sides of Dick Gregory*. Vee-Jay LP 4005 (1963).

Hope, Bob. *American is 200 Years Old*. Capitol T 11538 (1976).

Lehrer, Tom. *That Was the Year that Was*. Reprise RS–6179 (1969).

Little, Rich. *Rich Little, Politics and Popcorn*. Mercury SRM 1617 (1971).

Meader, Vaughn. *The First Family*. Cad 3060 25060 (1963).

National Lampoon. *The Missing White House Tapes*. Blue Thumb BTS 6008 (1974).

Paulson, Pat. *Pat Paulson for President*. Mercury SR 61179 (1968).

Rogers, Will. *Will Rogers Radio Broadcasts*. Mark 56 659 (n.d.).
———. *The Wit and Wisdom of Will Rogers*. Caedmon TC 2046 (n.d.).

Russell, Mark. *Wild, Weird, Wired World of Watergate*. Deep Six 0000001 (1973).

Sahl, Mort. *The New Frontier*. Reprise R 5003 (1961).

Vidal, Gore. *An Evening with Richard Nixon*. Ode SP 77015 (1972).

White, Slappy. *Elect Slappy White Vice-President*. Laff A 159 (1972).

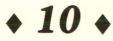

♦ *10* ♦

Folklore Methodology and American Humor Research

Elliott Oring

OVERVIEW

The serious study of tales, songs, riddles, proverbs, customs, and other forms that are today designated "folklore" began with the nineteenth century in Europe. Strongly influenced by romantic-nationalistic feelings, such materials were gathered among the peasantry and believed to be the detritus of a culture and ideology long gone—the culture of an aboriginal folk, who had lived upon the land, uncorrupted by Greek, Roman, or even Christian influence,[1] Even as the study of these materials was taken up in Britain with less nativistic motivations later in the century, the basic orientation toward these materials remained the same; they were relics—cultural survivals from ages past, no longer "at home" in their contemporary environments.[2]

When the study of folklore was undertaken in the United States at the turn of the century, the concept of folklore was redefined. The large cultural and historical discontinuities between the aboriginal population and those who came to inhabit the continent created enormous difficulties in the conceptualization of an American folklore. Consequently, folklore was viewed less as relics of the distant past than as unwritten traditions maintained through time, even if many of those traditions originated abroad.[3]

This shift in the conceptualization was significant for the study of folklore in general and for the study of humor in particular. Those early scholars who saw folklore as a way to reconstruct the remote past, particularly past beliefs, ideas, and philosophies, lavished their attentions upon tales, proverbs, riddles, calendar customs, and superstitions because these were felt to contain germs of the religiophilosophical systems of ancient or primitive folk. There was little attention to humor in this endeavor, since humor was regarded as trivial and unrelated to the serious philosophical systems of the past. Humor was collected only because it was a component of folktales, and folktales—particularly magic tales—were regarded as crucial in the reconstruction of these past religious ideologies. Basically, humor was incidental to the inquiry. If proverbs, riddles, and other sayings were regarded as "folk-wit," it was more in the sense of "knowledge" or "wisdom" than humor.[4]

With the American emphasis upon "oral tradition," origins became of less concern and all traditions became objects for study, including humorous ones. The collecting of humorous songs and tales proceeded with great energy, with only the obscene materials creating any dilemmas for their enthusiastic collectors. The assumption of these collectors was that tradition, both humorous and non-humorous, was on the wane and needed to be recorded. But the bits of folklore they collected were also compared and related to other known traditions, so that some larger "tradition" could be apprehended and a picture of folklore migration and spread could be constructed.

There was no end to the traditions that could be collected. In time, attention began to turn from mere accumulation to the tasks of explanation and interpretation. Furthermore, attention began to focus upon orally transmitted stories, songs, and speech that reflected contemporary situations, circumstances, and events. Folklore began to be viewed less as an artifact from the past and more as an expression of the present. New conceptualizations of folklore as "verbal art"[5] or "artistic communication in small groups"[6] emerged. Humorous expression, as a type of artistic communication, could be studied in its own right. Its forms and dynamics could be explored with less attention to questions of history and tradition.

Each conceptualization of folklore—as survival, oral tradition, and artistic communication—has left its impression upon the field. Each has had an important influence on the way folklorists conduct their research today. The survivalistic perspective initiated the widespread collecting and preservation of folklore. The characterization of folklore as "oral tradition" encouraged folklorists to trace the relationships of folklore forms through time and space and gave rise to the great comparative indexes. The realization that folklore was a living artistic expression directed attention to the contemporary contexts that shaped that expression. Collecting, indexing, and contextualization emerged as methodological concerns that characterized the folkloristic enterprise. These aspects of folklore methodology are exceedingly relevant to the study of American humor as well.

COLLECTING

Since folklore was originally conceived to be a survival from the remote past in imminent danger of dying out, the initial impetus of folklore research was the wholesale collection of extant folk traditions. Little of this collecting was directed toward the documenting of humorous traditions per se, but there was a concerted effort to preserve American folktale and song traditions, and within this collected corpus, a great deal of oral American humor as well. Large numbers of "raw" texts were consequently published in the pages of the *Journal of American Folklore*, the *Memoirs of the American Folklore Society*,[7] and in other folklore journals that were originally created by folklore societies to champion particular American regions. Intensive regional collections of American folklore also found their way to publication.

Although these early efforts at collecting were often crude by today's standards, early collectors managed to capture some sense of the oral expressions that were stored in the memories of everyday American (although primarily rural) people. The importance of these materials becomes particularly clear to the student of Americn humor when it is realized how much of the characterization of American humor is based upon literary or subliterary sources. The almanacs, sketchbooks, theatrical pieces, and memoirs that have served as the primary resources for the conceptualization of American humor[8] may give an accurate representation of what Americans read but do not necessarily give an accurate representation of what they know or tell. Of course, the literary and subliterary sources are absolutely crucial in any reconstruction of American folklore and American humor prior to the final decade of the nineteenth century, when field collecting began in earnest,[9] but it is unlikely that anything approaching a complete picture, whether in past centuries or in our own, can be drawn from media sources alone.

Collections by contemporary folklorists are different in several ways than those of their predecessors. Contemporary folklorists are likely to have had graduate training in folklore[10] and to have been exposed to a variety of theoretical perspectives that inform the collecting enterprise. These folklorists are more likely to address humorous traditions directly—not merely as an adjunct of the folktale—and to place considerably more emphasis upon contemporary and even ephemeral humorous expressions. A quest for materials with discernible links to past traditions is no longer *de rigueur*. There is also a much greater emphasis upon the social and cultural contexts in which folk expression takes place. Consequently, fewer collections of texts are published by folklorists. Those that do appear usually include a description of the fieldwork, transcription, and editing processes that preceded publication, sociological and other data on the tellers and their audience, and comparative notes on the tales themselves. Published collections that are unaccompanied by such critical apparatuses are generally those that are motivated by the regional or ethnic pride of an enthusiastic amateur, or published as children's entertainment. Such popularizations are unlikely to prove reliable representations of oral traditions of narrative or humor.

If raw texts are not published as frequently today as they were in the past, they are still available to the researcher. Thousands upon thousands of texts are deposited in folklore archives. Unlike the archives found in Europe that may be state funded and staffed by professional archivists and field collectors, American folklore archives are almost invariably established in a university by a faculty folklorist who teaches several sections of an introductory folklore course. Undergraduate students are urged to collect and document folklore in fulfillment of their course requirements, and the materials they submit may be indexed and stored in an archive. Donations of field materials by professional and amateur folklorists also regularly occur. Although the quality of archival materials is likely to be uneven, these archives often provide an excellent sample of regional folk traditions—with humorous traditions prominently represented. The accessibility of archival materials will depend to a great degree upon the resources of the folklore program in which it is housed. Those universities with active graduate programs are likely to have a greater number of trained archivists sifting, sorting, and indexing the submitted collections.

The folklorist's penchant for accumulating texts is still very much alive. A folkloristic analysis is more likely to be directed to a corpus or repertoire rather than a single text. Even a short interpretive article may include dozens of texts either collected by the researcher or drawn from archival sources. Folklorists have continued to collect and document humorous texts, including: bop jokes, elephant jokes, sick jokes, obscene jokes, handicap jokes, light bulb jokes, ethnic jokes, and Auschwitz jokes. In addition to these joke forms, they have also documented the humorous riddles, proverbs, proverbial comparisons, graffiti, nicknames, slangs, rituals, routines, dramas, and Xerox lore that, for the most part, have been omitted from the description of American humor.

INDEXING

The early comparative interests of folklorists led to the compilation of numerous large indexes or catalogues of folk materials, particularly of prose narratives. The intention was to list and classify folk narrative plots and motifs to establish some standard for the identification of orally collected narratives and to contribute to the establishment of their connection to older and broader streams of folk tradition. The most well-known of these indexes is *The Types of the Folktale*, Stith Thompson's twice-revised edition of Antti Aarne's *Verzeichnis der Marchentypen*.[11] *The Types of the Folktale* attempts to classify the plots of orally collected tales found in Europe and west Asia (and in those lands inhabited by emigrants from these areas), and assigns to each distinct plot its own identifying number. In addition, an attempt is made to provide bibliographic references to each indexed tale from printed and archival collections. The classification is broadly divided into five categories: (1) Animal Tales, (2) Ordinary Folktales, (3) Jokes and Anecdotes, (4) Formula Tales, and (5) Unclassified Tales. Each of these categories contains some humorous or jocular materials with categories 3 (Types 1200–1999) and 4 (Types 2000–2399) being exclusively comprised of such materials.

Even more ambitious than the index of types was Stith Thompson's *Motif-*

Index of Folk-Literature.[12] In this six-volume opus, Thompson attempted to catalog the individual elements that comprise traditional narrative literature. In the *Motif-Index*, Thompson did not limit himself to the elements of orally collected European tales but, drawing upon worldwide sources—both popular and literary—he cataloged the elements of myth, fable, ballad, romance, jest, and exemplum as well. The organization of the motifs is from "the mythological and the supernatural toward the realistic and humorous," with Chapters J "The Wise and the Foolish," K "Deceptions," amd X "Humor" containing the greatest number of humorous motifs. The index of motifs makes no attempt at full bibliographic reference but is content with one or two illustrative citations for each motif.

The compilation of type and motif indexes was part and parcel of the larger concern for the chronological and geographical distribution of individual folktales and the hypothesizing of "original" forms—an enterprise that occupied European and American folktale scholars from the turn of the century through the 1950s. The indexes proved indispensible in the identification of an individual tale tradition and its relations as well as in providing a first step in the amassing of numerous tale analogues necessary for the study of its historical and geographical vicissitudes.

Ernest W. Baughman's *Type and Motif-Index of the Folktales of England and North America* also explores some generally comparative questions concerning the influence of English folk narrative tradition upon the English-language traditions of North America. By comparing the distribution of types and motifs from the two areas, he confirmed a number of suspicions long held by students of folk narrative, most notably that American narrative tradition is characterized to a *much* greater extent by humorous tales and motifs than English tradition—particularly by tales of lying and motifs of hyperbolic exaggeration. Baughman tentatively credits the American landscape, the expanding frontier, and media dissemination for the popularity of these narrative types.[13]

Despite the fact that historic-geographic studies are no longer in vogue, the indexes of types and motifs continue to serve folklorists and are of use to the student of humor as well. Such indexes provide the beginnings of a comparative perspective within which the study of specific humorous forms can be grounded. By first attending to comparative concerns, the student of a particular form of humorous expression may (1) be directed to certain fruitful questions that might otherwise have escaped notice, or (2) avoid certain methodological problems that often attend analyses that are otherwise culturally or regionally circumscribed.

For example, the following humorous narrative was told by a black college student to the other members of his class:

Well, this joke that I want to tell is about the Black man, the White man, and the Chinese man, and Jesus Christ. Jesus Christ said . . . he would let the one that throws the javelin the farthest into heaven. And he wanted to know if all of these three men would participate, and of course all of them wanted to get into heaven and of course wanted to participate. So he gave the javelin to the Chinese man. So the Chinese man hobbles up and says, "Ah so, Jesus Christ, I want to throw the javelin too." He throws it tremendously far; he throws it across the United States. So the White man says, "Look out Chinese man, give me this javelin." And so he get this javelin and he throws the javelin halfway around the world. And so the White man looks at Jesus Christ and Jesus Christ says, "Ah, that's very nice, that's very good." He says, "What about you nigger? What you gonna do?" So the nigger says, "I can beat these people." So he picks up this javelin and he hurls the javelin all away around the world and it's still in orbit today. So Jesus Christ looks at all three of these individuals and he says, "Gee, you all did so well, I think I'm gonna let all of you into heaven." And he says, "You know, when you get to heaven you get a present. So you can go back there in my little room and pick out whatever you like to pick out." So the Chinese man, he goes into this back room and comes out and he has a bowl of rice. He says, "Thank you Jesus Christ." And the White man goes in there and he comes out with North America, and he says "Thank you Jesus Christ." And the Black man comes out stepping with this little jive-ass move, had a little pot of gold in hand, he says [high high-pitched voice] "Bye J.C."

Not a single member of the class to whom this story was told laughed or smiled. Undoubtedly they were bothered by the highly explicit ethnic content, the use of the term "nigger," as well as by an inability to identify anything in the final words of the black man that would constitute a genuine joking punch line.

It might be possible to dismiss this as a poorly remembered or ill-formed joke, and indeed, the teller described learning it many years before when he was in junior high school. But this joke seems very much connected with motif *A1671.1: Why the Negro Works*, which concerns the giving of packages to the Negro and white man. The Negro gets first choice and takes the bigger package which contains a plow or tools. The white man is left with the smaller package which contains writing implements or knowledge.[14] In some versions, the giving of packages is preceded by a foot race.[15] In other words, this joke would seem to be a variant of a well-established black-American folktale. This identification would also explain why the "joke" lacks an identifiable punch line, since punch lines are not characteristic of traditional tales. Furthermore, it raises the question as to whether this joke reflects a change in black self-image and expression. Most tales containing motif *A1671.1* were collected in rural areas in the 1950s. They are aetiological tales that explain the traditional order of white management of black labor. Our example was collected in the 1980s and it does not suggest that the black is subservient, even though the white man emerges with all of "North America." Have black-Americans reshaped their traditional tales in accordance with a more aggressively secure identity? Such an hypothesis would seem to be supported by other examples.[16] Ultimately, the answer to this question is not the issue. At issue is the realization that without the access to the comparative data that the indexes afford, such questions cannot even be framed.

Most folklorists consult the major indexes as a preliminary step in the study of any particular folklore text or repertoire. Although the aims of their inquiry may not be broadly comparative, they find that even a focused analysis may be informed by a comparative perspective. At least the tendency to regard a body of material as unique or peculiar to the individual or group under study is significantly reduced. The characterization of some humorous text as particularly "American" might be suspended until the consultation of the basic indexes has been carried out. It is true that these indexes are neither complete nor statistically representative of extant folk humor; nevertheless, they may help the scholar to avoid some of the more egregious errors that have been made in characterizing the uniqueness of a society's humorous repertoire.[17]

CONTEXTUALIZATION

In the 1950s and 1960s, the assumption that folklore was necessarily a survival from the distant past—or the maintenance of a venerable tradition—began to be questioned. After all, the materials that folklorists were collecting were clearly alive and meaningful in the present. That these materials were somehow tied to and reflected past realities required demonstration. Myths, tales, riddles, proverbs, were not survivals de facto. Furthermore, numerous expressive forms that were clearly contemporary in their content in many ways paralleled the materials that had been previously regarded as survivals. The notion that folklore consisted of relics from the past in danger of dying out was itself dying. Folklore was very much a part of the present, and the kinds of materials that had captured the imagination of folklorists were not only alive but continuing to be born anew. This shift from a past to a present orientation was, to some extent, part of the same shift taking place in anthropology where the concentration upon the reconstruction of past cultures (baseline ethnography) was giving way to the description and analysis of contemporary situations of change and adaptation. It had been sufficient for the folklorist to record and document *texts* exclusively when folklore was viewed as an object from the past. The folklorist's text was the record of what was believed to have survived. But with the formulation of folklore as an aspect of the present, new definitions of what was to be recorded and documented were required. Folklorists began to concern themselves seriously with the *contexts* of folklore expression. These contexts to which folklorists began to attend and which have come to comprise a major concern of their field investigations can be roughly categorized as cultural context, individual context, and social context.

Cultural Context

Cultural context refers to the concepts, values, and attitudes that inform upon the meaning of a piece of folklore. Studies of American humor have not attended to the explication of cultural context to any great extent, since these studies have been conducted by American researchers who have regarded that context as a given. The study of humor in other societies has not allowed such an assumption of context. The humor of another society often cannot even be perceived as humor if an explication of cultural context is not attempted.[18] Consider the following American-Jewish joke:

A Jew recently arrived in the United States from Eastern Europe. On his first Sabbath in New York, he goes for an afternoon walk in a nearby park. There he sees a man sitting on a bench smoking a cigar and reading a Yiddish newspaper. "America is a wonderful place," he says to himself. "Here even the *goyim* can read Yiddish."

Many readers will automatically recognize the humor in this brief narrative. Others may require some basic deciphering even to recognize it as a joke. To understand the "point" of this story it is necessary to recognize that Yiddish is the mother tongue of Eastern European Jews, and that many of the Jews who came to the United States from the villages and cities of Eastern Europe during the heyday of immigration at the turn of the century were orthodox, extremely observant Jews, adhering closely to the commandments and injunctions set forth in or derived from the Bible and Talmud. One of these injunctions is, "Observe the Sabbath and keep it holy." For the orthodox Jew, it would be a violation to make any kind of fire let alone smoke on the Sabbath. Furthermore, the word "goyim" must be recognized as the Yiddish word for non-Jews. One last idea is necessary for understanding this joke. Many Yiddish-speaking Jews who came to America from Europe were not observant. Some had given up their religious observances in Europe, while more had abandoned them in their adaptation to American society. Given these cultural data, the above joke should become clear. The newly arrived orthodox Jew has heard that America is a wonderful place filled with marvelous things. As he walks in the park on the Sabbath, he sees a man smoking a cigar and reading a Yiddish paper. As the orthodox protagonist coming from the sheltered and somewhat closed environment of the European Jewish village is unable to conceive that a Jew could be smoking on the Sabbath, he assumes that the person reading the paper must be a Gentile. Consequently he finds the depiction of America as a wonderful place confirmed because in America even the Gentiles read Yiddish.

The cultural data required to understand even this brief joke are extensive. Even though the joke may be understood intuitively by many, in making *explicit* the range of ideas and attitudes relevant to the understanding of this joke, one is forced to acknowledge several joke themes that otherwise might be overlooked: the narrowness of the East European, Jewish, worldview; the attitudes of European and American Jewry toward Gentiles; the image of America as a wonderland; and the basis of a Jewish identity devoid of religious observance or affiliation.

One way to get at the cultural context of humor is to encourage the tellers and listeners to discuss their jokes, to explain them, to comment upon the action and characters—to elicit what has been called an *oral literary criticism* of the humor.[19] But beyond the kinds of associations that informants explicitly provide, the folklorist must be sensitive to a wide range of ideas, behaviors, values, and attitudes that may contribute to an interpretation of the humorous expression but that fall outside the purview of informants' commentary. This sensitivity primarily results from a sustained ethnographic involvement with the community under investigation.

Individual Context

Individual context refers to those aspects of individual situation, experience, and disposition that inform upon the understanding of a folklore expression. Why does an individual choose to tell a particular joke on a particular occasion? Why do certain jokes or anecdotes become favorites to be performed over and over again? Why does an individual's joke repertoire seem to cluster about a very few themes? In order to answer questions of individual motivation, the humorous expressions must be contextualized. The life history of the individual, the development of his or her expressive repertoire, as well as psychological dispositions must be explored. For example, the following joke was collected from a Los Angeles lawyer in his late thirties who reported telling it to "a lot" of people within a very short period of time:

A fellow who had been in analysis for ten years told his psychiatrist that he felt he had had enough. The psychiatrist thought about it and agreed that it was time to terminate and that this would be his last session. Early the next morning the fellow calls the psychiatrist and tells him in an excited voice, "I know we terminated last time but there is something you should know." The psychiatrist asks, "What is it?" The fellow says, "Well, last night I dreamt that you were my mother." The psychiatrist says, "That is significant. You'd better get right down here." The guy says, "I'll grab a cup of coffee and be right over." And the psychiatrist says, "Coffee! You call that breakfast?"

A number of questions arise concerning the instant prominence that this joke assumed in the informant's humorous repertoire. It seems significant, however, that at the very time that this joke became prominent, the informant had been undergoing therapy with a variety of psychiatrists and psychologists to deal with his inability to sustain relationships with women. On a number of occasions he had expressed his concern that his problem was perhaps insoluble and that the therapy might just as well be terminated. He feared that his problem might stem from his relationship with his mother—some unresolved Oedipus complex. The informant did not recall, however, an interview several months prior to his adoption of the joke in which he related how he had been visiting his parents and got into an argument with his mother because he was preparing to leave the house to go somewhere having had only a cup of coffee for breakfast.

The significance of this joke to its teller is likely to be informed by such contextual data. Certainly, psychologists have not been negligent in investigating the emotional and cognitive bases of humor, but they have tended to focus upon the individual appreciation of humorous materials introduced under experimental conditions. Considerably less emphasis has been given to the exploration of an individual's natural repertoire and style. Although only a few folklorists have been willing to utilize depth psychological methods and interpretive techniques, many regularly record extensive life history data in the attempt to provide some individual context for the lore they record. As with the cultural context, oral literary criticism is also an important technique for establishing individual context.

Social Context

Social context is concerned with the social situation and interactional system in which a particular piece of folklore is expressed. The factors of social context include participants' identities and roles, physical setting, and the cultural codes and rules that govern interaction in such circumstances. The emphasis upon social context in contemporary folklore studies has been significantly influenced by developments in sociolinguistics and symbolic interaction.

How social context shapes the use and informs upon the meaning of narrative is illustrated in one folklorist's analysis of the following joke:

A man once came to a rabbi to ask a *shayle* [question] regarding ritual purity.
He says, "What is it? What did you do?"
He says, "I didn't say the prayer before the meal."
He says, "How come?"
He says, "Because I didn't wash my hands."
He says, "Well, why didn't you wash your hands?"
He says, "Because I wasn't eating Jewish food."
He says, "How come you weren't eating Jewish food?"
He says, "Because I was eating in a Gentile restaurant."
He says, "How come?"
He says, "Because it was *Yom Kippur*, the Day of Atonement. . . . and the Jewish restaurants were closed."

This joke concerns the confession of a small sin that reveals the existence of much more serious transgressions. What begins with the seeming oversight of failing to say grace before a meal is quickly transformed into deliberate violations of Jewish dietary law and the prescribed fast on the Day of Atonement. While the understanding of this story requires considerable familiarity with the cultural context, its performance on one occasion can only be understood with reference to aspects of the social context. This joke was used as a parable to comment upon the behavior of an informant's brother who had repeatedly promised his children that he would take them to the movies only to renege each time. Finally he agreed to take them to the show very late in the evening. By that time, they no longer wanted to go and were angry with him. He could not understand why they were angry and asked his sister, "What have I done?" She responded with the above story. Barbara Kirshenblatt-Gimblett has shown in detail how this joke was used strategically in the course of a social interaction, how it articulated with the events that transpired, and why another joke with a similar structure could not be used by the informant with the same effect.[20]

The folklorists' emphasis of social, cultural, and individual contexts in the recording and analysis of folklore expressions has contributed to a conceptualization of folklore as the study of *performance*, the attention to the act of artistic communicative expression that extends far beyond the referential content of reportable "texts." This reformulation of the scope of folklore study has led to the expansion of the folklore inquiry in general and humor inquiry in particular. Folklorists are currently investigating the humorous performances of talkers, pitchmen, puppeteers, as well as the creators of humorous material artifacts. They are expanding the range of those materials with which researchers in American humor must contend. Today, folklorists are probably the most prominent ethnographers of American humor.

CONCLUSION

Folklore is not a unified field of inquiry, and folklorists are allied with a variety of disciplines including literature, anthropology, sociology, linguistics, history, and musicology. They study a broad spectrum of folklore expressions from a variety of cultures throughout the world, although they are inclined to the study of their own culture and society than are their anthropological colleagues who have come to be identified with the exotic. The interpretations and explanations that folklorists have offered of the phenomena that they study are as diverse as the range of problems that have occupied their interests. Their theories are often related to or borrowed from those in neighboring disciplines. Indeed, it would be difficult to identify a theoretical perspective that is truly unique to folklore. Nevertheless, as the field has developed, certain general tendencies, strategies, and perspectives have come to be regarded as characteristic of the folkloristic approach. These basic accumulative, comparative, and contextual orientations have been outlined because they are relevant to the study of American humor. The study of humor in America is an enormously complex undertaking. There is no single approach that can be said to offer the "key" to the inquiry. Folkloristic perspectives expand the field of inquiry. They multiply the data with which the researcher must contend as well the dimensions of the phenomena to be apprehended. American humor cannot be reduced to a psychological or sociological or literary problem. It is more than any one of these and perhaps more than the sum of them all.

NOTES

1. Jacob Grimm, *Teutonic Mythology*, 4 vols, trans. from 4th ed. with Notes and Appendix by James Steven Stalleybrass (New York: Dover, 1966), Vol. 1, p. 10.

2. Sir James George Frazer, *Folk-Lore in the Old Testament*, 3 vols. (London: Macmillan, 1919), Vol. 1, pp. vii–xi.

3. William Wells Newell, *Transactions of the New York Academy of Sciences* 9 (1890): 134–36.

4. E. Sidney Hartland, "Folk-Lore Terminology," *The Folk-Lore Journal* 2 (1884): 343.

5. William R. Bascom, "Folklore and Anthropology," *Journal of American Folklore* 66 (1953): 283–90.

6. Dan Ben-Amos, "Toward a Definition of Folklore in Context," *Journal of American Folklore* 84 (1971): 3–15.

7. In the first issue of *Journal of American Folklore*, William Wells Newell published "English Folk-Tales in America," (1888): 227–34. In the same issue Alcee Fortier published "Louisianian Nursery-Tales," 140–47. Her complete collection emerged as the second volume of the Memoirs of the American Folk-Lore Society, *Louisiana Folk-Tales in French Dialect and English Translation* (Boston: Houghton, Mifflin, 1895).

8. Constance Rourke, *American Humor* (New York: Doubleday Anchor, 1953 [originally published by Harcourt, Brace in 1931]), pp. 237–44.

9. Francis Lee Utley, "Folk Literature: An Operational Definition," *Journal of American Folklore* 74 (1961): 198.

10. There are Ph.D. programs in folklore at Indiana University, University of Pennsylvania, University of Texas, University of California at Los Angeles, and Memorial University, St. John's, Newfoundland. M.A. programs or concentrations in folklore are offered at Western Kentucky University, Utah State University, Wayne State University, University of Oregon, University of California at Berkeley, and University of North Carolina.

11. Antti Aarne, *The Types of the Folktale*, trans. and enlarged by Stith Thompson, 2nd rev. ed. (Helsinki: Suomalainen Tiederakatemia, 1964).

12. Stith Thomas, *Motif-Index of Folk-Literature*, 6 vols., rev. ed. (Bloomington: Indiana University Press, 1955).

13. Ernest W. Baughman, *Type and Motif-Index of the Folktales of England and North America* (The Hague: Mouton, 1966), pp. xv–xvi.

14. Newman I. White, ed., *The Frank C. Brown Collection of North Carolina Folklore* (Durham, N.C.: Duke University Press, 1952), Vol. 1, p. 633.

15. Richard M. Dorson, *Negro Folktales in Michigan* (Cambridge, Mass.: Harvard University Press, 1956), p. 215.

16. Roger D. Abrahams, *Deep Down in the Jungle: Negro Narrative Folklore from the Streets of Philadelphia* (New York: Aldine, 1970), pp. 70–73.

17. Alan Dundes has been best at identifying such errors: see Alan Dundes, "An Experiment: Suggestions and Queries from the Desk, with a Reply from the Ethnographer," in *Structural Analysis of Oral Tradition*, ed. Pierre Maranda and Elli Kongas Maranda (Philadelphia: University of Pennsylvania Press, 1971), pp. 295–96; Frank Hamilton Cushing, "The Cock and the Mouse," in *The Study of Folklore,* ed. Alan Dundes (Englewood Cliffs, N.J.: Prentice-Hall, 1965), p. 274, note 4.; Bernard Wolfe, "Uncle Remus and the Malevolent Rabbit," in *Mother-Wit from the Laughing Barrel: Readings in the Interpretation of Afro-American Folklore,* ed. Alan Dundes (Englewood Cliffs, N.J.: Prentice-Hall, 1973), p. 533n.

18. For example, see Stanley Brandes, *Metaphors of Masculinity: Sex and Status in Andalusian Folklore* (Philadelphia: University of Pennsylvania Press, 1980), and Elliott

Oring, *Israeli Humor: The Content and Structure of the Chizbat of the Palmah* (Albany: State University of New York Press, 1981).

19. Alan Dundes, "Metafolklore and Oral Literary Criticism," *The Monist* 50 (1966): 505–16.

20. Barbara Kirshenblatt-Gimblett, "A Parable in Context: A Social Interactional Analysis of Storytelling Performance," in *Folklore: Performance and Communication*, ed. Dan Ben-Amos and Kenneth S. Goldstein (The Hague: Mouton, 1975), pp. 105–30.

BIBLIOGRAPHICAL SURVEY

Collecting

Numerous examples of humorous narratives, riddles, proverbs, and folk speech have been published in the pages of *Journal of American Folklore, Western Folklore* (originally *California Folklore Quarterly*.) *Southern Folklore Quarterly, New York Folklore* (originally *New York Folklore Quarterly*), *Kentucky Folklore Record, Keystone Folklore Quarterly, North Carolina Folklore Journal, Tennessee Folklore Society Bulletin,* as well as the *Publications of the Texas Folklore Society.* Some of these journals and publications have been indexed: see Tristram P. Coffin, *An Analytical Index to the Journal of American Folklore, Vols. 1–67, 68, 69, 70,* Publications of the American Folklore Society No. 7 (Philadelphia: American Folklore Society, 1958); James T. Bratcher, *Analytical Index to the Publications of the Texas Folklore Society: Volumes 1–36* (Dallas: Southern Methodist University Press, 1973); Joan Ruman Perkal, *Western Folklore and California Folklore Quarterly Twenty-five Year Index: Volumes I–XXV, 1942–1966* (Berkeley: University of California Press, 1969); as well as the index included at the back of each volume of *Western Folklore.*

Some early regional collections that emphasize texts, including humorous materials, are Emelyn E. Gardner's *Folklore from the Schoharie Hills, New York* (Ann Arbor: University of Michigan Press, 1937); Newman Ivey White, ed., *The Frank C. Brown Collection of North Carolina Folklore,* 7 vols. (Durham, N.C.: Duke University Press, 1952); Austin E. Fife and Alta S. Fife's work on Mormon folklore, *Saints of Sage and Saddle* (Bloomington: Indiana University Press, 1956); Richard M. Dorson's collection in Upper Peninsula Michigan, *Bloodstoppers and Bearwalkers* (Cambridge, Mass.: Harvard University Press, 1952), as well as his *Negro Folktales in Michigan* (Cambridge, Mass.: Harvard University Press, 1956). Vance Randolph did extensive collecting in the Ozarks and published a great deal of his material. Among his publications that include or emphasize humorous narratives are: *Who Blowed Up the Church House? and Other Ozark Folktales* (New York: Columbia University Press, 1952), *Hot Springs and Hell and Other Folk Jests and Anecdotes from the Ozarks* (Hatboro, Penn.: Folklore Associates, 1965), and *Pissing in the Snow and Other Ozark Folktales* (Urbana: University of Illinois Press, 1976). Randolph also compiled *Ozark Folklore: A Bibliography,* Folklore Institute Monograph Series Vol. 24

(Bloomington: Indiana University Research Center for Language Sciences, 1972) with whole sections devoted to tall tales and jests, see pp. 97–231. More recent collections of folklore that are more oriented to the cultural context in which the humorous lore is expressed include Patrick B. Mullen, *I Heard the Old Fisherman Say: Folklore of the Texas Gulf Coast* (Austin: University of Texas Press, 1978); George Carey, *A Faraway Time and Place: Lore of the Eastern Shore* (Washington, DC: Robert B. Luce, 1971); Roger D. Abrahams, *Deep Down in the Jungle: Negro Narrative Folklore from the Streets of Philadelphia* (New York: Aldine, 1970); and Robert D. Bethke, *Adirondack Voices: Woodsmen and Woodlore* (Urbana: University of Illinois Press, 1981).

Many scholars outside the field of folklore are not aware of the existence of folklore archives, even those that are located at their own university campuses. The best-known American folklore archives are: Library of Congress (Archive of Folk Culture, Washington, DC 20540); Indiana University (Folklore Institute, 504 North Fess, Bloomington IN 47405); University of California, Berkeley (Department of Anthropology, Berkeley CA 94720); University of California, Los Angeles (Center for the Study of Comparative Folklore and Mythology, 1037 GSM-Library Wing, Los Angeles CA 90024); University of Detroit (4001 West McNichols Road, Detroit MI 48221); University of Maine (Northeast Archives of Folklore and Oral History, South Stevens Hall, Orono ME 04469); University of Nebraska (Omaha NE 68182); University of Oregon (Randill V. Mills Memorial Archive, Department of English, Eugene OR 97403); University of Pennsylvania (Folklore and Folklife, Room 415, Logan Hall CN, Philadelphia PA 19104); University of Texas (Center for Intercultural Studies in Folklore and Ethnomusicology, Austin TX 78712); Utah State University (Fife Folklore Archive, Department of English, UMC 32, Logan UT 84322); Wayne State University (448 Purdy Library, Detroit MI 48202); Western Kentucky University (Universities Library, Bowling Green KY 42101). The compilation of Peter Aceves and Magnus Einarsson-Mullarky, *Folklore Archives of the World: A Preliminary Guide, Folklore Forum* Bibliographic and Special Series No. 1 (November 1968) contains many inaccuracies but was a first attempt to list all known folklore archives. A copy may be ordered from the *Folklore Forum* at the Folklore Institute of Indiana University (504 North Fess, Bloomington IN 47405) if it is not available in libraries.

Numerous articles have appeared in a variety of journals calling attention to, documenting, and analyzing contemporary joke cycles. For examples, see Maurice Crane, "Bop Jokes," *Journal of American Folklore* 73 (1960): 249–50; Elliott Oring, "Everything is a Shade of Elephant: An Alternative to a Psychoanalysis of Humor," *New York Folklore* 1 (1975): 149–59; Simon J. Bronner, " 'What's Grosser than Gross?': New Sick Joke Cycles," *Midwestern Journal of Language and Lore* 11 (1985): 39–49; Special issue of *Journal of American Folklore* on "Folklore and Obscenity," 75 (1962); Mac E. Barrick, "The Helen Keller Joke Cycle," *Journal of American Folklore* 93 (1980): 441–49; Judith B. Kerman, "The Light-Bulb Jokes: Americans Look at Social Action Processes," *Journal of American Folklore* 93 (1980): 454–58; Alan Dundes, "Polish Pope Jokes," *Journal of American Folklore* 92 (1979): 219–22; Alan Dundes, "Auschwitz Jokes," *Western Folklore* 42 (1983): 249–60.

There are many nonnarrative forms of folk humor. For examples of riddles and proverbs, see the *Frank C. Brown Collection of North Carolina Folklore* cited earlier; for proverbial comparisons, see Cathy M. Orr, "Folk Comparisons from Colorado," *Western Folklore* 35 (1976): 175–208; for graffiti, see Alan Dundes, "Here I Sit—A Study of American Latrinalia," *The Kroeber Anthropological Society Papers* 34 (1966): 91–105; for nicknames, see John A. McGeachy III, "Student Nicknames for College Faculty," *Western Folklore* 37 (1978): 281–96; for slangs, see Inez Cardozo-Freeman, "Rhyming Slang in a Western Prison," *Western Folklore* 37 (1978): 296–305; for examples of rituals, routines, and dramas, see Bill Ellis, "The Camp Mock-Ordeal: Theater as Life," *Journal of American Folklore* 94 (1981): 486–505; Elliott Oring, "Dyadic Traditions," *Journal of Folklore Research* 21 (1984): 19–28; and Joseph F. Tuso, "A Folk Drama—'What the Captain Means Is'—Or that Interview You Never Saw on T.V.," *Folklore Forum* 5 (1972): 25–27; for Xerox lore see, Alan Dundes and Carl R. Pagter, *Work Hard and You Shall Be Rewarded: Urban Folklore from the Paperwork Empire* (Bloomington: Indiana University Press, 1978). These examples are not exhaustive nor is the range of forms in which humor is regularly embedded exhaustively listed.

Indexing

Antti Aarne's *The Types of the Folktale: A Classification and Bibliography*, translated and enlarged by Stith Thompson, 2nd rev. ed. (Helsinki: Suomalainen Tiederakatemia, 1964) and Stith Thompson, *Motif-Index of Folk-Literature*, 6 vols., rev. ed. (Bloomington: Indiana University Press, 1955) are the standard indexes of tale types and motifs. Not only do they refer to a large number of other indexes of tale types and motifs, but they serve as the model for most recent indexing efforts. Ernest W. Baughman's *Type and Motif-Index of the Folktales of England and North America* (The Hague: Mouton, 1966) closely follows these models. Some recent indexes that have been published since Aarne and Thompson's works include Stanley L. Robe, *Index of Mexican Folktales, Including Narrative Texts from Mexico, Central America and the Hispanic United States* (Berkeley: University of California Press, 1973); Ørnulf Hodne, *The Types of the Norwegian Folktale* (Oslo: Universitetsfolaget, 1984); and Erastus O. Arewa, *A Classification of the Folktales of the Northern East African Cattle Area by Types* (New York: Arno, 1980).

Erotic and obscene types and motifs were generally neglected in the major indexes. Those that do appear are described in rather vague terms. Gershon Legman called for a motif index of erotic humor in "Toward a Motif-Index of Erotic Humor," *Journal of American Folklore* 75 (1962): 227–48. Although something less than a type of motif index, Legman's *Rationale of the Dirty Joke:*

An Analysis of Sexual Humor, First Series (New York: Grove, 1968) and *Rationale of the Dirty Joke: An Analysis of Sexual Humor, Second Series* (New York: Breaking Point, 1975) constitute a finding list of obscene jokelore useful for preliminary comparative purposes. However, Frank Hoffman's *Analytic Survey of Anglo-American Traditional Erotica* (Bowling Green, Ohio: Bowling Green Popular Press, 1973) is the only genuine index of erotic types of motifs in English.

For indexes and finding lists of nonnarrative forms of humorous expression, see Richard Reuss, "An Annotated Field Collection of Songs from the American College Student Oral Tradition" (M.A. thesis, Indiana University, 1965); G. Legman, *The Limerick: Examples with Notes, Variants and Index* (New York: Bell Publishing, 1974) and *The New Limerick* (New York: Crown, 1977); Archer Taylor, *English Riddles from Oral Tradition* (Berkeley: University of California Press, 1951); Archer Taylor, *The Proverb and an Index to the Proverb* (Hatboro, Penn.: Folklore Associates, 1962).

For indexes that relate to specific American joke traditions, see William M. Clements, *The Types of the Polack Joke, Folklore Forum* Bibliographic and Special Series No. 3 (November, 1969) and "The Polack Jokes in 1970: An Addendum," *Folklore Forum* 4 (1971): 19–29. Also see Jan Harold Brunvand, "A Classification for Shaggy Dog Stories," *Journal of American Folklore* 76 (1973): 42–68. For an example of an early comparative study of a popular contemporary joke, see Paul Franklin Baum, "The Three Dreams or 'Dream Bread' Story," *Journal of American Folklore* 30 (1917): 378–411.

Contextualization

Two of the essays that inspired the attention to context are William Bascom, "Four Functions of Folklore," *Journal of American Folklore* 67 (1954): 333–49 and Alan Dundes, "Texture, Text, and Context," *Southern Folklore Quarterly* 28 (1964): 251–65. Much discussion has revolved around the text/context dichotomy: D.K. Wilgus, "The Text is the Thing," *Journal of American Folklore* 86 (1973): 241–52; Steven Swann Jones, "Slouching towards Ethnography: The Text/Context Controversy Reconsidered, " *Western Folklore* 38 (1979): 42–47; Dan Ben-Amos, "The Ceremony of Innocence," pp. 47–52; Steven Swann Jones, "Dogmatism in the Contextual Revolution," pp. 52–55; Robert A. Georges, "Toward a Resolution of the Text/Context Controversy," *Western Folklore* 39 (1980): 34–40; Yigal Zan, "The Text/Context Controversy: An Explanatory Perspective," *Western Folklore* 41 (1982): 1–27; and Katherine Young, "The Notion of Context," *Western Folklore* 44 (1985): 115–22.

Virtually all folklorists make reference to the cultural context in the explication of obscure humor. Cultural context may also prove crucial to the interpretation of otherwise understandable humor. See, for example, some of the essays of Alan Dundes, "Misunderstanding Humor: An American Stereotype of the Englishman," *International Folklore Review* 2 (1982): 10–15; "The Dead Baby Joke Cycle," *Western Folklore* 38 (1979): 145–57; "Jokes and Covert Language

Attitudes: The Curious Case of the Wide-Mouth Frog,'' *Language in Society* 6 (1977): 141–47.

European folklorists have been sensitive to aspects of individual context since the nineteenth century. American folklorists have also been stimulated by their researches, particularly in their studies of songmakers, craftspeople, and tale tellers. For examples of studies of oral humorists that attend to the individual context, see Mody C. Boatright, *Gib Morgan: Minstrel of the Oil Fields*, Texas Folklore Society Publication No. 20 (Dallas: Southern Methodist University, 1945); William Hugh Jansen, *Abraham "Oregon" Smith: Pioneer, Folk Hero, and Tale-Teller* (New York: Arno Press, 1977); and James P. Leary, "George Russell: The Repertoire and Personality of a North Country Storyteller," in *Folklore on Two Continents: Essays in Honor of Linda Dégh*, edited by Nikolai Burlakoff and Carl Lindahl (Bloomington, Ind.: Trickster Press, 1980), pp. 354–62.

Folklorists in the United States have perhaps been slightly more open to the exploration of unconscious individual motivations than their European colleagues. See Thomas A. Burns with Inger H. Burns, *Doing the Wash: An Expressive Culture and Personality Study of a Joke and Its Tellers* (Norwood Penn.: Norwood Editions, 1976) or the 1972 dissertation upon which it is based. Also see Elliott Oring, ed., *Humor and the Individual* (Los Angeles: California Folklore Society, 1984).

Microstudies of social context in particular joke telling sessions can be found in Harvey Sacks, "An Analysis of the Course of a Joke's Telling in Conversation," in *Explorations in the Ethnography of Speaking*, edited by Richard Bauman and Joel Sherzer (New York: Cambridge University Press, 1974), pp. 337–53; and Steve Bartlett, "Social Interaction Patterns of Adolescents in a Folklore Performance," *Folklore Forum* 4 (1971): 39–67. For studies of humorous folklore in social context with a broader scope, see Richard Bauman, "The La Have Island General Store: Sociability and Verbal Art in a Nova Scotia Community," *Journal of American Folklore* 85 (1972): 330–43; Richard Tallman, "Where Stories are Told: A Noval Scotia Storyteller's Milieu," *American Review of Canadian Studies* 5 (1975): 17–41; James P. Leary, "Recreational Talk among White Adolescents," *Western Folklore* 39 (1980): 284–99; Michael Bell, *The World from Brown's Lounge: An Ethnography of Black Middle-Class Play* (Urbana: University of Illinois Press, 1983); Dan Ben-Amos and Kenneth S. Goldstein, eds., *Folklore: Performance and Communication* (The Hague: Mouton, 1975); Kay L. Cothran, "Talking Trash in the Okefenokee Swamp Rim, Georgia," *Journal of American Folklore* 87 (1974): 340–56; Amanda Dargan and Steve Zeitlin, "American Talkers: Expressive Styles and Occupational Choice," *Journal of American Folklore* 96 (1983): 3–33.

ADDITIONAL SOURCES

Apte, Mahadev L. *Humor and Laughter: An Anthropological Approach*. Ithaca, N.Y.: Cornell University Press, 1985.

Bauman, Richard. *Verbal Art as Performance*. Rowley, Mass.: Newbury Publishers, 1978.

Ben-Amos, Dan and Kenneth S. Goldstein, eds. *Folklore: Performance and Communication*. The Hague: Mouton, 1975.

Dorson, Richard M., ed. *American Folklore and the Historian*. Chicago: University of Chicago Press, 1971.

————. *Handbook of American Folklore*. Bloomington: Indiana University Press, 1983.

Dundes, Alan. "The American Concept of Folklore." *Journal of the Folklore Institute* 3 (1966): 226–49.

Oring, Elliott, ed. *Humor and the Individual*. Los Angeles: California Folklore Society, 1984.

Paredes, Americo, and Richard Bauman, eds. *Towards New Perspective in Folklore*. Austin: University of Texas Press, 1972.

Toelken, Barre. *The Dynamics of Folklore*. Boston: Houghton Mifflin, 1979.

Index

Aarne, Antti, 227
Adams, Joey, 115
Ade, George, 10–11
Adventures of Huckleberry Finn, The, 9
Adventures of Tom Sawyer, The, 9
Agee, James, 71, 85
Algonquin Roundtable, 12, 13
Allen, Fred, 94–95
Allen, Woody, 1–2, 75–76, 170–172
"Allen's Alley," 94
"All in the Family," 98
Allport, Gordon W., 163
American Bibliopolist, The, 49
American Humor, 207
American literary humor
  bibliographical survey of, 23–28
  historical development of, 2–17
  influence of jest books and almanacs, 3
  issues of, 17–21
  overview of, 1–2
  popular stage, 4
America's Humor, 17
A New Home—Who'll Follow, 143
Animal Farm, 196
Anthony, Norman, 58–59
Antihero, 72–73

Arbuckle, Fatty, 69
Arnez, Desi, 92
Arnez, Nancy L. and Clara B. Anthony, 180–181
"Artemus Ward," 7
Aunt Maguire Letters, 144
Austin, James C., 20, 27

Bails, Jerry and Hames Ware, 42
Ball, Lucille, 97
Ballard, Kaye, 114
Ballyhoo, 58–59
Bangs, John Kendricks, 10
Baughman, Ernest W., 217
B. C., 3
Becker, Stephen, 44
Bee, The, 52–53
Beetle Bailey, 38
Benchley, Robert, 13, 14
Benny, Jack, 94–95, 169
Berger, Phil, 100, 132
Berle, Milton, 96
Bier, Jesse, 7, 11, 17–18, 23, 26
Bierce, Ambrose, 9–10, 199–200
Big Bear of Arkansas, The, 6
Biglow, Hosea, 5

Biglow Papers, 5
"Bill Arp," 7
Birdofredom Sawin, 5
Black comedy, 78–79
Black humor, 17–18, 172–179
  humorists, 15–16
Blair, Walter, 2, 3, 4, 5, 6, 157
Blair, Walter and Hamlin Hill, 10, 12,
  13, 14
Blondie, 38
Bloom County, 38
Bombeck, Erma, 17, 149
"Borscht Belt," 115
Bradstreet, Anne, 139
Breathed, Berk, 38
Broadcast humor
  bibliographical survey of, 104–106
  formats of comedy programming in,
    91–93
  historical development of, 93–100
  overview of, 91–93
  racial, ethnic, and regional stereotypes
    in, 94, 97
  situation comedy in, 96–99
  television comedy in, 95–100
  themes and issues of, 101–103
Brooks, Mel, 78
Broom Hilda, 38
Brother Jonathan, 4
Browne, Dik, 38
Bruce, Lenny, 169–170
Bruère, Martha Bensley and Mary Rita
  Beard, 158
Bryant, John, 98, 105
Buckingham, Willis J., 20
Bunny, John, 68–69
Burrows, Abe, 109
Byrd, William, 138, 139
Byron, Stuart and Elisabeth Weis, 83

Cable TV, 100
Calinescu, Matei, 18
Cambridge, Godfrey, 178
Cameron, Ian, 86–87
Cantor, Joanne, 92
Capp, Al, 38
Capra, Frank, 74–75
Carell, Stanley, 84

Carpet-Bag, 55
Carson, Johnny, 99–100, 119
Cartoon Carnival, 60
Catalogue of Copyright Entries: Periodicals, 64
Ceasar, Sid, 96
Chaplin, Charlie, 69–70
Charney, Maurice, 25
Chase, Chevy, 87
Chicago humorists, 10
Clark, Lewis Gaylord, 54–55
Clemens, Samuel, 7, 8–9. *See* Twain,
  Mark
Clemens, Samuel and Charles Dudley
  Warner, 197
Clowns, 111
Cohen, Hennig, 8
Cohen, Sarah Blacher, 25
Colonial humor, 2
Comic art, 57
Comic columns, 51
Comics, the
  adventure comic strip, 7, 37–38
  bibliographical survey of, 41–47
  comic art, defined, 39
  conventions of comic strip, 36
  history of, 36–38
  overview of, 35–36
  relation to patterns of America, mainstream humor, 40–41
  research issues and problems, 38–41
  satire, in comic strips, 38
  soap opera strips, 38
Contrast, The, 4
Cooper, James Fenimore, 8
Corliss, Richard, 121
"Cosby Show, The," 99, 121
Cott, Nancy, 141
Couperie, Pierre, 44
Cracker-barrel Yankee, 72
Crackerbox humor, 11, 12
Crockett, David, 5

Dance, Daryl, 176–177
Daniels, Les, 46
Davies, Christie, 180
Davis, Jim, 38
DeMuth, James, 26

Dennie, Joseph and Royall Tyler, 53
Devil's Dictionary, 199–200
"Different Strokes," 102
Dodge, Mary Abigail, 145–146
Doonesbury, 38
Down east humorists, 4
Dr. Strangelove or: How I Learned to Stop Worrying and Love the Bomb, 79
Dudden, Arthur P., 166, 202, 203
Duffey, Bernard, 10
Dundes, Alan, 180
Dunne, Finley Peter, 11, 200–201
Durgnat, Raymond, 83

Education of Henry Adams, The, 203
Egg and I, The, 148
Ellison, Ralph, 172
Estren, Mark James, 46
Experimental Fiction of Ambrose Bierce, The, 19
"Evening at the Improv," 100

Fairbanks, Douglas, Sr., 69
Farmer's Weekly Museum, 53
Fashion, 143
Faulkner, William, 15
Female Quixotism, 142–143
Feminine Mystique, The, 149
Fern Leaves From Fanny's Portfolio, 145
Film comedy
  as affected by:
    changes in humor, 72–73
    economics, 73–74
  bibliographical survey of:
    books, 82–85
    shorter works, 85–88
  and censorship, 74
  overview and historical development:
    post-World War II era, 75–79
    silents, 67–72
    studio era, 72–75
  themes and issues of, 79–81
Fink, Mike, 5
Fisher, Rhoda and Seymour Fisher, 123, 133
Fleisher, Michael L., 42
Folklore, archives of, 215–216

Folklore, shifting conceptualization of, 213–214
Folklore methodology and American humor research:
  bibliographical survey of:
    additional sources, 229–230
    collecting, 225–227
    contextualization, 228–229
    indexing, 227–228
  collecting, 214–216
    literary influence on, 215
  contextualization:
    conclusion, 223
    cultural context, 219–221
    individual context, 221–222
    social context, 222–223
  indexing, 216–219
  overview, 213–214
Folklorists, contemporary, 215
Foxx, Redd, 178
Franklin, Benjamin, 1, 2, 3, 50, 198
Franklin, Joe, 112, 117, 132
  Joe Franklin's Encyclopedia of Comedians, 112
Freneau, Philip, 2
Freud, Sigmund, vii
Friedan, Betty, 149

Gale, Stephen H., 14
Game and quiz shows, 100
Garfield, 38
Gentlemen Prefer Blondes, 147
"Geoffrey Crayon." *See* Irving, Washington
Georgia Scenes, Characters, and Incidents, 5
Gibson, Charles Dana, 57
Gifford, Denis, 45
Gleason, Jackie, 96
Goldman, Albert, 167
Good Humor, 60
Goulart, Ron, 44
Greenfield, Jeff, 206
Gregory, Dick, 178
Grote, David, 101
Group, The, 140
Guilded Age, The, 197

Habegger, Alfred, 153
Hagar the Horrible, 38
Harris, George Washington, 6
Hart, Johnny, 38
Harte, Bret, 8
Hauck, Richard Boyd, 27
HBO, 100
Helmbold, George, 53
Herriman, George, 38
High Life in New York, 143–144
Hobbes, Thomas, 163
Holley, Marietta, 144–145
"Honeymooners, The," 96
Hooper, Johnson J., 6
Hope, Bob, 75–76, 127
Horn, Maurice, 42–43, 44–45
Hubbard, Kin, 11
Hughes, Langston, 11
Humor in periodicals
    almanacs, 50
    American periodical humor:
        literary burlesque in, 55
        social issues in, 55–56
    annual collections of humor, 51
    bibliographical survey of, 63–64
    domestic comedy in, 59
    historical development of, 52–60
    key issues for research, 60–63
    local color in, 57
    overt sensuality in, 58
    overview of, 49–52
    and satire, 54
    war comedy in, 59
Hutcheon, Linda, 19

"I Love Lucy," 97
Independent Balance, 53
Inge, M. Thomas, 15
Inspector Clouseau, 71
Irish humor, 165–166
Irving, Washington, 3–4, 53

"Jack Downing," 4
Jackson, Shirley, 148
Janus, Samuel, 126–127
"Jesse B. Semple," 11
Jewish humor, 166–172
"John-Mash" stories, 172–175

Jolson, Al, 168
Journal of American Folklore, 215
Journal of Madam Knight, The, 139
Judge, 56–57

Kael, Pauline, 86
Kaplan, Peter W., 86–87
Keaton, Buster, 69–70
Keillor, Garrison, 17
Kelly, Walt, 38
Kempkes, Wolfgang, 42
Kenney, Howland W., 140
Kerr, Jean, 148
Kerr, Orpheus C., 49
Kerr, Walter, 83
"Keystone Kops," 68
Kirkland, Caroline, 143
Kirshenblattf-Gimblett, Barbara, 223
Knickerbocker Magazine, 54–55
Knight, Sarah Kemble, 139–140
Kornfeld, Eve, 141
Kovacs, Ernie, 97
Krazy Kat, 38
Kubrick, Stanley, 79
Kunzle, David, 44
Kurtzman, Harvey, 59

Ladies of Castile, The, 140
Lafave, Lawrence, 164
Lake Wobegone Days, 17
Landmann, Salcia, 182
Langdon, Harry, 71
Lardner, Ring, 12–13
Last Laugh, The, 100
"Laugh-In," 100
"Laurel and Hardy," 71
Lauter, Paul, 23
Lawrence, D. H., 163
Leach, Jim, 81
Lear, Norman, 98
Levin, Harry, 25
Levine, Lawrence, 175
Lewis, Jerry, 76
Life, 56–57
Li'l Abner, 38
Lincoln, C. Erik, 181
Literary comedians, 7, 10
"Little magazines," 57

Lloyd, Harold, 70–71
Locke, David Ross, 7
Longstreet, Augustus Baldwin, 5
Loos, Anita, 147
Lowell, James Russell, 5

Mabley, Jackie, 178–179
MacDonald, Betty, 148
Machiavelli, Niccolo, 196
MacNelly, Jeff, 38
Mad Magazine, 59
Magazines, 50
Maltin, Leonard, 83
Mannell, Roger, 164
Marc, David, 91, 105
Marquis, Don, 12
Martin, Dean, 76
Martin, Steve, 121
Martin, Wendy, 139
"Martin Dooley," 200
"Marx Brothers, The," 73, 168–169
"Mary Tyler Moore Show," 99
"M*A*S*H," 99
Mast, Gerald, 72, 82–83, 85
Matthews, Brander, 49
Mattingly, Garrett, 196
McCarey, Leo, 71
McGee, Paul and Jeff Goldstein, 104
McLean, Albert, Jr., 113, 114
Memoirs of the American Folklore Society, 215
Mencken, H(enry) L(ouis), 12, 201–202
Mintz, Lawrence, 110, 167, 177–178, 188
Misogyny (in humor), 10, 14
Mitz, Rick, 105
Monaco, James, 87
Morris, Linda A. F., 153, 157
Motif—Index of Folk Literature, 216–217
Mott, Frank Luther, 63
Mowatt, Anna Cora, 143
"Mr. Dooley," 11
Murphy, Eddie, 76
Murray, Bill, 76
Murray, Judith Sargent, 141
Murrell, William, 43
Myers, Russel, 38

My Opinions and Betsey Bobbett's, 144–145
Mysterious Stranger, The, 9

Nash, Ogden, 174
National Lampoon, The, 59–60
Neal, Joseph C., 54
Newspaper columnists, 10–13, 16–17
New Yorker, 58
Nilsen, Don L. F., 25
Normand, Mabel, 69

Olson, Stephanie Koziski, 103 n.8
Omnium Gatherum, The, 53
"One Day at a Time," 102
"On Humbling our Rebellious Rebels," 198
"Oral literary criticism," 220–221
Orwell, George, 196
Ostropolier, Hershl, 166
O'Sullivan, Judith, 44
Ott, Fred, 67–68
Outcault, Richard, 36
Overstreet, Robert M., 42

Parker, Brant, 38
Parker, Dorothy, 13, 147
Parody film, 78
Parton, Sara Willis, 145
Paulding, James Kirke, 53
Peanuts, 38
Perelman, S(idney) J(oseph), 14
Perry, George and Alan Aldridge, 44
Personality comedian, 75–76
"Petroleum V. Nasby," 7
Philadelphia Tickler, 53
Pogo, 38
Political humor
    bibliographical survey of, 208–209
    cartoons of, 204
    competition in, 205
    consequences of, 195–196
    decline of, 202
    directed at politicians, 197
    directed at politics, 197
    discography of, 211
    and freedom, 204–205
    historical development of, 198–205

influence of mass communications,
    203–204
  key issues for research of, 205–208
  overview of, 195–198
  by politicians, 196–197
  rise of, 203
Poor Richard's Almanack, 3
Popular Culture Airwaves Bulletin, 101
Populist cracker-barrel, 77–78
Porter, William Sidney, alias "O.
    Henry," 12
Porter, William Trotter, 54–55
Poussaint, Alvin, Dr., 121–122
Prince, The, 196
Puck, 56–57, 167

Racial and ethnic humor
  bibliographical survey of:
    Afro-American humor, 188–189
    Jewish humor, 189
    other groups, other issues, 189–190
  historical context of, 165–179
  issues of, 179–183
  overview of, 163–165
Radcliffe-Brown, A. R., 182
Radio Comedy, 93
Radio comedy, 93–94, 95
Ramano, Ann, 102
Randolph, Vance, 225
Reitberger, Reinhold and Wolfgang
    Fuchs, 45
Rice, Dan, 113
Richards, David, 120
Rinehart, Mary Roberts, 152
Robbins, Trina and Catherine Yronwode,
    45
Robinson, David, 83
Robinson, Fred Miller, 27
Robinson, Jerry, 44
Rogers, Will, 11, 74–75, 202
Ross, Harold, 13
Rourke, Constance, 207–208
Rowson, Susanna Haswell, 141
Runyan, Damon, 12

Sack of Rome, The, 140
Safety Last, 70

Sahl, Mort, 169
Salmagundi, 53
Sanburn, Kate, 151, 152, 157
Sarris, Andrew, 86
Saturday Night Live, 87–88, 100, 119
Schlatter, George, 98
Schmitz, Neil, 21
Schulz, Charles, 38
Schwartz, Tony, 120
Screwball comedy, 72, 73, 74, 76, 77
Sellers, Peter, 71
Sennett, Mack, 68
Sennett, Ted, 84
Sheridan, Martin, 43
Shillaber, Benjamin Penhallow, 55
Shoe, 38
"Simon Suggs," 6
Singer, I. B., 182
Skinner, Cornelia Otis, 148
Slaves in Algiers, 141
Sloane, David E. E., 63
Smith, Charles Henry, 7
Smith, John, 138, 139
Smith, Seba, 4, 199
Sneeze, 67–68
*Some Adventures of Simon Suggs, Late of
    the Tallapoosa Volunteers*, 6
Southwestern humor, 5, 6–7
  in humor periodicals, 55
Spirit of the Times, The, 54–55
Stand-up comedy
  bibliographical survey, 131–133
  comedians in, 120
  in comedy clubs, 119–120
  functions of, 110
  historical development of, 110–122
  influence of film, 116, 117, 121
  influence of radio, 116
  influence of record albums, 117
  influence of television, 119, 121
  overview of, 109–110
  predecessors to stand-up comedy:
    burlesque, 113–114
    clown, 111, 112
    jester and fool, 112
    minstrelsy, 113
    trickster, 111, 112

vaudeville, 114–115
  themes and issues, 123–130
Stephens, Ann, 143–144
Steranko, James, 46
Sullivan, Ed, 96
"Sut Lovingood," 6

Talk shows, 99–100
Tandy, Jennette, 4
Tenney, Tabitha, 142–143
"Texas Star Theater," 96
Theory of Parody, A, 19
Thompson, Stith, 216–217
Thompson, William Tappan, 6
Thoreau, Henry David, 8
Thorpe, Thomas Bangs, 6
Thurber, James, 13–14
Toast of the Town, The, 96
Toelken, Barre, 124–125
Tomlin, Lily, 120
"Tonight Show, The," 119
Towsen, John H., 111, 112, 133
"Traveller Returned, The," 141–142
Trotter, Elizabeth Stanley, 152
Trudeau, Garry, 38
Tuckey, John S., 21
Tully, John, 3
Twain, Mark, vii, 200
Type and Motif—Index of the Folktales of
  England and North America, 217
Types of the Folktale, The, 216

Vanity Fair, 56
Veron, Enid, 27

Viorst, Judith, 149
"Virtue Triumphant," 141–142

Walker, Mort, 38, 44
Walker, Nancy, 145
Wallace, Ronald, 19
Warren, Mercy Otis, 140–141
Waugh, Coulton, 43
Weber, Brom, 15
Wertham, Frederic, 45
Wertheim, Arthur Frank, 93, 95, 105
West, Mae, 74
West, Nathaniel, 15
Whelan, Richard, 87–88
Whicher, Frances, 144
White, E(lwyn) B(rooks), 14
Widow Bedott Papers, The, 144
Wilde, Larry, 126, 132
"William Honeycomb," 52
Williams, Bert, 176
Wit of Women, The, 151
Wizard of Id, The, 38
Women's humor
  bibliographical survey of, 156–159
  domestic humor, 148–149
  feminist humor in, 149–150
  historical development of, 138–150
  overview of, 137–138
  themes and issues of, 150–154
Wright, Steve, 122

Yates, Norris, 11, 146
Yellow Kid, The, 36
Young, Chic, 38
"Your Show of Shows," 96

About the Contributors

JOSEPH BOSKIN is Professor of History and Afro-American Studies at Boston University, where he is also Director of the Urban Studies and Public Policy Program. His research has focused on the relationship between social conflict and alienation. Among his publications are *Seasons of Rebellion: Protest and Radicalism in Recent America, Humor and Social Change in Twentieth Century America,* and *Sambo: The Rise and Demise of an American Jester.* He is currently working on a project relating social change and joke cycles from the 1950s to the present.

JOSEPH DORINSON is the Chairman of the Department of History at Long Island University/Brooklyn Campus. He is the author of several articles on Jewish, Afro-American, and ethnic humor, and a forthcoming book on Jewish humor. Professor Dorinson is active in various civic associations and he admits to being a part-time standup comedian as well as a specialist in American Social History.

ZITA DRESNER is an Associate Professor of English at the University of the District of Columbia. Her Ph.D. dissertation deals with twentieth-century American women humorists and she has continued to do research and write on women's humor, most recently focusing on eighteenth-and nineteenth-century writers. She is also currently working on an anthology of American women humorists.

WES D. GEHRING received a Ph.D. in American film comedy from the University of Iowa. He has written books on Leo McCarey, Charlie Chaplin, W.C. Fields, the Marx Brothers, and screwball comedy. His articles on comedy have appeared in numerous journals. Gehring's current project is a book on American film genres. A professor of film in Ball State University's Telecommunications Department (Muncie, Indiana), he was recently cited as the university's "outstanding researcher, 1985–1986."

M. THOMAS INGE is the Robert Emory Blackwell Professor of Humanities at Randolph-Macon College in Ashland, Virginia. He edited the three-volume *Handbook of American Popular Culture* for Greenwood Press and is preparing for the same publisher the *Handbook of American Popular Literature*. Inge taught the first course on American humor ever offered at Moscow State University in the Soviet Union.

LAWRENCE E. MINTZ is Associate Professor of American Studies at the University of Maryland. He has written articles on various aspects of American popular culture including several dealing with American humor. From 1974 to 1984 Professor Mintz was an editor of *American Humor: An Interdisciplinary Newsletter*. Experiences teaching in France and consulting with Portuguese educators have led him to develop a recent interest in teaching American Studies abroad.

STEPHANIE KOZISKI OLSON is a printmaker, cartoonist, and writer with an avid interest in American Indian culture. Her interest in standup comedy developed during her graduate work in American Studies at the University of Maryland. She has worked as an art teacher and consultant with several Indian tribes and for the Smithsonian Institution; currently she is a program specialist in the Design Arts Program of the National Endowment for the Arts.

ELLIOTT ORING is Professor of Anthropology at California State University, Los Angeles, and serves as a Research Associate in the center for the Study of Comparative Folklore and Mythology at UCLA. He has published essays on humor, folklore, and symbolism in a variety of journals, and is a former editor of *Western Folklore*. His books include: *Israeli Humor: The Content and Structure of the Chizbat of the Palmah* (1981), *The Jokes of Sigmund Freud: A Study of Humor and Jewish Identity* (1984), *Humor and the Individual* (1984), and *Folk Groups and Folklore Genres: An Introduction* (1986).

NANCY POGEL is Professor of American Thought and Language at Michigan State University. Her articles and reviews on film comedy, literary humor, and American literature have appeared in *Literature/Film Quarterly, American Literature, Mid America*, and *American Humorists*. She is the author of a recent book on Woody Allen. With Paul Somers, Jr., she has co-authored an essay on

"Editorial Cartooning" in *The Handbook of Popular Culture* (Greenwood Press, 1980).

DAVID E. E. SLOANE is Professor of English at the University of New Haven (Connecticut) and author of *Mark Twain as a Literary Comedian* (1979), *The Literary Humor of the Urban Northeast, 1830–1890* (1983), and *American Humor Magazines and Comic Periodicals* (1987), as well as articles on humor, realism, business writing, and linguistics.

PAUL P. SOMERS, JR., is Professor of American Thought and Language at Michigan State University and a contributing editor of *National Lampoon*. He has published numerous articles on American literature and humor, as well as a book on Johnson J. Hooper. He is coauthor, with Nancy Pogel, of an essay on "Editorial Cartooning" in *The Handbook of Popular Culture*.

STEPHEN J. WHITFIELD holds the Max Richter Chair in American Civilization at Brandeis University, where he has taught since 1972. He currently serves as Chairman of the Department of American Studies. His most recent book is *A Critical American: The Politics of Dwight MacDonald* (1984). He has served as a Fulbright Professor at the Hebrew University in Jerusalem and as book review editor of *American Jewish History*.